W9-BCQ-959

U.S.
Constitution

JUL 18

for
dummies®
A Wiley Brand

U.S.
Constitution

2nd Edition

by Dr. Michael Arnheim
Constitutional expert

U.S. Constitution For Dummies®, 2nd Edition

Published by: **John Wiley & Sons, Inc.,** 111 River Street, Hoboken, NJ 07030-5774, www.wiley.com

Copyright © 2018 by John Wiley & Sons, Inc., Hoboken, New Jersey

Media and software compilation copyright © 2018 by John Wiley & Sons, Inc. All rights reserved.

Published simultaneously in Canada

For general information on our other products and services, please contact our Customer Care Department within the U.S. at 877-762-2974, outside the U.S. at 317-572-3993, or fax 317-572-4002. For technical support, please visit https://hub.wiley.com/community/support/dummies.

Wiley publishes in a variety of print and electronic formats and by print-on-demand. Some material included with standard print versions of this book may not be included in e-books or in print-on-demand. If this book refers to media such as a CD or DVD that is not included in the version you purchased, you may download this material at http://booksupport.wiley.com. For more information about Wiley products, visit www.wiley.com.

Library of Congress Control Number: 2018941628

ISBN: 978-1-119-38729-9; ISBN 978-1-119-38736-7 (ebk); ISBN 978-1-119-38748-0 (ebk)

Manufactured in the United States of America

10 9 8 7 6 5 4 3 2 1

Contents at a Glance

Table of Contents

Introduction

O kay, so you bought this book (or you got it as a present, or you borrowed it, or you're browsing through it in a bookstore). Obviously, you have some interest in the U.S. Constitution, but maybe you're afraid the Constitution isn't really that interesting.

Well, you're in luck. Even if you don't find the Constitution itself to be the most riveting read, it's a never-ending source of debates and arguments. And we all know how interesting debates and arguments can be!

About This Book

This book explains the Constitution simply and thoroughly, including all the juicy controversy it evokes. Whether you're a student, a lawyer, or just a concerned citizen, I hope you find it to be both a good read and a great resource.

You don't have to read this book from cover to cover, and you don't have to read the chapters in order. I've written each chapter so it can be understood on its own; if it refers to topics that aren't covered in that chapter, I tell you where to find information about that topic elsewhere in the book. Using the Table of Contents or the Index, feel free to identify topics of the greatest interest to you, and dive in wherever you want. Even if you dive into the middle or end first, I promise I won't let you get lost.

I cover the entire Constitution in this book, but I don't give each article or amendment equal attention. That's because some parts are more important, more difficult to understand, more controversial, or more relevant to modern society than others. If I believe a particular part of the Constitution requires or deserves more explanation than another, I give it lots of real estate in the pages that follow. Parts that are easier to understand or less important to your 21st-century life get less space in the book.

Throughout the book, I offer not just facts but also a variety of opinions about constitutional issues that have created debate for more than 200 years. In some cases, the opinions belong to Supreme Court justices, advocates for or against specific rights, or any number of other sources. In other cases, the opinions are my own — and I alert you to that fact. I may sometimes try to persuade you of the

rightness or wrongness of a certain opinion, but you're welcome to disagree —
that's the fun and the privilege of becoming a more informed citizen!

Conventions Used in This Book

Whenever I quote or refer to a specific part of the Constitution, I tell you the name
of that part. You'll often see this reference in the form of an *article*, a *section*, and
maybe a *clause* — for example, Article I, Section 8, Clause 3. If you turn to the
Appendix at the back of the book, where the text of the Constitution is provided,
you can see that it's broken into seven articles, some of which are divided into
sections. If a section contains more than one paragraph, I refer to each paragraph
as a clause. So if you're looking for Clause 3 within Section 8 of Article I, just find
the third paragraph in that section.

The amendments to the Constitution appear in the Appendix after the main body
of the document (and after the list of people who signed it). It's pretty easy to
locate an amendment, as long as you aren't too rusty on Roman numerals.

When you see the term *the Constitution*, it always refers to the U.S. Constitution.
Each of the 50 states also has its own constitution, but if I'm referring to one of
those, I include the state name (such as *the Virginia Constitution*). Similarly, when
I refer to *the Supreme Court, the high court,* or just *the Court,* that means the
U.S. Supreme Court. If I refer to a state supreme court, I always give the name of
the state concerned (such as *the Texas Supreme Court*).

You can't learn about the Constitution without being introduced to some legal,
political, and other jargon, but I do my best in this book to ease you into the constitutional vocabulary. If I use a term that I suspect may not be familiar to you, I
put that term in italic and provide a definition or explanation nearby.

Icons Used in This Book

Throughout this book, you find small pictures in the margins. These *icons* highlight
paragraphs that contain certain types of information. Here's what each icon means:

CONTROVERSY

The Constitution is nothing if not controversial, and this icon highlights paragraphs that explain what all the debate is about. If you want to know why people
can't seem to figure out what this document means even after 200-plus years,
head toward these icons.

IN MY OPINION

Where there's debate, there are opinions, and I won't pretend not to have some of my own. Where you see this icon, you'll know that I'm offering my perspective on the subject at hand, and I don't necessarily expect you to agree!

REMEMBER

The Remember icon sits beside paragraphs that contain information that's worth committing to memory. Even if you're not studying for an exam on the Constitution, you may want to read these paragraphs twice.

TECHNICAL STUFF

This icon denotes material that may fall into the "too much information" category for some readers. If you like to know lots of details about a topic, the information in these paragraphs may thrill you. If details aren't your thing, feel free to skip these paragraphs altogether.

Beyond the Book

To gain some additional insight into the U.S. Constitution, beyond the written words of this book, head to `www.dummies.com/cheatsheet/usconstitution` for an easily accessible reference guide.

Where to Go from Here

That depends on why you're reading this book. If you're a student who needs help understanding how and why the Constitution was created, what it says, and why it's still so important, I'd suggest that you start at the beginning.

If you picked up this book because you want to understand the debate about a certain issue (such as gun rights), check the Table of Contents or Index and flip to the chapter where that debate is explored. (In the case of gun rights, that'd be Chapter 15.)

If you're planning to start a campaign to impeach a government official who rubs you entirely the wrong way, perhaps Chapter 13 will be your cup of tea.

If you want to very quickly get a sense of why constitutional issues can cause tempers to flare, flip to Chapter 25 and read about just five of the many debates that keep people talking.

The law as stated in this book is correct, to the best of my knowledge, as of Presidents' Day, February 19, 2018.

1

Getting Started with the U.S. Constitution

Chapter **1**

Identifying the Main Principles and Controversies of the Constitution

Most of the stuff written about the Constitution is boring and hard to understand. But it doesn't have to be. And frankly, it shouldn't be, because the Constitution is pretty important — yes, important to *you* in your daily life.

In this book, I do my best to explain the Constitution in simple language. And in this chapter, I offer a broad introduction to the Constitution: what it is, who created it, the principles it does and doesn't discuss, and the areas of controversy that keep it in the headlines even today.

Defining "Constitution"

First, what exactly *is* a constitution? Okay, here goes. A constitution is a sort of super-law that regulates the way a country or state is run. How helpful is that as a definition? Not very? So let's be more specific, and this time let's focus specifically on the Constitution of the United States.

The U.S. Constitution is the supreme law of the nation controlling the following main features (plus a few more):

>> The functions and powers of the different branches of the government: the President, the Congress, and the courts

>> The way in which the President and the Congress are elected and how federal judges are appointed

>> The way government officials — including the President and the judges — can be fired

>> The relationship between the federal government and the states

>> Your rights as a citizen or inhabitant of the United States

REMEMBER

The word "constitution" can mean *either* the physical paper document *or* constitutional law as defined by the U.S. Supreme Court, which includes a number of features that don't actually appear in the document, such as the rights to privacy, abortion, and gay marriage. These additional features are mainly a product of the so-called "living constitution" approach to the Constitution (as a document), which believes that the Constitution needs to be constantly reinterpreted to take account of changes in prevailing social, political, and moral values. On the other hand, strict constructionists, textualists, and originalists interpret the Constitution (as a document) sticking closely to the perceived original meaning of the words in question. I discuss the different approaches to constitutional interpretation in Chapter 3.

Knowing When and Why the Constitution Was Created

The Constitution emerged from a meeting called the Philadelphia Convention, which took place in 1787. (That meeting has since come to be known also as the *Constitutional Convention*.) The Convention was held because the *Articles of Confederation* — the document that had been serving as the country's first governing constitution — were considered to be weak and problematic (see Chapter 2). The stated goal of the Convention was to revise the Articles of Confederation, but the outcome was much more than a mere revision: It was a new form of government. See Figure 1-1 for a look at a scene from the Convention.

FIGURE 1-1: George Washington presiding over the Constitutional Convention, 1787.

The 55 delegates to the Philadelphia Convention came to be known as the *Framers* of the Constitution. They represented 12 of the 13 states (Rhode Island didn't send a delegate), and they included some familiar names, such as George Washington, Alexander Hamilton, and James Madison.

The Convention lasted from May 25 to September 17, 1787. In the end, only 39 of the 55 delegates actually signed the Constitution. Three delegates refused to sign it, and the rest had left the Convention before the signing took place.

For the Constitution to take effect, it had to be *ratified* — or confirmed — by nine states. Special conventions were summoned in each state, and the Delaware, New Jersey, and Georgia conventions ratified the Constitution unanimously. But some of the other states saw a pretty fierce battle for ratification. In New York, for example, the Constitution was ratified only by 30 votes to 27.

Ratification was achieved in 1788, and the Constitution took effect with the swearing in of President George Washington and Vice President John Adams on April 30, 1789.

DISTINGUISHING THE FOUNDERS FROM THE FRAMERS

The term *Founding Fathers* was (probably) coined by President Warren G. Harding about 100 years ago. *Founding Fathers,* or simply *Founders,* refers to the political leaders of the struggle for American independence against Britain. It includes the American leaders in the Revolutionary War, the signatories of the Declaration of Independence, and also the Framers of the Constitution (or simply, *Framers*).

The Founders include George Washington, Benjamin Franklin, Alexander Hamilton, John Jay, John Adams, Thomas Jefferson, James Madison, James Monroe, Patrick Henry, and Tom Paine.

The term *Founding Fathers* overlaps somewhat with the term *Framers of the Constitution,* but the two terms are not identical in meaning. The term *Founders* is much broader than the term *Framers* because it covers all the leaders in the fight for American independence, including all the delegates to the Philadelphia Convention who drafted the Constitution. So all the Framers were Founders, but not all the Founders were Framers!

Thomas Jefferson, for example, drafted the Declaration of Independence and was one of the leading Founders of the United States. But he was not involved in the drafting of the Constitution because he was on official business in France at the time. So Jefferson was a very prominent Founder, but he was not a Framer.

Summarizing the Main Principles of the Constitution

In broad strokes, here are the principles you find in the Constitution:

>> **Liberty:** The Framers of the Constitution aimed to establish a form of government that gave the people as much individual freedom as possible, by guaranteeing them

- Religious freedom

- Freedom of speech

- Freedom to defend themselves with arms

>> **Federalism:** The United States started out as 13 separate British colonies, which banded together to throw off the British yoke. At first, in 1777, the

colonies formed a loose alliance under the so-called *Articles of Confederation* (not to be confused with the similarly named Confederacy proclaimed by the seceding southern states in the 1860s). But the need for a stronger central government resulted in the drafting of the U.S. Constitution, which was ratified in its original, unamended form in 1788. The Constitution established a *federal* system of government, which gave the central or federal government certain clearly defined and limited powers, reserving the remaining powers to the states or to the people.

» **Separation of powers:** The Framers of the Constitution were very anxious to prevent any one person or institution from becoming too powerful. So the Constitution keeps the three branches of government separate. These branches are the Executive (the President), Legislative (Congress), and Judicial (the law courts). But a system of "checks and balances" cuts across this separation. So, for example, Congress passes laws, but the President can veto them. Similarly, the President has the power to appoint Cabinet officers and federal judges, but his appointments are subject to the "advice and consent" of the Senate. And the Supreme Court can check any perceived abuse of the power of Congress by striking down laws that the Court rules are unconstitutional.

» **Due process:** "Due process of law" is one of the main buzz phrases of the Constitution — according to the Supreme Court. You may assume that this phrase would refer simply to *procedure,* or how things should be done, like whether or not you are allowed a jury trial. But the Supreme Court has widened its interpretation of the phrase greatly to include *substantive due process,* or what rights the Constitution actually confers or protects. As a result, the Court has interpreted the Constitution as guaranteeing a bunch of controversial "fundamental rights," including

- An expansion of the rights of those suspected or accused of crimes

- An expansion of minority rights

- Privacy

- Abortion

Here are some of the principles you may assume are addressed in the Constitution, but aren't:

» **Democracy:** The words *democracy* and *democratic* don't figure anywhere in the text of the Constitution. In its original form, the Constitution was not democratic, and the House of Representatives was the only directly elected part of the federal government. The Constitution became democratic as a result of the rise of President Andrew Jackson's Democratic Party in the 1830s (see Chapter 6).

>> **Equality:** Equality was also not one of the principles of the Constitution in its original form.

- Slavery formed an integral part of the Constitution until the Civil War. For example, Article IV, Section 2, Clause 3 provided in its original, unamended form that runaway slaves who escaped from a slave state to a free state had to be "delivered up" to their original owners. The whole structure of the House of Representatives also depended on slavery. In its original form, Article I, Section 2 of the Constitution apportioned the representation of the various states according to the numbers of their free population — plus three-fifths of their slaves. This "three-fifths rule" cynically used the slave population (who of course didn't have the right to vote) to give the slave states more representation in the House than they would otherwise have had.

- Women didn't have the right to vote in the U.S. as a whole until 1920, though some states had allowed women to vote before then.

THE FEDERALIST PAPERS

When the U.S. Constitution emerged from the Philadelphia Convention after being signed by delegates from each of the 12 participating states, it still had to be ratified, or confirmed, by the states, each of which summoned a special convention for this purpose. Fierce controversy reigned.

In October 1787, Alexander Hamilton, a leading member of the Convention and a dedicated upholder of the Constitution, started publishing a series of articles explaining and justifying the Constitution. Hamilton got James Madison, another leading Convention delegate, to join him. John Jay, another Founding Father (although not a Convention delegate) also contributed some articles.

The series of articles was titled *The Federalist* and was described as "a Collection of Essays written in favor of the New Constitution." Hamilton himself wrote 51 of the 85 articles, Madison contributed 27, and Jay wrote 5.

Although they were written before the Constitution took effect, these essays show tremendous insight into the problems of government and have been cited ever since as embodying an authoritative interpretation of the Constitution.

- To this day, the interpretation of the anti-discrimination (or equal treatment) amendments to the Constitution remains highly controversial. The most controversial amendment is the Fourteenth, which can be invoked either in support of affirmative action or in opposition to it. Those Supreme Court justices who support affirmative action see it as a necessary part of the anti-discriminatory thrust of the Due Process Clause of the Fourteenth Amendment, while those justices who oppose affirmative action see it as itself just another form of discrimination.

Identifying Some Areas of Controversy

The whole text of the Constitution takes up just a few pages of print; see the Appendix if you don't believe me. So why do you need to read a book this long in order to understand it? The old-fashioned language of the Constitution sometimes needs to be explained. And there are a few — actually surprisingly few — genuine ambiguities in the text. But, for the most part, you can blame it on the lawyers and the judges — particularly the U.S. Supreme Court — who have made a major production out of a pretty simple, straightforward document.

How come there's such major disagreement about what the Constitution means? There are essentially three reasons:

>> **Old-fashioned language:** The English language has changed since the horse-and-buggy era when most of the Constitution was written (but perhaps not as much as you may think). Consider the following examples:

- Article III, Section 3 contains the phrase "Aid and Comfort" in connection with committing treason. Does this mean that you'll go to jail if you give the enemy milk and cookies? Not quite. The phrase was lifted straight out of the old English Treason Act of 1351. The word *comfort* comes from a Latin root meaning *to strengthen.* So, giving the enemy "Aid and Comfort" means actively assisting the enemy and strengthening him, whether by means of arms, money, or intelligence.

- The biggest changes have occurred in punctuation. So, for example, the Fifth Amendment ends with this prohibition: *nor shall private property be taken for public use, without just compensation.* Some commentators have claimed to notice a smudge in the original handwritten version of the Bill of Rights, which they take to be a comma between "taken" and "for," making "for public use" a bracketed phrase. They conclude from this that the Constitution allows the government to take private property for purposes other than "for public use."

Even if there's meant to be an additional comma in there, this interpretation is plainly wrong. First, in the 18th century commas were strewn around much more liberally than today, without affecting the meaning. Second, the idea that the government can just take private property whenever it feels like it goes clean against the whole tone and tenor of the Constitution.

>> **Ambiguity:** There are a few passages in the Constitution where the meaning is genuinely in doubt. Here are two examples:

- **Do individuals have the right "to keep and bear Arms"?** The Supreme Court says yes, but the wording of the Second Amendment is not at all clear. I discuss this important question in Chapters 12 and 15.

- **If the President dies, does the Vice President become President or only Acting President?** Article II, Section 1 of the Constitution is genuinely ambiguous. The Twenty-Fifth Amendment, which came along only in 1967, says that in these circumstances the Veep does become President. But the problem was actually solved in practice by John Tyler, back in 1841. See Chapters 10 and 22 for all the details.

>> **Interpretation:** Many of the disputes about the meaning of the Constitution arise out of different approaches to constitutional interpretations by justices of the Supreme Court. Here are just a few of the most controversial constitutional issues:

- **Can Congress pass any laws it likes?** The Supreme Court says no. But some commentators disagree with this interpretation and read Article I, Section 8 of the Constitution very widely. In particular, they interpret the power of Congress to "pay the Debts and provide for the common Defence and general Welfare of the United States" as meaning that Congress can pass any laws it likes. This reading is almost certainly wrong, and James Madison said so himself. I tackle this question particularly in Chapter 9.

- **Does the President have the power to lock up "enemy combatants" and deny them access to the U.S. courts?** In the 2008 case *Boumediene v. Bush,* by a majority of 5 to 4, the U.S. Supreme Court said no. However, in June 2012 the Court declined, without comment, to take up appeals filed on behalf of seven Guantanamo detainees who claimed that they had not had a "meaningful opportunity" to challenge their detention.

- **Is the death penalty kosher?** Yes, but it does depend on the method used. Lethal injection is now the favored method — and the Supreme Court says it's not "cruel and unusual punishment." But the Supreme Court has also held that it's unconstitutional to execute minors and the mentally ill. In *Glossip v. Gross* (2015), the Supreme Court held by a majority of 5 to 4 that the use of the drug midazolam was not unconstitutional. Justice Breyer used his dissent to launch an attack on the constitutionality of capital punishment of any kind. "Welcome to Groundhog Day" was Justice Scalia's sarcastic response, referring to earlier attacks on capital punishment in cases such as *Furman v. Georgia* (1972), in which a 5–4 majority succeeded in temporarily banning the death penalty as unconstitutional. In April 2017, the Supreme Court was again confronted with a problem with midazolam, which its manufacturers were no longer prepared to supply for the purpose of execution. The state of Arkansas was anxious to execute a number of death-row inmates before its stock of midazolam reached its expiration date. Newly appointed Justice Neil Gorsuch formed part of the 5–4 majority allowing all but one of the executions to go ahead.

- **Can a school district assign students to public high schools on the basis of race alone?** In 2007, by 5 votes to 4, the Supreme Court said no. Writing for the majority, Chief Justice John Roberts held that "The way to stop discrimination on the basis of race is to stop discriminating on the basis of race." Why, then, we may ask, do school districts in a number of states still require parents to fill out a form asking "What race(s) do you consider your child?" The form often lists more than 50 "races" to choose from. The short answer to my question posed above is simply that the school districts concerned have not yet reached the goal of a color-blind educational policy.

- **Is gay marriage constitutional?** Marriage doesn't figure in the U.S. Constitution at all. It was considered to be a matter for individual states to decide. But in *Obergefell v. Hodges* (2015), by a majority of 5 to 4 the U.S. Supreme Court ruled that marriage is a fundamental right guaranteed to same-sex couples by both the Due Process Clause and the Equal Protection Clause of the Fourteenth Amendment to the Constitution. The ruling requires all states to issue marriage licenses to same-sex couples and to recognize same-sex marriages solemnized in other jurisdictions. In his dissenting opinion, Justice Scalia scathingly characterized the majority opinion as "lacking even a thin veneer of law" and as descending "to the mystical aphorisms of the fortune cookie." See Chapter 23 for more on this case.

- **Are states allowed to secede from the Union?** The Supreme Court says no. The last time secession was tried, it took a civil war to end it. Since that time a number of groups have advocated the secession of a state, a city, or a tribe, but no serious attempt has been made. (One such group, the Alaskan Independence Party, hit the news during the 2008 election campaign because of alleged links with Sarah Palin, the Republican vice presidential candidate.)

This is just the tip of the iceberg when it comes to constitutional controversies, and I devote a good deal of space in this book to sifting through them and offering my own humble opinions of the Supreme Court's interpretations. If the Constitution weren't a source of so much debate within the halls of government, perhaps it wouldn't be nearly as interesting to read and learn about. Luckily for you, that isn't the case!

Chapter **2**

Probing Underlying Concepts: Big Thinkers, Big Thoughts

The United States started out as 13 British colonies that overthrew the British yoke — which was no joke at all! The American Revolution and the War of Independence led to the birth of a new nation and a new form of government enshrined in a written constitution — which, with a number of changes, has survived for more than 200 years.

Although the United States was born out of a bitter struggle with Britain, the leading citizens of the new nation — including the Framers of the Constitution (see Chapter 1) — were of British stock. They were educated men steeped in English law and familiar with British political institutions and philosophy.

No wonder, then, that the U.S. Constitution drew on these British sources — but no wonder either that it departed from British traditions in some major ways too, sometimes deliberately and sometimes accidentally.

In this chapter, I discuss some of the British constitutional documents, political writings, and doctrines that were most venerated by the Founders of the United States, including:

>> Magna Carta

>> Habeas corpus

>> The rule of law

>> Natural law

>> The consent of the governed

>> Republicanism

Building on Magna Carta

Magna Carta (Latin for "Great Charter") is a document dating back to the year 1215 containing a number of concessions made by King John of England to his rebellious barons.

What relevance could this kind of document possibly have to the United States nearly eight centuries later? The Founding Fathers used Magna Carta as a justification for the Declaration of Independence and later as a precedent for some features of the U.S. Constitution.

Such is the veneration accorded this document in the United States that in 1957 the American Bar Association erected a memorial to Magna Carta in England. And a 1297 reissue of Magna Carta (sold at auction in 2007 for $21.3 million!) sits in a glass case in the National Archives rotunda in Washington, D.C. — right beside the original texts of the Declaration of Independence and the U.S. Constitution.

If you take the trouble to read Magna Carta, you'll probably find it just about as riveting as a phonebook — even if you speak Latin at home, because that is the language in which Magna Carta is written.

The good bits of Magna Carta are few and far between. Here's the most quoted provision:

> *No free man shall be arrested or imprisoned, or deprived of his rights or property, or outlawed or exiled . . . except by the lawful judgment of his equals or by the law of the land.*

Here are a few examples of ways Magna Carta may have influenced the Founding Fathers, as evidenced in the Declaration of Independence and the U.S. Constitution:

REMEMBER

>> **Taxation without representation:** Did Magna Carta prohibit taxation without representation? Clause 12 of the original promised "no scutage or aid shall be imposed on our kingdom, except by the common council of our kingdom." *Scutage* and *aid* were two feudal taxes on knights and barons alone. But did this mean that a tax could be imposed only with the consent of those subject to it? Possibly. The American patriots sure thought so. When in 1765 the British Parliament passed the Stamp Act taxing everything from newspapers to playing cards and dice, the Massachusetts Assembly declared the act "against the Magna Carta and the natural rights of Englishmen, and therefore . . . null and void." I discuss the concept of "the consent of the governed" in connection with the Declaration of Independence later in the chapter.

>> **Trial by jury:** Did Magna Carta — in particular the clause quoted earlier in this section — guarantee trial by jury? The clause supposedly guaranteed everyone the right to be tried by their "equals," or fellow citizens. In fact, this right took a lot longer to be established in England — and it has now largely been lost there, except in cases of serious crime. But the right to a jury trial sure is alive and well in the United States and is enshrined in the Sixth and Seventh amendments to the Constitution, which I deal with in Chapter 18.

>> **Habeas corpus:** Did Magna Carta guarantee *habeas corpus* — the right to take legal action to end unlawful detention? Not exactly, but Magna Carta was a trailblazer for this later right. The passage from Magna Carta quoted earlier in this section promises that nobody is to be imprisoned except after a proper trial. But this right didn't become available right away. As late as 1628, King Charles I had five knights imprisoned "by his majesty's special command-ment." Habeas corpus became a major issue in the ensuing English Revolution, resulting in Charles I's execution. Habeas corpus was eventually incorporated into statute in 1679.

This important privilege (not a right) is now enshrined in Article I, Section 9 of the U.S. Constitution: "The Privilege of the Writ of Habeas Corpus shall not be suspended, unless when in Cases of Rebellion or Invasion the public Safety may require it." Habeas corpus became a hot-button issue in the final year of the Bush Administration with regard to detention in Guantanamo Bay: *Boumediene v. Bush* (2008).

Respecting the Rule of Law (or the Rule of Lawyers?)

The rule of law is commonly regarded as a fundamental principle of the Western world, and of the United States in particular. The phrase *rule of law* sounds impressive. But what exactly does it mean?

At its simplest, the rule of law just means that nobody is above the law. This principle was used as a stick to beat the old absolute monarchs of Europe — like King Louis XIV of France, who famously boasted, "I am the state," or even the weak Louis XVI, who is reported as asserting, "It's legal because I wish it."

The counterblast to such exorbitant claims was put by the English political philosopher James Harrington as "the empire of laws and not of men." John Adams adapted this concept slightly and introduced it into the Massachusetts Constitution of 1780 as "A government of laws and not of men." In its most euphonious form, it became "A government not of men but of laws." This high-sounding ideal was echoed by Chief Justice John Marshall in the leading case of *Marbury v. Madison* (see Chapter 23).

REMEMBER

But how can law rule? Laws are just words on paper. They are therefore subject to interpretation — by courts, judges, and lawyers (who argue their interpretations of laws to the courts and hope that their interpretations will be accepted). An anonymous wag put his finger on this truth and retorted that what the Founding Fathers were really likely to establish was "A government not of laws, but of lawyers."

This throwaway line has proved prophetic, and even some Supreme Court justices have admitted that the meaning of the U.S. Constitution changes in accordance with the changing views of the Court. In the words of Chief Justice Charles Evans Hughes, "We are under a Constitution, but the Constitution is what the judges say it is."

IN MY OPINION

This oft-quoted remark comes from a speech that Hughes gave as governor of New York in 1907, long before becoming a Supreme Court justice. But he was already pompous enough to add, "and the judiciary is the safeguard of our liberty and our property under the Constitution." Susette Kelo, who nearly lost her lovely salmon-pink Victorian cottage because of a particularly unjust decision by the U.S. Supreme Court in 2005, would probably not agree with Hughes's comment! (See my discussion of eminent domain in Chapter 17.)

The principle of the rule of law doesn't figure in the U.S. Constitution in so many words. The closest thing to the rule of law that appears in the Constitution is the Supremacy Clause in Article VI, which reads as follows:

> *This Constitution, and the Laws of the United States which shall be made in Pursuance thereof; and all Treaties made, or which shall be made, under the Authority of the United States, shall be the supreme Law of the Land; and the Judges in every State shall be bound thereby, any Thing in the Constitution or Laws of any State to the Contrary notwithstanding.*

This clause clearly places federal law above state law, but does it give the U.S. Constitution higher status than the rest of federal law? Article V sure makes it difficult to amend the Constitution, but that in itself doesn't prove that the Constitution trumps all other laws.

Chief Justice John Marshall, in the case of *Marbury v. Madison*, went to great lengths to show that the Constitution has higher status than any other law and that "a law repugnant to the Constitution is void." This was a new judge-made principle and enabled the Supreme Court to arrogate to itself the power of judicial review — which was to become its strongest weapon against the other branches of the federal government. See Chapter 23 for a full discussion of *Marbury v. Madison*.

The power of the Supreme Court to strike down laws found to be unconstitutional is now taken for granted. But was that the intention of the Founding Fathers? Thomas Jefferson objected strongly to the way the Supreme Court "usurped" the right "of exclusively explaining the Constitution," commenting that, "The Constitution on this hypothesis is a mere thing of wax in the hands of the judiciary, which they may twist and shape into any form they please."

A more accurate prediction about the Constitution would be hard to find!

Analyzing the Concepts Underlying the Declaration of Independence

The American colonists had an ambivalent attitude toward the British Constitution. Their leaders steeped themselves in the traditions of the British Constitution and generally identified with the revolutionary spirit that had led to the execution of one king — Charles I in 1649 — and the expulsion of another — James II in 1689. They regarded themselves as entitled to the same rights as natural-born Englishmen but found themselves treated at best as second-class subjects.

At first they appealed to King George III for redress of their grievances. But when their heartfelt pleas fell on deaf ears, they decided to throw off the British yoke altogether and declare their independence.

But on what basis could they justify this revolutionary step? Although they felt excluded from the British Constitution — because they were denied a voice in the British Parliament — they invoked the principles underlying Britain's embryonic democratic system, most notably the principles of "No taxation without representation" and "Government by consent of the governed."

Thomas Jefferson took just 17 days to construct the case for American independence in the Declaration of Independence, whose rolling prose and unforgettable phrases were based on a blend of traditional British principles with some European ideas. See Figure 2-1 for a look at some who helped construct the Declaration of Independence.

The Declaration of Independence, adopted on July 4, 1776, by the Second Continental Congress, marks the birth of the United States as a new nation — or does it? Upon closer inspection, the Declaration actually announces the birth of not one but 13 new nations — each of the former colonies being a separate nation. See Chapter 7 for more on this aspect of the Declaration.

FIGURE 2-1:
An idealized reconstruction of Benjamin Franklin, John Adams, and Thomas Jefferson composing the Declaration of Independence. The Declaration was mainly the work of Jefferson.

Source: Jean Leon Gerome Ferris

But, whether the Declaration announced one birth or a litter of 13, it was a document essentially justifying the throwing off of British colonial rule.

The Founding Fathers were not natural revolutionaries. They were educated, well-to-do men of property and pillars of society who wouldn't normally have been mixed up in violence or war. So, what impelled these solid citizens to become involved in a bloody conflict that lasted six years?

REMEMBER

The slogan that first rallied opposition to Britain was "No taxation without representation." The American colonies had elected legislatures, but the British Parliament could override these colonial legislatures and pass laws without consulting them. The Stamp Act of 1765 was an example of this: It slapped a tax on everything from newspapers to playing cards and dice — without any consultation with the colonists. The high-handedness of this action rankled the colonists.

Did the colonists have a legal right to consent to decisions that affected them? Not under the British Constitution as understood at the time. So the colonists had to look elsewhere.

England had itself had a revolution — or two revolutions, to be precise — in the 17th century. The colonists naturally found themselves drawn to the rhetoric of those revolutionaries, who had relied a good deal on Magna Carta, to which they gave a very broad interpretation.

But Magna Carta wasn't enough on its own to justify throwing off the British colonial yoke. Magna Carta belonged to a bygone feudal age. Most of the rights contained in Magna Carta were concessions made by King John to the barons and didn't apply to ordinary people. During the English revolutions of the 17th century, the opponents of the Crown glamorized and reinterpreted Magna Carta in ways that were not always very convincing. The American Founders adopted the same expansive approach to Magna Carta, but they also used the following concepts that are reflected in the Declaration of Independence:

>> Natural law

>> "[U]nalienable Rights"

>> Consent of the governed

>> Republicanism

Invoking the law of nature

The Declaration of Independence opens with a claim on behalf of the American "people" to "the separate and equal station to which the Laws of Nature and of Nature's God entitle them."

The concept of the law of nature (or natural law) goes back to ancient Greece and Rome, and it was commonly equated with the law of God (or divine law) and also with the law of nations.

REMEMBER

Natural law theory said that man-made law — or *positive law* — was valid only if it conformed to the moral standards laid down by natural law, which was rational, universal, unchanging, and everlasting. The only problem with natural law was that there was no agreement about its content, as it was unwritten and existed only in the minds of its adherents. For example, was slavery in accordance with natural law? Some natural law advocates said yes, others no.

The Declaration of Independence claimed that the American states were entitled to independence from Britain on the basis of the supposed natural law principle that each nation, or "people," has the right to national self-determination. That supposed principle formed no part of the British Constitution — and was not even recognized in international law (with major modifications) until the 20th century.

Securing "unalienable Rights"

Natural law was popular among educated Americans in the late 18th century. But the problem with natural law was that those who supported it could disagree violently about its content. So, although the Founders relied on natural law, it provided a pretty shaky foundation for American independence. The Declaration of Independence is on firmer ground when it declares that it's the people's right — and even their duty — to overthrow a despotic government and to replace it with a government that will protect their "unalienable Rights."

This assertion is proclaimed in ringing tones:

> We hold these truths to be self-evident, that all men are created equal, that they are endowed by their Creator with certain unalienable Rights, that among these are Life, Liberty and the pursuit of Happiness. That to secure these Rights, Governments are instituted among Men, deriving their just powers from the consent of the governed.

These are just about the most sacred words of any American founding documents, but we need to delve just a little beneath their surface. Let's take a look at some of these rolling phrases:

>> **We hold these truths to be self-evident:** This is an admission that these "truths" can't be proved.

>> **All men are created equal:** How could this statement be reconciled with slavery? Thomas Jefferson himself, the author of the Declaration of Independence, was a slave owner, as were many other Founding Fathers. Similar wording in the Massachusetts Constitution of 1780 led to a legal challenge to slavery in the state courts, which effectively ended slavery in that state. But slavery was legally abolished throughout the nation only with the ratification of the Thirteenth Amendment in 1865 (see Chapter 20).

CONTROVERSY

>> **Creator:** Does the appearance of this word — and the appeal "to the Supreme Judge of the world" later on in the Declaration of Independence — mean that the United States is based on acceptance of religious belief? The last verse of the U.S. national anthem, "The Star-Spangled Banner," contains the words "And this be our motto: 'In God is our trust'." The motto "In God We Trust" has appeared on the penny since 1909, and since 1956 it has been the official national motto of the United States. But is this public display of religious belief in accordance with the First Amendment? I discuss this important subject in Chapter 14.

>> **Unalienable Rights:** The word *unalienable* — in modern English, *inalienable* — refers to something that can't be taken away, or even given away. Inalienable rights are therefore fundamental rights that automatically belong to every human being. They can be seen as God-given rights or as rights conferred by natural law — similar therefore to what are commonly labeled *natural rights.* Not everybody believes that such rights actually exist. The British philosopher Jeremy Bentham famously declared, "The idea of rights is nonsense and the idea of natural rights is nonsense upon stilts."

>> **Life, Liberty and the pursuit of Happiness:** This phrase is a variant on the phrase "lives, liberty, and property" that appeared in the Articles of Association of the First Continental Congress in 1774. *The pursuit of Happiness* is broader than *property* and harder to pin down. In the case of *Loving v. Virginia,* decided in 1967, the U.S. Supreme Court struck down a Virginia statute outlawing interracial marriage, on the ground that "The freedom to marry has long been recognized as one of the vital personal rights essential to the orderly pursuit of happiness by free men."

Even the term *Liberty* is hard to define. In *Meyer v. Nebraska,* the U.S. Supreme Court decided in 1923 that a Nebraska law banning the use of a foreign language as the medium of instruction to kids in grade school was unconstitutional and a denial of the "liberty" protected by the Due Process Clause of the Fourteenth Amendment. Justice Anthony Kennedy commented in 2000 that, had *Meyer*'s case been decided more recently, it probably would have been based not on the Fourteenth Amendment but rather on the First Amendment's protection of freedom of speech, belief, and religion.

"Deriving their just powers from the consent of the governed"

The Declaration of Independence goes on like this:

> *[T]o secure these rights, Governments are instituted among Men, deriving their just powers from the consent of the governed.*

In other words:

REMEMBER

>> The purpose of government is to safeguard the rights of the people.

>> The only legitimate type of government is one based on popular consent.

What exactly is meant by "consent of the governed"? By putting these words into the Declaration of Independence, Thomas Jefferson gave early notice that the government of the new United States was to be based on consent. New state constitutions soon followed suit, with elected governors and legislatures. And the government of the United States itself was designed on the same pattern, although it was at first confined, under the Articles of Confederation, to a Congress made up of delegates appointed by the state legislatures. (I discuss the Articles of Confederation later in this chapter.)

But how genuine was the claim that the governments set up by the American patriots did, indeed, govern by consent of the governed? It doesn't take much scrutiny to see that the American Revolution was not a democratic revolution. Instead, it was the overthrow of a colonial power by a wealthy elite, who then naturally stepped into the shoes of their former colonial masters.

In fact, the Framers never claimed to be democrats, and the word *democracy* doesn't appear anywhere in the U.S. Constitution (see Chapter 1). In establishment circles in the American colonies — as in England — *democracy* was a dirty word:

>> John Adams, the future president, attacked the proposals of the radical Thomas Paine as "so democratical, without any restraint or even an attempt at equilibrium or counterpoise, that it must produce confusion and every evil work."

>> James Madison, often described as "Father of the Constitution" and also a future president, was no fan of democracy either. Indeed, he attacked it in even stronger terms than the more conservative Adams. Here's what Madison said about democracy:

> >> *Democracy is the most vile form of government . . . democracies have ever been spectacles of turbulence and contention: have ever been found incompatible with personal security or the rights of property: and have in general been as short in their lives as they have been violent in their deaths.*

The Founders just didn't trust the ordinary people and deliberately kept them at arm's length, as can be seen from the way they drafted the Articles of Confederation and then the U.S. Constitution. Keep reading to see what I mean.

Establishing a Republic

The Founding Fathers weren't democrats, so what were they? The concept that they embraced was *republicanism*. John Adams — the same John Adams who attacked democracy — waxed lyrical in his praise of republicanism. Here's how Adams defined it:

> *A government, in which all men, rich and poor, magistrates and subjects, officers and people, masters and servants, the first citizen and the last, are equally subject to the laws.*

As you start reading this definition, you get the impression that it's going to be egalitarian — based on the equality of all people. But the last phrase gives the game away. Republicanism, according to this definition, isn't about any power that the people *have* but about a power that they are *under*. In a republic, says Adams, everybody is equally under the law.

This definition of republicanism ties in with Adams's better-known statement of the goal aimed at by the newly independent states. As I note earlier in the chapter, this objective was so fundamental to Adams that he incorporated it into the Massachusetts state constitution: "A government of laws and not of men."

REMEMBER

Adams's ideal was not one of people power at all. Rather, his ideal was one in which the people were subservient to laws made by an elite group (of which he was a prominent member) — with the last word on the interpretation of those laws going to judges drawn from the same elite group.

Democracy doesn't figure in the U.S. Constitution at all — but republicanism sure does. Article IV, Section 4 says:

> *The United States shall guarantee to every State in this Union a Republican Form of Government.*

There is no precise definition of *Republican,* but Adams's views on the subject are a reflection of the Framers' thinking (although Adams himself didn't attend the Constitutional Convention, as he was serving as U.S. ambassador to Britain at the time).

Getting rid of the king

The absence of a king is an important aspect of republicanism. The main body of the Declaration of Independence is taken up with a long list of grievances against King George III. Most of these grievances start with the word "He," referring to the King in person.

The truth is that King George did not call all the shots personally. He delegated a lot of his power to his ministers, and he just didn't have a great deal of power. (Later in life, after the American Revolutionary War, the poor guy was replaced by his son as Regent because King George suffered from serious mental illness.)

As a result, the King was in reality no longer head of government but only head of state — an increasingly purely ceremonial position in which the King represented the nation but was under pressure to become politically neutral.

This British model of government in which the head of state is separate from the head of government has spread around the world — not only among monarchies but also widely among republics, including Germany, Italy, Poland, India, and Israel.

REMEMBER

But the American revolutionaries didn't understand these subtleties about British rule. As far as they were concerned, their main enemy was King George. For this reason, among others, the form of government of the United States of America wasn't about to be a monarchy; it would be a republic with a president who combined the positions of head of government and head of state — in other words, an executive presidency. The Framers never even realized that the separation between head of state and head of government was possible, let alone desirable.

Leaving democracy out of the U.S. Constitution

The U.S. Constitution was not intended to set up a democracy. Here's why:

REMEMBER

>> The Senate was not originally directly elected, but made up of members appointed by the state legislatures.

>> The President was not elected by the people but by an Electoral College. The Electoral College system still exists, but, thanks to the rise of political parties, it has been short-circuited and is therefore more democratic than the Framers ever intended. (I discuss presidential elections in Chapter 10.)

>> Even elections to the House of Representatives — the only body directly elected under the original version of the U.S. Constitution — were not truly democratic, because the right to vote was narrowly restricted in the early days of the republic. It took more than a half century before the United States could be described as a democracy. The movement toward democracy was largely the achievement of a political party that started out by calling itself the Republican Party, then the Democratic-Republican Party, and later, under Andrew Jackson — who was President from 1829 to 1837 — simply the Democratic Party (see Chapter 6).

DISTINGUISHING *CONFEDERATION, FEDERATION,* AND *UNION*

The word *confederation* is not the same as *federation*. Let's take a moment to disentangle these terms.

Confederation: This is the weakest type of association between a number of independent regions, cantons, or states. The central government barely exists and is in control only of foreign affairs and defense. The best example of a confederacy or confederation is Switzerland, though since 1848 it has really been a federation rather than a confederation.

America has had two totally unconnected confederacies at two different times:

- The confederacy that lasted from 1777 until 1788, governed by the Articles of Confederation. However, the Articles stated at the beginning that "The Stile of this Confederacy shall be: 'The United States of America.'"

- The Confederate States of America, the 11 breakaway southern states that seceded from the United States, resulting in the Civil War in 1861.

Federation: The U.S. Constitution established a federal system of government, in which quite extensive powers were delegated to the national, or federal, government. But any powers not delegated to the federal government were — and still are — retained by the states or by the people. See more on this topic in Chapter 19, which deals with the Tenth Amendment.

Union: The word *union* appears quite a few times in the U.S. Constitution in reference to the federal government, and it's still often used in that sense: for example, the President's annual "State of the Union" address. In fact, *union* is a misnomer as a description of a federal system. Strictly speaking, the word *union* refers to a much more centralized system of government where all power is concentrated in the national government, as in present-day France.

IN THIS CHAPTER

» Understanding why the Constitution is not self-explanatory

» Considering whether some constitutional provisions are obsolete

» Exploring some constitutional ambiguities

» Scrutinizing major omissions from the Constitution

» Analyzing conflicting schools of interpretation

Chapter **3**

Untangling Some Confusion and Ambiguities

The U.S. Constitution is only a few pages long (see the Appendix). It makes a pretty neat pocket-size pamphlet.

Why do you need to read this big book when you can just read the Constitution itself? One reason is that my publishers need to make a few bucks. (It's not for *my* benefit — we authors only get peanuts!)

Seriously, though, there are many reasons why everybody — and I do mean *everybody* — needs help to understand the Constitution. I explore these reasons in this chapter so you can begin to understand why this short document is such a source of confusion and debate.

Listing Some Sources of Confusion

Here are some of the key reasons the Constitution is such a difficult document to digest:

>> **Technical language:** The Constitution is a statement of law, so it's not surprising that it contains some legal jargon. For example, *ratifying* an amendment is not the same thing as ratting on that amendment! To *ratify* an amendment means to confirm it. To change the Constitution, it's necessary for an amendment to be proposed and then ratified. (The Fifth Amendment deals with the process of amending the Constitution. For more on that subject, see Chapter 5.)

>> **Old-fashioned language:** Most of the Constitution was written more than 200 years ago. The meanings of some words have changed a bit since then. For example, what is the meaning of the word *compact* — as in, "No State shall, without the Consent of the Congress . . . enter into any Agreement or Compact with another State, or with a foreign Power"? In modern English, *compact* often refers to something that occupies very little space. As a noun, *compact* can mean a small cosmetic case containing face powder. But in the clause that I just quoted from Article I, Section 10 of the Constitution, *compact* means an agreement or an alliance. So, the quoted words mean that individual states are not allowed to pursue their own foreign policy. This provision gives the federal government a lock on foreign policy.

>> **Old-fashioned ideas:** Just as a lot of the language of the Constitution is old-fashioned, so are some of the ideas and values that it expresses. For example, the Seventh Amendment guarantees a right to trial by jury in any civil suit "where the value in controversy shall exceed twenty dollars." In 1791, when the Bill of Rights (including the Seventh Amendment) was ratified, the average wage earner made only about $16 a week. Times have certainly changed. But in this case, the discrepancy is not important. If anything, it's good that the threshold for jury trial is so low, because that means that trial by jury is available for almost all civil suits.

>> **Obsolete concepts:** The Constitution is based on old concepts and ideas. But does that mean the Constitution is no longer relevant to the present day? Some people have leveled this accusation against the Constitution. I examine this serious charge in this chapter (see the upcoming section "Discarding Out-of-Date Ideas?").

>> **Ambiguity:** The Framers of the Constitution were educated, articulate men. But even these intellectual giants made a few boo-boos. I take a look at some of the unintended ambiguities in the Constitution in this chapter (see "Clarifying Uncertainties").

- » **Omissions:** Some of the most important constitutional concepts and institutions don't actually figure in the text of the Constitution at all. These missing features include democracy, political parties, the death penalty, privacy, and abortion. The death penalty does at least rate a couple of indirect mentions in the text of the Constitution. But the rest of these missing concepts don't get any mentions at all. I tackle this topic in the section "Giving Some Important Principles the Silent Treatment."

- » **Interpretation:** The U.S. Supreme Court has made a lot of major changes to the Constitution — without altering a single word of the text. This is the most important reason why just picking up and reading the Constitution doesn't really tell you what it means. See the section "Interpreting the Constitution" to find out more.

Discarding Out-of-Date Ideas?

It's easy to criticize the Constitution as being past its sell-by date. The Framers recognized the danger that later generations might want to keep changing the Constitution in accordance with shifting political fashions. That's why the Framers deliberately made the Constitution so difficult to amend. (See Chapter 5 for a discussion of the official and unofficial ways that the Constitution has been changed.)

Here are just three of the many constitutional provisions that have been singled out for attack as obsolete:

- » **The right to bear arms,** contained in the Second Amendment, has always been controversial, but is it also obsolete? That depends on how it's interpreted. If you interpret the amendment as giving individuals the right to buy and use guns, the amendment appears obsolete to those people who view that right as part of a long-gone Wild West culture. But that same interpretation is seen as sensible and relevant to modern life if viewed from the perspective of human rights — and it's the interpretation now accepted by the Supreme Court. On the other hand, if you interpret the Second Amendment as protecting gun ownership and usage only by people who participate in state militias, the amendment may be seen as obsolete. That's because the National Guard, which is the modern successor to the militia, has since 1933 been a component of the U.S. Army (and its members sure don't have to provide their own weapons!). But *that* narrower interpretation is seen by its supporters as relevant to the need for gun control. See Chapter 15 for all the details and debates surrounding this amendment.

>> **The right to trial by jury,** guaranteed for criminal trials by the Sixth Amendment and for civil trials by the Seventh Amendment, may be seen by some as anachronistic. Jury trial originated in England, but it has disappeared there from practically all civil trials, and even in criminal trials it's available in far fewer cases than it used to be. However, as a practicing trial lawyer, I would prefer to try a case in front of a bunch of ordinary folk than in front of any judge you could name.

>> **The Electoral College system** for picking the President, as laid down by Article II, Section 1 of the Constitution and modified by the Twelfth Amendment, is often criticized as obsolete because it doesn't appear to be democratic. There's actually confusion here between two different things: the *Electoral College* system on one hand and, on the other, the *winner-take-all* system.

In most states these two systems are combined. That means that the winner of the presidential race in a particular state usually takes *all* the electoral votes of that state. So, if the Democratic candidate gets 60 percent of the votes in California and the Republican candidate gets 40 percent, all 55 of California's electoral votes go into the Democratic column. But the Constitution doesn't actually demand this approach. The Constitution only says that the electoral vote for a state is calculated by adding the number of representatives for that state in the House of Representatives to the number of senators (which is always two).

REMEMBER

If California preferred, it could adopt a *split vote* system. For example, California could decide to split the electoral vote in the same proportion as the popular vote. So, if the Democratic candidate won 60 percent of the vote, that candidate would get 60 percent of California's 55 electoral votes, which is 33 votes, and the Republican candidate would get the remaining 22.

If every state adopted this form of the Electoral College system, the Electoral College system would produce the same result as a straight popular-vote system calculated without reference to state boundaries — which is what most critics of the Electoral College system are angling for.

Whether a state goes for the winner-take-all system or for a split vote system is entirely a matter for that state to decide. At present, Nebraska and Maine are the only two states that operate a form of split vote. And that system did actually produce a split vote in Nebraska in 2008 and Maine in 2016.

Clarifying Uncertainties

The Constitution has a reputation for being unclear or even ambiguous at times. If it weren't, the members of the Supreme Court might have a lot more free time on their hands! Consider just two examples:

>> Does the Second Amendment give individual citizens the right "to keep and bear Arms"? Or does it restrict the right to members of militias or their modern equivalent? James Madison, who drafted the amendment, must have known what he intended it to mean, but he didn't express it very clearly. As I explain in Chapter 15, proponents of both sides of the gun rights debate find support for their arguments within the murky structure of this one-sentence amendment.

>> What happens if the Vice President takes the reins when the President dies or resigns? Is the Veep actually the President or just the acting President? Article II of the Constitution is clear as mud, and the issue became very real when William Henry Harrison died in 1841 and Vice President John Tyler took over as President. Tyler refused to be just an acting President, and he set a precedent that was followed by every subsequent Veep. But it was only in 1967 that the Twenty-Fifth Amendment finally settled the issue in crystal-clear language. For much more detail on this topic, see Chapters 4 and 22.

Giving Some Important Principles the Silent Treatment

The whole idea of a written constitution is to lay everything on the line. Chief Justice John Marshall famously remarked, "The government of the United States has been emphatically termed a government of laws, and not of men."

But how can this ambitious ideal ever be achieved if the Constitution omits all mention of some of the most important principles on which that Constitution is based?

Here are some important principles and institutions that don't figure in the text of the Constitution at all:

>> **Democracy:** As I explain in Chapter 1, the words *democracy* and *democratic* don't figure anywhere in the text of the Constitution. Is the United States a democracy? It sure wasn't in the early days of the Republic.

The Founders didn't trust the ordinary people. *Democracy* was a dirty word as far as they were concerned. Voting rights were restricted to property owners, and the House of Representatives was the only directly elected federal institution. Senators were appointed by the state legislatures, and the President was elected by an Electoral College. (The Electoral College system is still in place today, but it's now largely nominal. The existence of parties has short-circuited the Electoral College and democratized presidential elections. See my discussion in the earlier section "Discarding Out-of-Date Ideas?")

The U.S. Constitution doesn't read as a blueprint for a democracy — simply because democracy wasn't on the agenda as far as the Founders were concerned.

>> **Political parties:** The Constitution contains not a single reference to political parties, but political parties are the lifeblood of the Constitution. The competition between the parties has made the United States much more democratic than it would otherwise have been.

Parties started crystallizing quite early on, but the Framers didn't recognize their importance. As a result, the 1800 presidential election was a mess — and the Twelfth Amendment was needed to remedy the situation. (I discuss the Twelfth Amendment in Chapter 20.)

The United States has always had two main parties competing for power — at first Federalists and Democratic Republicans, then later Whigs and Democrats, and, since 1854, Republicans and Democrats. This two-party system gives voters a choice and prevents power from being concentrated in the hands of one group.

>> **The death penalty:** The Constitution doesn't specifically allow or disallow the death penalty, but both the Fifth and the Fourteenth amendments refer to it. The Fifth Amendment opens with these words:

No person shall be held to answer for a capital, or otherwise infamous crime, unless on a presentment or indictment of a Grand Jury.

A *capital crime* means a crime carrying the death penalty. Which crimes were these? The amendment doesn't say, but it takes it for granted that such crimes exist. Murder is the most common capital crime, but it's usually a state crime rather than a federal crime — and the Fifth Amendment refers purely to federal law.

The Fourteenth Amendment does refer to state law, and the Due Process Clause in Section 1 of that amendment recognizes the death penalty:

nor shall any State deprive any person of life, liberty, or property, without due process of law.

For a state to deprive somebody of life by due process of law can only mean that execution was a recognized sentence in 1868, when the Fourteenth Amendment was ratified. So, how come the Constitution doesn't say in so many words that capital punishment is okay as long as certain due process is given? Because the Constitution doesn't restate the whole of the criminal law, which had always imposed the death penalty for murder, treason, and other "infamous" crimes.

REMEMBER

The presence of these references to capital punishment in the Fifth and Fourteenth amendments, side by side with the ban on "cruel and unusual punishments" in the Eighth Amendment, makes it crystal clear that capital punishment *in itself* was not viewed as being cruel and unusual. However, the *mode* of execution could well make a difference as far as the Eighth Amendment is concerned. For example, execution by boiling in oil or by tearing the offender limb from limb would undoubtedly qualify as "cruel and unusual punishments."

Execution by lethal injection is acceptable, according to the 2015 U.S. Supreme Court ruling in the case of *Glossip v. Gross.* The case arose out of a challenge by two men sentenced to death by lethal injection in Kentucky. Ralph Baze was convicted of murdering a sheriff and deputy sheriff who were trying to serve him with a warrant. Thomas Bowling was convicted of killing a husband and wife after ramming their car. The test used by the U.S. Supreme Court for "cruel and unusual punishments" is whether the punishment in question carries the risk of inflicting "unnecessary pain." In the words of Chief Justice John Roberts, writing for the majority on the court, "Kentucky has adopted a method of execution believed to be the most humane available, one it shares with 35 other States." For more on the death penalty see Chapter 18.

>> **Privacy:** The word *privacy* also doesn't figure anywhere in the text of the Constitution. However, in the case of *Griswold v. Connecticut,* decided in 1965, Justice William O. Douglas, writing for the majority, found the right to privacy in the "penumbras" formed by "emanations" of guarantees contained in the First, Third, Fourth, and Fifth amendments. Concurring judgments cited also the Ninth and Fourteenth amendments.

Justice Potter Stewart disagreed, stating: "With all deference, I can find no such general right of privacy in the Bill of Rights, in any other part of the Constitution, or in any case ever before decided by this Court." But the powerful dissent by Stewart, joined by Justice Hugo Black, wasn't enough to block this far-reaching reinterpretation by the majority on the Court. (For more on this subject, see Chapter 5.)

CONTROVERSY

>> **Abortion:** The newfound right to privacy served as the springboard to a right of abortion in certain circumstances. This controversial right was established by the Court in *Roe v. Wade,* which I discuss in Chapter 5.

Interpreting the Constitution

Chief Justice Charles Evans Hughes famously remarked that, "We are under a Constitution, but the Constitution is what the judges say it is, and the judiciary is the safeguard of our liberty and our property under the Constitution." The Chief Justice was right to point out that the meaning of the Constitution keeps changing as a result of judicial interpretation and reinterpretation, without any change in the words on paper.

Changing the Constitution

Hughes was not criticizing the courts for this process but was actually praising them. Not everyone would agree with this view. Here are some of the reasons for opposing judicial changes to the Constitution:

>> Article V of the Constitution makes it clear that the only way that the Constitution can be changed is by formal amendment, which requires a two-thirds majority in both houses of Congress and ratification by three-fourths of the state legislatures.

>> The Framers deliberately made amendment difficult, so that any change would command broad general support.

>> The Supreme Court justices are unelected, are appointed for life, and are removable only by impeachment. This means that the justices are independent and not answerable to the electorate or to anybody else.

>> Supreme Court justices who interpret the Constitution in ways that depart from the text are effectively rewriting that document by imposing their own views on it.

The reply to these points is along the following lines:

>> The Constitution was mostly written more than 200 years ago. It's impossible to get back to the original intention of the Framers — even if we wanted to.

>> To remain relevant and meaningful, the Constitution must be interpreted afresh by each new generation, as a "living Constitution."

>> This process of interpretation in the light of changing political, social, and moral values doesn't amount to unauthorized amendment but is needed to make sense of the Constitution and to apply it to the modern age.

Identifying methods of interpretation

The classification of the different schools of constitutional interpretation is messy, to say the least. But here's a bird's-eye view of the main divisions:

>> **Living Constitution:** This school of thought sees the Constitution as a living and breathing document that must be interpreted and reinterpreted according to society's changing needs. On the present Supreme Court, Justices Breyer, Ginsburg, Kagan, and Sotomayor generally adhere to this approach. As Justice Breyer puts it, the Constitution's values don't change, but they "must be applied to a world that changes every five minutes." And: "George Washington did not know about the Internet, but he did know about free speech. And the values of free speech have to apply to today's world that includes an Internet." The late Justice Antonin Scalia attacked this approach as undemocratic by wanting "matters to be decided not by the people, but by the justices of the Supreme Court."

>> **Strict constructionism:** This label is used to refer to a literal approach to constitutional interpretation. Thomas Jefferson favored this approach, which took a narrow view of the powers of the federal government as against the states. Chief Justice William Rehnquist was often described as a strict constructionist, as are Justices Clarence Thomas and Scalia. Scalia rejected the label. "Strict constructionism," explained Scalia, "is a degraded form of textualism that brings the whole philosophy into disrepute. I am not a strict constructionist, and no one ought to be — though better that, I suppose, than a nontextualist. A text should not be construed strictly, and it should not be construed leniently; it should be construed reasonably, to contain all that it fairly means."

   Scalia went on to provide an illuminating example from the criminal case of *Smith v. United States* (1993). The question before the Supreme Court was whether Mr. Smith had "used" a firearm in the course of committing a drug-related crime. Smith had wished to buy some cocaine, for which he had offered an unloaded gun in payment. Did this amount to "using" a gun in connection with the drug trafficking offense? The majority on the Court, made up of six justices, were satisfied that it did. Scalia dissented and explained his dissent as follows: "The phrase 'uses a gun' fairly connoted use of a gun for what guns are normally used for, that is, as a weapon. When you ask someone 'Do you use a cane?' you are not inquiring whether he has hung his grandfather's antique cane as a decoration in the hallway."

>> **Textualism:** Judges who are referred to by politicians and the media as strict constructionists nowadays tend to prefer to be regarded as *textualists, formalists,* or *originalists*. These labels are not identical, but they overlap to a considerable extent. *Originalism* is essentially an approach to the Constitution, while *textualism* is concerned with other legislation. So, there

is no contradiction between being both a textualist and an originalist. Scalia referred to himself as "first of all a textualist, and secondly an originalist."

Textualists are also often regarded as conservatives (check out Figure 3-1 for a picture of liberal and conservative justices), but there is some confusion here. Conservative judges normally have a certain reverence for *stare decisis* — the doctrine of binding precedent, that courts should adhere to previous decisions. But what should a textualist do when his reading of the Constitution disagrees with a previous Supreme Court decision? In those circumstances, some of them, like Thomas, tend to jettison *stare decisis.* Scalia is on record as remarking: "Clarence Thomas doesn't believe in *stare decisis*, period. If a constitutional line of authority is wrong, he would say, let's get it right. I wouldn't do that."

FIGURE 3-1: (From left to right) Justices Sandra Day O'Connor (retired), Sonia Sotomayor, Ruth Bader Ginsburg, and Elena Kagan, October 2010. The three current justices are all thought of as "liberal," while O'Connor, nominated by President Reagan and starting out as essentially "conservative," later became the swing vote on the Court.

Source: Steve Petteway, photographer for the Supreme Court of the United States

>> **Originalism:** This term is now applied to several different shades of legal opinion, which share the view that the Constitution had a clear and definite meaning at the time it was drafted and that to interpret the Constitution, a court must get back to that original meaning.

Justice Neil Gorsuch, a Trump appointee who took his seat in April 2017, has been described as a textualist in statutory interpretation and an originalist in regard to constitutional interpretation. He is also known to be an advocate of natural law, having written his Oxford doctoral dissertation on assisted suicide and euthanasia (he is against both). In Gorsuch's first criminal case as a Supreme Court Justice, his vote tipped the scales against eight death row inmates from Arkansas who were petitioning the Court for a stay of execution in *McGehee v. Hutchinson* (2017). Gorsuch wasn't swayed by Justice Breyer's impassioned plea in support of a stay of execution on the ground that "Apparently the reason the State decided to proceed with these eight executions is that the 'use by' date of the State's execution drug is about to expire."

REMEMBER

The most influential branch of this school of thought, claiming adherents such as Scalia, stresses *original meaning* at the expense of *original intent* — the meaning of the text as it would have been understood by a reasonable person at the time it was drafted, rather than some secret purpose that the Framers may have had. Critics of this approach have pooh-poohed as unrealistic the attempt to recapture the meaning of a text as it was understood more than 200 years ago.

The sight of judges beating one another over the head with old dictionaries can be entertaining. In 1994, Scalia, relying on a raft of dictionaries, ruled that the word *modify* meant no more than "to make minor changes." He rejected the argument, based on *Webster's Third New International Dictionary* published in 1976, that *modify* could also refer to the making of major or fundamental changes.

If this is the sort of mess a court can get into on the basis of word meanings of the late 20th century, how easy can it be to reach the original meaning of texts drafted in the late 18th century? Interpreting the Constitution on the basis of its meaning at the time it was written sure makes sense. The problem may be that none of the high court justices were trained as a historian, a linguist, or a philologist.

Chapter **4**

Catching a Bird's-Eye View of the Constitution

s the Constitution complicated, hard to understand, and boring? You betcha! Okay, so don't read it yet. Read this chapter first.

In this chapter, I introduce you to the Preamble — the introduction — to the Constitution, as well as to the seven articles of the Constitution itself. I deal with the subject matter of these seven articles in detail in later chapters.

My goal in this chapter is to look beneath the surface of the Constitution and identify what I consider the most important (and sometimes disputed) issues it addresses. I also reveal that some of the most important principles that formed the basis of the Constitution don't actually figure in the text at all. This chapter doesn't deal with any of the 27 amendments to the Constitution. Those are covered in Parts 4 and 5.

Presenting the Preamble: "We the People . . ."

"We the People" are the best-known words of the U.S. Constitution. They are the opening words of the *Preamble* — the almost lyrical introduction to the Constitution:

> *We the People of the United States, in Order to form a more perfect Union, establish Justice, insure domestic Tranquility, provide for the common defence, promote the general Welfare, and secure the Blessings of Liberty to ourselves and our Posterity, do ordain and establish this Constitution for the United States of America.*

The language of the Preamble is very different from that of the rest of the Constitution. The Constitution is essentially a legal document, but the Preamble reads more like a political statement. Let me examine the wording more closely:

» *We the People of the United States . . . do ordain and establish this Constitution for the United States of America:* Did "the people of the United States" really "ordain and establish" the Constitution? Yes and no. The delegates to the Philadelphia Convention who drafted the Constitution in 1787 were not directly elected; they were selected by their state legislatures. But the Constitution was then submitted for ratification to a directly elected convention in each state.

» *in Order to form a more perfect Union:* This clause refers to the perceived failure of the Articles of Confederation, the first American constitution, which had been in effect since 1777. The Philadelphia Convention drafted a Constitution that aimed "to form a more perfect Union" — a closer union than the loose association of sovereign states that existed under the Articles of Confederation.

» *[in Order to] establish Justice, insure domestic Tranquility, provide for the common defence, promote the general Welfare, and secure the Blessings of Liberty to ourselves and our Posterity:* This is an impressive list of objectives. The Articles of Confederation weren't able to deliver these goals. They didn't even set up any national law courts. The states were at one another's throats. And Congress wasn't able to offer protection against foreign enemies or the Native American tribes. But the Framers were confident that their new Constitution could secure these benefits for their own age and for the future. They turned out to be right!

Article I: Setting Up the Congress

Article I is by far the longest article of the Constitution (see the Appendix). Section 1 of that article reads as follows:

> All legislative Powers herein granted shall be vested in a Congress of the United States, which shall consist of a Senate and House of Representatives.

At first sight this section looks as though it gives Congress total legislative power — the power to make any laws it likes. The very first word, "All," certainly contributes to this impression. But that impression is false.

The most important word in this section is not "All" but the easily missed "granted." This important section can be rewritten like this:

REMEMBER

» The Constitution grants the federal government certain limited legislative powers — the power to pass laws on certain matters, but not on just anything.

» The Constitution grants *all* these *limited* legislative powers to a Congress.

» The Congress shall consist of two houses: a Senate and a House of Representatives.

Sections 2 through 7 of Article I spell out who can run for election to each branch of Congress, how often those elections take place, how many members each branch has, and (in broad terms) how the business of Congress is to be run. I discuss these topics in Chapter 11.

But by far the meatiest sections of Article I are Section 8, which lists the powers of Congress, and Section 9, which details specific limits on congressional power. In the following sections, I explain two reasons that Section 8, in particular, deserves special attention.

Magnifying the commerce power

Over the years, the Constitution has been interpreted in such a way that the most important part of Article I, Section 8 is the *Commerce Clause,* which confers on Congress the power

> To regulate Commerce with foreign Nations, and among the several States, and with the Indian Tribes.

CONTROVERSY

The U.S. Supreme Court has at times interpreted this clause — and particularly Congress's power over interstate commerce — so widely as to embrace virtually all economic activities. This interpretation is a far cry from what the Framers appear to have intended because the wording of the clause places interstate commerce slap bang between international trade and trade with the Native American tribes. This positioning can only mean that interstate commerce must be understood in the same limited way as the other two categories. I deal more fully with the Commerce Clause in Chapter 9.

(Mis)interpreting the "necessary and proper" clause

The "necessary and proper" clause of Article I, Section 8 is also important, but it too has suffered at the hands of greedy feds. This clause gives Congress the power

> To make all Laws which shall be necessary and proper for carrying into Execution the foregoing Powers, and all other Powers vested by this Constitution in the Government of the United States, or in any Department or Officer thereof.

Once again, it's easy to be unduly influenced by the opening words, "To make all Laws." But a close reading of the rest of the clause appears to indicate a serious limitation. The key words are "necessary and proper." Does this phrase apply to *all* congressional legislation? If it does, then it clearly acts as a limitation on the power of Congress.

IN MY OPINION

In the leading case of *McCulloch v. Maryland*, decided in 1819, Chief Justice John Marshall disagreed with this interpretation and held that, far from restricting the power of Congress, the "necessary and proper" clause actually extended that power. My own view is that Marshall was wrong about this and that his interpretation of this clause is one of his many "twistifications" (a phrase that Thomas Jefferson coined).

Article II: Hailing the Chief

Section 1 of Article II begins with these words:

> The executive Power shall be vested in a President of the United States of America.

Section 2 adds:

> *The President shall be Commander in Chief of the Army and Navy of the United States, and of the militia of the several states, when called into the actual service of the United States.*

REMEMBER

In addition to his executive and military powers, the President's approval is needed for a bill to become an Act of Congress. If the President doesn't approve a bill, he is commonly said to *veto* it. The presidential veto kills the bill concerned (but the veto can be overridden by a two-thirds majority in both houses of Congress). These legislative powers of the President are found in Article I, Section 7 of the Constitution.

The President is also Head of State of the United States (see Figure 4-1 for a look at four former presidents), a position that isn't mentioned in the Constitution at all — because the Framers didn't recognize it as a separate position. I discuss this and the other powers of the President in Chapter 10.

FIGURE 4-1:
Presidents Reagan, Ford, Carter, and Nixon in October 1981. While the President has great power as Head of State, it is a position not recognized in the Constitution.

Source: White House Photo Office

Listing presidential powers and duties

Article II is surprisingly brief. The only presidential powers and duties that are specifically enumerated are the following:

>> The power to make treaties — subject to confirmation by the Senate.

>> The power — subject to confirmation by the Senate — to appoint "Ambassadors, other public Ministers and Consuls, judges of the supreme Court, and all other Officers of the United States, whose Appointments are not herein otherwise provided for."

>> The power to fill casual vacancies in the Senate that occur during congressional recesses.

>> The duty to report to Congress on the state of the union (the origin of the annual State of the Union Address).

>> The power to recommend legislation to Congress.

>> The power to call a meeting of one or both houses of Congress "on extraordinary Occasions" — a power that has been exercised by 16 presidents.

>> The power to adjourn Congress "in Case of Disagreement" between the two Houses "with Respect to the Time of Adjournment."

>> The right to "receive Ambassadors and other public Ministers" representing foreign nations.

>> An obligation to "take Care that the Laws be faithfully executed" — a really important duty.

>> The power to appoint all officers of the United States armed forces.

Finally, Article II, Section 4 contains one of the best-known features of the Constitution — the provision for the impeachment of "The President, Vice President and all civil Officers of the United States." I discuss impeachment in Chapter 13.

Identifying the real issues

This list of presidential powers and duties looks boringly straightforward. So how come different presidents have exercised such different degrees of power? You need only compare a weak president like James Buchanan with his immediate successor, Abraham Lincoln, to notice the difference — or, say, a strong president like Theodore Roosevelt with his weak hand-picked successor, William Howard Taft.

The reason for these contrasts is the divergent interpretations of the Constitution that these different presidents embraced. These days, the main areas of dispute include

>> Presidential power in regard to war

>> Presidential power in regard to homeland security

>> The President's role in regard to healthcare

I discuss all these topics in Chapter 10.

Article III: Understating Judicial Power

Article III, which sets forth the power of the judiciary, looks pretty straightforward — and mind-numbingly dull. Here's Section 1:

> *The judicial Power of the United States shall be vested in one supreme Court, and in such inferior Courts as the Congress may from time to time ordain and establish. The judges, both of the supreme and inferior Courts, shall hold their Offices during good Behaviour.*

REMEMBER

The provision allowing federal judges to hold office "during good Behaviour" is effectively the same as saying "for life." That's why the battle over who will receive a coveted appointment to a federal judgeship is often protracted and heated. Quite a number of Supreme Court justices — including Chief Justice William Rehnquist and Justice Antonin Scalia — died in harness.

Article III, Section 2 lists the types of cases that the federal courts are empowered to hear. The U.S. Supreme Court is the most important court in the nation. The "inferior" federal courts include the U.S. courts of appeals, U.S. district courts, and also specialist courts such as the U.S. bankruptcy courts and the U.S. Tax Court.

There is only one surprise in the list of judicial functions in Article III: It includes cases "between a State and Citizens of another State," which were later excluded by the Eleventh Amendment (see Chapter 20).

CONTROVERSY

The most important power of the U.S. Supreme Court doesn't figure in the text of the Constitution at all. This is the power of *judicial review,* which I discuss at length in Chapter 12. In brief, here's what judicial review means: It allows the Supreme Court to decide whether a federal or state law is in violation of the U.S. Constitution. If the Court finds that a law conflicts with the Constitution, it declares the law unconstitutional. This means that the law (or the relevant part of the law) is *void,* or of no effect.

Because of judicial review, the Supreme Court is extremely powerful — arguably more powerful than either of the other two branches of government. The Court can strike down a law that has been passed by both houses of Congress and signed by the President! In the words of Chief Justice Charles Evans Hughes, "the Constitution is what the judges say it is."

Two key questions come to mind, both of which I discuss in Chapter 12:

>> **How come this great power of the Supreme Court isn't spelled out anywhere in the text of the Constitution?** The Framers of the Constitution may not have intended for the Court to wield such power; the Court arrogated the power of judicial review to itself. Chief Justice John Marshall started the ball rolling with a famous 1803 opinion in *Marbury v. Madison* — a case I discuss in Chapter 23.

>> **Was the Court's decision to give itself the power of judicial review wrong?** Probably. But nonetheless, the power remains intact today.

Article IV: Getting Along with the Neighbors — and Uncle Sam

The first sentence of Section 1 of Article IV is known as the *Full Faith and Credit Clause.* It reads as follows:

> *Full Faith and Credit shall be given in each State to the public Acts, Records, and judicial Proceedings of every other State.*

This clause appears to mean that every state has to recognize the laws and court decisions of every other state. But the Supreme Court established a "public policy" exception to the operation of this clause. In 1939, the Court ruled that "there are some limitations to the extent to which a state may be required by the full faith and credit clause to enforce even the judgment of another state in contravention of its own statutes or policy."

It is possible for a state to get around the "full faith and credit" rule. Between 1996 and 2004, 39 states passed laws defining marriage as the union of a man and a woman. Most of these laws also explicitly prohibited the state from honoring same-sex marriages solemnized in other states and in foreign countries. But the U.S. Supreme Court decision in *Obergefell v. Hodges* (2015) made same-sex marriage legal throughout the U.S. and obliged all states to recognize same-sex marriages performed in all other states.

The opening sentence of Section 2 of Article IV, the Privileges and Immunities Clause, is less controversial. It reads as follows:

> *The Citizens of each State shall be entitled to all Privileges and Immunities of Citizens in the several States.*

But even this clause has had its problems — especially when it has come up against the clause modeled on it in the Fourteenth Amendment, which I discuss in Chapter 21.

Article V: Changing versus Amending the Constitution

Article V lays down the rather complicated procedure required for amending the Constitution — or, to be precise, four alternative routes that can be adopted for this purpose. With one exception — the Twenty-First Amendment, repealing Prohibition — the procedure adopted for every amendment has been the same, namely:

>> Proposal by a two-thirds majority in both houses of Congress

>> Ratification by three-fourths of the state legislatures

The Framers deliberately (and cleverly) made the procedure for amending the Constitution as complicated and elaborate as possible — because they didn't want their handiwork undone by the shifting breezes of political fashion. On the face of it, the Framers appear to have achieved their objective: Since the ratification of the Bill of Rights (the first 10 amendments) all at once in 1791, only 17 amendments have been made to the Constitution — in the space of more than two centuries.

REMEMBER

Does this remarkable fact mean that, with the exception of these 17 amendments, the Constitution today is the same as it was in 1791? No, not at all. It means only that the wording of the Constitution hasn't been changed by formal amendment. There have been plenty of changes, accomplished by judicial interpretation. The power of the Supreme Court is such that it is able to "amend" the Constitution — sometimes quite radically — by interpreting a word or phrase. I discuss this topic in Chapter 5.

Article VI: Fudging Federalism

The most important part of Article VI is the Supremacy Clause, which reads as follows:

> This Constitution, and the Laws of the United States which shall be made in Pursuance thereof; and all Treaties made, or which shall be made, under the Authority of the United States, shall be the supreme Law of the Land; and the judges in every State shall be bound thereby, any Thing in the Constitution or Laws of any State to the Contrary notwithstanding.

This clause purportedly has the following effects:

>> It sets federal law above state law.

>> It makes the U.S. Constitution the highest law in the nation.

>> It also places international treaties above state law.

I explore these effects, and the questions they raise, in Chapter 7.

Article VII: Ratifying the Constitution

A nice, easy one at last! Article VII of the Constitution, the last part of the original, unamended Constitution, sets out the requirement for ratifying the Constitution. It's now purely of historical interest and doesn't apply to the ratification of amendments, which is governed by Article V.

Chapter **5**

Changing the Constitution by Amendment and Interpretation

How does the Constitution change? Only with difficulty. The Framers of the Constitution believed that they'd hit the jackpot. They had thought and debated long and hard about the best form of government, and they wanted to make sure that future generations wouldn't mess up their perfect construction by adding or subtracting bits arbitrarily. Benjamin Franklin, one of the Framers, described the Constitution as creating a system of government that was "near to perfection." So the Framers deliberately made the Constitution very hard to change — not impossible, just very complicated.

I'm talking here about *amendments*: official, formal changes to the Constitution. But there is another, less formal kind of change — through decisions of the U.S. Supreme Court *interpreting* the Constitution. You won't find that type of change even mentioned in the Constitution because the Framers never imagined change could come about in that way. It simply wasn't supposed to happen.

Some of the most important changes to the Constitution have been made as a result of Supreme Court decisions. These include:

>> Banning racial segregation

>> Expanding the rights of people charged with crimes

>> Declaring a right to privacy

>> Establishing a (limited) right to abortion

>> Legalizing same-sex marriage

I come back to judge–made changes later in the chapter. But first I discuss the type of change allowed by the Constitution: amendment.

Noting the Four Paths to an Amendment

Article V of the Constitution provides for no fewer than four different ways of amending the Constitution. Ready for some fancy footwork?

>> Congress proposes an amendment — passed by a two-thirds majority of both houses. This amendment is then *ratified* (confirmed) by the legislatures of three-fourths of all the states.

>> Congress proposes an amendment — passed by a two-thirds majority of both houses. This amendment is then ratified by special conventions in three-fourths of the states.

>> Two-thirds of the state legislatures ask Congress to call a national convention. This convention proposes an amendment, which is then ratified by the legislatures of three-fourths of the states.

>> Two-thirds of the state legislatures ask Congress to call a national convention. This convention proposes an amendment, which is then ratified by special conventions in three-fourths of the states.

Whew! A lot of this technical detail is of academic interest only. The first of the four ways of amending the Constitution has by far the greatest practical significance. This method has been used for 26 of the 27 amendments ratified so far. The second method was used only once — for the Twenty–First Amendment, which repealed the Eighteenth Amendment (Prohibition). And the third and fourth routes for amendment provided by the Constitution have never been used.

REMEMBER

The President is not involved in the amendment process at all. He can neither propose an amendment nor veto it. This is surprising, to say the least, because Article I, Section 7 of the Constitution gives the President the right to approve or disapprove "Every Order, Resolution, or Vote" needing the agreement of the House and the Senate. Doesn't this cover amendments as well? On the basis of Article I, Section 7, it sure looks like it. But Article V, the article that deals with amending the Constitution, doesn't mention the President at all.

In *Hollingsworth v. Virginia*, decided in 1798, the Supreme Court ruled that the President had no say in regard to amendments, and this is still the position today. Presidents have occasionally signed proposed amendments nevertheless, to give them extra support. In 1861 President James Buchanan signed a pro-slavery proposed amendment for this reason, and in 1865 Abraham Lincoln followed his example by signing the Thirteenth Amendment abolishing slavery.

Explaining What Happens in Practice

As is so often the case, the words of the Constitution raise more questions than they answer. Let me tackle a few of these questions:

>> **Two-thirds of both houses of Congress can propose an amendment. Does this mean two-thirds of all members?** No. Only two-thirds of those present and voting at the time — provided there's a *quorum* (more than half of the members) present in each house.

>> **What exactly is meant by a *convention?*** A convention is a meeting of delegates, and Article V provides for two different kinds of conventions: a national convention for proposing amendments and state conventions for ratifying amendments.

>> **Who gets to be chosen as a member of a national convention?** The only national constitutional convention in U.S. history was the initial Philadelphia Convention that drafted the U.S. Constitution in 1787. The 55 delegates were not elected, but selected by the state legislatures. States have recently made more than 500 requests for a national convention, but Congress has remained resistant to all such requests. The method of choosing delegates to any future convention is undecided.

>> **What powers would a national convention have?** A national convention would be permitted to propose amendments but not to ratify them. Why? Because Article V of the Constitution leaves the "Mode of Ratification" up to Congress. But a national convention would in practice have unlimited power to propose amendments or even a radical rewriting of the Constitution — which is probably why Congress is reluctant to agree to another national convention.

>> **Who gets to be chosen as a member of a state convention?** The only time state conventions were ever called was in 1933, to ratify the Twenty-First Amendment. Different states had different arrangements. But a common method was for the voters in the state concerned to elect delegates from a list chosen by the state governor in consultation with other state officials.

>> **What powers does a state convention have?** State conventions can ratify proposed amendments but can't themselves propose any amendments. The Twenty-First Amendment is the only one that has been ratified by this method.

THE *PROPOSED* AMENDMENTS WHICH DIDN'T QUITE MAKE IT

Six amendments to the Constitution cleared the first hurdle of congressional approval but were never ratified. Here they are:

- **Article 1 of the original Bill of Rights, 1789:** This proposed amendment was intended to ensure that the size of the House of Representatives would continue to grow with the population. It stipulated that, as the population grew, "there shall not be less than two hundred Representatives, nor more than one Representative for every fifty thousand persons." It was ratified by 11 states and is still technically open, needing ratification by 27 more states to become part of the Constitution. But this is most unlikely ever to happen, as the Reapportionment Act of 1929 capped the size of the House of Representatives at 435 members.

- **Foreign titles of nobility and gifts, 1810:** This proposed amendment stripped of their citizenship any U.S. citizen who accepted any foreign title of nobility or "any present, pension, office or emolument of any kind whatever" from a foreign power. It was ratified by 12 states and is still technically open, needing ratification by 26 more states to be adopted as part of the Constitution. This proposed amendment was an extension of Article I, Section 9, Clause 8 of the Constitution, known as the Emoluments Clause, which became topical under the Trump Administration. The main difference between the Emoluments Clause and the proposed amendment is that the amendment contained a definite, and harsh, penalty for breach.

- **Corwin Amendment, 1861:** This is probably the most intriguing of the six failed amendments. This proposed amendment was the brainchild of lame-duck President James Buchanan in a last-ditch attempt to avert a civil war. Without using the word *slavery*, the amendment guaranteed the preservation of slavery in all states where it already existed, without, however, dealing with the vexed question of slavery in the territories or new states. Congress passed this proposed amendment with the requisite two-thirds majority in both houses just two days before the end of Buchanan's term, and the President, in an unprecedented move, signed it himself. The widespread support for this amendment in Congress even after the representatives of seven southern states had withdrawn shows that the North had more tolerance of southern slavery than might have been expected. And two days later the new President, Abraham Lincoln, alluding in his Inaugural Address to the proposed amendment and to the preservation of southern slavery in particular, declared: "I have no objection to its being made express and irrevocable." Ohio and Maryland then ratified the amendment, and Lincoln's own state, Illinois, did so as well, though its ratification was technically invalidated. But it was too late to avert civil war. Had Congress approved the amendment in time for it to be ratified before Buchanan's term expired, there's just a chance that the lives of 620,000 men may have been spared.

- **Child Labor Amendment, 1926:** This proposed amendment gave Congress "power to limit, regulate, and prohibit the labor of persons eighteen years of age." It was ratified by 28 states and needs to be ratified by an additional 10 states to become part of the Constitution. But this is unlikely to occur, as the Fair Labor Standards Act of 1938, which the Supreme Court approved in 1941, achieves essentially what the amendment was intended to do.

- **Equal Rights Amendment (ERA), 1972:** This proposed amendment was intended to guarantee equal rights for women. The main section of the amendment is very brief: "Equality of rights under the law shall not be denied or abridged by the United States or by any State on account of sex." After its passage by Congress in 1972, the ERA was sent to the states with a seven-year deadline for ratification by the requisite 38 states. However, only 35 states had ratified it by the time of the deadline, and in the meantime, 4 states rescinded their ratification, though the acting governor of Kentucky vetoed the rescinding resolution of that state's legislature. In 1982, the U.S. Supreme Court ruled that an attempted extension of the deadline was unconstitutional. The reason for the controversy surrounding the ERA was that, despite massive support, it also aroused a good deal of opposition among women. Phyllis Schlafly, a leading activist against the ERA, argued that the amendment "would lead to women being drafted by the military and to public unisex bathrooms." Opponents of the ERA also claimed that the Equal Pay Act of 1963 and the Civil Rights Act of 1964 made the ERA unnecessary.

- **Washington D.C. Voting Rights Amendment, 1978:** This proposed amendment would have accorded Washington, D.C., the same representation as a state. The deadline for ratification was seven years, during which time only 16 states ratified it. One reason for the failure of this amendment was that it would have repealed the Twenty-Third Amendment, ratified in 1961, which gave the nation's capital three Electoral College votes in presidential elections but no voting representation in Congress (see Chapter 22).

In the 200-plus years that the Constitution has been in force, no fewer than 5,000 — that's right, 5,000 — amendments have been introduced in Congress. Of these, only 33 have gotten over the two-thirds hurdle to be formally proposed, and of these just 27 have made it through the ratification process to become part of the Constitution. This figure of 27 includes the first 10 amendments, which were all ratified together on December 15, 1791, and are collectively known as the *Bill of Rights*. This leaves the amazingly small total of 17 amendments in the whole period from 1791 to the present day.

Listing the Amendments

Here's a rundown of all 27 amendments that have made it into the U.S. Constitution:

>> First Amendment: Freedom of speech, religion, and assembly

>> Second Amendment: Right to bear arms

>> Third Amendment: Ban on quartering of soldiers

>> Fourth Amendment: Unreasonable search and seizure

>> Fifth Amendment: Grand juries, double jeopardy, self-incrimination, due process, and the taking of private property for public use

>> Sixth Amendment: Jury trial and other rights of defendants in criminal trials

>> Seventh Amendment: Trial by jury in civil suits

>> Eighth Amendment: Cruel and unusual punishments

>> Ninth Amendment: Rights retained by the people

>> Tenth Amendment: Powers reserved to the states or to the people

>> Eleventh Amendment: Ban on lawsuits brought by citizens of one state against another state

>> Twelfth Amendment: Electing the President and Vice President

>> Thirteenth Amendment: Abolishing slavery

>> Fourteenth Amendment: Rights of citizenship, obligations of the states, due process

>> Fifteenth Amendment: Ban on racial discrimination in voting

>> Sixteenth Amendment: Income tax

>> Seventeenth Amendment: Direct election of senators

>> Eighteenth Amendment: Prohibition

- >> Nineteenth Amendment: Women's right to vote

- >> Twentieth Amendment: Fixing new term dates for the President and Congress

- >> Twenty-First Amendment: Repealing Prohibition

- >> Twenty-Second Amendment: Presidential term limits

- >> Twenty-Third Amendment: Voting rights for Washington, D.C.

- >> Twenty-Fourth Amendment: Banning poll tax as a bar to voting rights

- >> Twenty-Fifth Amendment: Death, removal, resignation, or incapacity of the President

- >> Twenty-Sixth Amendment: Voting age reduced to 18

- >> Twenty-Seventh Amendment: No pay increases for Congress until after the general election

I give each amendment its due in Parts 4 and 5 of this book.

Debating the Need for Judge-Made Law

CONTROVERSY

Article V of the Constitution lays down pretty clear procedures for amending the Constitution, providing a choice of four routes. Isn't this enough? Take a look at the Supreme Court building in Figure 5-1. Should the "Guardians of the Law" be allowed to make changes to the Constitution?

Dissenting views to restricting change

The objections to limiting constitutional change to the methods set out in Article V are as follows:

- >> The Article V procedures are cumbersome and slow.

- >> As a result, we are stuck with a Constitution that is largely the product of a bygone age.

- >> This situation makes it difficult for the Constitution to respond to changes in society and politics.

- >> The old-fashioned language of the Constitution has to be interpreted and made relevant to modern society.

- >> The U.S. Supreme Court is very well-suited to making the Constitution relevant to modern society.

FIGURE 5-1:
Front facade, U.S. Supreme Court, Washington, D.C. The sculpture represents the "Authority of Law" or "Guardian of Law." The tablet of laws held by the figure is inscribed with the word LEX, Latin for "law."

Maintaining proper amendment procedure

On the other side are people who argue that we should stick to the proper Article V procedure for amending the Constitution. They believe that it's just plain wrong for judges to rewrite the Constitution. Here are some of the reasons supporting this view:

>> The Article V procedures ensure that changes to the Constitution are made only after due consideration and with wide support.

>> The principles enunciated in the Constitution are timeless.

>> The Constitution should not become the plaything of changing fashions.

>> The language of the Constitution does have to be interpreted, but that is not the same thing as changing its meaning.

>> If judges rewrite the Constitution according to their own predilections, this can only lead to disagreement over what the Constitution means.

>> The U.S. Supreme Court — made up of unelected judges — is not entitled to change the Constitution.

>> It's simply undemocratic, or even anti-democratic, for judges to rewrite the Constitution according to their own likes and dislikes.

IN MY OPINION

Which of these two points of view is right? You're welcome to make up your own mind, but my own view is that it's wrong for judges to try to amend the Constitution.

Sampling judge-made amendments

Here are a few examples of changes to the U.S. Constitution made by decisions of the Supreme Court:

>> **Privacy:** In *Griswold v. Connecticut* (1965), the Supreme Court discovered a right of privacy lurking in "emanations" from the "penumbras" (shadowy surrounds) of certain guarantees in the Bill of Rights. This was the only way in which the majority on the Court could get over the serious problem identified by Justice Potter Stewart, dissenting: "I can find no such general right of privacy in the Bill of Rights, in any other part of the Constitution, or in any case ever before decided by this Court."

>> **Abortion:** Justice Harry Blackman, writing for the majority of the Supreme Court in *Roe v. Wade* (1973), admitted that "The Constitution does not explicitly mention any right of privacy." However, "the Court has recognized that a right of personal privacy does exist under the Constitution." This right of privacy, the majority on the Court concluded, includes a woman's right to terminate her pregnancy — an absolute right up to the end of the first trimester (weeks 1 to 12) and after that when it's necessary to protect a woman's health. Justice Byron White (dissenting) condemned the majority decision as "an exercise of raw judicial power," adding, "I find nothing in the language or history of the Constitution to support the Court's judgment." And even Justice Ruth Bader Ginsburg, a strong pro-choice advocate, has criticized *Roe v. Wade* as "heavy-handed judicial intervention" in an issue that should rather have been left to the democratic political process. Opposition to *Roe* comes chiefly from those who believe in the "right to life" of the unborn child. And it's also possible to argue that abortion should not just be a woman's right to choose but should also involve the husband or father, whose right even to be notified was rejected by the Supreme Court in *Planned Parenthood v. Casey* (1982).

>> **Affirmative action:** In the landmark case of *Brown v. Board of Education* (1954), the Supreme Court ruled that racial segregation of students in public schools was unconstitutional because it violated the Fourteenth Amendment, which prohibits states from denying anyone "the equal protection of the laws." *Brown,* like the Fourteenth Amendment on which it was based, was concerned with equal rights. But when it failed to lead to racial equality, President John F. Kennedy issued an Executive Order (which is not supposed to change the law) requiring government employers to

"take affirmative action" in selecting applicants for government posts. This marked the beginning of widespread affirmative action, especially in education. In *Regents of the University of California v. Bakke* (1978), the Supreme Court found the quota system operated by the University's Medical School unconstitutional, while still allowing race to be taken into account in admissions. In 2007, in a case involving a Seattle and a Kentucky school district, Chief Justice John Roberts famously concluded his plurality opinion with the words: "The way to stop discrimination on the basis of race is to stop discriminating on the basis of race." Or, as Justice Clarence Thomas put it, the Constitution is "color-blind." The greatest victory against affirmative action to date came in *Schuette v. Coalition to Defend Affirmative Action* (2014), in which six justices of the Supreme Court upheld a Michigan Initiative supported by 58 percent of voters, which amended the state constitution by banning affirmative action (with some exceptions) "in the operation of public employment, public education, or public contracting." However, affirmative action is far from dead, and was again upheld by the Supreme Court for university admissions in the second *Fisher v. University of Texas* case decided in 2016.

» **Same-sex marriage:** In *Obergefell v. Hodges* (2015), the Supreme Court decided by a 5–4 majority that marriage is a fundamental constitutional right guaranteed to same-sex couples as much as to male-female couples. Chief Justice Roberts penned a strong dissent: "The majority's decision is an act of will, not legal judgment. The right it announces has no basis in the Constitution or this Court's precedent . . . The Court invalidates the marriage laws of more than half the States and orders the transformation of a social institution that has formed the basis of human society for millennia, for the Kalahari Bushmen and the Han Chinese, the Carthaginians and the Aztecs. Just who do we think we are?"

» **Money in politics:** Unlike all the other cases in this section, *Citizens United v. Federal Election Commission* (2010) may be regarded as a conservative decision. It arose out of a challenge by a conservative nonprofit organization called Citizens United to the McCain–Feingold Act of 2002, which prohibited corporations and labor unions from funding "electioneering communications" within 30 days before a primary or 60 days before a general election. Citizens United wanted to air on TV an advertisement of its own political documentary titled *Hillary: The Movie* during the 2008 Democratic Party presidential primaries. The majority opinion written by Justice Anthony Kennedy struck down McCain–Feingold as a violation of the First Amendment's protection of freedom of speech, which prohibits any restriction on political expenditure by corporations and labor unions. In joining the decision of the Court, Justice Antonin Scalia claimed that there was no reason why the right of freedom of speech under the First Amendment didn't include "the freedom to speak in association with other individuals, including association in the corporate form." Justice John Paul Stevens concluded his robust dissent with the observation that the American people had "fought against the distinctive corrupting potential of corporate electioneering since the days of Theodore Roosevelt. It is a strange time to repudiate that common sense. While American democracy is imperfect, few outside the majority of this Court would have thought its flaws included a dearth of corporate money in politics."

2

We the People: How the United States Is Governed

Chapter 6

Scrutinizing Sovereignty: Who Rules America?

"We the People" rule the U.S. of A. Right? Ummm, well, maybe not. The President and a few other big hitters are involved too. Here are the main contenders for the title of ruler of the United States:

» We the People

» The President

» The Congress

» The states

» The U.S. Supreme Court

» The Council on Foreign Relations, the Trilateral Commission, and the Bilderberg Conference

I examine the claims of each of these contenders in turn. My conclusion is that sovereignty isn't held by any one single person or institution — sovereignty is shared among the first five institutions that I have just listed. But that doesn't mean that all five institutions have an equal share. They do not, but the degree of dominance that any one institution enjoys at any one time varies in accordance with circumstances and with the personalities concerned.

Introducing "We the People"

The phrase "We the People" entered history when it appeared in the Preamble (or introduction) to the U.S. Constitution (see Chapter 4). The Preamble is a fanfare proclaiming the nature and purpose of the Constitution. It doesn't form part of the Constitution as a legally enforceable instrument. But courts sometimes cite the Preamble as evidence of the Framers' intentions in drafting the Constitution as a whole.

REMEMBER

Does the use of the phrase "We the People" mean that the Framers claimed to be establishing a democracy? Not at all. Ancient constitutions and legal systems claimed to have been handed down by a god, a king, or some semi-divine law-giver. The Framers tacitly rejected these models and claimed a popular basis for the U.S. Constitution — but that is not the same as claiming that the system of government established by that constitution was a democracy. Indeed, neither the word *democracy* nor the word *democratic* figures anywhere in the text of the Constitution (see Chapter 1).

Ordaining and establishing a Constitution

The Preamble claims that "We the People . . . do ordain and establish this Constitution for the United States of America." Is this claim true? The Constitution was drafted by the Philadelphia Convention made up of 55 delegates from 12 of the 13 states. (Rhode Island refused to participate.) The 55 delegates included most of the Founding Fathers of the nation, with the notable exceptions of John Adams and Thomas Jefferson, who were both serving in Europe at the time. Jefferson described the Convention as "an assembly of demigods" but regretted their decision to conduct their deliberations behind closed doors.

Who picked these demigods? *Not* "We the People." They were selected by the state legislatures, which in turn were elected. But only about 15 percent of the adult white male population had the right to vote. So "We the People" rings a bit hollow as far as the drafting of the Constitution is concerned.

But "We the People" at least ratified (confirmed) the Constitution, right? Not exactly. Ratification was entrusted to a specially elected convention in each of the 13 states (except Rhode Island). So "We the People" had only an indirect say on ratification.

MAKING DEMOCRACY FASHIONABLE

The acceptability of democracy as a political ideal can be gauged from the use of the word *democratic* as a party political label.

Historians often refer to the political party founded in 1791 by Thomas Jefferson and James Madison as the Democratic-Republican Party, but in fact both Jefferson and Madison referred to themselves simply as Republicans and to their party as the Republican Party down to 1823. (That party had nothing to do with the modern Republican Party, by the way.)

Adherents of the party of Jefferson and Madison were sometimes called *democrats* — not by themselves but as an insult by their opponents, who equated *democrats* with *Jacobins,* the most extreme French revolutionaries. Ex-President George Washington himself said of a "professed Democrat" that "he will leave nothing unattempted to overturn the Government of this Country."

At the party's first national convention, held in 1832, it was still calling itself the Republican Party. It officially changed its name to the Democratic Party only in 1844. By this time *democratic* had become a positive political label — thanks largely to Andrew Jackson, who was instrumental in extending voting rights to all adult white males.

REMEMBER

The Constitution did not aim to establish a democracy. Instead, the Framers were aiming to establish "a *Republican* Form of Government" — which was not the same thing at all. See Chapter 2 for an explanation.

Resolving to preserve democracy

The first six presidents were all members of a wealthy elite. The election of Andrew Jackson to the presidency in 1828 broke with that aristocratic tradition.

Andrew Jackson's form of democracy

Jackson was an unabashed populist. The first plank in the program of *Jacksonian democracy* was the extension of voting rights to all white men, sweeping away property qualifications. Jackson also repeatedly called for a constitutional amendment to abolish the Electoral College system, which he saw as an undemocratic way of electing the President.

But Jackson was no liberal. His populism extended only to the white population; he was himself a slave owner. And his belief in the *Manifest Destiny* of the United States to expand westward and control the whole of North America from the Atlantic to the Pacific Ocean resulted in a less than sympathetic attitude toward Native Americans.

As a result of Jackson's two-term strong presidency followed by the single term of the skillful Democratic Party organizer, Martin Van Buren, and that of the much underrated James K. Polk, populist democratic ideals became widely accepted in the 1840s.

Abraham Lincoln's vision of democracy

By the time of Abraham Lincoln, who was first elected President in 1860, democracy had become quite respectable. Lincoln concluded his famous Gettysburg Address with a solemn pledge that has echoed down the years:

> *We here highly resolve that these dead shall not have died in vain — that this nation, under God, shall have a new birth of freedom — and that government of the people, by the people, for the people, shall not perish from the earth.*

This is pretty heady stuff. But what exactly does it mean? Lincoln delivered his speech on November 19, 1863, just a few months after the bloody battle of Gettysburg. The occasion was the dedication of the Soldiers' National Cemetery in Gettysburg, Pennsylvania.

Lincoln didn't use the word *democracy*, but his three rhythmical phrases — "government of the people, by the people, for the people" — are commonly taken as a definition of democracy.

Was Lincoln holding up democracy as an ideal for the future? Yes, but he also seems to have thought that it already existed. Indeed, the theme of his two-minute address was that the cause of the Union in the Civil War was the cause of democracy.

But did Lincoln really have the right to cast himself as the spokesman for democracy? His own election to the presidency in 1860 was anything but a landslide. Although he won a majority of electoral votes, he carried only 18 states out of 33 and got less than 40 percent of the popular vote. His election to the presidency was the most divisive in American history. When Lincoln was declared the winner of the 1860 presidential election, seven southern states seceded even before his inauguration.

Lincoln's identification with democracy also has another problem, because government "by the people" looks very much like *direct democracy*, which has never existed in the United States.

Defining democracy

The word *democracy* comes to us from the Greek *demokratia*, meaning the "power of the people."

But can the people ever rule themselves? Well, it did happen in ancient Athens — sort of. The citizens all met together in the *Ekklesia*, or Assembly, and deliberated. But only adult males had the rights of citizenship. Women, slaves, and resident aliens had no civic rights. Athens had about 30,000 citizens at its height — about 10 percent of the population.

REMEMBER

Athenian democracy was *direct democracy.* That form of government would be impossible in the United States today with a population of around 325 million! Instead, the type of democracy that exists now is *indirect* or *representative democracy* — in which the people don't run the government themselves but pick other people to do it for them.

So, how does an indirect democracy stand up to Lincoln's three-part test?

>> **Government of the people:** This is ambiguous. Does it mean that the people are doing the governing or that they are *being* governed? If the former, then it's the same as "government by the people." If the latter, then it could apply to any form of government. Any government is automatically a government *of* the people in that sense. It doesn't have to be a democratic form of government. A monarchy, a dictatorship, an oligarchy — all are governments *of* the people, but they aren't governments *by* the people.

>> **Government by the people:** This is the elusive one. Government *by* the people, in the sense of direct democracy, has never existed in the United States — and could never exist. So what was Abe Lincoln thinking of? Or did he just figure that it had a nice ring to it as part of a threesome?

>> **Government for the people:** Every government of every kind everywhere in the world always maintains that it governs in the interests of its people — or *for* the people. This is not a specifically democratic feature at all.

In fairness to Abe, he probably figured that the sort of indirect, representative democracy that we have in the United States was actually government *by* the people — a pretty dangerous assumption to make by a guy who got into the White House with just 39.8 percent of the popular vote. However, he did become popular enough to make it on to the $5 bill (see Figure 6-1). Perhaps being outspoken has its advantages!

Testing for democracy today

But what about today? Is the United States a true democracy in the 21st century? Yes and no.

Here are some points **in favor of** and *against* classifying the United States as a democracy:

>> **Everybody 18 years or older has the right to vote.** *But the voters are usually presented with a choice of one out of only two candidates — if that. The really important election often is not the general election but the Democratic or Republican primary.*

>> **Voters can also pick the candidates for the political party of their choice by participating in the primaries.** *But the choice in primaries is usually among a bunch of millionaires — or candidates bankrolled by political action committees (PACs) funded by corporate money.*

>> **Office-holders are mostly restricted to comparatively short terms, like four years for the President and two years for members of the House of Representatives.** *Although presidents are limited to two elected terms, representatives and senators can be reelected indefinitely — and quite often are!*

>> **More posts are filled by popular election than in most other countries — often including state judges, mayors, school boards, and (previously) even dogcatchers.** *But most elective positions are at the state level. It's a pity federal judges aren't elected too!*

>> **Popular or citizens' initiatives, propositions, or referenda are the closest thing in the United States today to ancient direct democracy. They allow the voters a direct say in no fewer than 24 states plus the District of Columbia.** *But initiatives are just votes on specific issues — a far cry from decision-making on a day-to-day basis. Also, initiatives exist purely at the state level. Moves to allow national initiatives have never gotten very far.*

>> **The United States has a healthy two-party system that guarantees competition.** *But quite a number of districts — and even whole states — are routinely in the red or blue column.*

>> **The views represented in U.S. political institutions span a wide range.** *But third parties and independents have little chance of being elected — largely because of the winner-take-all electoral system.*

So, do "We the People" rule the roost? No, because the power of the people is indirect — and it can also happen, as in 2016, that someone can be elected President with a majority of electoral votes but a minority of the popular vote. Yet, "We the People" must certainly be regarded as having *some* share of sovereignty at least. Let us now turn to the power of the President, which I examine in more detail in Chapter 10.

Hailing the Chief

The President of the United States is commonly said to be the most powerful person in the world, but how much power does he exercise in the United States?

From the beginning, critics of the Constitution were afraid that the President would become too monarchical. For example, Patrick Henry, the radical revolutionary, characterized the Constitution as "squinting towards monarchy." To counter these fears, George Washington discouraged people from addressing him as "Your Excellency," preferring the more republican appellation, "Mr. President."

REMEMBER

The Framers were careful to incorporate into the Constitution the principle of the *separation of powers* coupled with a system of *checks and balances*. The purpose of this arrangement was to prevent any one of the three branches of government — Executive, Legislative, and Judicial — from becoming too powerful.

Here are the points **in favor of** and *against* regarding the President as sovereign:

>> **The President combines the position of head of state with executive power, so his dominance over the federal government is guaranteed.** *Not so. Periods of strong presidential power have alternated with periods when the President was pretty insignificant compared to Congress and the Supreme Court. Abraham Lincoln was a strong President, but the presidents who preceded and succeeded him were mostly pretty weak. After the strong presidencies of Theodore Roosevelt and Woodrow Wilson, Congress became dominant again, until the so-called "imperial presidency" of Franklin D. Roosevelt. In 1973, Watergate dealt a severe blow to presidential power, but Ronald Reagan put the presidency on a*

strong footing again, which benefited Bill Clinton, George W. Bush, Barack Obama, and Donald Trump.

>> **The President has control over foreign affairs and defense, especially in times of war.** *Sure, but the War Powers Act allows Congress to limit presidential war powers. The Senate also has the power to block presidential appointees. And the Supreme Court can clip the President's wings too, as happened with President George W. Bush in regard to Guantanamo Bay, and with Donald Trump over his travel ban.*

>> **The President can veto bills that have passed Congress, and a presidential veto can be overridden only by a two-thirds majority in both houses of Congress.** *True, but vetoes can backfire, as President Bill Clinton found out when his deadlock with Congress over the budget twice paralyzed the federal government for months.*

At the time of this writing, the power of the President is great but certainly not unchallenged. A particularly sharp thorn in the side of President Trump is the appointment of Robert Mueller III as special counsel with the power to investigate the President without the President having the direct power to fire him. I turn now to Congress, which I examine more closely in Chapter 11.

Congress: Flexing Its Lawmaking Muscle

In 1884, when a young Woodrow Wilson wrote a book about the U.S. constitutional practice, he titled his book *Congressional Government.* He wrote, "The actual form of our present government is simply a scheme of congressional supremacy." Nobody could write that today — and Wilson himself actually turned out to be a strong President, although he was thwarted by Congress in regard to his pet project, the League of Nations (a forerunner of the United Nations), which the U.S. never joined.

The President can veto any bill passed by both houses of Congress, but that veto can be overridden by a two-thirds majority in both houses. This overriding has occurred comparatively rarely. Here's a rundown of the situation since 1981, when Ronald Reagan entered the White House:

>> **Barack Obama:** Congress overrides President Obama's veto of the Justice Against Sponsors of Terrorism Bill of 2016, which allows families of victims of the 9/11 terrorist outrage of 2001 to sue Saudi Arabia. This was the only time that an Obama veto was overridden.

- **》 George W. Bush:** Congress overrides President George W. Bush's veto of the Medicare Improvements for Patients and Providers Bill of 2008. This was one of four of George W.'s vetoes that were overridden by Congress.

- **》 William Clinton:** Congress overrides President Clinton's veto of the Private Securities Litigation Reform Bill of 1995, which was designed to limit frivolous lawsuits. Clinton's veto was overridden on only one other occasion.

- **》 George H.W. Bush:** Congress overrides President George H.W. Bush's veto of the Cable Television Consumer Protection and Competition Bill of 1992. This was the only override of a veto by President Bush 41.

- **》 Ronald Reagan:** Congress overrides President Reagan's veto of the Comprehensive Anti-Apartheid Bill of 1986, which imposes sanctions on South Africa. This was one of four of Reagan's vetoes that were overridden by Congress.

But the conflict between the President and Congress pales into insignificance by comparison with the conflict between the Supreme Court and the other two branches of government. See the next section.

Giving the States Their Due

Do the states have a share in the sovereignty of the United States? Absolutely. The history of the United States could easily be written in terms of the tensions between state and federal power.

"Incorporation" is the key issue in the relationship between the states and the feds — the question of how much of the Bill of Rights applies to the states as well as to the federal government. Why is this called "incorporation"? Because the question is whether the Bill of Rights (or any part of it) is *incorporated* into the Fourteenth Amendment by one of three provisions in that amendment: (a) the "due process" clause; (b) the "privileges or immunities" clause; and (c) the "equal protection of the laws" clause.

After many twists and turns, the U.S. Supreme Court now recognizes the whole of the first eight amendments as applying to the states as well as to the federal government, with only two small exceptions: the Fifth Amendment provision for indictment by a grand jury and the Seventh Amendment right to a jury trial in civil lawsuits. In other words, these two features are left to the states. Currently, only about half the states use grand juries for indictments. But jury trials are available at the request of either party in a civil suit in every state except Louisiana.

Other important state-based issues include the following:

>> **State sovereign immunity:** See Chapter 7.

>> **Presidential elections:** The national popular vote takes second place to the state-based electoral college system. The winning candidate needs a majority of electoral votes, with or without a majority in the popular vote. For example, in 2016 Donald Trump was elected president with a majority of electoral votes but a minority in the popular vote. See Chapter 10.

I deal with the power of the states in Chapters 7 and 20.

The High Court: Saying What the Law Is

The Supreme Court certainly deserves to be up there with the President and the Congress as a sharer in sovereignty.

This idea would have come as a shock to the Framers. The Constitution establishes the principle of the separation of powers, in which the three branches of government — the Executive, Legislative, and Judicial branches — are all equal, and each acts as a check and balance against the others.

However, one of the leading Framers of the Constitution, Alexander Hamilton, was convinced that, with separation of powers, the judiciary "will always be the least dangerous" to the other two branches of government because it lacked either the power of the sword or the power of the purse.

From a present-day vantage point, Hamilton's view of the judiciary as a shrinking violet seems almost laughable. For example, Hamilton spoke of the power to "prescribe the rules by which the duties and rights of every citizen are to be regulated." This is a perfect description of one of the many powers exercised by the Supreme Court — but Hamilton attributed it to Congress!

REMEMBER

Hamilton wrote the words that I have just quoted in 1788. He could not have known how completely the role of the Supreme Court was to be transformed by Chief Justice John Marshall, who held office from 1801 to 1835. In the famous case of *Marbury v. Madison*, decided in 1803, Marshall said,

> *It is emphatically the province and the duty of the judicial department to say what the law is.*

These words are so important and so often quoted that they can now be seen inscribed on the wall of the Supreme Court Building behind John Marshall's statue.

But where in the Constitution does it say that the Supreme Court has this huge power? Nowhere. So, where did Marshall get this idea from? It was one of his many *twistifications* — Thomas Jefferson's word to describe the way in which Marshall's mind worked. (And Jefferson ought to have known, as the two men were distant cousins and lifelong foes.)

Jefferson, the third President, recognized the danger of judicial activism. He wrote these words during his presidency in 1804, the year after *Marbury v. Madison*:

> But the opinion which gives to the judges the right to decide what laws are constitutional, and what not, not only for themselves in their own sphere of action, but for the legislature and executive also, in their spheres, would make the judiciary a despotic branch.

Charles Evans Hughes, Chief Justice from 1930 to 1941, famously said, "We are under a Constitution, but the Constitution is what the judges say it is." This looks like a cynical recognition of the power of the Supreme Court. But Hughes then went on to say, "and the judiciary is the safeguard of our liberty and our property under the Constitution." So, he recognized the power of the judges but saw it as a power for good.

It's impossible to disagree with Hughes's assessment of the power of the Supreme Court, but not everyone would agree with his characterization of that power as benign.

I deal with the judiciary in Chapter 12. And in Chapter 5 I list a few of the ways in which the U.S. Supreme Court has "amended" the Constitution without being permitted to do so under the Constitution — which lays down a very specific and quite elaborate procedure for amending the Constitution that does not involve the courts at all.

Uncovering Conspiracies

Conspiracy theories have been around forever. Any organization or group of people that was a bit separate from the rest of society, a bit different, or a bit secretive was likely to find itself targeted as holding the controlling power behind the scenes. The theory behind this kind of thinking is that the Constitution is just a front for the exercise of power by some group or groups. Groups that have been targeted in this way include the Jews, the Catholic Church, and the Freemasons.

Three associated organizations — the Council on Foreign Relations, the Trilateral Commission, and the Bilderberg Conference — have been attacked in recent years as being the secret power-brokers not only over the United States but also internationally. Here's a brief rundown on these three organizations:

>> **The Council on Foreign Relations** is a private, U.S.-based organization established in 1921 and dedicated to a study of foreign policy. Its members include Republicans, Democrats, and independents. It is widely believed to have had considerable influence on U.S. foreign policy, including the normalization of relations with Red China.

>> **The Trilateral Commission** is a private association of about 350 members established in 1973. The idea behind it was to develop closer economic cooperation between North America, Europe, and Japan. Its membership is said to include former Secretary of State Henry Kissinger; former U.S. presidents Jimmy Carter, George H.W. Bush, and Bill Clinton; former Vice President Dick Cheney; and Senator John McCain.

>> **The Bilderberg Group, Club, or Conference** is the strangest of the three associated organizations, as its 130 members meet only once a year. The group was founded in 1954 to counter growing anti-American sentiment in Western Europe by fostering mutual understanding between Europe and the United States. There are generally two invitees from each participating nation: one conservative and one liberal. The membership of this club overlaps to quite a marked extent with that of the Trilateral Commission and to some extent also with that of the Council on Foreign Relations.

The membership of the three organizations includes a lot of influential names. But are they influential because of their membership, or are they members because they were already influential? The latter seems to be the case.

The three organizations have been accused of aiming to establish a single world government or "New World Order," in which the United States would lose its separate identity and become absorbed into an international state ruled by a small elite. But if that is the plan, it doesn't appear to have made much headway so far.

Chapter **7**

Defining Federalism

The United States has a federal system of government, right? Right. Anytime somebody doesn't like what the federal government is doing, he blames "the feds." And when you come across a government acronym starting with the letter "F," chances are it stands for *Federal* (think FBI, FCC, FDIC . . .).

REMEMBER

The United States has a federal system of government, but the word *federal* doesn't figure anywhere in the text of the Constitution. This fact raises some pretty important questions, which I tackle in this chapter:

» What is federalism?

» How do we know that the United States has a federal system of government?

» Has U.S. federalism changed over time and, if so, how?

Tracing the Origins of U.S. Federalism

A federal system of government is one in which power is shared between the *federal* government — the central or national government — and the state, provincial, or regional governments. The United States is the oldest federal nation in the world, but it sure isn't the only one. Just a few of the other countries that also have federal systems of government are Argentina, Australia, Austria, Brazil, Canada, Germany, India, Mexico, and Nigeria.

Analyzing the founding documents

The United States began life as 13 separate British colonies, which united in opposition to their treatment by the British government of the day — particularly against the imposition of taxes by the British Parliament, on which the American colonies were not represented. This opposition was expressed in the slogan "No taxation without representation."

The Declaration of Independence

The Declaration of Independence of July 4, 1776, was headed "The unanimous Declaration of the thirteen united States of America." We are now used to using the term "The United States of America" as referring to one single country. But that phrase didn't have the same meaning back in 1776 — as can be seen from a close reading of the text of the Declaration. The concluding part of the Declaration is particularly revealing. It declares

> *That these United Colonies are, and of Right ought to be Free and Independent States; . . . and that as Free and Independent States, they have full Power to levy War, conclude Peace, contract Alliances, establish Commerce, and to do all other Acts and Things which Independent States may of right do.*

REMEMBER

The Declaration of Independence is commonly taken to mark the beginning of the existence of the United States of America as a nation. The Declaration certainly severed all ties with Britain, but it did not create a single new country. Instead, it created 13 separate new countries. Notice that the language of the Declaration is all in the plural. The key to its meaning lies in the last sentence that I have quoted. Each of the states, says the Declaration, has the power to make war and peace! And the end of the quoted passage contains an assertion that the 13 colonies are "Independent States."

The Articles of Confederation

The Articles of Confederation, passed by Congress in 1777 and formally ratified in 1781, served as the constitution of the United States from 1777 until 1788.

REMEMBER

A *confederation* is a weaker form of association between states than a *federation*. The best-known confederation is Switzerland, although even that has since 1848 been a federation rather than a confederation, but with a very weak — almost nonexistent — central government. Power resides in the governments of the 26 cantons that together form the "Swiss Confederation."

The American Articles of Confederation recognized the sovereignty of each of the 13 states. Article II of this document made the position quite clear:

> Each state retains its sovereignty, freedom, and independence, and every power, jurisdiction, and right, which is not by this Confederation expressly delegated to the United States, in Congress assembled.

The Congress was the only central institution established by the Articles of Confederation. The Congress was not an elected body but was made up of delegates appointed by each of the state legislatures for a year at a time. Congress had power only over foreign affairs and defense. The Articles of Confederation did not establish any form of central executive power or any national courts. The Articles established not a single country but merely "a firm league of friendship" among the 13 sovereign states.

Forming "a more perfect Union"

The form of government set up under the Articles of Confederation was hopelessly weak, and conflicts among the states arose. George Washington and some other leading figures recognized the need for a new constitution "to form a more perfect Union." So a "Grand Convention" was called to meet in Philadelphia in May 1787. Its original purpose was to revise and amend the Articles of Confederation, but the Convention ended up drafting a whole new instrument of government: the U.S. Constitution.

The first printed draft of the Constitution, dated August 6, 1787, is significantly different from the final version approved by the Convention only a few weeks later, on September 17, 1787. Instead of the now-familiar "We the People of the United States" in the Preamble, the earlier draft had a list of all the states:

> We the People of the States of New Hampshire, Massachusetts, Rhode-Island and Providence Plantations, Connecticut, New York, New Jersey, Pennsylvania, Delaware, Maryland, Virginia, North Carolina, South Carolina, and Georgia, do ordain, declare and establish the following Constitution for the Government of Ourselves and our Posterity.

The change from this formulation to "We the People of the United States" signals a last-minute shift in emphasis from the states to the national government.

However, both versions of the Constitution assert the supremacy of the U.S. Constitution and federal law over the state constitutions and laws. In the final version of the Constitution, this fundamental principle is found in the so-called "Supremacy Clause" in Article VI:

> This Constitution, and the Laws of the United States which shall be made in Pursuance thereof; and all Treaties made, or which shall be made, under the Authority of the United States, shall be the supreme Law of the Land; and the judges in every State shall be bound thereby, any Thing in the Constitution or Laws of any State to the Contrary notwithstanding.

REMEMBER

Does the Supremacy Clause mean that the federal government can simply ride roughshod over the states and do whatever it likes? No. The Supremacy Clause gives supremacy to the federal (or union) government subject to the limits imposed upon it by the Constitution. But the Constitution is not at all clear about the status of the states and their relationship with the federal government. Above all, are the states sovereign? And what is the meaning of *sovereignty* anyway? I tackle these questions in the next section.

Defining sovereignty

A *sovereign* state is one that has complete legal independence. For example, the United Kingdom is a sovereign state, but Scotland is not. Scotland forms part of the United Kingdom and enjoys a high degree of *autonomy*, or self-rule, but Scotland does not have complete legal independence.

REMEMBER

The United States started out as 13 British colonies that declared themselves individually independent as 13 sovereign states. In 1777, these 13 sovereign states banded together under the Articles of Confederation, which recognized each of the states as sovereign.

This loose association of sovereign states didn't work out too well, which is why the U.S. Constitution was created. But the Constitution didn't directly address the question of whether the 13 states were still sovereign or whether they had surrendered some of their independence to the federal government.

A sovereign state automatically enjoys *sovereign immunity*, meaning that it can't be prosecuted for any crime or sued in a civil court unless the sovereign state itself gives permission for that to happen. (That's why cars belonging to the representatives of foreign nations can ignore parking tickets — a serious problem in Washington, D.C., and New York City!)

Are the states of the United States sovereign, and do they enjoy sovereign immunity? The Eleventh Amendment, which was intended to settle this issue, can be interpreted in four different ways! The most generally accepted, though vague, answer to these tricky questions is that the states are *not* sovereign in the fullest sense of that term and that they therefore enjoy only partial immunity from suit. For more on this discussion, see Chapter 20.

Can a state secede from the union?

Can a state lawfully secede from the United States of America? The Constitution doesn't provide an answer to this crucial question.

When 11 southern states did in fact secede in 1860–1861 and constituted themselves into the Confederate States of America — or the *Confederacy*, as it's commonly known — their action was condemned as "rebellion," and a bloody civil war ensued. Check out Jefferson Davis, president of the Confederate States of America and charged with treason, in Figure 7-1.

FIGURE 7-1:
Jefferson Davis, president of the secessionist Confederate States of America, 1861-65. Although charged with treason and kept in jail for two years, he was never put on trial. He lived for 24 years after the end of the Civil War, dying in 1889 at the age of 81.

Source: Julian Vannerson

In *Texas v. White* (1869) the Supreme Court declared secession to be unconstitutional, but the authority of that decision is now questioned in some quarters. Chief Justice Chase, who wrote the majority opinion, was anxious to rule that secession was unconstitutional, and it's easy to see why:

>> The year was 1869, and Texas and the other secessionist states were in the throes of Reconstruction.

>> Chase himself had been Secretary of the Treasury in Lincoln's cabinet.

>> Chase and four other justices who sat on *Texas v. White* were Lincoln appointees.

So, did the Supreme Court have an ulterior political motive for declaring that secession was unconstitutional? You betcha!

Testing State Sovereignty: Some Recent Supreme Court Decisions

Just when it may have looked as though the problems about states' rights had been laid to rest, a flurry of blockbuster cases came before the courts that all went to the heart of federalism. These cases are the following:

>> **Voting Rights Act:** In *Shelby County v. Holder* (2013), the Supreme Court struck down as unconstitutional a provision of the Voting Rights Act of 1965 on the grounds that it conflicted with the constitutional principles of federalism and "equal sovereignty of the states." The offending provision of the 1965 Act required certain states to obtain "preclearance" from the U.S. Attorney General or the U.S. District Court for the District of Columbia that any proposed change to their voting laws or practices did not discriminate against protected minorities. The states in question were nine mostly southern states (plus seven component parts of states), selected on the ground that they had discriminated by means of poll taxes and literacy tests. In *Shelby County v. Holder,* the U.S. Supreme Court in a 5–4 decision effectively disbanded the whole "preclearance" system. The majority was made up of the four "conservative" justices plus Justice Kennedy, with the liberal members of the Court dissenting. Chief Justice Roberts, for the majority, pointed out that the preclearance provisions did not treat all states equally, as was required, but discriminated against certain (mostly southern) states.

>> **Voter ID:** The ruling in *Shelby* means that challenges to changes in electoral law in the states previously covered by the preclearance system now have to be decided on a case-by-case basis. The current bone of contention concerns voter ID, which is an issue controlled by the states. Conservatives tend to favor photo ID as a voting requirement while some liberals oppose it as discriminatory of minorities and the poor. Surprisingly perhaps, a 2005 bipartisan report by a commission headed up by ex-President Jimmy Carter recommended that voter ID be made mandatory and that eligible voters would be issued free photo ID cards. This sensible proposal has never been implemented. However, in *Crawford v. Marion County Election Board* (2008), the Supreme Court by 6 votes to 3 upheld as constitutional an Indiana law requiring photo

ID for voting but also allowing those unable to afford a photo ID to vote if they executed a sworn affidavit to that effect — although Indiana's ID cards are free. Interestingly enough, the leading opinion was written by Justice John Paul Stevens, who is generally thought of as a liberal.

Yet objections to photo ID for voting continue to be voiced. Individual states have enacted various voter ID qualifications — some requiring photo ID, others requiring non-photo ID (with some being stricter and others less strict), and no fewer than 18 states (plus D.C.) requiring no ID at all in order to vote. Public opinion is broadly supportive of voter ID. A 2012 Pew poll showed an overall majority of 77 percent in favor of photo ID, made up of 95 percent of Republicans, 83 percent of independents, and 61 percent of Democrats. Those favoring photo ID are chiefly concerned with preventing voter fraud, while those opposing it tend to regard the requirement of a photo ID as discriminating against minorities and the poor. The most common form of photo ID is a driver's license, which minorities and the poor are less likely to have. However, in most states it's possible to obtain a "non-driver ID card" from the Department of Motor Vehicles upon payment of a small fee ($29 in California, $13 in New York).

CONTROVERSY

>> **Voter fraud:** What about the danger of voter fraud, another issue affecting the states, which control and administer voting in elections. This issue was highlighted by President Trump's claim that between 3 and 5 million votes cast in the 2016 presidential election were illegal? This extreme claim was probably motivated by Trump's pique at losing the popular vote to Hillary Clinton by almost 3 million votes. The idea of widespread voter fraud has been widely pooh-poohed even by a number of Republican office-holders. In May 2017 President Trump issued an executive order creating a Presidential Advisory Commission on Election Integrity. Yet 44 states plus the District of Columbia have refused to play ball, some declining to give any information and others agreeing to give only partial information to the commission.

The issue of voter fraud certainly raises emotions on both sides. In the 1960 election, which put John Kennedy into the White House, rumors of vote-rigging were rife, particularly in Texas and Cook County, Illinois, where Mayor Daley of Chicago ran a very efficient Democratic Party machine. Recounts revealed very few irregularities, but the type of voter fraud that was widely believed to exist would not have been revealed on a recount, consisting as it did in the impersonating of dead voters. As the conservative-leaning *Chicago Tribune* put it: "Once an election has been stolen in Cook County, it stays stolen." In regard to the 2016 election, former New York Mayor Rudy Giuliani (Republican) remarked: "Dead people generally vote for Democrats rather than Republicans" because the inner cities tend to be controlled by the Democratic Party. "So what they do is they leave dead people on the rolls and then they pay people to vote [as] those dead people, four, five, six, seven, eight [times] . . . Maybe if Republicans controlled the inner cities, they'd do as much cheating as Democrats." Because of President Trump's allegations of voter fraud, the 2016 election has proved particularly controversial, but a 2012 report by the Pew Charitable Trust based on research conducted by RTI International, a nonprofit, nonpartisan research institute, found that

- "Approximately 24 million — one of every eight — voter registrations in the United States are no longer valid or are significantly inaccurate."

- "More than 1.8 million deceased individuals are listed as voters."

- "Approximately 2.75 million people have registration in more than one state."

Of course, these figures don't equate to fraudulent voting statistics but do reveal the wide scope of opportunities for voter fraud. The same report also highlighted the fact that at least 51 million citizens, or more than 24 percent of the eligible population, appeared "to be unregistered in the United States." It's important to note that the whole issue of voter registration and ID is a matter for the states.

>> **Immigration:** The issue in the case of *Arizona v. United States* (2012) was whether a state law usurped the federal government's authority to regulate immigration. The U.S. Supreme Court struck down the most sensitive sections of the state law in question, with Justice Kennedy writing the majority opinion with the support of "liberal" justices.

The background to the case is as follows. Arizona, a state bordering on Mexico, has long had a problem with illegal immigration. In 2010 it had approximately 460,000 undocumented migrants, a fivefold increase since 1990. In January 2010 the Arizona state legislature began considering tough new measures. The killing of Robert Krentz and his dog close to the Mexican border in March 2010 gave the legislation an extra impetus. In April 2010 the Arizona legislature passed the law, commonly referred to as SB 1070, which had widespread support among voters in the state. One of the most controversial sections made it a misdemeanor to work or seek work without proper authorization. Another such section allowed the arrest without warrant of foreigners believed on the basis of "probable cause" to be removable from the United States. Governor Jan Brewer of Arizona characterized the dispute as being "about the fundamental principles of federalism under which every state has a right to defend its people." But the case was decided under the Supremacy Clause (Article VI, Clause 2) of the Constitution, which gives the federal government what Justice Kennedy described as "broad" and "undoubted" authority to regulate immigration and aliens. The offending sections of the state law were struck down as being "preempted" by federal law. Justice Antonin Scalia, dissenting, rejected this whole argument on the basis of state sovereignty: "As a sovereign, Arizona has the inherent power to exclude persons from its territory, subject only to those limitations expressed in the Constitution or constitutionally imposed by Congress. That power to exclude has long been recognized as inherent in sovereignty."

>> **"Obamacare":** The Patient Protection and Affordable Care Act, or the Affordable Care Act (ACA), nicknamed "Obamacare," was a federal statute signed into law by President Obama in 2012. One of its most important and controversial provisions was the "individual mandate" requiring everybody (with the exception of those covered by an employer-sponsored health plan, Medicaid, Medicare, or some other public insurance program) to buy insurance or pay a penalty for refusing to do so. Twenty-eight states challenged the individual mandate in court and also objected that by requiring Medicaid expansion the law placed an unfair financial burden on state governments. These challenges culminated in the U.S. Supreme Court case of *Florida v. U.S. Department of Health and Human Services* consolidated with *National Federation of Independent Business v. Sebelius* (2012). In the Supreme Court the states won on the Medicaid issue. The federal government defended the individual mandate on the basis of the powers of Congress under the Commerce Clause or, alternatively, under the "Necessary and Proper Clause." These arguments failed, but by 5 votes to 4 the Supreme Court upheld the individual mandate on a completely different basis altogether: as an exercise of Congress's taxing power. Chief Justice Roberts, writing for the majority, explained: "The Affordable Care Act's requirement that certain individuals pay a financial penalty for not obtaining health insurance may reasonably be characterized as a tax. Because the Constitution permits such a tax, it is not our role to forbid it, or to pass upon its wisdom or fairness."

>> **Same-sex marriage:** Marriage doesn't figure in the Constitution, and it has traditionally been left to the states. But challenges to state laws about marriage can end up in the U.S. Supreme Court. Same-sex marriage has aroused the most recent controversy. In *Obergefell v. Hodges* (2015), the Supreme Court decided by 5 votes to 4 that the right to marry is guaranteed by the Constitution to same-sex couples as much as to male-female couples, and that state laws banning same-sex marriage violated the Due Process and Equal Protection Clauses of the Fourteenth Amendment. The majority opinion, written by Justice Kennedy and supported by the "liberal" wing of the Court, placed same-sex marriage on a broad constitutional foundation, declaring that: "The Constitution promises liberty to all within its reach," that the fundamental rights embodied in the Fourteenth Amendment's Due Process Clause "extend to certain personal choices central to individual dignity and autonomy," and that this extension includes a right to marry. Justice Scalia, in a scathing dissenting opinion, attacked the majority opinion as "lacking even a thin veneer of law," and descending "to the mystical aphorisms of the fortune cookie."

Foreign Affairs: Looking at the Influence of Treaties

Remember the first part of the Supremacy Clause? Where it states: *This Constitution, and the Laws of the United States which shall be made in Pursuance thereof; and all Treaties made, or which shall be made, under the Authority of the United States, shall be the supreme Law of the Land.* It may seem strange to find international treaties up there, above state law, as part of "the supreme Law of the Land." And the 1920 U.S. Supreme Court decision in *Missouri v. Holland,* which upheld the constitutionality of the Migratory Bird Treaty Act of 1918, has been characterized as meaning that "the protection of an international duck takes precedence over the constitutional protections of American citizens." The leading authority on this question is still the Supreme Court decision in *Reid v. Covert* (1957), in which the court held that: "No agreement with a foreign nation can confer power on the Congress, or on any other branch of Government, which is free from the restraints of the Constitution." In *Medellin v. Texas* (2008), the Court held that an international treaty is not binding on domestic federal or state law unless Congress has enacted a statute to implement it or unless the treaty itself is "self-executing."

Who has the power to make an international treaty? Article II, Section 2, Clause 2 of the Constitution gives that power to the President, "by and with the Advice and Consent of the Senate . . . provided two thirds of the Senators present concur." There have been some exceptions to this rule, notably NAFTA (the North American Free Trade Agreement), which was ratified by being passed as an Act of Congress and signed into law by President Clinton in December 1993. For more on this, see Chapter 10.

Perhaps even more importantly: Who has the power to repeal a treaty? As a treaty, once agreed, automatically becomes part of U.S. federal law, Congress can repeal it in the same way as any other legislation, with presidential approval. But can the President repeal a treaty unilaterally, without congressional approval? Amazingly, there is no Supreme Court ruling on this, although several presidents have taken it upon themselves to pull the U.S. out of an international treaty. When President Jimmy Carter unilaterally terminated a defense treaty, his authority to do so was challenged by Senator Barry Goldwater and other members of Congress. But the Supreme Court declined jurisdiction and dismissed the case without hearing oral argument, on the ground that it was a "political question." Similarly, when President George W. Bush unilaterally withdrew the U.S. from the Anti-Ballistic Missile Treaty, which had been in force since 1972, the courts again declined to interfere. Right at the start of his term, President Donald Trump pulled the U.S. out of the 12-nation Trans-Pacific Partnership. At the time of this writing, he has also indicated his intention to renegotiate or withdraw from NAFTA with Canada and Mexico, and has announced that he will withdraw the U.S. from the Paris climate change accords.

IN THIS CHAPTER

» **Understanding the implications of the separation of powers**

» **Exploring the membership and functions of the federal government's three branches**

» **Bringing checks and balances into the mix**

» **Checking on executive orders**

Chapter **8**

Separation of Powers: Checking and Balancing

The separation of powers is one of the fundamental principles of the U.S. Constitution — right up there with federalism, democracy, the rule of law, and judicial review. And like these other principles, the separation of powers is not specifically mentioned in the text of the Constitution.

What exactly is the meaning of *separation of powers*? At its simplest, this doctrine refers to separation between the three branches of government:

» **Legislative:** Congress, the lawmaking branch of government

» **Executive:** The President, who has the duty under Article II, Section 3 of the Constitution to "take Care that the Laws be faithfully executed"

» **Judicial:** The Supreme Court justices and other judges who interpret and enforce the law through the courts

We must examine separation of powers from four angles:

>> The membership of the three branches of government

>> The functions of the three branches of government

>> The purpose of separation of powers

>> Checks and balances between the three branches

I discuss each of these topics in this chapter along with the validity of executive orders, but first I trawl the text of the Constitution for any cryptic references to separation of powers.

No Moonlighting for the President

Although the Constitution never uses the phrase *separation of powers*, it does contain some oblique references to that principle. This fact is significant, because it shows that separation of powers was embedded in the Constitution from the beginning but the Framers took the principle for granted.

Here are the references to separation of powers in the Constitution:

>> Article I, Section 1 gives Congress "all legislative Powers" under the Constitution. This means that the other two branches of government are not allowed to be involved in legislation. (In reality, they both *are* involved, as you see when you look at the workings of checks and balances later in this chapter.)

>> Article III, Section 1 similarly reads, "The judicial Power of the United States shall be vested in one supreme Court, and in such inferior Courts as the Congress may from time to time ordain and establish." Although this section doesn't say "All judicial Power," the phrase "The judicial Power" makes it clear that the courts are to have *all* judicial power, excluding the other two branches of government from judicial activities.

>> Article II, Section 1 forbids the President from receiving any payment from the United States or any of the states besides his salary as President. This means that the President isn't allowed to moonlight as a senator or a judge. Here's the actual wording: "The President shall, at stated Times, receive for his Services, a Compensation . . . and he shall not receive within that Period any other Emolument from the United States, or any of them."

President Donald Trump waived the presidential salary of $400,000. But his failure to divest himself fully of his properties and hand them over to a genuinely "blind trust" could possibly cause him trouble — for example, if it can be shown that certain policies of his (like his executive order repealing environmental protection for wetlands) benefit him financially as a real estate developer and golf course owner. The President is exempt from the conflict of interest statutes that are applicable to other officeholders, but there's a general unwritten principle against using public office for private gain.

>> Article I, Section 9, the "Emoluments Clause," says that no U.S. government official "shall, without the Consent of the Congress, accept of any present, Emolument, Office, or Title, of any kind whatever, from any King, Prince or foreign State." This clause was incorporated into the Constitution after the King of France gave Benjamin Franklin a diamond-studded snuffbox. It was then mostly forgotten, and the U.S. Supreme Court has never addressed it. President Obama's $1.4 million Nobel Peace Prize wasn't a problem, because it didn't come from a government source. Interest in this obscure clause was reawakened by the election of Donald Trump with his vast international business empire. Some even suggested that the very existence of the Trump International Hotel, situated at 1100 Pennsylvania Avenue NW, less than a mile down the road from the White House, might itself fall foul of the emoluments clause, acting as it does as a powerful magnet for foreign dignitaries visiting Washington, D.C. But nothing has happened since a failed attempt to take President Trump to court for infringing on the clause.

TECHNICAL
STUFF

TRACING THE ORIGINS OF SEPARATION OF POWERS

The Framers of the Constitution constantly had before their eyes the examples of Britain and Europe. They adopted what they liked from these systems, modified the features that they thought needed tweaking, and rejected the rest.

In France, Spain, and other so-called *absolute monarchies,* a great deal of power was concentrated in the hands of the King. King Louis XIV of France famously remarked, "I am the state."

The American Founding Fathers greatly admired the writings of Baron de Montesquieu, an 18th-century French aristocrat who praised the British Constitution for its supposed separation of powers. In fact, Montesquieu had an exaggerated impression of the degree of separation of powers that actually existed in the British Constitution.

The Framers of the U.S. Constitution had no firsthand experience of the workings of the British Constitution. They simply accepted Montesquieu's analysis of the British Constitution, together with his theoretical framework.

Keeping the Branches Apart

Would it be possible to have strict separation between the members of the three branches of government without strict separation of functions? Yes, it would — and that is the case with the U.S. Constitution. For example, the President can never be a member of the legislature or the judiciary, but he does exercise some legislative functions and actually appoints the federal judiciary. (To be more precise, the President nominates the federal judges, who must be confirmed by the Senate. If they are confirmed, the President appoints them as federal judges.) Take a look at Figure 8-1 to see an illustration of the interplay between the executive and legislative branches, with the President (head of the executive branch) addressing a joint session of Congress (legislative branch) together with members of the Supreme Court (judicial branch). The Vice President (executive branch) is there in his capacity as president of the Senate (legislative branch), and the Speaker of the House of Representatives (legislative branch) presides over the proceedings. The sections that follow explore the membership and functions of each branch of the U.S. government.

FIGURE 8-1: Convergence of the executive and legislative branches: President George W. Bush, delivering the State of the Union address in January 2007, with Vice President Dick Cheney (as president of the Senate) and Speaker Nancy Pelosi (the first female Speaker).

Source: White House photographer David Bohrer

Membership

Separation of powers is strictly observed in regard to membership of the three branches of government:

- » No member of the legislature — Congress — is allowed to hold an executive position at the same time.

- » No member of Congress is allowed to hold a judicial post — as a Supreme Court justice or other judge — at the same time.

- » Neither the President — the executive head of the nation — nor any member of his Cabinet is allowed to combine that position with a seat in Congress.

- » Neither the President nor any member of his Cabinet is allowed to combine that position with a judicial post.

- » No justice of the Supreme Court or any other judge is allowed to combine that judicial position with a Cabinet post or a seat in Congress.

The President comes to Congress every year to give the State of the Union address, but he or she is not a member of Congress. That's why the Congress generally goes wild when the President arrives, with everyone wanting to shake his hand or even get his autograph — and why large numbers of normally staid legislators jump to their feet every few minutes during the President's speech.

It's unthinkable that the President could be a member of Congress while serving as President, even though that kind of combination is quite normal (even obligatory) in many other countries, like Britain, Ireland, and Germany. But where in the U.S. Constitution does it say that the President is not allowed to combine these two positions? The only reference to this rule is the oblique prohibition that we've already looked at in Article II, Section 1:

> *The President shall, at stated Times, receive for his Services, a Compensation . . . and he shall not receive within that Period any other Emolument from the United States, or any of them.*

Does this mean that it's okay for an incumbent President to serve as a member of Congress as long as he doesn't get a paycheck for doing so? Umm, no.

The same rule applies to the President's Cabinet, to which the President delegates some of his executive power. Cabinet members, including the Secretary of State, the Secretary of the Treasury, and the Attorney General, are not allowed to combine that position with a seat in Congress.

But why doesn't the Constitution spell out this prohibition more directly? The Philadelphia Convention that passed the Constitution recognized the need for strict separation between the three branches in their *membership* while retaining flexibility of *function*. But the Convention stopped short of putting this two-pronged rule into words — except in the oblique manner that I've already mentioned. The reason for this omission is unknown, but the rule of strict separation among the membership of the three branches has nevertheless been religiously followed at all times.

Not only is it unconstitutional to hold office in more than one branch of the government at the same time, but it's also illegal under state law in many states even to *run* for more than one office at the same time. When Lyndon Johnson was picked as John Kennedy's vice presidential running mate in the 1960 presidential race, Johnson also ran for a third term in the U.S. Senate — just in case the Kennedy–Johnson ticket lost the election. Johnson had to get Texas law changed in order to be permitted to run for both offices at the same time — in what came to be called "Lyndon's law." Johnson won both elections, but he made no attempt to hold down both positions. As soon as his second term in the Senate ended on January 3, 1961 — and before being inaugurated as Vice President — Johnson resigned his Senate seat, and with it his position as Senate majority leader. (He soon regretted having to give up this powerful position because as Vice President he was almost totally sidelined by President Kennedy!)

Functions

Strictly speaking, the Legislative branch should legislate, the Executive branch should "take Care that the Laws be faithfully executed," and the Judicial branch should interpret and enforce the law through the courts — and each branch should stay away from the functions of the other two branches.

But there are two problems with this theory:

>> In practice, overlap between the functions of the three branches can't be entirely avoided — and in some important situations, overlap is quite deliberate.

>> If each of the three branches kept religiously to its own specific functions and didn't stray into the preserve of the other branches, the branches couldn't act as checks and balances on one another.

I discuss the first problem here and the second in the next section, "Checking and Balancing."

Some of the overlap between the three branches of government is the result of a genuine desire of one branch to help out another. For example, after Congress has passed a law, the Executive branch must enforce it. Sometimes, enforcing a law may involve making additional rules. But this practice has come under attack. A Supreme Court ruling in 1825 established what's called the *non-delegation doctrine*. Chief Justice John Marshall in *Wayman v. Southard* held that "important" matters can't be delegated, but Congress may delegate the power to one of the other branches of government "to fill up the details." For example, Congress delegates to executive agencies, such as the Food and Drug Administration and the Internal Revenue Service, the power to make detailed regulations in the areas that they cover.

The U.S. Supreme Court has given its blessing to Congress's delegation of power to other government bodies. Here's the test that the court applies in deciding whether a particular delegation is kosher or not:

> *Congress simply cannot do its job absent an ability to delegate power under broad general directives. Accordingly, this Court has deemed it "constitutionally sufficient if Congress clearly delineates the general policy, the public agency which is to apply it, and the boundaries of this delegated authority."*

The Supreme Court has only rarely struck down Acts of Congress delegating power to the other branches of government. An exception to this trend was the 1998 case *Clinton v. City of New York*, in which the Supreme Court struck down the Line Item Veto Act of 1996, which allowed the President unilaterally to delete individual items of expenditure approved by Congress. The idea behind the act was to allow the President to cut *pork barrel spending* — government spending that benefits a particular region rather than the nation as a whole. Most state governors have long had this power. President Ronald Reagan asked for a line item veto in his State of the Union address in 1986, saying, "Give me the authority to veto waste, and I'll take the responsibility, I'll make the cuts, I'll take the heat."

Surprisingly, perhaps, the Line Item Veto Act of 1996 originated not with the Democratic President but with his Republican opponents, who had just won control of both houses of Congress in the 1994 midterm elections. President Bill Clinton then also eagerly embraced the idea of a line item veto. So, what was wrong with the act? In a nutshell, the objection to the line item veto is that it allows the President to legislate, contrary to the principle of the separation of powers.

MUSCLING IN ON THE OTHER BRANCHES OF GOVERNMENT

Since the United States was founded, the three branches of government have jockeyed for position, with each trying to get one over on the other branches. Here are a few examples:

- **Legislative courts:** From an early date, Congress tried to break the courts' lock on litigation by setting up its own courts for certain purposes. The U.S. Supreme Court hit back by narrowly restricting the scope of the power of these legislative courts. In *Murray's Lessee v. Hoboken Land & Improvement Co.,* decided in 1856, the Court ruled that a legislative court couldn't hear "a suit at the common law, or in equity, or admiralty" — in other words, any regular lawsuit. This left only "public rights" determinations to the legislative courts — cases between a citizen and the government.

- **The Supreme Court strikes back:** In a 1982 case called *Northern Pipeline Co. v. Marathon Pipe Line Co.,* a plurality of the Supreme Court struck down an Act of Congress that had set up bankruptcy courts with wide jurisdiction. The main objection to these bankruptcy courts was that they posed a "serious threat that the exercise of the judicial power would be subject to incursion by other branches." Not that the Supreme Court had ever heard many bankruptcy cases!

- **Jurisdiction stripping:** Article III, Section 2 of the Constitution says, "[T]he supreme Court shall have appellate Jurisdiction . . . with such Exceptions . . . as the Congress shall make." Justice Felix Frankfurter commented, "Congress need not give this Court any appellate power: it may withdraw appellate jurisdiction once conferred." Was Frankfurter right? Absolutely. The Illegal Immigration Reform and Immigrant Responsibility Act of 1996 provides a good example of Congress's exercise of the power to restrict the power of the courts. Under this act, if the Immigration and Naturalization Service (INS) refuses to grant a particular person asylum, no federal court — including the high court — is permitted to review that decision.

- **Guantanamo Bay:** Could Congress exclude the jurisdiction of the courts in regard to detention in Guantanamo Bay? The Military Commissions Act (MCA) of 2006 did just that. The MCA established special "military commissions" to try "alien unlawful enemy combatants engaged in hostilities against the United States." In the 2008 case *Boumediene v. Bush,* the U.S. Supreme Court ruled 5 to 4 that the MCA was unconstitutional and that foreign detainees held in Guantanamo Bay *did* have the right to challenge their detention in the ordinary U.S. courts. Justice Antonin Scalia, in his dissenting opinion, held that the majority's "analysis produces a crazy result."

It's important to distinguish these examples of competition among the different branches of government from the checks and balances between them that the Framers deliberately inserted into the Constitution to prevent concentration of power in too few hands.

Checking and Balancing

Here's what James Madison said in the *Federalist Papers* in support of separation of powers:

> *The accumulation of all powers, legislative, executive, and judiciary, in the same hands, whether of one, a few, or many, and whether hereditary, selfappointed, or elective, may justly be pronounced the very definition of tyranny.*

Madison and the other Framers considered separation of powers essential in order to avoid "tyranny." But the Constitution went much further than the mere separation of powers — it also established an elaborate system of checks and balances.

REMEMBER

The concept of checks and balances is in one sense a natural extension of separation of powers, but in another sense the two concepts — separation of powers and checks and balances — are actually in opposition to each other.

On its own, separation of powers should just mean that each branch of government would go its own merry way without interference from any other branch. But this arrangement isn't practical, because the boundaries between the three branches of government aren't clear-cut. Plus, the Framers deliberately introduced overlaps between the functions of the three branches so that they could act as checks and balances on one another.

Keeping each branch in line

Here are the most important checks and balances built into the Constitution. I look first at checks on Congress, then at checks on the President, and lastly at checks on the judiciary. Here are the checks on Congress:

>> **The President's veto power:** Under Article I, Section 7 of the Constitution, the President has the power to veto — or block — any bill passed by both houses of Congress. This is a really powerful tool against the legislature in the hands of the executive. Congress can override a presidential veto, but only by a two-thirds majority in both houses, which is notoriously difficult to achieve.

>> **The Veep:** The Vice President is a member of the executive branch of government, and he is also President of the Senate by virtue of Article I, Section 3 of the Constitution. But, although he has the right to preside over the Senate, the Vice President is not a member of that legislative body, can't participate in debates there, and can't vote except to break a tie. So, his potential to keep the Senate in check is very limited — especially since most

Veeps don't spend a lot of time presiding over the Senate. They tend to leave that to the *president pro tem* of the Senate, the senior senator of the day.

CONTROVERSY

>> **Judicial review:** The most serious check on congressional power doesn't appear in the text of the Constitution at all but was read into it by Chief Justice John Marshall in the famous 1803 case of *Marbury v. Madison,* which I discuss in Chapter 23. Marshall's highly controversial ruling is still accepted today. It gives the Supreme Court the power to strike down any law passed by Congress or any of the state legislatures if the Court finds that law unconstitutional. I discuss the effect of this ruling later in this chapter and also in Chapter 12.

Now for the main checks on the President:

>> **Impeachment:** Impeachment is the best-known check on the President because it can result in his or her removal from office. But impeachment has been used only twice — against Andrew Johnson in 1869 and against Bill Clinton in 1999. Neither Johnson nor Clinton was removed from office, but Richard Nixon's resignation in 1974 was in reaction to a serious threat of impeachment.

In impeachment proceedings, the House of Representatives prosecutes and the Senate sits as a jury and decides the case. A two-thirds majority is needed for a conviction. The Chief Justice presides over the trial, which represents a further check on both the President and the Congress on the part of the judiciary. I discuss impeachment in Chapter 13.

>> **"Advice and Consent":** Article II, Section 2 of the Constitution gives the President the "Power, by and with the Advice and Consent of the Senate, to make Treaties, provided two thirds of the Senators present concur." This provision seriously cramps the President's style in foreign policy matters. Similarly, the President's power to appoint ambassadors, Supreme Court justices, and other federal officials is exercised "by and with the Advice and Consent of the Senate" — which translates in practice into sometimes quite lengthy and acrimonious confirmation hearings. I deal with the presidency in Chapter 10.

>> **Commander in Chief:** Article II, Section 2 of the Constitution makes the President Commander in Chief of the armed forces. But under Article I, Section 8, Congress has the power "to declare War." The precise relationship between the President and Congress in regard to war remains the subject of intense debate. I discuss this issue in Chapters 10 and 11.

>> **Choosing the President:** If no candidate running for President obtains a majority (more than 50 percent) of the electoral votes, the Twelfth Amendment provides that "the House of Representatives shall choose immediately, by ballot, the President" — with each state having one vote. This

provision has been used twice. The Senate has the same power in regard to choosing the Vice President.

>> **Judicial review:** The Supreme Court has a similar power in regard to decisions of the President and other members of the executive branch as it has in regard to Congress. The Court can set aside an executive decision as unconstitutional. This derives from the power of the Supreme Court to interpret the Constitution — a right that doesn't figure in the text of the Constitution, but which derives from Chief Justice John Marshall's ruling in *Marbury v. Madison*, which I discuss in Chapter 23.

What about checks on the judiciary by the other two branches? There are remarkably few:

>> **Impeachment:** The main check on the judiciary is impeachment. Many more judges have been impeached than presidents. Only one of these judges was a Supreme Court justice, and he was acquitted. But no fewer than 13 other federal judges have been impeached, 7 of them being removed from the bench and a couple others choosing to resign. As with presidents, the threat of impeachment can be as effective as a successful impeachment conviction. Justice Abe Fortas — nominated by President Lyndon Johnson to become Chief Justice — is reliably thought to have resigned rather than face impeachment. As with presidential impeachments, the House of Representatives prosecutes and the Senate tries the case. But the Vice President presides — not the Chief Justice as in the impeachment of a president.

>> **Appointment:** Supreme Court justices and other federal judges are appointed by the President subject to confirmation by the Senate. But Article III, Section 1 of the Constitution allows them to "hold their Offices during good Behaviour" — in other words, for life, subject only to removal by impeachment.

>> **Pardons:** Article II, Section 2 of the Constitution gives the President the "Power to grant Reprieves and Pardons for Offences against the United States, except in Cases of Impeachment." Is this power a check on the judiciary? Yes, in a sense, because a pardon cancels the sentence without cancelling the conviction.

Considering the judiciary's special position

The judiciary has fewer checks on its power than either of the other two branches of government because, once appointed, a federal judge is there for life unless he really steps out of line sufficiently to be impeached.

REMEMBER

The judiciary also exercises more control over the other two branches than those branches have over the judiciary. Judicial review is the killer weapon in the hands of the U.S. Supreme Court, which can use it against the President as well as against Congress, and also against the states.

Interestingly enough, this nuclear weapon doesn't figure anywhere in the text of the Constitution. The Supreme Court arrogated this power to itself back in 1803 in the case of *Marbury v. Madison*, and it has clung to this power ever since. That ruling is doubly worrying in regard to the doctrine of the separation of powers, for two reasons:

>> It gave the judiciary the exclusive right to interpret the Constitution, a power that the Constitution itself doesn't confer on them. Such was the skill of Chief Justice John Marshall that his "twistifications of the law" (Thomas Jefferson's term) have become accepted as valid constitutional law. Jefferson's own take was quite different:

    My construction of the Constitution is . . . that each department [or branch of government] is truly independent of the others and has an equal right to decide for itself what is the meaning of the Constitution in the cases submitted to its action; and especially where it is to act ultimately and without appeal.

>> It gave the judiciary the power to add to its own power simply by means of a high court decision — which is also nowhere to be found in the Constitution, and is in any case contrary to the whole principle of the separation of powers.

Above all, the effect of *Marbury v. Madison* is to give a group of unelected justices the power to strike down as unconstitutional any laws passed by a democratically elected Congress. Here's Jefferson's take on that ruling:

> *The Constitution . . . meant that its coordinate branches should be checks on each other. But the opinion which gives to the judges the right to decide what laws are constitutional and what not, not only for themselves in their own sphere of action but for the Legislature and Executive also in their spheres, would make the Judiciary a despotic branch.*

Right away in 1804, Jefferson recognized the danger of runaway power in the hands of the Supreme Court. He was President at the time yet was powerless to stop that development — even though it was not sanctioned by the Constitution. And none of his successors has been able to stop the inexorable growth of judicial power either. For more on this subject, see Chapter 12.

Pondering the legality of executive orders

Presidential executive orders, which have been around forever, have now become a serious problem. What exactly are *executive orders?* They are legally binding but are not laws. Huh? This is where confusion creeps in. Executive orders are only supposed to be instructions by the President to federal agencies within the Executive branch of government. It's a complete no-no for an executive order to trump (no pun intended!) any existing law or any part of the U.S. Constitution. So, in keeping with the Constitution's directive for checks and balances, the President can't lawfully use executive orders to go behind the back of Congress and legislate on his own.

Examples of executive orders

In recent years, executive orders have become particularly controversial. For example, in 2006, Harry Reid, the Democratic Senate Majority Leader at the time, remarked of President George W. Bush: "In matters ranging from domestic spying to the use of torture, the current President has effectively declared himself above the law." However, none of President Bush's executive orders was challenged in court. Check out the following examples of executive orders to get a feel for how presidents have worked around the rule.

Washington was the first

CONTROVERSY

George Washington issued the first executive order in 1789. But the earliest controversial executive order was Abraham Lincoln's 1861 suspension of habeas corpus. (*Habeas corpus* is an important constitutional privilege allowing an arrested person to challenge in court the lawfulness of his or her detention.) Lincoln's order was challenged in the well-known case *Ex parte Merryman,* in which Chief Justice Roger Taney roundly condemned the President's order on the ground that only Congress could suspend habeas corpus. Lincoln just ignored the Chief Justice's ruling.

Obama and Osama

President Obama's 2011 order to hunt down and kill al-Qaeda leader Osama bin Laden, which may have been expected to be problematic, was widely welcomed. The reaction of retired Supreme Court Justice John Paul Stevens was typical: "It was not merely to do justice and avenge September 11, [but] to remove an enemy who had been trying every day to attack the United States . . . I haven't the slightest doubt it was entirely appropriate for American forces to act" as they did. By contrast, a deadlocked Supreme Court blocked in 2016 President Obama's executive order protecting about 4 million undocumented immigrants from deportation, affirming the decision of the U.S. Fifth Circuit Court of Appeals.

Trump's travel ban

Donald Trump ostentatiously started signing controversial executive orders as soon as he was inaugurated, including one to cut federal funding for so-called "sanctuary cities" (cities that give a certain amount of protection to undocumented immigrants), and another to authorize the building of a much-touted wall along the U.S. border with Mexico. But these orders were more rhetorical than real. An order that was implemented right away was a travel ban that blocked for 90 days the admission into the U.S. of all citizens of seven majority-Muslim countries. This order ran into immediate judicial challenges. Courts in three states issued temporary restraining orders against the most important parts of the travel ban, with only the U.S. District Court for Massachusetts finding in favor of the President's order. The government's appeal against the temporary restraining orders to the U.S. Court of Appeals for the Ninth Circuit was unsuccessful. President Trump then issued a revised executive order revoking and replacing the original one. This corrected some of the most serious problems with the original order by, for example, dropping Iraq from the list of countries affected and by exempting valid green-card holders from the ban's operation ban. However, the revised order didn't fare much better than the original one in the courts. A negative ruling by a judge in Hawaii elicited this dismissive comment from Attorney General Jeff Sessions: "I really am amazed that a judge sitting on an island in the Pacific can issue an order that stops the President of the United States from what appears to be clearly his statutory and constitutional power."

The legal justification relied upon for President Trump's travel ban was chiefly the Immigration and Nationality Act (INA) of 1952, which allows the President to "suspend the entry of all aliens or any class of aliens" that he "finds . . . would be detrimental to the interests of the United States." This would appear to give the President unlimited power in this area. However, a 1965 amendment to the INA restricts presidential power by providing that "no person shall receive any preference or priority or be discriminated against in the issuance of an immigrant visa because of the person's race, sex, nationality, place of birth, or place of residence." Opponents of the Trump travel ban latched on to this restriction together with the Establishment Clause of the First Amendment and constitutional rights to procedural due process and "equal protection of the laws." "The clearest command of the Establishment Clause," held the Supreme Court in *Larson v. Valente* (1982), "is that one religious denomination cannot be officially preferred over another." Opponents of the travel ban were not slow to cite anti-Islamic remarks by Trump and members of his team in the 2016 presidential election campaign. Former New York City mayor Rudy Giuliani told Fox News on January 29, 2017, that Trump had asked him to show him how to impose a travel ban on Muslims that would be legal. A memo prepared by a commission set up by Giuliani in response to this request was later ordered by a judge to be turned over. Can such documents be used in court as evidence of the "intent" behind the travel ban? That's a question that will almost certainly end up before the U.S. Supreme Court when the matter is finally decided. In the meantime, on June 26, 2017, the Supreme Court allowed a version of the travel ban to go into effect.

Reviewing administrative regulations

Congress passed the Administrative Procedure Act (APA) in 1946 as a check on the numerous federal administrative agencies that President Franklin Roosevelt established. The APA allows judicial review of these agencies. APA litigation blocked a number of regulations that the Obama administration promulgated. These include the Department of Labor's new overtime regulations that would have increased the minimum wage, which were blocked by a preliminary injunction issued in November 2016 by a federal district court. President Trump ordered some federal agencies and departments to change course. However, to alter regulations previously finalized, an agency must follow the detailed procedures set out in the APA. The APA doesn't provide a cause of action against the President. But, as the Supreme Court ruled in *Franklin v. Massachusetts* (1992), based on the leading case of *Youngstown Sheet & Tube Co. v. Sawyer* (1952), "the President's actions may still be reviewed for constitutionality." But the APA enables challenges to be filed against the relevant federal agencies directed to carry out an executive order, and such challenges can be based on non-constitutional grounds as well, if found to be arbitrary, capricious, or contrary to a federal statute.

Trumping the President

Does the President have immunity from suit while he is in office? A sitting President can be sued in federal court over activities prior to his election as President. The Supreme Court established this ruling in 1997 in the sexual harassment case brought by Paula Jones against President Bill Clinton. This ruling applies to federal (but possibly not state) civil suits only, and not to criminal prosecutions. And crimes allegedly committed by the President while in office can only be the subject of impeachment, and then only if they rise to the level of "Treason, Bribery, or other High Crimes and Misdemeanors." I discuss impeachment in Chapter 13.

At the time of his election as President, Donald Trump was facing at least 75 civil suits. One of these, a class action brought in federal court by a number of former students alleging fraud on the part of Trump University, was settled in March 2017 for $25 million.

Assigning a special counsel

Much more troubling to Trump than these civil suits was the appointment in May 2017 of former FBI director Bob Mueller as special counsel to oversee the previously confirmed FBI investigation of the Russian government's efforts to interfere in the 2016 presidential election, specifically including "any links and/or coordination between the Russian government and individuals associated with the campaign of President Donald Trump." As Attorney General Jeff Sessions had recused himself from the Russian investigation, Deputy Attorney General Rod Rosenstein made the appointment, adding: "My decision is not a finding that crimes have been committed or that any prosecution is warranted. I have made no such determination."

Why, in that case, it may be asked, was a "special counsel" needed at all? Especially as there were already no fewer than four congressional committees looking into Russia's alleged interference in the 2016 election: two Senate committees and two committees of the House of Representatives. Parallels were already being drawn with Watergate, even by Senator John McCain. But one crucial difference was that the Watergate investigation, which eventually led to the resignation of President Richard Nixon, was sparked off by an undoubted crime, a break-in at the headquarters of the Democratic National Committee in the Watergate building in Washington, D.C. Another difference was that Archibald Cox, the (original) special counsel in the Watergate matter, was appointed by the Attorney General with the specific authorization of President Nixon himself. By contrast, the appointment of Bob Mueller as special counsel in the "Russiagate" matter was made without any authority from President Trump, who indeed was only informed of it after the order making the appointment had already been signed. Trump was far from happy about the appointment, calling it a "witch hunt."

Noting internal conflict

It's important to note that both the FBI and the Deputy Attorney General, who appointed the special counsel to oversee the FBI investigation, are part of the Executive branch of the government headed up by the President. What constitutional or legal authority is there for executive officials to act independently of the President — their boss — and indeed against his will? This is a very different matter from an investigation of executive actions by Congress, which is part of the checks and balances inherent in the separation of powers.

REMEMBER

It's really important to understand just how exceptional the appointment of a special counsel is, because it essentially creates internal conflict within the Executive branch of government, setting lower officials against their own boss, the President. The very appointment itself — regardless of the outcome of any investigation — therefore potentially weakens the President. Moreover, Bob Mueller's appointment is probably unlawful.

The legal basis for Mueller's appointment as special counsel can be found in an obscure Justice Department regulation, 28 CFR 600.1, headed "Grounds for appointing a Special Counsel," which reads as follows: "The Attorney General, or in cases where the Attorney General is recused, the Acting Attorney General, will appoint a Special Counsel when he or she determines that criminal investigation of a person or matter is warranted"; that this "would present a conflict of interest for the Department or other extraordinary circumstances"; and "That under the circumstances, it would be in the public interest to appoint an outside Special Counsel to assume responsibility for the matter."

Establishing criminality

Is Bob Mueller as special counsel engaged in a criminal investigation? That is the crucial question. An operation becomes a "criminal investigation" only when it's clear that a crime has been committed — as in the Watergate burglary. But in the present case, Deputy Attorney General Rod Rosenstein categorically denied that he had "determined" that any crime had been committed. Yet, according to the law, a special counsel can only be appointed to conduct a "criminal investigation," meaning that there has to be a crime to investigate. Which must mean that Bob Mueller's appointment as special counsel was invalid.

What possible crimes could be involved here? There are three main contenders:

>> **Logan Act:** There has been much discussion of the obscure Logan Act of 1799, which makes it illegal for a U.S. citizen to engage "without authority of the United States" in "any correspondence or intercourse with any foreign government or any officer or agent thereof" with the intention of influencing that foreign government. The penalty laid down in the act is a fine or up to three years in jail, or both. However, nobody has ever been convicted under the act. If Bob Mueller uncovers "collusion" with Russia on the part of any U.S. citizen, the Logan Act may come into play.

>> **Foreign Agents Registration Act (FARA):** This law, originally passed in 1938, requires the registration of anyone representing a foreign power in a "political or quasi-political capacity." There are currently over 1,700 lobbyists representing more than 100 countries registered under FARA. Breaches of the act may give rise to either a criminal prosecution or a civil suit. There have been no successful criminal prosecutions since 1966. It has been informally suggested that one or more of President Trump's associates or appointees may have fallen foul of FARA, but at the time of this writing, no prosecutions or civil suits have been launched.

» **Obstruction of justice:** This is by far the most serious potential offense that could conceivably arise out of the "Russiagate" investigation. Yet at the time of this writing, it appears to have no basis. Professor Alan Dershowitz (a self-confessed "very proud" Hillary Clinton supporter in the 2016 election) opined that "Even if the [Trump] campaign coordinated — which there is no evidence of — but coordinated activities with Russia, and even if Russia and the campaign said 'gee, wouldn't it be better if Trump were elected?' That's political wrongdoing, but it's just not a crime." Dershowitz added that Trump's firing of FBI Director James Comey would not amount to obstruction of justice, because the President has "a constitutional and statutory right to do that."

Chapter **9**

Doing Business: The Commerce Clause

C ongress is the Legislative branch of the federal government — the branch that makes laws. But Congress can't pass just any laws it likes. Its lawmaking powers are limited by the Constitution as part of the delicate balancing act that the Constitution performs between the federal government and the states.

Article I, Section 8 of the Constitution lists the powers of Congress. It's a pretty long list — but don't worry, I'm not going to bore you with it here. (You can turn to the Appendix if you're dying with curiosity.)

Article I, Section 8, Clause 3 — known as the *Commerce Clause* — contains probably the most important of these listed powers. Here's what the Commerce Clause says:

> *The Congress shall have Power . . . To regulate Commerce with foreign Nations, and among the several States, and with the Indian Tribes.*

As usual, there's more to these few words than meets the eye.

How the Commerce Clause Was Born

The Commerce Clause owes its existence to the economic conflicts between the states during the period under the Articles of Confederation, which were in force from 1781 until the ratification of the U.S. Constitution in 1788.

Under the Articles of Confederation, the national government was extremely weak and had no power to regulate the economy. The states were essentially independent of one another. In 1787 James Madison wrote to George Washington in exasperation at the way the states continued "to harass each other with rival and spiteful measures dictated by mistaken views of interest." Madison added that "the national Government should be armed with positive and compleat authority in all cases which require uniformity; such as the regulation of trade, including the right of taxing both exports & imports."

But how far does the Commerce Clause reflect Madison's view on this important subject? The poor little guy (he was only 5 foot 3¾ inches tall) was often thwarted in the Constitutional Convention.

Interpreting the Commerce Clause

The courts have pored over practically every word in the Commerce Clause. Here are some of the issues associated with the definitions of certain words and phrases:

- » **Power:** The question here is whether the Commerce Clause gives Congress *exclusive* power to regulate commerce — particularly over interstate commerce — or whether the states have a *concurrent* power (a power running parallel to that of Congress). I discuss this tricky question in the next section.

- » **Commerce:** Two hundred years ago, *commerce* referred primarily to the buying and selling of goods and commodities. But, in the leading case of *Gibbons v. Ogden,* decided in 1824, Chief Justice John Marshall held that it also included navigation. Since then, the term *commerce* has been narrowed and widened at different times, according to the changing views of the Supreme Court justices.

- » **Regulate:** *To regulate* was defined by Marshall as meaning "to prescribe the rule by which commerce is to be governed."

- » **"Commerce with foreign Nations":** It is not at all surprising that Congress was given the power to regulate foreign trade, because foreign affairs generally were the concern of the national government and not of the states.

>> **"among the several States":** As Marshall put it, this phrase "may very properly be restricted to that commerce which concerns more states than one" — now generally called *interstate* commerce. The definition of this term has fluctuated in accordance with the views of the justices of the Supreme Court over time. The ruling definition of *interstate commerce* is now very broad, covering the movement of pretty much any goods or services — or even people — across state lines.

>> **"with the Indian Tribes":** Native Americans were recognized from the foundation of the Republic as being separate from the United States. However, in an 1831 case the Supreme Court decided that the Cherokee nation was not an independent state but a "denominated domestic dependent nation." By referring to Native Americans separately from foreign nations, the Commerce Clause supports this high court view.

Hunting Down the Dormant Commerce Clause

On the face of it, the Commerce Clause gives Congress the power "to regulate Commerce." But the U.S. Supreme Court has long held that lurking within the simple and positive wording of the Commerce Clause is a "Dormant Commerce Clause," prohibiting any state law that discriminates against interstate commerce — even in regard to a matter where federal legislation is completely silent. The Dormant Commerce Clause doctrine therefore gives the U.S. Supreme Court permission to strike down any such state laws. But not all justices of the Supreme Court believe in the existence of a Dormant Commerce Clause, or what they prefer to call a "negative" Commerce Clause, at all. The Dormant Commerce Clause theory is a bit like a flying saucer. Those who believe in it are passionate in its support, while skeptics are dismissive of the whole idea.

Looking at double taxation and the Dormant Commerce Clause

The conflict between these two schools of thought on the Commerce Clause came to a head in the case of *Comptroller of Treasury of Maryland v. Wynne* (2015). This was a case about double taxation. Maryland required its citizens to pay Maryland income tax on all their income, no matter where it came from and without regard to any taxes that they may have had to pay in other states. So, for example, if a Maryland resident earned $100,000 in Maryland and another $200,000 from other states, that resident would be assessed Maryland income taxes for the full $300,000, even if that resident was also paying income taxes on the out-of-state $200,000 to other states.

Brian and Karen Wynne, a married couple living in Maryland, earned income in 39 different states. Under Maryland law, the Wynnes were obliged to pay income tax to Maryland not only for the income that they earned in-state but also for their out-of-state earnings, on which they also had to pay income tax to other states. The Wynnes claimed an income tax credit for all the income tax paid to other states. Maryland refused to give the Wynnes a credit against the Maryland county-based income taxes while allowing a credit against state-wide income taxes.

The Wynnes won before Maryland's Court of Appeals, the state's highest court. By 5 votes to 4, the U.S. Supreme Court upheld this decision. One point of interest in this case was the unusual lineup, with the majority, led by the conservative Justice Alito, also including the very liberal Justices Breyer and Sotomayor, against whom was ranged an exceptional alliance between the conservative Justices Scalia and Thomas with the liberal Justices Ginsburg and Kagan.

Passing judgment

Justice Alito, writing for the majority, based his opinion squarely on the doctrine of the Dormant Commerce Clause, holding that "Maryland's tax scheme is inherently discriminatory and operates as a tariff . . . discriminating against interstate commerce."

Justice Scalia, dissenting with characteristic exuberance, rejected the whole "negative Commerce Clause" idea, which he labeled "a judicial fraud," adding: "The Court claims that the doctrine 'has deep roots.' So it does, like many weeds." As a textualist, Scalia opined: "The fundamental problem with our negative Commerce Clause cases is that the Constitution does not contain a negative Commerce Clause. It contains only a Commerce Clause. Unlike the negative Commerce Clause adopted by the judges, the real Commerce Clause, adopted by the People, merely empowers Congress 'to regulate Commerce with foreign Nations, and among the several States, and with the Indian Tribes.' The Clause says nothing about prohibiting state laws that burden commerce. Much less does it say anything about authorizing judges to set aside state laws *they believe* burden commerce."

Justice Clarence Thomas began his dissenting opinion in much the same vein as Scalia's: "The negative Commerce Clause has no basis in the text of the Constitution, makes little sense, and has proved virtually unworkable in application, and, consequently, cannot serve as a basis for striking down a state statute." But his emphasis is on "the deference we owe to the duly enacted laws of a State — particularly those concerning the paradigmatically sovereign activity of taxation."

In her dissent, Justice Ruth Bader Ginsburg, joined by Justices Scalia and Kagan, put forward a completely different and quite ingenious argument. Other residents of the same county of Maryland as the Wynnes who also earned $2.67 million in taxable net income — but whose earnings were all in-state — would have paid the same amount of income taxes *to Maryland* as the Wynnes. It would be unfair, argued Ginsburg, if the Wynnes were allowed tax credits against taxes paid to other states, because "the Wynnes enjoyed equal access to the State's services but will have paid . . . less to cover the costs of those services than similarly situated neighbors who earned their income entirely within the State." Which of these diverse arguments is right? On the face of it, Justice Ginsburg's position looks like a liberal argument from fairness. But that impression is quickly dispelled upon closer examination, because no liberal would suggest that access to state services should be allocated in proportion to taxes paid. By that argument, someone on welfare would be entitled to less access to state services than someone contributing more in state taxes — an argument that Justice Ginsburg would be most unlikely to embrace.

Justice Scalia's dissent, based as it is on a literal reading of the Constitution, sounds rather pedantic and does not concern itself with the patent unfairness suffered by the Wynnes. And Thomas's dissent is equally doctrinaire.

So does that mean that Justice Alito's motley majority got it right? Probably, though not necessarily on the basis of the shadowy and highly dubious Dormant Commerce Clause doctrine, but simply on the basis of a rejection of double or multiple taxation in the interest of fairness.

Tracing the Changing Meaning of the Commerce Clause

The commerce power is one of the most important powers that the Constitution entrusts to Congress. So, Supreme Court justices favoring the federal government have tended to adopt a broad interpretation of the clause, while justices favoring states' rights have generally taken a narrow view of the clause.

In 1824, there was debate about whether even a commercial activity like navigation fell within the commerce power. But within half a century the high court had greatly widened its interpretation of the Commerce Clause. In 1877, Chief Justice Morrison Waite ruled that, as the power to regulate commerce was "intrusted to the general government for the good of the nation, it is not only the right, but the duty, of Congress to see to it that intercourse among the States and the transmission of intelligence are not obstructed or unnecessarily encumbered by State legislation."

Protecting freedom of contract

The next phase in the life of the Commerce Clause was a restrictive interpretation by the high court of government power — state as well as federal — to regulate commerce.

CONTROVERSY

The period between 1905 and 1937 is often termed the *Lochner* era, named for the controversial Supreme Court decision striking down a New York labor law that limited the number of permissible hours of work in bakeries. The majority on the Court held that the state law violated the *freedom of contract* of employers and employees alike. They also ruled that freedom of contract was an integral part of the liberty protected by the Due Process Clause of the Fourteenth Amendment. So, by infringing on this right, the New York law was unconstitutional. (I discuss the Due Process Clause and the Lochner case in more detail in Chapter 17.)

The *Lochner* decision itself was not based on the Commerce Clause. But the principle of freedom of contract soon became a useful weapon against the commerce power of Congress.

Introducing the Four Horsemen and the Three Musketeers

The stage was set for a major battle in the Supreme Court between the supporters of federal regulation of the economy and the champions of freedom of contract.

The doctrine of freedom of contract was still dominant when Franklin Delano Roosevelt (FDR) was elected President in 1932. FDR's New Deal took the form of a series of radical programs embodied in congressional legislation. Four justices on the Supreme Court — nicknamed the Four Horsemen (of the Apocalypse) — were staunch conservatives who fought the New Deal tooth and nail. Luckily for the Horsemen, they found an ally in Justice Owen Roberts, who often provided the swing vote giving the Horsemen a majority on the court. The liberal wing of the court — nicknamed the Three Musketeers — was no match for the Horsemen when they had Roberts in tow.

Between 1935 and 1937 the conservative majority struck down one after another of the New Deal programs as unconstitutional.

FDR was sick of the way the Four Horsemen thwarted him repeatedly in the Court by, as he put it, "reading into the Constitution words and implications which are not there, and which were never intended to be there."

Not a single vacancy on the Supreme Court bench opened up during FDR's first term, so the President wasn't able to name any new justices. But, bolstered by two landslide victories and an overwhelming majority in both houses of Congress, FDR decided to play the Horsemen at their own game — the game of constitutional interpretation.

Article III of the Constitution establishes a Supreme Court, but nowhere does the Constitution say how many members that court should consist of. Roosevelt therefore proposed a law giving the President the power to appoint an additional Supreme Court justice for every sitting member of the Court who had reached the age of 70½. This measure would immediately have allowed FDR to appoint six more justices, which would have given him indirect control over the court — something that even some of his staunchest supporters opposed as an abuse of presidential authority.

In the end, Roosevelt didn't need his court-packing scheme to get the Supreme Court on his side. The threat of it was enough. The turning point came when Justice Roberts switched sides — the famous "switch in time that saved nine" (justices) in *West Coast Hotel v. Parrish*, decided in 1937. (There is still some doubt whether Roosevelt's plan really was the reason for Roberts's sudden switch, because it appears that Roberts had written his opinion before the President even announced his proposal.)

West Coast Hotel v. Parrish signaled the end of the *Lochner* "freedom of contract" era. With a pro-New Deal majority on the court, it was inevitable that federal power under the Commerce Clause would grow exponentially.

Signaling the feds' control of the economy

The first sign of this growth in federal power came in *National Labor Relations Board (NLRB) v. Jones & Laughlin Steel Corporation*, decided in 1937. But that decision was by no means the most extreme manifestation of the control over the economy that the federal government had now obtained. That honor probably goes to a 1942 case about a small farmer and his small allotment: *Wickard v. Filburn.*

The Agricultural Adjustment Act of 1938 — part of FDR's vast New Deal program — restricted the area that farmers could use for growing wheat. The idea was to keep wheat prices stable by controlling production.

Roscoe Filburn was a small farmer in Ohio. He produced 239 bushels more wheat than his federal quota allowed him. So he was hit with a penalty amounting to 57 percent of the market value of his excess production.

Roscoe pointed out that he didn't sell any of his excess wheat production. Not only did none of his wheat crop enter interstate commerce, but also none of it ever left his farm. All his wheat was consumed right there by himself, his family, his poultry, and his livestock. Roscoe figured that this explanation gave him an ironclad case against the feds — but he hadn't reckoned on the new pro-government approach of the Supreme Court.

The question before the high court in the case of *Wickard v. Filburn* was quite simple: Was the law setting production quotas in keeping with the Commerce Clause — even when the wheat crop in question never left the state where it was grown?

Amazingly, the high court ruled unanimously in favor of the federal legislation. It held that if Filburn had not grown and consumed his excess wheat, he would have had to buy it from someone else — which is commerce. In the words of Justice Robert H. Jackson, writing for the Court, "Even if [Filburn's] activity be local, and though it may not be regarded as commerce, it may still, whatever its nature, be reached by Congress if it exerts a substantial economic effect on interstate commerce."

IN MY OPINION

Justice Jackson was not noted as a comedian, but was this a joke? Did he really say "though it may not be regarded as commerce"? Yep, he sure did. So, that must mean that even something that's not commerce at all — let alone *interstate* commerce — can still be regulated by the feds under the Commerce Clause! But that's not all he said. How about the phrase "if it exerts a substantial economic effect on interstate commerce"? Seriously, how could 239 bushels of wheat exert a substantial effect on anything?

Using the Commerce Clause to advance civil rights

The high court's decision in Filburn's case was a signal that allowed the feds to muscle in on pretty much any economic activity. Not surprisingly, the feds took the opportunity to use their economic power to further their political program — including, above all, civil rights. Federal legislation outlawed segregation, and the Supreme Court under Chief Justice Earl Warren was quick to support this legislation in any way it could, including using the Commerce Clause. One leading example of this kind occurred in a case involving an Atlanta motel.

The Heart of Atlanta Motel in Atlanta, Georgia, offered accommodation only to white people. This policy was directly contrary to federal law. The Civil Rights Act of 1964 specifically outlawed racial discrimination "in any place of public accommodation" if its operations "affect commerce."

The owner of the motel filed suit in federal court arguing that, in passing this provision, Congress exceeded its powers under the Commerce Clause. A unanimous Supreme Court ruled that the ban on racial discrimination in public accommodations was well within Congress's powers under the Commerce Clause. The Court also noted that three-fourths of the motel's guests came from outside Georgia, so the business clearly affected interstate commerce.

Turning back the federal tide?

The *Heart of Atlanta* case was no isolated example. The Commerce Clause was a convenient tool in the hands of the Supreme Court to bring the states to heel. But the Court itself was beginning to change, most notably after the appointment of William Rehnquist as Chief Justice in 1986. Rehnquist was a conservative who tended generally to favor states' rights in what came to be called "the new federalism."

In *United States v. Lopez,* decided in 1995, the Supreme Court at last struck down a federal law on the ground that it went beyond the permissible limits of the Commerce Clause. This was the first high court decision since 1937 to restrict congressional authority to legislate under the Commerce Clause.

"Appropriating state police powers under the guise of regulating commerce"

United States v. Morrison, decided in 2000, was another case in which the high court struck down part of a well-intentioned federal statute. The law in question was the Violence Against Women Act (VAWA), and the relevant provision allowed female victims of gender-based violence to file civil suits in federal court.

Justice Clarence Thomas, concurring with Chief Justice Rehnquist, charged Congress in the VAWA with "appropriating state police powers under the guise of regulating commerce." This statement puts the majority decision in a nutshell.

REMEMBER

It's important to note that the high court did not invalidate the whole of VAWA but only the part allowing a civil remedy in federal court. The rest of VAWA — mainly providing funding for the investigation and prosecution of sexual violence in the *criminal* courts — is still alive and well. Congress reauthorized it in 2005, and President George W. Bush signed it into law in 2006 — with the addition of relief for male victims of domestic violence and indecent assault.

Taking a step backward

IN MY OPINION

After the successful check on the feds in *United States v. Morrison,* we find ourselves back in 1942. In *Gonzales v. Raich,* decided in 2005, the high court upheld a federal law banning the use of marijuana for medicinal purposes — although a California state law allowed such use. Angel Raich, who brought the case, used only in-state marijuana. In the words of Justice Thomas, dissenting, Raich's "local cultivation and consumption of marijuana is not 'Commerce . . . among the several states'." The result of this sad case was the same as that in the remarkably similar case of *Wickard v. Filburn* — victory for the feds over the little person, over the states, and over the correct interpretation of the Commerce Clause.

Missing an opportunity?

Obamacare was one government policy which its supporters generally expected to be vindicated by the Commerce Clause. The chief feature of Obamacare considered by the U.S. Supreme Court in *Federation of Independent Business v. Sebelius* (2012) was the "individual mandate" requiring most Americans to take out health insurance whether they felt they needed it or not — and to pay a penalty if they failed to do so. The majority on the Court upheld the constitutionality of Obamacare, more properly called the Patient Protection and Affordable Care Act, but, to general surprise, did not do so on the basis of the Commerce Clause but on the basis that the imposition of the individual mandate with its penalty provision was a valid exercise of Congress's taxing power. In the words of Chief Justice Roberts, writing for the majority: "The individual mandate cannot be upheld as an exercise of Congress's power under the Commerce Clause. The Clause authorizes Congress to regulate interstate commerce, not to order individuals to engage in it. In this case, however, it is reasonable to construe what Congress has done as increasing taxes on those who have a certain amount of income, but choose to go without health insurance. Such legislation is within Congress's power to tax."

3

Assessing the Three Engines of Government: The President, Congress, and the Judiciary

IN THIS CHAPTER

» Determining eligibility for the presidency

» Explaining how the President is elected

» Examining the President's veto power

» Appointing judges, Cabinet officers, and others

» Claiming executive privilege

» Commanding and deploying the troops?

Chapter **10**

Examining the Role of the President

The President of the United States is commonly described as the most powerful person in the world. So it's pretty important to understand how the President is chosen and exactly what powers and responsibilities the President has under the Constitution. That's what this chapter is all about.

Being "eligible to the Office of President"

Thinking about running for president? Want to know if you qualify? Article II, Section 1 of the Constitution lays down the requirements for eligibility:

> *No person except a natural born Citizen, or a Citizen of the United States, at the time of the Adoption of this Constitution, shall be eligible to the Office of President; neither shall any Person be eligible to that Office who shall not have attained to the Age of thirty five Years, and been fourteen Years a Resident within the United States.*

In other words, to be eligible for the office of President, you have to be

» "[A] natural born" U.S. citizen — but see the discussion that follows

» At least 35 years old

» A U.S. resident for at least 14 years

Do you really need to have been born a citizen of the United States to become President? A close reading of the quoted section shows that you don't — provided you became a U.S. citizen by June 21, 1788. The only snag is that you'd have to be more than 220 years old to qualify under that rule!

Interpreting "natural born Citizen"

Does the term "natural born Citizen" mean that you have to be born in a state of the United States? Or is it good enough if you were born in a U.S. territory? Barry Goldwater, the Republican presidential nominee in 1964, was born in Arizona Territory before it became a state, but his right to run for President was never seriously questioned. The same applied to John McCain, who was born to U.S. parents (his father was an admiral) at a U.S. military base in the Panama Canal Zone, which was a territory of the United States at the time.

Was Barack Obama "eligible to the office of President"? After his election in 2008 and reelection in 2012, and after he served two full terms as President, Obama's eligibility is no longer moot. But the so-called "birthers" (a name for those who contested Obama's citizenship), including Donald Trump, challenged Obama's eligibility on the ground that he was not really born in Hawaii as he claimed but in Kenya, where his father came from. "Birthers" were skeptical about the "short form" Hawaiian birth certificate released by the Obama presidential campaign in June 2008, and the authenticity of a "long form" Hawaiian birth certificate in April 2011 was also challenged by some as a forgery made with image editing software. On October 24, 2012, Donald Trump announced: "If Barack Obama opens up and gives his college records and applications, and passport application and records, I will give to a charity of his choice, a check immediately for $5 million." Obama did not take the bait. However, on September 16, 2016, after being elected as the Republican Party presidential nominee, Trump put the "birther" controversy to rest by declaring: "President Barack Obama was born in the United States. Period." See Figure 10-1 for a look at President Trump.

FIGURE 10-1: Donald Trump, who would become the 45th U.S. president, is greeted at a White House reception by an uneasy looking President Ronald Reagan in 1987. Trump, who was born in New York, has questioned other elected officials' eligibility.

Trump also raised doubts about the right of Senator Ted Cruz to run for President in 2016. Cruz was born in Canada to a Cuban father and an American mother. At the time of his birth, his father was not a U.S. citizen, but his mother was a U.S. citizen born in Delaware. According to the Cruz campaign, she lived in Canada under a work permit and at no time applied for Canadian citizenship or permanent residence. Cruz acquired U.S. citizenship at birth and moved to the U.S. at the age of 4. But he also had Canadian citizenship, which he subsequently renounced. Professor Laurence Tribe, who taught both Cruz and Obama constitutional law at Harvard, remarked that the constitutional questions surrounding Cruz's eligibility were "murky and unsettled."

The key to figuring out a person's eligibility lies in the meaning of the term "natural born Citizen," which appears only once in the U.S. Constitution — in regard to the Presidency but not in regard to any other office. That's why there has never been any doubt about Ted Cruz's eligibility to serve as a U.S. senator, for which the only requirement as far as citizenship is concerned is that you have to have been a U.S. citizen for at least nine years. So even a foreigner who became a citizen of the U.S. by naturalization would be eligible to become a senator. But why is there a different requirement for the presidency? Probably because the Founders were anxious to prevent anyone who could be suspected of having even the slightest hint of a foreign connection from becoming President.

But what does "natural born Citizen" actually mean? Under English law there were no citizens, only subjects, and the term "natural-born subject" certainly was known under English law at the time of the drafting of the U.S. Constitution. Here's a relevant quote from the great English jurist William Blackstone, written in 1765: "Natural-born subjects are such as are born within the dominions of the crown of England." This, Blackstone explains, is based on the principle "that every man owes natural allegiance where he is born." But what about foreign-born children of natural-born subjects? They were "to all intents and purposes" natural-born subjects themselves, said Blackstone, in accordance with certain statutes. Those statutes did not of course apply to the United States. So the most likely meaning of the phrase "natural born Citizen" is someone actually born in the United States, which would exclude Ted Cruz. If Cruz or anyone else with a similar problem were again to become a presidential candidate, the whole question would have to be looked at again and probably go to the U.S. Supreme Court to be decided. (Please note that the interpretation of arcane or archaic phrases in the Constitution will vary according to the school of thought of the interpreter. The three main schools of thought are textualists, originalists, and those believing in a "living Constitution." I deal with this in Chapter 12.)

Looking at the two-term rule

CONTROVERSY

Another controversy surrounding eligibility to be President is whether a former two-term President could lawfully run for election as Vice President. This was raised in connection with the possibility that Bill Clinton might become Hillary Clinton's running mate. Then, if she died or resigned, he would become President for a third term.

The suggestion is preposterous because the Twenty-Second Amendment states categorically that "No person shall be elected to the office of the President more than twice." The pro-Clintonites argue that this amendment is a prohibition only on being *elected* President, but not on becoming President by some other route, like being elected as Veep and then succeeding to the presidency on the resignation of the President. For a discussion on the Twenty-Second Amendment, see (appropriately enough) Chapter 22.

"[E]ligible to the Office of President" just means "able to be *elected* to the office of President." This phrase in Article II, Section 1 dovetails with the Twenty-Second Amendment, and also with the Twelfth Amendment, which provides that "no person constitutionally ineligible to the office of President shall be eligible to that of Vice-President of the United States." In short, if you can't be elected President, you also can't be elected Vice President. Reading the three constitutional texts together, we get this: *A former two-term President can't be elected to a third term as President, and he also can't be elected as Vice President.*

IT'S A TWO-PARTY SYSTEM

To run for President, it helps to be a billionaire. It also helps to have been nominated as the candidate of one of the two major political parties, Democratic or Republican. Nomination can be achieved only by winning enough *primary elections* — contests within one of the major parties — to ensure the support of a majority of pledged delegates at the party convention.

These are not constitutional requirements, but in practice it's almost impossible for a third-party candidate to be elected President. In 1912, ex-President Theodore Roosevelt, running on a Progressive Party (or "Bull Moose") ticket, made a strong showing as a third-party candidate. He received 88 electoral votes, far superior to incumbent Republican President William H. Taft's 8 electoral votes. But what Roosevelt really accomplished was putting Democratic nominee Woodrow Wilson into the White House (with 435 electoral votes).

More surprisingly, in 1992, Ross Perot, a 62-year-old billionaire who had never held public office, picked up 18.9 percent of the popular vote. Although Perot got no electoral votes because he didn't get a majority in any one state, he arguably cost incumbent President George H. W. Bush the election and put Bill Clinton into the White House.

In fact, in the 2016 election there were no fewer than 32 candidates for President who received at least 1,000 votes or were on the ballot in at least one state. But besides the Democratic and Republican candidates, there was only one who made it onto the ballot in all 50 states plus the District of Columbia, and that was the Libertarian candidate, Gary Johnson. Jill Stein, the Green Party candidate, appeared on the ballot in 44 states plus DC. Stein ended up with 1.07 percent of the national popular vote, with Johnson at 3.28 percent. All the other candidates polled a total of 1.3 percent of the vote. The lion's share of the popular vote, 94.27 percent, was shared between the Democrats and the Republicans, with Hillary Clinton taking 48.18 percent and Donald Trump 46.09 percent.

What's the reason for the perpetuation of the two-party system? It's a direct result of the winner-take-all arrangement. Voters perceive a vote for a third party or an independent as a wasted vote.

Picking a President

The Constitution goes into great detail on presidential elections, but much of what it says on that subject is obsolete or misleading.

The biggest problem in regard to the constitutional rules for presidential elections is the Framers' total disregard of the existence of political parties, which they scorned as "factions" but which came to play a major role in elections.

Examining the modern electoral system

Let's take a look at how the President gets elected today:

>> **How many electors does each state get?** Each state chooses electors equal in number to the total of the representatives from that state plus the 2 senators from that state. So, for example, at present Florida has 29 electors because it has 27 representatives and 2 senators. A state with a small population, like Wyoming, may have only 1 representative, but, like all states, it has 2 senators. So Wyoming is entitled to 3 electors.

>> **Who elects the electors?** The Constitution leaves it up to each state legislature to decide how the electors for that state are chosen. Today, the electors are always directly elected. I discuss this point more in a minute.

>> **What is the Electoral College?** The term *Electoral College* is commonly used to refer to the electors of all the states together. But the phrase *Electoral College* doesn't figure in the text of the Constitution. And the Electoral College never meets together as a national body — only as 51 separate groups of electors (one for each state plus one for Washington, D.C., which has three electors).

REMEMBER

>> **What about the popular vote?** The real election — the vote by the people — doesn't rate a mention in the Constitution! The reason for this omission is that in the early days, the people didn't get to vote for the President at all. The state legislatures would often choose the electors themselves, and the electors would then pick the President according to their own personal preferences. Democracy triumphed only through the rise of the party system, under which the voters in each state were presented with a slate of electors for each party. Voters picked the slate of the political party of their choice. The electors were *pledged* to support the presidential candidate of one or the other particular party. So, in choosing, say, the Republican slate, a voter was actually voting for the Republican presidential candidate.

>> **What is the short ballot?** Nowadays, the whole Electoral College system is usually short-circuited. Most states use the so-called *short ballot,* which just shows the names of the presidential candidates themselves. Anonymous slates of electors still lurk behind the candidates' names, but the voters are given the impression — which is almost invariably correct — that they are picking the President directly themselves.

>> **What happens when the electors meet?** The electors then meet in their respective states and formally cast their votes. They vote separately for the

President and for the Vice President. But the whole of this stage of the election is a charade because the electors almost always vote for the candidates to whom they have pledged their support. Can an elector step out of line and refuse to vote for his pledged candidate? Sure, but it doesn't happen all that often. (In Chapter 25, I discuss the so-called *faithless elector*.)

» **Who tallies the formal vote count?** Each state certifies the number of votes cast by its electors for the different candidates. These certificates are sent to Washington, D.C., and are opened at a joint sitting of both houses of Congress. The electoral votes from all the states are then tallied up, and the official result is formally announced.

» **What happens if a candidate gets a majority?** If the presidential candidate with the most votes has more than 50 percent of the total number of electoral votes cast, that candidate becomes President. The same applies to the candidates for Vice President.

» **What happens if no presidential candidate gets a majority?** If the top-scoring presidential candidate doesn't receive a majority of electoral votes, or if two candidates tie, the election is thrown into the House of Representatives, which chooses the President from the three top-scoring candidates. Here each state has only one vote. To become President, a candidate needs 26 states to vote for him. This procedure has been used twice, in 1800 and 1824 — and should probably also have been used in 2000. This arrangement gives a great advantage to the smaller states. For example, it gives Alaska the same say as California, although under the normal Electoral College system Alaska has only 3 electoral votes to California's 55.

» **What happens if no vice-presidential candidate gets a majority?** If no vice-presidential candidate gets the requisite majority in the normal Electoral College process, the Senate picks the Vice President. Support from 51 out of the 100 senators is needed for victory.

Exploding some myths about the Electoral College

CONTROVERSY

Presidential elections are so important that it would be surprising if they weren't surrounded by a few myths. The commonest myth is that the Electoral College system is by its very nature undemocratic. This fallacy is based on the assumption that the *winner-take-all* system, or plurality voting system, is a necessary part of the Electoral College system.

The winner-take-all arrangement sure is unfair because a difference of one vote out of millions can switch all the electoral votes of a state from one party's column to the other. Here's how the system works.

Let's take a hypothetical state with 12 electoral votes. In a presidential election, let's assume that 2,000,000 votes are cast for the Democratic ticket in that state and that the Republican ticket garners 1,999,999 votes — just one vote fewer. The winner-take-all arrangement dictates that in those circumstances, all 12 electoral votes for that state stand in the Democratic column.

In that scenario, the winner at least has a majority — more than 50 percent — of the votes. But the same rule applies where the winner has only a *plurality*: less than 50 percent but more votes than any other candidate.

This doesn't look like a very fair outcome — and it also makes disputed elections and recounts much more likely. The close vote in Florida in the 2000 election is an excellent example of this problem.

The election result in our hypothetical state appears unsatisfactory, to say the least. But is that outcome the fault of the Electoral College system, as is generally assumed? No, the problem is caused not by the Electoral College system itself but by the winner-take-all arrangement that is associated with it. But isn't winner-take-all part and parcel of the Electoral College system? The two systems are generally found together, but that isn't necessarily so.

REMEMBER

The winner-take-all arrangement is

>> Not a necessary part of the Electoral College system

>> Not laid down by the Constitution

>> Not used by all states

Explaining the Nebraska and Maine "congressional district method"

Can you really have the Electoral College system without winner-take-all? Sure. Two states have already taken the step of separating these two features. These states are Nebraska and Maine, which allow the electoral vote to be shared between the parties in accordance with the proportion of the vote each party gets.

Maine has four electoral votes, based on its two congressmen plus its two senators. The state is divided into two congressional voting districts. Let's assume the following results in a hypothetical presidential election:

>> Statewide vote: Democrat 60 percent, Republican 40 percent

>> District 1: Democrat 80 percent, Republican 20 percent

>> District 2: Democrat 40 percent, Republican 60 percent

In this hypothetical situation, the Nebraska–Maine "district method" gives two electoral votes to the Democratic ticket for winning the statewide popular vote, plus a third electoral vote for winning in District 1, while the Republicans pick up one electoral vote for winning in District 2. The overall result is then a 3:1 split of the electoral vote, instead of the winner-take-all approach which would give all four electoral votes to the Democrats.

Until 2008, neither Nebraska nor Maine had ever actually split its electoral votes because Nebraska was normally overwhelmingly Republican, while the Democrats have always had big majorities in Maine since the system was introduced there in 1972. However, in the 2008 presidential election, Senator Barack Obama, the Democratic Party candidate, was awarded one of Nebraska's five electoral votes, with the remaining four electoral votes going to Senator John McCain, the Republican flag-bearer. In 2012, neither Nebraska nor Maine had a split vote. But in 2016, one of Maine's electoral votes went to Donald Trump, with Hillary Clinton taking the remaining three. Nebraska gave all five of its electoral votes to Trump.

A simpler version of this system was proposed for Colorado in 2004, but it was roundly rejected by an almost two-thirds majority of the voters. The proposal was for the state's electoral votes to be split in proportion to the votes cast for each ticket. So, if the Democrats received 55 percent of the votes and the Republicans received 45 percent, Colorado's nine electoral votes would have been split 5:4.

Those campaigning against the change argued that, because presidential elections in Colorado tend to be close, four of Colorado's nine electoral votes would always go to the loser, so that Colorado's influence on the election would amount to only one electoral vote — five minus four. The logic of this argument may be flawed, but it played well with Colorado voters.

On the basis of the Colorado experience, the winner-take-all method of calculating electoral votes looks set to survive as the dominant system for the foreseeable future.

But what about scrapping the Electoral College altogether and going to a pure nationwide popular vote system?

Picking the President by popular vote?

The biggest objection to the Electoral College system is that it has on five occasions — most recently in 2016 — denied victory to the winner of the popular vote. I must stress once again that these supposedly "stolen elections" were the product not of the Electoral College system itself but of the winner-take-all arrangement that is usually, but not necessarily, associated with it.

In the 2016 election, the Democratic candidate, Hillary Clinton, polled 48.18 percent of the popular vote to Republican Donald Trump's 46.09 percent. In actual numbers, this meant that Clinton garnered nearly 2.87 million more votes than her Republican rival.

The situation in the 2000 election was more complicated. George W. Bush *would* have been elected President with 273 electoral votes to 264 electoral votes for Al Gore if the electoral vote in each state had been split in proportion to the popular vote in that state. This was very much the same result as was finally certified in the actual election of 2000 — but it would have been done without the intervention of the U.S. Supreme Court!

Instead of the legal circus that actually occurred in 2000, under the Constitution the election ought to have been thrown into the House of Representatives. In that scenario, Bush would have won hands-down because he had 30 states in his column against only 20 (plus the District of Columbia) for Gore.

However, on the basis of the popular vote alone, Gore would have won because he ended up with about 543,000 votes more than Bush. Scrapping the Electoral College altogether and replacing it with a pure popular vote system would require an amendment to the U.S. Constitution. What chance such an amendment would have of being adopted is hard to say, but it would face concerted opposition from those favoring states' rights, from the smaller states generally, and probably from most conservatives.

REMEMBER

Although pure popular election looks simple, democratic, and modern, it has problems of its own. For example, would a plurality of the popular vote be enough to win the election, or would the winning candidate need to have a majority? If the latter, would there have to be a runoff election — or would the House of Representatives have to decide, as under the present system? I discuss the arguments for and against popular election in Chapter 20.

Canning the President

Firing a President — known as *impeachment* — is just as important as picking a President in the first place. So how come impeachment gets only this itsy-bitsy paragraph here dedicated to it? In fact, impeachment has a whole chapter of its own in this book: Chapter 13. Check it out.

Signing, Vetoing, and Pocketing Legislation

Article I, Section 7 of the Constitution gives the President an important power against Congress: the power to stop any bill passed by both houses of Congress from becoming law. This is known as the *presidential veto power*, although the word *veto* doesn't appear anywhere in the Constitution.

Here's a summary of how the President's veto power works.

>> Every *bill* (proposed law) has to pass both the Senate and the House of Representatives by a majority in each house.

>> After passing both houses, a bill is sent to the President for his approval.

>> If the President approves the bill, he signs it, which makes it law — he *signs it into law*.

>> If the President doesn't approve a bill, he can veto it by returning it unsigned to Congress with his objections.

>> Congress then reconsiders the vetoed bill. A two-thirds majority in both houses is needed to override the President's veto.

>> If the President has not returned a bill within ten days of it being sent to him, it becomes law anyway, without the President's signature.

>> If the President doesn't sign the bill, and if Congress adjourns before the ten-day period is up, the bill doesn't become law. This provision is called the *pocket veto*.

REMEMBER

A pocket veto is better for the President than an ordinary veto because a pocket veto kills a bill stone-dead. If Congress still wants the bill passed, the bill must start life again in the next session and go through the whole procedure from the beginning.

In the 1938 case of *Wright v. United States,* the Supreme Court approved the possibility of Congress appointing agents to send and receive messages on behalf of Congress during an adjournment to stop the President from taking unfair advantage of the pocket veto rule. That practice is now routinely used. The agent is usually either the clerk of the House of Representatives or the secretary of the Senate, depending on the house where the bill originated.

Appointing Key Positions

Article II, Section 2 of the Constitution says that the President

shall nominate, and by and with the Advice and Consent of the Senate, shall appoint Ambassadors, other public Ministers and Consuls, judges of the supreme Court, and all other Officers of the United States, whose Appointments are not herein otherwise provided for, and which shall be established by Law.

This provision gives the President the power to make a lot of important appointments: Supreme Court justices, other federal judges, Cabinet officers, and diplomats, to mention but a few. But all appointments are subject to the confirmation of the Senate. The Senate has blocked presidential appointments so frequently that the phrase "Advice and Dissent" is now often jocularly used instead of the phrase "Advice and Consent" that appears in the Constitution.

CONTROVERSY

The Senate has sometimes exercised its power to advise and consent in such a way as to amount to a veto over the President's power to appoint qualified officials. This power has been exercised more savagely in recent times than previously. Besides actually voting a nomination down, the Senate can tie a nomination up in committee for so long that it has to be withdrawn, or senators seeking to block a nomination can keep talking indefinitely to stop a vote on the nomination from being taken — a technique known as a *filibuster*. Here are a few examples of these tactics:

>> The Senate started blocking presidential appointments very early on. In 1795, by 14 votes to 10, the Senate voted down George Washington's nomination of John Rutledge as Chief Justice of the United States. This rebuff to Washington appears to have been motivated by a combination of opposition to Rutledge's political views and a feeling that he was mentally unstable.

>> The degree of support enjoyed by a President in the Senate is an important factor determining how that body is likely to react to any particular nomination. Vice President John Tyler, who succeeded to the presidency on the death of the Whig President William Henry Harrison in 1841, had more of his nominees to the Supreme Court rejected by the Senate than any other President — four nominees, some of whom were rejected twice. The reason for this was that the Senate had a majority of Whigs, whom Tyler had angered by vetoing all their proposed legislation. He was then expelled from the Whig party and became known as "the man without a party."

>> In 1987, the Senate rejected President Ronald Reagan's nomination of Judge Robert Bork by 58 votes to 42. Bork was extremely well-qualified for the appointment in terms of knowledge, intellect, and integrity. He was rejected because of his extremely conservative views on politics and on the role of the judiciary.

» Justice Clarence Thomas, nominated to a seat on the Supreme Court by President George H. W. Bush in 1991, was subjected to probably the most embarrassing hearings of any presidential nominee ever. Thomas faced opposition both on the grounds of his conservative views and because of allegations of sexual harassment leveled against him by Anita Hill, a former colleague of his at the U.S. Equal Employment Opportunity Commission. Thomas managed to weather the storm, and he was confirmed by the Senate by 52 votes to 48.

» The nomination by President George W. Bush of John Bolton, an outspoken conservative, as the Permanent U.S. Representative to the United Nations, was blocked in May 2005 by a Democratic Party filibuster in the Senate. The President appointed Bolton anyway while the Senate was in recess — which is specifically allowed under the Constitution as a temporary measure. Bush then renominated Bolton in 2006, but opponents kept a vote from being taken in the relevant Senate committee. Eventually, Bolton decided to step down when his recess appointment expired in December 2006.

Is the President bound by the so-called "Bobby Kennedy Law," an anti-nepotism measure? President John F. Kennedy's appointment of his brother Bobby Kennedy as Attorney General raised hackles in certain quarters. The law, passed in 1967 to prohibit such appointments in the future, says that "a public official" — specifically including the President — "may not appoint, employ, promote, advance. . . . any individual who is a relative of the public official." The law goes on to say that anyone appointed or employed "in violation" of that law "is not entitled to pay." So the appointment of President Trump's "first daughter," Ivanka, as a presidential advisor is presumably kosher, as she is unpaid. But what about the appointment of her husband, Jared Kushner, as a senior White House advisor? A Justice Department opinion issued just hours after President Trump's inauguration in 2017 said that the President had the power to appoint his son-in-law anyway, because of a subsequent 1978 law that trumps (no pun intended) the "Bobby Kennedy Law." The opinion admitted that even after 1978 the Office of Legal Counsel had stopped several presidents from appointing family members, but added: "Although our conclusion today departs from some of that prior work, we think that this departure is fully justified."

Hailing the Chief: The President's Administration

Article II, Section 1 of the Constitution says, "The executive Power shall be vested in a President of the United States of America." *Executive power* means the power to enforce the law and to administer — or run — the government on a day-to-day basis. This provision gives the President power over all aspects of the federal government: financial issues, domestic affairs, and foreign affairs (not to mention military matters, which I discuss separately a little later in this chapter).

The Constitution is silent on the way that the President is expected to perform this mammoth task. In practice, the President operates through a vast administrative machine — hence the description of a President's period in office as his *administration*.

Uncovering the secrets of Cabinet secretaries

The President's chief lieutenants in running his huge empire are his Cabinet secretaries, including the Secretary of State, Secretary of Defense, Secretary of the Treasury, Secretary of the Interior, and Secretary of Homeland Security.

What's with this title of *secretary*? It makes these high officers of state sound like jumped-up typists. The title of *secretary* originated in England, where the Secretary of State was originally the King's private secretary — and the word *secretary* reflected the fact that this office-holder really was the keeper of confidential information.

The secret about U.S. Cabinet secretaries is that their activities are not secret. The President *does* also have some more personal and more confidential advisers — in the Executive Office of the President, which I discuss a bit later in this chapter.

Article II, Section 2 contains the only reference to the Cabinet officers in the original, unamended Constitution:

> *[The President] may require the Opinion, in writing, of the principal Officer in each of the executive Departments, upon any Subject relating to the Duties of their respective Offices.*

This cryptic provision raises more questions than it answers. Does this brief clause envision a Cabinet at all, or just several separate government departments doing their own thing? And what's with "may require the Opinion, in writing"? Is that the only way that the President can communicate with his own Cabinet secretaries? What about Cabinet meetings? And can't the President give instructions to his Cabinet officers?

The Framers were probably in a hurry to go out to lunch when they drafted this baffling snippet, which is both too vague and too precise at the same time — if that makes any sense!

In practice, presidents have not been hamstrung by this curious clause. Some presidents have given their Cabinet officers a free hand, while others have tried to micromanage the whole enchilada.

Cabinet officers — and in particular secretaries of state — were much more important in the early days than they are today. In the first 60 years of the Republic, no fewer than six secretaries of state made it to the presidency, starting with Thomas Jefferson and ending with James Buchanan. Since then, not a single president has come from the ranks of the secretaries of state.

Here's a quick rundown of some important facts about Cabinet officers, most of whom (fortunately!) don't hit the headlines that often:

>> **How do you become a Cabinet officer?** The President can appoint whomever he likes to his Cabinet — subject to confirmation by the Senate. The Senate doesn't usually give the President as hard a time over Cabinet appointments as over his nomination of Supreme Court justices.

>> **How do Cabinet officers get fired?** The President doesn't have to consult the Senate or anybody else if he wants to fire a Cabinet secretary.

>> **What do Cabinet officers do?** Each Cabinet officer heads up a department of the federal government. For example, the Secretary of State, the most important Cabinet member, is in charge of foreign affairs. He or she is the boss of all ambassadors and ministers representing the United States in foreign countries. The Secretary of Defense is responsible for the whole defense establishment.

>> **Where do Cabinet officers figure in the presidential succession?** The importance of Cabinet officers is recognized by their presence in the order of succession on the death, resignation, or removal of the President. The Presidential Succession Act of 1947 places the Vice President in first position, followed by the Speaker of the House of Representatives and the President Pro Tempore of the Senate. But then comes the Secretary of State and all the other Cabinet secretaries in the order of seniority of their offices — so the Secretary of Homeland Security is last in line, because that office was created only in 2003. I discuss the question of succession to the presidency more fully in Chapter 22.

Unmasking the imperial presidency

The Founders took a lot of flak for creating what some critics saw as a monarchy. George Washington was often addressed as "Your Excellency," although he preferred the simpler, more republican-style "Mr. President," which became the normal form of address for all later presidents — except when they were being mocked. (John Adams was referred to as "His Rotundity" for being short and fat, and John Tyler was ridiculed as "His Accidency" for being the first Vice President to succeed to the presidency as a result of the previous President's death.)

REMEMBER

With a few notable exceptions — Andrew Jackson, Abraham Lincoln, and Theodore Roosevelt — the President's power rarely outmatched that of Congress in the period before the election of Franklin Delano Roosevelt in 1932. But then the power of the presidency rapidly escalated. On the basis of the Great Depression followed by World War II, FDR established what is sometimes called an "imperial presidency": a presidency with far greater powers than were envisioned by the Framers of the Constitution.

Unlocking the Executive Office of the President

The Executive Office of the President (EOP) first came into existence in 1939 and now comprises a staff of about 1,800 people who are directly responsible to the President. Staff in the EOP have the title "Assistant to the President" or "Special Assistant to the President." Senior officials in the EOP include the White House Chief of Staff and the White House Press Secretary. Most staff on the EOP don't have to be confirmed by the Senate — which is a great boon to presidents.

REMEMBER

For national security and foreign policy matters, presidents now rely to a great extent on the National Security Council (NSC), which is part of the EOP. The NSC was first set up during the presidency of Harry Truman in 1947. The President chairs this august body himself. Meetings of the NSC are regularly attended by Cabinet officers such as the Secretary of State, the Secretary of Defense, and the Secretary of the Treasury, as well as by the Vice President. However, the NSC, together with the White House Situation Room, is run by the National Security Adviser, who is directly responsible to the President. (This position's formal title is Assistant to the President for National Security.)

George W. Bush established the Homeland Security Council (HSC) in the wake of the 9/11 terrorist outrages in 2001. It mirrors the NSC on the domestic front. Like the NSC, the HSC forms part of the EOP and is chaired by the President himself. As with the NSC, the HSC is under a non-Cabinet official, in this case the Assistant to the President for Homeland Security and Counterterrorism.

Why aren't the NSC and the HSC under Cabinet officers, the Secretary of State and the Secretary of Homeland Security, respectively? Because it suits the President to keep more direct control of these important bodies by chairing their meetings himself and by placing their day-to-day running under handpicked "Assistants to the President" — who, if need be, can also be used as counterweights to overambitious or unduly independent Cabinet secretaries.

President Trump's appointment of his son-in-law, Jared Kushner, as "Senior Adviser to the President," or, more formally, "Assistant to the President and Senior Adviser," right after Trump's inauguration, raised quite a few eyebrows. Kushner's appointment was initially queried under the anti-nepotism law passed in reaction to President John Kennedy's appointment of his brother Robert as Attorney General. But the Department of Justice Office of Legal Counsel issued an opinion stating that "the President may appoint relatives to his immediate staff of advisors."

As simply an "adviser," Kushner's appointment does not need confirmation by the Senate, even though he has been given top-secret security clearance. But at the time of this writing, his position appeared to be under threat after it was reported that he had close ties with Russia, to the point of asking Russian Ambassador Sergey Kislyak to establish a "secret and secure communications channel" between the White House and the Kremlin which could not be monitored by U.S. security services.

Selling the President's legislative program

In spite of the separation of powers, the President is inevitably involved in legislation. The President's approval is needed for a law to be passed by Congress. But modern presidents don't just wait around for Congress to propose legislation: The President has his own legislative program as well.

The President used to connect with Congress through the Bureau of the Budget or the Office of White House Counsel. However, in 1953 President Dwight Eisenhower formalized the relationship between the executive and legislative branches by establishing a Legislative Affairs Office in the White House.

This arrangement still survives today, with a permanent Legislative Affairs Office of about 12 members under the Office of Management and Budget, which forms part of the Executive Office of the President. One of the tasks of the Legislative Affairs Office is to produce Statements of Administration Policy (SAPs) addressed to a house of Congress that set out the President's views on a particular bill or issue. During the second session of the 110th Congress alone, in 2008–2009, no fewer than 88 SAPs were issued.

Most modern presidents have recognized the importance of liaison with Congress for the implementation of the President's legislative program. Even before taking office, President Barack Obama named Phil Schiliro as Assistant to the President for Legislative Affairs, or simply the Director of Legislative Affairs.

Presidents have also employed more direct methods of persuasion in respect to policies dear to their hearts. The use of President Lyndon Johnson's famed

"Johnson Method" of twisting the arms of recalcitrant lawmakers came into its own in the push to have the Civil Rights Act signed into law in 1964. Bill Clinton appointed an "Intensive Care Unit" to promote the President's abortive health-care reform package in Congress. President George W. Bush had a hard time selling what became the Medicare Modernization Act to lawmakers in 2003.

The direct involvement of the President in healthcare reform is now taken for granted. In the 2008 presidential election, Barack Obama made healthcare one of his top priorities if elected, and the Affordable Care Act, or "Obamacare" as it was commonly called, was signed into law by President Obama on March 23, 2010. In 2012, by 5 votes to 4, the U.S. Supreme Court upheld the constitutionality of Obamacare — including the highly controversial individual mandate, on the surprising basis that it was a "tax" and not a "penalty." One of Donald Trump's prime election pledges was to "repeal and replace" Obamacare, which at the time of this writing has not yet been achieved.

President Obama's financial "bailout" plan — an extension of one first proposed by President George W. Bush in 2008 — and a major economic stimulus package together represent the closest involvement a President has had in legislation regulating the economy since FDR's New Deal in the 1930s. The bailouts after the 2008 financial crisis included propping up a number of banks and other financial institutions that were considered "too big to fail," meaning that the institutions concerned were so important to the economy as a whole that their failure would be catastrophic. A key measure designed to prevent a recurrence of the 2008 financial crisis was the Dodd-Frank Act, signed into law by President Obama in 2010, which tightened up regulation of the banks and other financial institutions. However, there was also a good deal of opposition to Dodd-Frank, notably from Donald Trump, who pledged in the 2016 presidential election to repeal it. At the time of this writing, Congress was in the process of attempting to repeal Dodd-Frank. In the words of North Dakota Senator Heidi Heitkamp, a critic of Dodd-Frank and the "too big to fail" mentality: "We tried to fix too-big-to-fail and we created too-small-to-succeed."

President Trump also pledged major tax cuts, and on December 22, 2017, he signed into law a hard-fought law known in the House of Representatives (but not in the Senate) as the Tax Cuts and Jobs Act of 2017, which permanently reduced the corporate tax rate from 35 to 21 percent. More controversially, it also reduced most individual taxes, but only until the year 2025. President Trump touted the measure in his State of the Union address on January 30, 2018: "Since we passed tax cuts, roughly three million workers have already gotten tax cut bonuses. Many of them, thousands and thousands of dollars per worker and it's getting more every month, every week." On the other hand, House Minority Leader Nancy Pelosi characterized the legislation as "designed to plunder the middle class to put into the pockets of the wealthiest 1 percent more money."

On the international trade front, President Trump has come out against the North American Trade Agreement (NAFTA), the Trans-Pacific Partnership (TPP), and the World Trade Organization (WTO), favoring bilateral treaties with individual countries instead. In June 2017, President Trump announced the U.S. withdrawal from the international Paris Agreement on Climate Change, though the withdrawal can't take place before November 4, 2020, which happens to fall on the day after the 2020 presidential election. After President Trump's announcement, the governors of 13 states and Puerto Rico formed the United States Climate Alliance to continue to abide by the Paris accord.

Battling Executive Privilege

The President has long claimed *executive privilege,* the right to withhold information from the courts or from Congress. The expressed ground for this claim is national security, or else the need for confidentiality within the Executive branch. The claim of executive privilege is ultimately based on the doctrine of the separation of powers, under which the three branches of government — the Executive, the Legislative, and the Judicial — are kept separate in terms of membership. (But there's a certain amount of overlap in function for the purpose of checks and balances.) I discuss the separation of powers in Chapter 8.

There have been some recent court battles involving executive privilege. President Bill Clinton crossed swords with the courts over his affair with intern Monica Lewinsky. Clinton unwisely invoked executive privilege in refusing to allow his aides to be called to testify about the affair. Clinton lost. A federal judge ruled that the aides could be called.

Clinton later agreed to waive executive privilege and testify before a grand jury himself — but only under certain conditions. In the words of independent counsel Kenneth W. Starr, "Absolutely no one is above the law." On the basis of evidence collected by Starr, Clinton became only the second President to be subjected to impeachment proceedings. (However, he was acquitted and served out the remainder of his second term. He left office in January 2001 with a 65 percent approval rating, the highest end-of-term rating of any President since Dwight D. Eisenhower 40 years earlier.)

President George W. Bush's administration also got involved in some battles over executive privilege. For example, the administration claimed executive privilege in declining to disclose information about Vice President Dick Cheney's energy task force. In the 2004 case *Cheney v. U.S. District Court for the District of Columbia,* the

Supreme Court ruled in favor of the administration. Here's an extract from the 7-to-2 ruling:

> While the President is not above the law, the Judiciary must afford Presidential confidentiality the greatest possible protection, recognizing the paramount necessity of protecting the Executive Branch from vexatious litigation that might distract it from the energetic performance of its constitutional duties.

President George W. Bush also invoked executive privilege over the firing of eight federal prosecutors. The administration refused to comply with a Senate Judiciary Committee subpoena requiring presidential advisers to testify before the committee. However, quite a number of Justice Department officials resigned — including Attorney General Alberto Gonzales.

The Bush administration also claimed executive privilege in relation to the death in Afghanistan — by "friendly fire" — of popular football player Pat Tillman, who had passed up a football contract offer of $3.6 million over three years to enlist in the U.S. Army.

Supreme Court Justice Anthony Kennedy identified the central problem in regard to claims of executive privilege:

> Once executive privilege is asserted, coequal branches of the Government are set on a collision course. The Judiciary is forced into the difficult task of balancing the need for information in a judicial proceeding and the Executive's Article II prerogatives. This inquiry places courts in the awkward position of evaluating the Executive's claims of confidentiality and autonomy, and pushes to the fore difficult questions of separation of powers and checks and balances.

This statement recognizes executive privilege as lurking within Article II of the Constitution. But the bottom line is that the Supreme Court has given itself the right to decide the limits of the President's powers — and of its own powers. Can that be what the Framers of the Constitution intended? See Chapter 12 for more discussion of the judiciary.

Making War versus Declaring War

The Founders clearly intended to split responsibility for national defense between the President and Congress. Article II, Section 1 gives the President total executive power. This broad power links up with Article II, Section 2, which says:

The President shall be Commander in Chief of the Army and Navy of the United States, and of the Militia of the several States, when called into the actual Service of the United States.

The problem is how the two passages relate to Article I, Section 8, which gives Congress the Power

To declare War . . .;

To raise and support Armies, but no Appropriation of Money to that Use shall be for a longer Term than two Years;

To provide and maintain a Navy;

To make Rules for the Government and Regulation of the land and naval Forces;

To provide for calling forth the Militia to execute the Laws of the Union, suppress Insurrections and repel Invasions;

To provide for organizing, arming, and disciplining the Militia, and for governing such Part of them as may be employed in the Service of the United States, reserving to the States respectively, the Appointment of the Officers, and the Authority of training the Militia according to the discipline prescribed by Congress.

REMEMBER

Don't forget, the Founders were well-bred 18th-century gentlemen who would have regarded war between nations as a sort of polite parlor game played by the rules of international diplomacy. So, Step 1 must be a formal declaration of war by Congress. Step 2 is the raising of an army, again by Congress. Step 3 is the calling out of the militia. It's only when you get to Step 4, the actual conduct of the war, that the President becomes involved as Commander in Chief by deciding on strategy and tactics and leading the troops into battle.

The first five full-scale international wars that the United States was involved in were all initiated with a formal declaration of war passed by Congress. These wars are the following:

>> The War of 1812 against Great Britain

>> The Mexican–American War of 1846–1848

>> The Spanish–American War of 1898

>> World War I, in which the United States was involved from 1917 to 1918

>> World War II, which for the United States lasted from 1941 to 1945

Controlling the President through the War Powers Act of 1973

After World War II, the United States became involved in the Korean War in 1950 without any declaration of war. President Harry Truman relied on United Nations resolutions as a justification for U.S. involvement and never sought congressional authorization.

CONTROVERSY

Some members of Congress weren't happy about this bypassing of Congress on the part of the President. The Vietnam War, which lasted from 1964 to 1973, aroused much fiercer resentment in Congress.

So, in 1973 Congress passed the War Powers Act, providing that

> *The constitutional powers of the President as Commander-in-Chief to introduce United States Armed Forces into hostilities, or into situations where imminent involvement in hostilities is clearly indicated by the circumstances, are exercised only pursuant to (1) a declaration of war, (2) specific statutory authorization, or (3) a national emergency created by attack upon the United States, its territories or possessions, or its armed forces.*

If any troops are already engaged, the President must pull them out within 60 days,

> *unless the Congress (1) has declared war or has enacted a specific authorization for such use of United States Armed Forces, (2) has extended by law such sixty-day period, or (3) is physically unable to meet as a result of an armed attack upon the United States.*

The act goes on to say that, "notwithstanding" the 60-day rule,

> *any time that United States Armed Forces are engaged in hostilities outside the territory of the United States without a declaration of war or specific statutory authorization, such forces shall be removed by the President if the Congress so directs by concurrent resolution.*

It's worth noting that President Richard Nixon vetoed this act, but his veto was overridden by a two-thirds majority in both houses of Congress.

Every President since 1973 has declared the War Powers Act unconstitutional — yet they have all been careful to comply with its requirements.

Preventing presidential precedents?

If every President has recognized the War Powers Act in practice while rejecting it as unconstitutional, who has the correct interpretation of the Constitution in this respect, the President or Congress? The answer is that both are partly right.

And, if presidents for the past 45 years have all complied with the act, why do they need to reject its validity? To free themselves from a law that limits presidential power, that's why. If the President admits that the act is constitutional, then all presidential actions complying with it since 1973 automatically become legally binding precedents subordinating the President to Congress.

Congress's case in favor of the constitutionality of the War Powers Act is, as is stated in Section 2(a) of the act itself, that the act fulfills "the intent of the framers of the Constitution of the United States" to "insure that the collective judgment of both the Congress and the President will apply to the introduction of United States Armed Forces into hostilities."

The President's position is exactly the opposite. Here's a statement of the constitutional position as seen from the President's point of view, taken from a 2003 legal brief from the administration of President George W. Bush:

> The Constitution vests the President with full "executive Power," and designates him "Commander in Chief" of the Armed Forces. Together, these provisions are a substantive grant of broad war power that authorizes the President to unilaterally use military force in defense of the United States' national security.

REMEMBER

The main difference between the President's position and that of Congress is that the President interprets his constitutional powers as Commander in Chief broadly, while Congress adopts a narrow interpretation of these powers. The President's role as Commander in Chief must surely mean that the President is in charge of military operations. To that extent the presidential approach is correct. But the power of the Commander in Chief appears from the Constitution to be triggered by a declaration of war, the deployment of troops, and the summoning of the militia (or nowadays, of the National Guard) — all of which are functions entrusted by the Constitution to Congress and not to the President.

Perhaps the most important provision in the War Powers Act is the recognition that insisting on a declaration of war or even congressional authorization is unrealistic and unnecessary in the event of "a national emergency created by attack upon the United States."

Chapter **11**

Giving Everyone a Voice: The House of Representatives and the Senate

The United States may be a democracy, but that doesn't mean that "We the People" get to elect every branch of the government directly. Citizens don't vote for Supreme Court justices, for example, and even the President is elected indirectly through that thing called the *Electoral College* (which I discuss in Chapter 10).

Where your vote has the most direct effect is in the legislative branch of government: the House of Representatives and the Senate. But I'd bet serious money that the vast majority of U.S. citizens can't name both senators currently representing their state plus the House representative elected from their district. Can you?

In this chapter, I explore the responsibilities of both houses of Congress. By the time I'm done, I hope you'll have a better understanding of just how important your vote can be and why, if you couldn't tick off the names of your senators and representative just now, you may want to get to know these folks a little better.

Making the Laws That Govern the Land

Article I, Section 1 of the Constitution states:

> *All legislative Powers herein granted shall be vested in a Congress of the United States, which shall consist of a Senate and House of Representatives.*

In a nutshell, this means that Congress has the power to create all federal laws. It can't do so in a vacuum — the President gets a say as well — but all laws are birthed in the two houses of Congress. Later in the chapter, in the section "Passing Legislation," I explain in detail the steps Congress takes to draft a bill, debate and modify it, and pass it into law.

One function, two houses

TECHNICAL STUFF

The fact that there are two houses of Congress means that it is *bicameral* — a word you probably learned in middle school. The Senate is sometimes referred to as the *upper house* and the House as the *lower house,* but the Constitution doesn't use these designations.

Why a bicameral legislature? George Washington supposedly explained the reasoning like this to Thomas Jefferson, who was pouring his tea into a saucer before drinking it. "Why did you do that?" Washington asked. "To cool it," came the reply. "Exactly so," explained Washington. "We pour the House legislation into the Senatorial saucer to cool it." The implication was that the House tended to be more partisan while the Senate was more of a deliberative body. Washington's observation still holds true today (because there are fewer senators than representatives, because senators serve longer terms than representatives, and because Senate rules are somewhat more relaxed).

REMEMBER

Strictly speaking, the term *congressman* or *congresswoman* should apply to a member of either house, but in practice it's used only for members of the House, who are also referred to as *representatives.* Members of the Senate are referred to only as *senators.* Each house is a bit coy when referring to the other. Each stops short of ignoring the other house altogether but never refers to it by name, calling it instead "the other body."

Keeping the President in the loop

Do the two houses of Congress have the power to pass any laws as long as they both agree? A federal law is known as an *Act of Congress*, and every Act of Congress starts with the formula "Be it enacted by the Senate and House of Representatives of the United States in Congress assembled."

REMEMBER

What about the President? Doesn't he play a role in legislation? Yes, he most certainly does. His approval is needed before a *bill* (a proposed law) can become an Act of Congress. He must respond to a bill within ten days (not counting Sundays) because if he doesn't, the bill becomes law automatically. The President can veto any bill, and Article I, Section 7 states that his veto can be overridden only by a two-thirds majority of both houses. Also, in practice many bills nowadays originate from the White House rather than from the *Capitol* (the building occupied by Congress). So it turns out that Congress does not have *all* legislative power after all.

TECHNICAL STUFF

WHO GETS TO ELECT THE HOUSE?

Since the day the Constitution was enacted, "the People" have had the right to elect the House of Representatives. But which people have that right? The Constitution isn't particularly helpful on that point. All it says is this, in Article I, Section 2:

> *The House of Representatives shall be composed of Members chosen every second Year by the People of the several States, and the Electors in each State shall have the Qualifications requisite for Electors of the most numerous Branch of the State Legislature.*

This seems a surprisingly vague and roundabout provision. But there's a reason for the murkiness. The right to vote in federal elections is based on the right to vote in state elections, and this right is left to the states to decide.

In the early days, voting rights weren't uniform across the country; they varied from state to state. Hence the provision that the right to vote for the House of Representatives would go to everyone entitled to vote for "the most numerous Branch of the State Legislature." (This is the lower house in those states — all except Nebraska — that have a *bicameral* or two-house legislature. In 41 states, the lower house is called the House of Representatives, in 5 states it's called the Assembly, and in 3 it's called the House of Delegates.)

Today, voting rights for the upper house, or state senate, are exactly the same as those for the lower house, but this was not always the case. Originally, voting rights for the lower house were more liberal.

Visiting the People's House

The two houses of Congress are equal under the Constitution, and both are needed for a law to be made, but each house has special features and functions that aren't shared with the other. In this section, I walk you through the particulars of the House of Representatives.

Representing the U.S. population

The people have always directly elected the House of Representatives (unlike the Senate, as I explain later in the chapter). Therefore, it's known as "the people's house." Since 1911 (except for the period from 1959 to 1963), the *House* (as it's commonly referred to) has had 435 voting representatives. The present makeup of the House is

>> 435 representatives from the 50 states

>> Non-voting delegates (one each) from Washington, D.C., and the territories of American Samoa, Guam, and the U.S. Virgin Islands

>> A Resident Commissioner from Puerto Rico

There's roughly one representative for every 710,767 U.S. residents (based on the 2010 census). Keep in mind I'm talking about *population* here, not the number of voters.

REMEMBER

Because representation is based on a state's population, it's possible for a state to gain or lose representatives as its population changes. These gains or losses take place during the *reapportionment* of House seats, which happens every ten years based on the U.S. Census. In 2010, for example, Texas gained four representatives, Florida gained two, and quite a few states either gained or lost one seat.

Although House seats are based on population, each state is entitled to at least one representative, no matter how small it is. Wyoming has way below 710,767 inhabitants but still has one representative in the House.

Respecting the power of the Speaker

The Framers of the Constitution make only one mention of the important office of Speaker of the House: "The House of Representatives shall chuse their Speaker and other Officers." They probably didn't think it was necessary to write a job description because the position was already familiar from colonial times and from the British Constitution, which says that the Speaker presides over debates without being allowed to participate in them.

REDISTRICTING AND GERRYMANDERING

Each of the 435 representatives in the House represents a voting district, referred to by state and number. For example, Nancy Pelosi represents the eighth Congressional District of California, which covers most of San Francisco. As populations shift, congressional voting districts sometimes have to shift as well. Otherwise, a district may be home to too many or too few residents to be represented by a single member of the House.

In 36 states, the state legislature does the redistricting, mostly subject to the governor's approval. Seven states have handed this important power to an independent bipartisan commission, though in 2 of these states, the state legislature has the final say. The remaining 7 states have only one representative each, so the problem doesn't arise.

The term *gerrymander* is the dubious legacy of Elbridge Gerry, who was governor of Massachusetts from 1810–1813 and Vice President from 1813–1814. Gerry proposed a redistricting bill for Massachusetts that blatantly favored his own Democratic-Republican party. One narrow, elongated district so resembled a lizard that it prompted someone to remark, "Salamander?" To which a wag retorted, "No, gerrymander." The name stuck, and Gerry went down to defeat for reelection as state governor.

There has been no shortage of charges of gerrymandering over the years. The object is to maximize the number of seats won by your own party without wasting too many votes. Two techniques of gerrymandering have been identified:

- Where the opposition party has a comfortable majority in a particular district, you add more opposition-dominated counties to it so that the opposition has, if possible, an 80 percent or 90 percent majority in that district. This strategy is called *packing.* The opposition party would carry that district anyway, but now a lot of its votes are wasted because it needs only a simple majority (50+ percent) to win. By packing an opposition-controlled district, you don't waste too many of your own party's votes.

- Next comes *cracking,* which is redistricting so that your party has a comfortable but not overwhelming majority in as many seats as possible. You *crack* a minority of opposition voters into those districts so that those votes are wasted without wasting too many of your own party's.

The Supreme Court has found that the Fourteenth Amendment, which I discuss in Chapter 21, provides some protection against gerrymandering. However, in a 2004 decision, *Vieth v. Jubelirer,* the Supreme Court found that claims related to political (but not racial) gerrymandering can't be resolved by the Court. In 2006, in *League of United Latin American Citizens v. Perry,* the Supreme Court ruled that one particular Texas

(continued)

(continued)

redistricting violated the Voting Rights Act but refused to invalidate the whole Texas redistricting plan because of lack of evidence of "partisan gerrymandering." Two justices, Scalia and Thomas, believed that claims of political gerrymandering aren't justiciable, or, in other words, aren't the business of the courts. And Chief Justice Roberts and Justice Alito noted that they were "taking no position" on whether claims of political gerrymandering were justiciable.

At the time of this writing, gerrymandering has once more reared its head in the case of *Gill v. Whitford,* an appeal by the State of Wisconsin against a federal district court ruling that the state's 2011 redistricting plan was unconstitutional. The objection to Wisconsin's redistricting was that, although the Republicans received only 49 percent of the statewide vote in 2012, they won 60 percent of the seats in the State Assembly. A ruling by the U.S. Supreme Court is pending, with 12 other states joining Wisconsin in its appeal. This reflects the importance of the question of redistricting and gerrymandering. Democrats object that in many states, Republicans are overrepresented in the House of Representatives by comparison with their proportion of the popular vote. The Republican response to this is that this is not the product of any deliberate bias but simply the result of the fact that Democratic voters tend to be concentrated in inner cities while Republican voters are more likely to be spread across the countryside.

The Speaker of the British House of Commons remains studiously neutral and has practically no political power. By contrast, the Speaker of the House of Representatives has an armory of powers, just about the least of them being the right to participate in debate and to vote — which is rarely exercised, except on constitutional amendments or other really important issues.

REMEMBER

The Speaker comes immediately after the Vice President in the line of succession to the presidency. This chain of succession isn't in the Constitution itself but in the Presidential Succession Act of 1947. Some people have questioned the constitutionality of this provision, but it has never been tested because no Speaker has ever succeeded to the presidency.

Presiding over debates, or not

The role of Speaker of the House has developed into one of the most powerful in the U.S. system of government. As is so often the case, the Speaker's true position is attributable more to party politics than to constitutional law. The Speaker is the presiding officer of the House, but that's just the start.

The function of actually presiding over debates is usually delegated to a representative of the Speaker's choosing. During debates, whoever is presiding is addressed as "Mr. Speaker" or "Madam Speaker," except when the House resolves itself into a *Committee of the Whole* — which is a fancy way of saying that the House considers itself to be a committee for the purpose of making changes (*amendments*) to bills. When that happens, the Speaker passes the gavel to another presiding officer, who is addressed as "Mr. Chairman" or "Madam Chairman." For important debates, the presiding officer will be a senior member of the majority party, but for routine debates it could be quite a junior representative.

The presiding officer decides whom to *recognize,* meaning whom to allow to speak in debates. He or she also rules on points of order, though such rulings can be appealed to the whole House. (Joseph Gurney Cannon, who served as Speaker from 1903 to 1911, ruled the House with an iron fist and supposedly recognized only the representatives he liked.)

Leading the House's majority party

The Speaker's most important role is as leader of the majority party in the House. (The House Majority Leader, who is subordinate to the Speaker, assists the Speaker in persuading the representatives of the majority party to support the party's legislative program.) Because the Constitution doesn't recognize the existence of political parties (see Chapter 10), it's not surprising that the Speaker's true role isn't even mentioned. But from this strong partisan base, the Speaker's power and influence flow.

The Speaker's chief concern is to make sure that the majority party's program is passed into law. The Speaker's influence extends to deciding which bill is considered when. Subject to the approval of the majority party's *conference* or *caucus* (a body made up of all representatives belonging to that party), the Speaker chooses 9 of the 13 members of the powerful Rules Committee (the other 4 coming from the minority party). The Rules Committee controls amendments, debate, and timetabling. Here's what I mean:

» **Amendments** are changes to a bill on its way to becoming an Act of Congress, or a law. These changes can be very important, and no bill goes through unchanged. Representatives propose amendments to bills. The Rules Committee sifts through these proposals and decides which amendments should be allowed to be considered by the whole House.

» **Debate,** or discussion, on a bill happens before the House votes on it. Representatives try to persuade their fellow members to vote either in favor of a bill or against it. Debate in the House isn't unlimited (in contrast with the Senate, which I discuss later in this chapter). The Rules Committee decides on the limits in the scope and time available for debate on any particular bill.

>> **Timetabling** is important because the fate of a bill may depend on the amount of time allowed for its debate. If the majority party leadership wants a bill passed quickly and without much publicity, the Rules Committee may allocate little or no debate time to it. But if the majority party leadership wants to create a big publicity campaign in favor of a bill, they're more likely to arrange a liberal debate schedule for it.

So by controlling the Rules Committee, the majority party and the Speaker have a stranglehold over the House.

Dancing with the President

When the White House is occupied by a President of the same party as the Speaker, the Speaker tends to defer to the President. But when the Speaker and President are from opposite parties, the Speaker can become essentially the leader of the opposition. For example, Speaker Tip O'Neill (see Figure 11-1) openly opposed President Ronald Reagan's domestic and defense policies; President Bill Clinton came up against a formidable foe in Speaker Newt Gingrich; and Speaker Nancy Pelosi took a strong line against President George W. Bush.

FIGURE 11-1:
Speaker "Tip" O'Neill had the longest uninterrupted tenure as Speaker, from 1977-1987. Most of this time was during the presidency of Ronald Reagan, with whom Tip had an ambivalent relationship. He described Reagan as "the most ignorant man who had ever occupied the White House." But, in private, the two men were on cordial terms, "friends after 6 pm," as Reagan put it.

Source: U.S. National Archives and Records Administration

But being members of the same party doesn't guarantee harmony either. At the start of the 20th century, Speaker Joseph ("Uncle Joe") Gurney Cannon didn't get on well with fellow Republican President Teddy Roosevelt, who was described by the Speaker as having "no more use for the Constitution than a tomcat has for a marriage license."

Controlling the nation's purse strings

REMEMBER

The House is in charge of the nation's finances — an enormous responsibility in a nation whose budget is in the trillions, and reason enough for you to get familiar with the person representing your home district. You wouldn't just hand your wallet over to a stranger in the grocery store and say, "I need some food. Can you buy it for me?" The U.S. government buys lots of things on your behalf — infrastructure, public education, the military — so it makes sense to know who's collecting your money to make those purchases.

Here's what Article I, Section 7 of the Constitution says about this responsibility:

> *All Bills for raising Revenue shall originate in the House of Representatives; but the Senate may propose or concur with Amendments as on other Bills.*

The first half of this provision means that the House alone can originate tax legislation, but the second half ensures that the Senate has influence as well.

REMEMBER

Why does the House get first dibs at crafting tax-related legislation? The Framers of the Constitution didn't forget the slogan that led to U.S. independence in the first place: "No taxation without representation." For the Senate to initiate tax bills would be unfair because in the Senate, small states are overrepresented in terms of their population and big states are underrepresented. The Framers knew that "the people's house" should have the principal voice in deciding how much of the people's money the government can claim.

But just because the House gets its paws on revenue legislation first doesn't mean the Senate is in a weak position. The power to add amendments to legislation is crucial. The reality is that when the Senate receives revenue legislation, it can add new provisions, change tax rates — alter it as much as its members (at least a majority of them) deem appropriate.

The flip side of raising money is spending it, which occurs thanks to *appropriation* bills: bills authorizing the spending of federal funds. The Constitution doesn't specify that the House is solely responsible for originating those bills, so in theory, they could originate in the Senate as well. And sometimes they do. However, the House wants to keep the upper hand in all financial legislation, so when the Senate does send it an appropriations bill, that bill usually gets ignored.

Deciding disputed presidential elections

The House also has another special power that the Senate doesn't have: the right to decide disputed presidential elections. The Twelfth Amendment, ratified in 1804, states that if no candidate has a majority of electoral votes, the election is taken to the House of Representatives. As I explain in Chapter 10, it's not enough for a winning candidate to have a plurality of electoral votes; that person must receive an absolute majority of more than 50 percent.

The House has exercised this power on two occasions: in 1800 (to elect Thomas Jefferson) and in 1824 (to elect John Quincy Adams). In 1876, in the midst of highly disputed election results, it delegated its power to an Electoral Commission, which ushered Rutherford B. Hayes into power.

Some people think the House should have been asked to decide the election of 2000, which instead was decided by the U.S. Supreme Court. The House gets involved in deciding a presidential election only after all the states have certified their election results. But in 2000, the presidential candidates rushed to court over the Florida election result before it was certified. So the House never got a look-in.

A couple of flaws exist with the House's power to decide a disputed election:

>> Each House member gets one vote. That may seem fair because the number of representatives in a state is determined by the state's population. The problem is that this system differs from the Electoral College system, which lets each state have as many votes as it has senators and representatives. In other words, a state with a small population (and only one representative in the House), like Alaska or Vermont, gets three votes in the Electoral College. But that same state gets only a single vote if the disputed election goes to the House.

>> The House has the power to choose the President, but the Senate has the power to choose the Vice President. If different parties control the two houses, this could result in having a Republican President and a Democratic Vice President, or vice versa.

IN MY OPINION

Why does this flaw exist? The Framers of the Constitution failed to appreciate the importance of political parties. As a result, Thomas Jefferson served as Vice President under John Adams, who belonged to a different party. Difficult as that situation was 200 years ago, it would be a serious problem in today's extremely partisan political environment. In my opinion, a better solution would be to throw disputed elections to both houses of Congress together, which would choose both the President and the Vice President.

Impeaching the President and other civil officers

The Constitution gives the House of Representatives "the sole Power of Impeachment." It then gives the Senate "the sole Power to try all Impeachments." This language means that in impeachment cases, the House of Representatives acts as the prosecutor and is empowered to bring the charges, and the Senate acts as the jury and decides the outcome or verdict. This is such an important function of the two houses of Congress that I devote an entire chapter to it: Chapter 13.

Declaring war

The Constitution splits war powers between the President and Congress. The President is Commander in Chief, but in Article I, Section 8, Congress is given the power to "declare War" and to "raise and support Armies."

Congress has exercised its power to declare war only five times during the whole history of the United States. The last time Congress declared war was in World War II. Congress didn't declare war in any of these major conflicts:

>> The Korean War

>> The Vietnam War

>> The Persian Gulf War

>> The war in Afghanistan

>> The Iraq War

CONTROVERSY

Congress did "authorize" all these military engagements, but that isn't the same thing as a declaration of war. Critics of presidential power say that all these wars were illegal because a legal war requires a congressional declaration of war. Those who defend the President's war powers say that Congress's constitutional power to "declare War" isn't the same as a power to commence or initiate war. The people who take this line of argument believe that the President as Commander in Chief can initiate a legal war without the need for a congressional declaration of war.

The War Powers Resolution (or Act) of 1973 says that, "in the absence of a declaration of war," the President has to submit a written report to Congress within 48 hours of sending U.S. troops into action in any foreign country. The act goes on to say that the President must withdraw these troops from the foreign country concerned within 60 days unless Congress has in the meantime either declared war or specifically authorized the President's decision to send the troops into the foreign country.

CAN YOU RUN FOR THE HOUSE OR SENATE?

If you plan to run for a seat in the House of Representatives, keep these requirements in mind:

- You have to be at least 25 years old.
- You have to have been a citizen of the United States for at least seven years.
- When elected you must be living in the state where the voting district that you represent is situated.

The Senate gets its name from a similar body in the Roman Republic. The name comes from the Latin word *senex,* which means "old man." So it's not surprising that senators have to be a little older than representatives. Here's the scoop on becoming a senator:

- You have to be at least 30 years old.
- You have to have been a citizen of the United States for at least nine years.
- When elected you must be living in the state that you represent.

TECHNICAL STUFF

Is the War Powers Act constitutional? Presidents have generally taken the view that the 1973 law is unconstitutional. So, every time a President has drafted a report required by that act, he has said that his report was "consistent with" the War Powers Act — not that it was "pursuant to" the act. Writing a report "pursuant to" a particular law means that the writer is acting in obedience to that law. But writing a report that is "consistent with" a particular law doesn't entail recognition of the validity or constitutionality of that law. The question of the constitutionality of the War Powers Act has not yet been tested in court. I tackle the serious and topical question of the President's war powers in Chapter 10.

Getting to Know the Senate

The Senate is an august body made up of just 100 members (2 from each state) who serve six-year terms — longer than those of any other elected officeholders in the federal government. The Senate has two ancestors:

>> The Senate of ancient Rome

>> The British upper house, the House of Lords

The Senate is the embodiment of *federalism*: a political system in which national and state governments share power. Hence the words emblazoned above the Dirksen Senate Office Building: "The Senate is the Living Symbol of Our Union of States."

REMEMBER

If the House of Representatives is "the people's house," the Senate is the states' house. James Madison wrote that "the government ought to be founded on a mixture of the principles of proportional and equal representation." The House of Representatives provides proportional representation: States are represented according to the size of their populations. The Senate provides equal representation for each state.

For example, California has 53 representatives for its 39 million inhabitants, and Wyoming has just 1 representative for its population of 580,000. But in the Senate, Wyoming and California get 2 members each. So in the House, the biggest states are dominant, but in the Senate, the smallest states have equal influence.

So important is this principle that Article V of the Constitution protects it in a way that no other provision is protected: "No State, without its Consent, shall be deprived of its equal Suffrage [right to vote] in the Senate." For example, say a constitutional amendment was proposed that said Alaska was henceforth to have only one seat in the Senate. Even if this amendment was ratified by the requisite three-fourths of all state legislatures, it would not take effect unless Alaska (through its elected officials) gave its consent.

Electing a senator

Originally, the Constitution called for senators to be chosen by each state's legislature rather than by popular vote. This arrangement worked okay at first, but it broke down under bitter party rivalries in the 19th century, which sometimes left senate seats vacant for years at a time.

In the late 19th century, some states started using a type of referendum that effectively allowed the direct election of senators. Popular pressure built up in favor of a constitutional amendment for the direct election of senators nationwide. About two-thirds of the states had already introduced direct election to the U.S. Senate by the time this reform became part of the Constitution through the ratification of the Seventeenth Amendment in 1913 (see Chapter 22). Unlike members of the House of Representatives, who are elected by their individual voting districts, each senator is elected by the state as a whole.

Direct popular election gave the Senate democratic credibility that it had lacked before, and with it came enhanced prestige. Senators now tend to refer to themselves not by their official designation as "senator *from* New Mexico" but rather as "senator *for* New Mexico," which sounds more democratic.

Of the two senators from a particular state, the one with the longer unbroken tenure is known as the *senior senator* from that state, and the other is known as the *junior senator.* But these titles don't reflect any difference in status. The official title of a senator takes this form: "The Honorable John Doe, the junior senator from Wyoming." But nowadays, we generally just write "Senator John Doe."

REMEMBER

Elections to the Senate are staggered. A *class,* made up of roughly one-third of the Senate, is up for election every two years. Senators' terms of office are arranged so that both seats from a particular state are never contested at the same time. And while senators enjoy longer terms than any other elected federal officials (six years), they can also run for reelection as many times as they like.

Presiding over the Senate

The Constitution gives the Vice President the job of presiding over the Senate. Here's what Article I, Section 3 of the Constitution says:

> *The Vice President of the United States shall be President of the Senate, but shall have no Vote, unless they be equally divided.*

In practice, the Veep doesn't often preside over the Senate. He's likely to have more important things to do, and in any case, he doesn't have an active role to play in the Senate. He can't participate in debate and can cast a vote only to break a tie. For this reason, the Constitution provides for the election of "a President pro tempore, in the Absence of the Vice President."

The position of *president pro tempore* ("president for the time being") usually goes to the most senior senator of the majority party. Election to this position is a great honor, and the president pro tempore ranks immediately after the Speaker of the House of Representatives in the line of succession to the presidency. But the president pro tempore of the Senate wields a lot less power than the Speaker of the House.

The functions of the office of president pro tempore aren't fixed. Each holder of the office molds it in his own image. When he chairs the Senate, the president pro tempore has full authority to administer oaths and to sign legislation on behalf of the Senate. In the absence of the Vice President, the president pro tempore presides together with the Speaker of the House when both houses of Congress sit together in joint sessions. The president pro tempore presides over the Senate as frequently or infrequently as he likes and quite often names other senators, sometimes even freshmen senators, to chair meetings of the Senate in his absence.

The president pro tempore forms part of the leadership of his party in the Senate, but his role in the party is subordinate to that of the majority leader. (In the House, by contrast, the Speaker is the leader of the majority party, as I explain earlier in this chapter.)

Advising and consenting

The Senate has some important powers not shared by the House of Representatives, most notably the power of "Advice and Consent." Here's what Article II, Section 2, Clause 2 says about this power:

> [The President] shall have Power, by and with the Advice and Consent of the Senate, to make Treaties . . .; and he shall nominate, and by and with the Advice and Consent of the Senate, shall appoint Ambassadors, other public Ministers and Consuls, judges of the supreme Court, and all other Officers of the United States, whose Appointments are not herein otherwise provided for . . .

CONTROVERSY

There has been some disagreement about what this provision means in practice. The text indicates that the President is meant to have both the power to nominate and the power to appoint. Some people argue that the Senate was intended to question or prevent those nominations and appointments only in cases of favoritism, incompetence, or fraud. But from the beginning, partisan politics influenced the Senate's power to advise and consent.

For example, George Washington's 1796 nomination of John Rutledge as the second Chief Justice was blocked by the Senate at least partly for political reasons (though Rutledge also had some mental problems). Since then, the Senate has blocked a lot of presidential nominations on a party political basis, including Judge Robert Bork's nomination to the U.S. Supreme Court by President Ronald Reagan.

Judges up for confirmation are now routinely asked questions about their views on privacy and abortion, which are just as much political as legal questions. Another technique favored by both parties in recent years is simply to delay the holding of hearings, which has left a good number of vacancies among federal circuit and district court judges, who form the backbone of the federal judiciary.

The views of the senators from a nominee's home state are often weighted in the Senate. The term *blue slip process* refers to this situation. The blue slip system has lately been expanded, giving a senator virtual veto power over appointments of judges not only from her home state but also from any other state in the circuit to which her home state belongs. (The states are grouped into 11 circuits for the federal court system.)

Passing Legislation

The main function of Congress is to make laws, and Congress is the federal lawmaking body in the United States. A law passed by Congress is known as an *Act of Congress*, which starts life as a bill. No fewer than 9,665 bills were introduced during the 114th Congress of January 2015–January 2017, but only 329 of these actually became law (and of those, 79 just renamed federal buildings). But where do all these bills come from? There are several possible sources:

>> **Lobbyists.** In 2016, there were 9,726 federally registered lobbyists. Lobbyists may even prepare the text of a bill for a sympathetic member to introduce.

>> **Election campaign promises or party platforms.**

>> **Petitions from citizen groups.**

>> **State legislatures.** They may pass *memorials* asking Congress to pass certain laws.

>> **Executive communications.** These may come from the President, a Cabinet member, or an independent agency.

TECHNICAL STUFF

An alternative way of proposing legislation is by *joint resolution,* which is practically indistinguishable from a bill except that it normally begins with a preamble explaining the need for the legislation. Like a bill, both houses of Congress must pass a joint resolution, and the President must accept or veto it. And like a bill, it becomes a law. Joint resolutions are used to authorize minor government expenditures, to create commissions and other bodies, and for other fairly technical legislation. But they can also be used for some pretty important stuff, like admitting new states into the Union (a power specifically reserved to Congress by Article IV, Section 3 of the Constitution) and proposing an amendment to the Constitution.

Tracking a bill's progress

A bill may start its life in either the House or the Senate. (As I explain earlier in the chapter, if the bill raises taxes, it must originate in the House, which has power over revenue.) The way in which bills are proposed differs between the two bodies:

>> In the House, a member wishing to introduce a bill places it in the *hopper,* a wooden box next to the rostrum. The bill, or at least its title, used to be read out before the whole House, but this practice is no longer followed.

>> In the Senate, the procedure may be more formal, with the sponsor introducing his bill from the floor. But the bill can also simply be left with the clerk without any comment.

The bill is referred to the appropriate standing committee, of which the House has 20 and the Senate 16. Each committee is led by a chairperson belonging to the majority party and a "ranking member" of the minority party. The committee may hold hearings and collect relevant evidence. I explain the committee process in detail in the next section.

If the committee is in favor of the bill, it is reported out of the committee and reaches the floor of the chamber concerned. (If the committee doesn't favor the bill, it can be killed without ever reaching the floor.) The House or Senate may then debate the bill and amend it. The debate process differs between the two houses.

Debating in the Senate

In the Senate, the presiding officer must recognize the first senator who rises to speak about a bill, but the majority and minority leaders are generally given first dibs. Senate speeches aren't required to be relevant to the bill being debated, and senators may usually speak for as long as they like.

REMEMBER

To delay or block a vote on a bill, senators can use a special tactic not available in the House: the *filibuster*. Essentially, to filibuster means to talk so long that the Senate can't actually vote on a bill or some other measure. The record is held by Senator Strom Thurmond, who filibustered the Civil Rights Act of 1957 by talking continuously for more than 24 hours.

Since 1917, it has been possible to end a filibuster by passing a *cloture* (French for "closure") motion. Originally, a two-thirds majority of senators actually present and voting was required for cloture. But in 1975 the rule was changed so that a fixed number of 60 senators was needed for cloture in most circumstances. This applied not only to votes on legislation but also to the confirmation of presidential nominees. In 2013 the Senate agreed to eliminate the use of the filibuster on all presidential nominees to the executive branch and all judicial nominees — except to the Supreme Court. In 2017 the Senate eliminated this one exception, so that Neil Gorsuch could be confirmed to the Supreme Court by a simple majority. In the event, Gorsuch was confirmed by a 54-45 vote.

Debating in the House

In the House, debate is much more tightly controlled. The presiding officer has a good deal of freedom to decide whom to recognize. The Rules Committee determines whether amendments to a particular bill are going to be allowed or not. Debate is normally limited to one hour: a half hour for each party. Each party appoints a *floor manager*, who allocates time to members who wish to participate in the debate. If a lot of members want to have their say, a member may be allocated 2 minutes or even just 30 seconds.

Voting

After the debate, the bill is put to a vote. The House uses several different forms of voting but nowadays generally uses an electronic vote. The Senate shuns such modern gadgetry. In that body, the typical manner of voting is by *roll call*: The clerk calls out the name of each senator in alphabetical order, the member votes "Aye" or "No," and the clerk repeats the member's vote. It's a time-consuming process. (Thank heavens there are only 100 senators.)

Moving to the other body

After a bill is passed by one house of Congress, it is sent to the other chamber, which may pass, reject, or amend it. If the second house amends the bill, a conference committee made up of members of both houses meets to reconcile the differences. Conference committees have, on occasion, departed from both versions in producing a composite bill. President Ronald Reagan once remarked, "If an apple and an orange went into conference consultations, it might come out a pear." For the bill to pass, both houses have to agree to the conference committee's version.

Landing on the President's desk

The bill is then ready to be presented to the President. The President may either sign it into law or veto it, and he offers a message giving the reasons for either action. A presidential veto can be overridden only by a two-thirds majority of both houses.

If the President does nothing, the bill automatically becomes law after ten days (excluding Sundays). However, if Congress adjourns during that ten-day period, the bill fails. This situation is known as a *pocket veto* because it's as if the President just puts the bill in his pocket and forgets about it. Unlike a regular veto, a pocket veto can't be overridden by Congress because the bill is not returned to Congress.

The pocket veto has recently attracted some controversy. If a President tries unsuccessfully to exercise a pocket veto on a bill, then the President's non-response allows that bill to become law automatically. To avoid this outcome, recent presidents have started using a so-called *protective return veto*. The President exercises a pocket veto but then returns the vetoed bill to Congress. President George H. W. Bush and President Bill Clinton both used this tactic. If it's successful, this type of veto kills the bill in question without any chance of a congressional comeback. But, just in case this tactic doesn't work, the President can at least be sure that he has vetoed the bill in the ordinary way and that it won't automatically become law.

Examining congressional committees

In his 1885 book on *Congressional Government*, future President Woodrow Wilson wrote, "It is not far from the truth to say that Congress in session is Congress on public exhibition, whilst Congress in its committee rooms is Congress at work."

There are no fewer than 200 congressional committees and subcommittees. Although the first committees were established in 1789, the present committee system dates from 1946.

Types of committees

There are three main types of congressional committees:

REMEMBER

>> **Standing:** Permanent committees within the House and the Senate.

>> **Select, or special:** Committees created by the House or Senate to do work not covered by existing standing committees.

>> **Joint:** Committees with members from the House and the Senate that tackle issues relevant to both. Most of these are standing committees, but a select committee can also be a joint committee.

There's a standing committee for most every branch of government, including Armed Services, Budget, Foreign Affairs (which in the Senate is called the *Foreign Relations Committee*), Judiciary, and Homeland Security. As I note earlier in the chapter, a powerful standing committee in the House is the Rules Committee. (Its counterpart in the Senate, known as the *Committee on Rules and Administration*, is much less powerful.)

At present there are only two select committees in the House:

>> The Select Committee on Energy Independence and Global Warming

>> The Permanent Select Committee on Intelligence

In the Senate, there are three select committees:

>> Ethics

>> Intelligence

>> A Special Committee on Aging

Committee powers

REMEMBER

Congressional committees have very wide powers, including the power to investigate and keep a check on the President, his Cabinet, and other executive branch officials. Committees may look into the effectiveness of laws that have been passed, the need for new legislation, and the performance of the executive (and to some extent of the judiciary).

Committees may hold hearings and can compel a witness to testify or to produce certain documents by issuing a subpoena. Witnesses who ignore a subpoena can be cited for contempt of Congress, which is similar to contempt of court. The penalty for this offense is a maximum of 12 months in jail.

CONTROVERSY

A debate has long raged about whether Congress can subpoena executive officials and compel their testimony. People who take this line are likely to reject executive privilege while upholding congressional privilege. For more on this topic, see Chapter 8 on the separation of powers.

Chapter **12**

"Saying What the Law Is": The Judicial System

The legislature, the executive, and the judiciary are the three branches of government. The legislature, or Congress, passes laws. The executive, or the President, must "take Care that the Laws be faithfully executed." But what is the function of the judiciary? It's more complex than you may imagine, and I start this chapter with a brief discussion of that function.

With the function of the judiciary defined, I then delve into discussions of how someone becomes a judge, why judges aren't subject to the same types of term limits as presidents and members of Congress, and how the courts have assumed greater powers than the Founding Fathers ever imagined.

Examining the Courts' Function

Section 1 of Article III of the Constitution says:

> *The judicial Power of the United States shall be vested in one supreme Court, and in such inferior Courts as the Congress may from time to time ordain and establish.*

But what exactly does this judicial power consist of? Section 2 of Article III was drafted to answer this question, and it's a mouthful. I'll let you turn to the Appendix if you're brave enough to read it, but here are the key points:

>> The U.S. Supreme Court has *original jurisdiction* over cases involving ambassadors and other diplomats, and cases in which a state is a party. This means that in these two types of cases alone, the Supreme Court can hear the case from the beginning, as a court of first instance.

>> In all other cases, the Supreme Court has only *appellate jurisdiction* — the power to act as an appeal court from lower federal courts or, in regard to certain matters, from state courts.

Defining jurisdiction

The appellate jurisdiction of the Supreme Court (and all other federal courts) is made up of two main categories: *federal question jurisdiction* and *diversity jurisdiction*. These terms don't actually appear in the text of the Constitution; they are a form of modern shorthand for what Article III, Section 2 says. Both of these categories are pretty technical, but here are the basic concepts involved:

>> *Jurisdiction* refers to the power of a court to hear a particular case or type of case. For example, if a citizen of Florida sues a citizen of Ohio in a dispute over real estate situated in Texas, the state courts of Florida, Ohio, and Texas all have jurisdiction to hear the case, but the courts of New Jersey would have no jurisdiction to hear it.

>> *Federal question jurisdiction* and *diversity jurisdiction* are the two main types of jurisdiction possessed by the federal courts:

 • *Federal question jurisdiction* essentially covers cases involving federal law.

 • *Diversity jurisdiction* covers cases where the plaintiff and the defendant are from different states, provided the amount of money in controversy is above a certain threshold, which is now set at $75,000 and is periodically adjusted to keep up with the times. The question here is what law is applicable. Should it be the law of the plaintiff's state, the law of the defendant's state, or federal law? Under the so-called *Erie Doctrine,* adopted by the high court in 1938, the Supreme Court (and other federal courts) must apply the substantive law of the state where the cause of action arose.

Applying the law

How do Supreme Court justices and other federal judges decide cases in practice? To put it at its simplest, they apply the law to the facts of the case. Trial courts spend a lot of time sorting out the facts, but the Supreme Court doesn't hear any live evidence, so it concentrates on the law.

Here are some of the important questions that the Supreme Court has to ask about the law:

>> What is the relevant law that is being challenged?

>> How should it be interpreted?

>> What are the relevant constitutional provisions?

>> How should they be interpreted?

>> Is the challenged law in keeping with the Constitution, or is it unconstitutional?

>> What previous relevant cases are there?

>> Should these cases be followed, distinguished, or overruled?

Appointments and Elections: Becoming a Judge

The President appoints federal judges, subject to confirmation by the Senate. Supreme Court justices, District Court judges, and judges of the federal Courts of Appeals are appointed "during good Behaviour" — meaning, for life. Other federal judges are appointed for long terms — for example, 15 years in the case of bankruptcy judges. Check out Figure 12-1 for a look at current members of the Supreme Court.

FIGURE 12-1:
The members of the U.S. Supreme Court as of June 2017. Neil Gorsuch, who replaced Antonin Scalia (died in office, February 2016), is in the back, right.

Source: Photograph by Franz Jantzen, Collection of the Supreme Court of the U.S.

State court judges, by contrast, are mostly chosen by popular election. No fewer than 39 states elect at least some of their judges, and 87 percent of all state judges in the nation are elected. In some states, judges are initially appointed by elected officials but can then be reappointed by means of retention elections. These elections may take the form of a "Yes" or "No" vote, where the judge in question is not running against anybody else. Yet, even in such cases, unpopular judges have been voted out. Chief Justice Rose Bird of California is an example. She was removed from office in 1986 on the basis of a sweeping vote against her.

Judging the election process

Here are some of questions to consider about popularly elected judges:

>> **Can anybody run for election as a judge?** No. In most states with elected judges, you have to be a member of the state bar to qualify.

>> **How does a lawyer become a judge?** Whenever a vacancy occurs between elections, the state governor appoints someone to fill the office temporarily. At election time, these appointees run as incumbents (and usually get elected).

>> **For how long do elected judges serve?** Terms vary from state to state, but a six-year term is common for the lower courts. Judges can run for reelection as many times as they want.

>> **How do voters pick a judge?** Here's how elections usually work:

- State bar associations sometimes rate the candidates. This may be helpful to voters, but it may also favor the more establishment-minded candidates or those who have been members of the local bar association for a long time.

- The candidates usually finance their campaigns using their own funds or by soliciting contributions, and they put out their own campaign literature.

- In most states, candidates for judgeships must run as individuals without party labels, but they often hint at their party affiliation.

- Candidates are not normally allowed to make specific campaign promises, but some give an indication that they are going to be tough on crime.

>> **Can candidates for judicial election announce their views on disputed political and legal issues?** Yes. That was the answer that the U.S. Supreme Court gave in the 2002 case known as *Republican Party of Minnesota v. White*. The Minnesota Supreme Court prohibited judicial candidates from revealing their views on most issues. By 5 votes to 4, the high court ruled that the Minnesota prohibition violated the First Amendment guarantee of freedom of speech. Justice Ruth Bader Ginsburg, writing for the minority, opined, "Judges are not politicians, and the First Amendment does not require that they be treated as politicians simply because they are chosen by popular vote."

Considering whether elections taint the judiciary

IN MY OPINION

Justice Ginsburg's remark goes to the heart of the matter. She seems to have assumed that judges are above politics and that they decide cases purely on the basis of law. In fact, judges have political views just like anybody else — and their political views can't help but color their legal decisions. Most judges are not too difficult to pigeonhole in terms of their political preferences — on the basis of which it's usually quite easy to predict how they are likely to rule.

This fact applies just as much to unelected U.S. Supreme Court justices as to elected state court judges. Justice Ginsburg is herself a prime example of a judge whose views on any given case can usually be predicted. She is one of the most politically liberal members of the Court, and her voting record on the Court matches her political outlook.

Justice Sandra Day O'Connor formed part of the majority in the *White* case, but she later said that she regretted her vote. O'Connor had herself started out as an elected judge in Arizona but favored the switch from elected to appointed judges that took place there in the 1970s. She said, "I watched the improvement of the judiciary in that state." Her preference? "If I could wave a magic wand . . . I would wave it to secure some kind of merit selection of judges across the country."

Even in her concurring opinion in *White*, Justice O'Connor took some sideswipes at elected judges. As she put it, "I am concerned that, even aside from what judicial candidates may say while campaigning, the very practice of electing judges undermines" the state interest in having an impartial judiciary.

O'Connor made the following attacks on elected judges (and my responses are in italic):

>> Elected judges are less likely to be impartial because they "cannot help being aware that if the public is not satisfied with the outcome of a particular case, it could hurt their reelection prospects." *Maybe. But is this necessarily a bad thing? It means that elected judges' rulings are more likely to be in tune with public opinion — in contrast with the decisions of U.S. Supreme Court justices, who do not answer to the people and can remain in office until they drop dead.*

>> "Contested elections generally entail campaigning. And campaigning for a judicial post today can require substantial funds . . . Even if judges were able to refrain from favoring donors, the mere possibility that judges' decisions may be motivated by the desire to repay campaign contributors is likely to undermine the public's confidence in the judiciary." *This sure looks bad. But should the whole system of elected judges be thrown out because of it? That would be throwing the baby out with the bathwater. Instead, why not introduce some campaign finance reform? North Carolina has already done that with the Judicial Campaign Reform Act, which mandates using public money to pay for judicial election campaigns.*

Understanding Judicial Independence without Accountability

The independence of the federal judiciary is enshrined in the Constitution. It's easy to miss because the relevant section doesn't actually include the word *independence* at all. Instead, the relevant provision is buried in this throwaway clause in Article III, Section 1:

> *The Judges, both of the supreme and inferior Courts, shall hold their Offices during good Behaviour, and shall, at stated Times, receive for their Services a Compensation, which shall not be diminished during their Continuance in Office.*

Bypassing term limits and salary concerns

What exactly is meant by "during good Behaviour"? Convicted criminals in jail are usually allowed time off for good behavior. Does that phrase have the same meaning as it does here? No.

"During good Behaviour" is the guarantee of judicial independence. It means that Supreme Court justices, federal district judges, and appeals court judges can't be fired by the President or anybody else for any reason — unless they are impeached and found guilty of "Treason, Bribery, or other high Crimes and Misdemeanors." I discuss impeachment in Chapter 13.

So, unless removed from office after impeachment, these top judges are appointed for life. Many of them resign of their own accord when they feel no longer able to cope with the demands of the job. But some have stayed in office until they dropped dead, like Chief Justice William Rehnquist, following the example of his idol, John Marshall, who died in office after serving as Chief Justice for 34 years.

The "during good Behaviour" provision is linked with a prohibition on reducing a judge's salary after his or her appointment. Justices and judges protected by these two provisions can certainly afford to be independent. No matter what views on law and politics they may espouse at the time of their appointments, they can change their minds as much as they like afterward.

Is that a bad thing? Not necessarily, but it means they can decide cases entirely according to their personal predilections — or "the whim of the gavel." This situation is particularly dangerous in the U.S. Supreme Court, which decides many highly sensitive political issues. The independence of the Supreme Court justices is independence without accountability. Nine unelected and unaccountable people can decide the fate not only of individuals but also of the nation as a whole. And all too often the decision is in the hands not of nine but of one — the swing vote. (I discuss the swing vote in detail later in this chapter.)

Chief Justice William Rehnquist termed judicial independence "one of the crown jewels of our system of government." Supreme Court justices owe their appointments to the President, but once in office they can take whatever line they like.

Consider some examples:

» In 1953 President Dwight Eisenhower picked Chief Justice Earl Warren for the top spot on the assumption that he was a conservative. When Warren turned out to be one of the most liberal justices of all time, Eisenhower reputedly remarked that Warren's appointment was "the biggest damned-fool mistake I ever made." But there was nothing Eisenhower or any other President could do about that.

>> More recently, Justices Harry Blackmun, John Paul Stevens, and David Souter also turned out to be much more liberal on the bench than was anticipated. Souter, appointed in 1990, was widely expected to adopt extremely conservative positions. The National Organization for Women held a rally to oppose his confirmation, and the then-president of that organization actually testified at Souter's confirmation hearing that his appointment would "end . . . freedom for women in this country." The NAACP also opposed Souter's confirmation, asking its members to write their senators to block his appointment to the Court. Yet Justice Souter emerged as one of the most liberal justices on the Court.

Grappling with issues the Constitution doesn't address

Such examples are what judicial independence is all about — or is it? Independence from direct political pressure is one thing. But what about independence from *indirect* political, social, and intellectual currents?

Some of the most contentious recent constitutional battles concern affirmative action, abortion, gay rights, and same-sex marriage. What did Benjamin Franklin, Alexander Hamilton, or James Madison think about these issues? The answer is nothing. None of these issues were in the air when the Constitution was being drafted, or for a very long time afterward.

REMEMBER

So, what does the Constitution have to say on these issues? The Constitution doesn't address any of them, precisely because the Framers weren't aware of them. Justices who adhere to the *living Constitution* school of thought read into the Constitution the broad doctrines that they claim to have found there by way of extrapolating from the words that actually figure in the text. On the other hand, *textualists, originalists,* and other justices loosely described as *strict constructionists* generally refuse to speculate on how the Framers would have reacted to modern problem issues but claim to stick to what the Constitution actually says. I explain each of these approaches to the Constitution in Chapter 3.

Making the Judiciary Paramount: Judicial Review

In *Marbury v. Madison*, decided in 1803, Chief Justice John Marshall claimed the power of judicial review for the courts, and in particular for the U.S. Supreme Court. I discuss this landmark case throughout the book and particularly in Chapter 23. (The nearby sidebar "John Marshall's conflict of interest" provides some background.)

JOHN MARSHALL'S CONFLICT OF INTEREST

One of the key problems with the case of *Marbury v. Madison* relates not to the decision itself but to the circumstances surrounding it.

The case arose out of lame-duck President John Adams's attempt to appoint a whole bunch of "midnight judges" — 16 circuit judges and 42 justices of the peace — the day before his term was due to end. These were all political appointees. Adams, a Federalist, had been deprived of a second term by his defeat at the hands of his own Vice President, Thomas Jefferson, a Democratic-Republican, in the 1800 election. So Adams decided to take his revenge by ensuring that the judiciary remained Federalist-dominated well beyond his presidency.

All these "midnight" appointments were rushed through the Senate. But the *commissions,* or official letters of appointment, still had to be delivered to each of the new appointees. Time ran out on Adams's presidency before all the commissions had been delivered — and without an official commission, an appointment could not take effect.

William Marbury was one of Adams's "midnight" justices of the peace whose commission was not delivered in time. President Thomas Jefferson ordered the new Secretary of State, James Madison, to withhold the commissions that hadn't been delivered, including Marbury's. So Marbury petitioned the U.S. Supreme Court to order Madison to deliver his commission to him.

Madison was the named defendant because delivering commissions to new appointees was one of the duties of the Secretary of State. Marbury's beef was with Madison for not delivering the commission to him. But the guy who really let Marbury down wasn't Madison — it was Madison's predecessor as Secretary of State, John Marshall. Yes, that's the very same John Marshall who presided over the case as Chief Justice. If ever there was a blatant example of a conflict of interest, this had to be it!

But that didn't stop Marshall from going on to expand the power of the Supreme Court — and of himself as Chief Justice — by means of judicial review.

Understanding the nature of judicial review

Almost all the cases heard by the Supreme Court today fall under the court's *appellate jurisdiction*, which I discuss earlier in the chapter. Since the passing of the Judiciary Act of 1925, the great majority of cases heard by the high court under this head are cases of judicial review — which, strictly speaking, are not appeals at all.

REMEMBER

An *appeal* is normally an application to a higher court contesting the decision of a lower court. In contrast, in a *judicial review*, the appellate court concerned reviews the lawfulness of a law passed by Congress or a state legislature, or a decision or other executive action taken by the President or a state.

Application for judicial review is made by filing a petition for a *writ of certiorari* with the appropriate appellate court. If the court agrees to hear the case, it is said to grant *certiorari*. This phrase does not mean that the court agrees with the petitioner — only that the court is prepared to hear the petitioner's case. An appellate court exercising the power of judicial review doesn't get to hear any live witnesses, and there is no jury — only a bench of judges. In the U.S. Supreme Court, an affirmative vote by any four of the nine justices is needed for *certiorari* to be granted. This is known as "the rule of four," the purpose of which is to prevent a majority of the Court from controlling the Court's docket. Every case in which *certiorari* has been granted is then heard by all nine justices sitting together — when a majority of at least five justices is needed for a final decision.

Judicial review doesn't figure in the wording of the Constitution. Yet early in the country's history, it became the mainstay of the power of the Supreme Court. Today, judicial review is more important than ever.

REMEMBER

Judicial review gives the U.S. Supreme Court the power to decide whether a federal or state law is in violation of the U.S. Constitution. If the Court finds that the law in question conflicts with the Constitution, the Court declares the law unconstitutional. This ruling means that the law (or the relevant part of the law) is *void*, or of no effect. Another way of describing this situation is to say that the Court *strikes the law down*, because the effect of the Court's decision is to strike the law (or the relevant part of the law) from the record as if it never existed in the first place.

Judicial review is more important today than ever before because:

>> The U.S. Supreme Court has expanded the scope of the Constitution to cover issues that the Framers never intended it to cover, such as abortion, affirmative action, and gay rights.

>> The high court has narrowed down the *political question* doctrine, which says that the courts should keep their hands off questions that are entrusted by the Constitution to one of the other branches of government, either the President

or the Congress. A good example of this development is the Supreme Court's determination of the presidential election of 2000 in *Bush v. Gore*.

>> The high court has interpreted the Due Process Clause of the Fourteenth Amendment so widely as to make practically the entire Bill of Rights applicable to the states as well as to the federal government — giving the Court far more control over the states than the Framers ever envisioned.

Tracing the origins of judicial review

If the Constitution didn't give the high court the power of judicial review, where did this power come from? There is considerable disagreement on this question. Here are some possible answers:

>> **Although judicial review isn't specifically mentioned in the Constitution, it's implied.** Alexander Hamilton took this position in the *Federalist Papers* even before the Constitution was ratified. (Note that the *Federalist Papers* were published precisely to win enough support for the Constitution to be ratified.) Hamilton's argument runs as follows:

- The Constitution is "fundamental law."

- Any law that conflicts with the Constitution is therefore void.

- Who should decide the constitutionality of a particular law? It's "rational to suppose" that the courts were intended to have this power because "The interpretation of the laws is the proper and peculiar province of the courts."

CONTROVERSY

The problem with this explanation is that judicial review is so important a power of the Supreme Court that, if the Framers really intended to give the Court this power, it's hard to understand why they didn't actually spell it out. The omission of any mention of judicial review from the text of the Constitution is unlikely to be accidental and may well indicate a deliberate decision not to give the Court this awesome power.

>> **The existence of a written constitution with the status of fundamental law makes judicial review necessary. Somebody has to decide whether any federal or state law is in conflict with the fundamental law — and who more appropriately than the courts?** How convenient! Why can't the legislature decide such conflicts? This solution is what the Virginia Constitution of 1776 provided for that state. (See the upcoming section "Considering alternatives for solving constitutional conflicts.")

>> **John Marshall invented judicial review in *Marbury v. Madison*.** Judicial review was discussed long before *Marbury* at the Constitutional Convention and in the state ratifying conventions — and it also figures in the *Federalist Papers.* But all this discussion makes it more rather than less likely that its omission from the Constitution was deliberate.

Noting Jefferson's response to *Marbury v. Madison*

Thomas Jefferson, a distant cousin and sworn enemy of John Marshall, was President at the time of *Marbury v. Madison.* Jefferson rejected what he called Marshall's "twistifications of the law" in claiming the power of judicial review for the Supreme Court. Here's what he wrote shortly after the *Marbury* ruling:

> *The opinion which gives to the judges the right to decide what laws are constitutional and what not, not only for themselves in their own sphere of action but for the Legislature and Executive also in their spheres, would make the Judiciary a despotic branch.*

Jefferson's fears proved well-founded. Judicial review gave the Supreme Court power over Congress and the President that was contrary to the whole idea of three coequal branches under the doctrine of separation of powers.

Considering alternatives for solving constitutional conflicts

If judicial review was abolished, how would conflicts between the Constitution and other laws be resolved? The 1776 Constitution of Virginia suggested an alternative approach. Section 7 of that Constitution's Bill of Rights read as follows:

> *That all power of suspending laws, or the execution of laws, by any authority, without consent of the representatives of the people, is injurious to their rights, and ought not to be exercised.*

We should not be surprised to learn that the Constitution of Virginia was mainly drafted by none other than Jefferson himself.

IN MY OPINION

The section in question clearly takes away from the judiciary the power of "suspending" and, therefore, also of setting aside any law. In other words, judicial review was not permitted under the Virginia Constitution. This power was given instead to the popularly elected legislature. This is not a bad solution and is much more in keeping with democratic principles than judicial review exercised by unelected judges.

Watching the Supreme Court's power seep into politics

Like Alexander Hamilton, James Madison saw judicial review as implied by the Constitution. But Madison's take on this possibility was very different from Hamilton's. Instead of justifying judicial review like Hamilton, Madison foresaw and deplored the danger of judicial review. Here's what Madison wrote on October 15, 1788:

> In the State Constitutions, and, indeed, in the Federal one also, no provision is made for the case of a disagreement in expounding them; and as the Courts are generally last in making their decision, it results to them, by refusing or not refusing to execute a law, to stamp it with its final character. This makes the Judiciary Department paramount in fact to the Legislature, which was never intended and can never be proper.

The problem has turned out in practice to be far more serious than Madison could have predicted, largely because of the bold intrusion of the high court into politics.

The *political question* doctrine is potentially one of the most valuable constitutional doctrines. It springs from the fundamental doctrine of the separation of powers. The doctrine requires the courts to decline jurisdiction in a case which the Constitution has entrusted to either the executive or the legislature.

Here are a couple of recent examples of the application of this doctrine:

» In *Goldwater v. Carter,* decided in 1979, Senator Barry Goldwater and other members of Congress challenged President Jimmy Carter's right to break a treaty with Taiwan — thereby favoring Red China — without consulting the Senate. The U.S. Supreme Court threw out the application on the ground that it raised a political question "because it involves the authority of the President in the conduct of our country's foreign relations." The Court left open the question of the constitutionality of the President's action.

» In *Nixon v. United States,* decided in 1993, a federal judge, Walter Nixon (no relation to the former President), challenged the handling of an impeachment trial by the Senate. Nixon had been convicted of perjury before a grand jury but refused to resign from office even after he had been jailed. The Senate then impeached and removed him from office. The Supreme Court unanimously threw out his application on the ground that impeachment was under the control of Congress and the Court had no right to get involved.

Cases like these are obvious political questions. But what about all the other issues in which the Court gets involved, like abortion, gay rights, or the election of the

President? Aren't these actually political questions too? That argument has never been used in relation to those issues. Yet other countries around the world have laws about abortion and gay rights that are decided by legislators, not judges.

For the courts to become embroiled in such highly fraught political debates could easily be interpreted as judicial activism at its worst, usurping the role of the other branches of government. On the other hand, the very existence of a written constitution makes it likely that almost any issue of importance is likely to find its way sooner or later into a high court docket.

Justice Ruth Bader Ginsburg has recognized that for the Court to have made abortion a constitutional issue could also have harmed the pro-choice cause that she favors. Here's what she said about *Roe v. Wade* long before she took her seat on the Supreme Court: The court's ruling terminated "a nascent democratic movement to liberalize abortion law." And: "Heavy-handed judicial intervention was difficult to justify and appears to have provoked, not resolved, conflict."

Casting the Swing Vote

With judicial review as its main weapon against the President, Congress, and the states, the power of the Supreme Court grew unchecked. For nine unelected judges to exercise this kind of power has often been criticized as undemocratic. But at certain times, the power has been exercised not by nine judges but by one — the wielder of the swing vote. If judicial review is by its very nature undemocratic, then unbridled judicial review power exercised by a single judge can only be regarded as anti-democratic in the extreme. In this section, I present some key examples of the power of the swing vote.

Under Chief Justices William Rehnquist and John Roberts, Justices Sandra Day O'Connor and Anthony Kennedy were able to flex their muscles by casting swing votes. Since O'Connor's retirement in 2005, Kennedy has exercised disproportionate influence by holding in his hands the determination of a number of sensitive cases — which also often gave him the right to write the majority opinion for the court. For example:

>> Kennedy's swing vote put George W. Bush into the White House in the 2000 decision in *Bush v. Gore.*

>> His vote also gave victory to the conservatives on the Court in *Boy Scouts of America v. Dale,* which allowed the Boy Scouts to exclude gays from membership as scoutmasters. But in *Lawrence v. Texas,* decided in 2003, he joined O'Connor and the liberals on the court to strike down a Texas law criminalizing homosexual intercourse.

» On abortion, Kennedy has taken the side of the liberals. In *Planned Parenthood of Southeastern Pennsylvania v. Casey,* decided in 1992, his vote produced a controlling plurality that struck down a Pennsylvania law requiring a husband to be notified before an abortion could be performed. In this case, Kennedy initially supported the four conservative justices — thus producing a majority — in favor of striking down *Roe v. Wade.* However, at the last minute Kennedy switched his swing vote to save *Roe v. Wade.*

» The debate on partial-birth abortion in *Stenberg v. Carhart* in 2000 saw Kennedy on the side of the conservative minority.

» Kennedy has generally adopted a liberal line on capital punishment. In *Roper v. Simmons,* decided by 5 votes to 4 in 2005, Kennedy wrote the opinion for the majority, ruling that it was unconstitutional to execute Christopher Simmons for a murder committed when he was under 18.

Despite the horrendous nature of the murder, Kennedy ruled that "The Eighth and Fourteenth Amendments forbid imposition of the death penalty on offenders who were under the age of 18 when their crimes were committed." His opinion was that no exceptions are allowed to this blanket ruling, which effectively strikes down provisions in the death penalty laws of 20 states. I discuss the *Simmons* case in more detail in Chapter 21.

» However, in *Kansas v. Marsh,* decided in 2005, Kennedy gave the conservatives a 5–4 majority in another capital punishment case. The issue here was whether a defendant could be sentenced to death where the mitigating factors and aggravating factors were of equal weight. A Kansas law said yes. The question before the high court was whether this law was unconstitutional. As a result of Kennedy's swing vote, the Court upheld the Kansas law.

» Kennedy wrote for the 5–4 liberal majority in the 2008 case *Kennedy v. Louisiana,* which ruled that state laws imposing the death penalty for child rape are unconstitutional. In crimes against individuals, Kennedy held, "the death penalty should not be expanded to instances where the victim's life was not taken."

» The very next day after handing down this liberal ruling, Kennedy gave a 5–4 victory to the conservative wing of the court in the important gun-rights case *District of Columbia v. Heller* (see Chapter 15).

» In yet another historic case decided in 2008, *Boumediene v. Bush,* Kennedy wrote for the liberal 5–4 majority that he had created, ruling that foreign detainees at Guantanamo Bay had the right to challenge their detention according to the principles of habeas corpus under the U.S. Constitution.

CONTROVERSY

» Kennedy also gave a 5–4 victory to the more liberal wing of the Court in the highly contentious 2005 case of *Kelo v. City of New London* about "eminent domain" under the Fifth and Fourteenth amendments. I discuss this case in Chapter 23.

>> In the landmark case of *Citizens United v. FEC* (2010), Kennedy wrote the majority opinion, this time tipping the balance in favor of the conservatives on the Court. See Chapter 23.

>> In 2015 Kennedy went to bat for the liberals on same-sex marriage, writing the 5–4 majority opinion in *Obergefell v. Hodges.*

These examples are merely a selection of *some* of the important cases whose outcome has been determined by Justice Kennedy's views. I pick on him only because he has managed to place himself in a pivotal position on the current Court.

Can it be right that a single unelected judge should have this kind of power? Since John Kennedy's election to the presidency, there has been much speculation about the power of the Kennedy clan. But in fact Justice Anthony Kennedy — no relation to the former President — has for 30 years exercised more power and influence than all the members of the Kennedy clan put together.

REMEMBER

The reason for this concentration of power in the hands of a single judge is twofold:

>> The tremendous power wielded by the U.S. Supreme Court, in particular in regard to judicial review

>> The absence of a common approach to constitutional interpretation, resulting in the division of the Court into two opposed ideological blocs

Labeling Supreme Court Justices

Supreme Court justices can be classified in a number of different ways, which can sometimes cut across one another. Following are discussions of a couple of basic divisions. For the different schools of interpretation, see Chapter 3.

Stare decisis/free exercise of power

Stare decisis, or the doctrine of *precedent,* means that judges are expected to follow previous decisions on the same legal issues. The U.S. Supreme Court pays lip service to this ancient doctrine but is not formally bound by it and has, in fact, overruled its own decisions in well over 100 cases in the past half-century. In general, *stare decisis* is a conservative doctrine — both politically and judicially conservative.

But what is a strict constructionist judge to do when his own view of what the Constitution means is contradicted by a longstanding high court precedent? Does he go with his own view of what the text of the Constitution means, or does he follow the precedent, even though he thinks it's wrong? Justices Antonin Scalia and Clarence Thomas — both conservatives — differ in this respect. As Scalia put it, Thomas "doesn't believe in *stare decisis,* period. If a constitutional line of authority is wrong, he would say let's get it right. I wouldn't do that."

What about believers in a "living Constitution"? Such justices wouldn't regard it as a big deal to break with precedent when they thought it was wrong. For example, in *Brown v. Board of Education,* decided in 1954, the liberal-dominated Supreme Court under Chief Justice Earl Warren had no trouble departing from the 1896 high court ruling in *Plessy v. Ferguson,* which had accepted racial segregation.

Judicial activism/judicial restraint

The term *judicial activism* is almost always used as a derogatory or negative label to refer to the exercise of judicial power that goes beyond its proper limits. Judges pilloried by critics as guilty of judicial activism are typically accused of

REMEMBER

» Making law instead of applying and interpreting it

» Legislating from the bench

» Ruling by the whim of the gavel

» Deciding cases on the basis of their own political predilections

Nobody ever claims to be a judicial activist. This label is pinned on judges by their critics — including other judges. Chief Justice William Rehnquist expressed himself anxious "to prevent judges from roaming at large in the constitutional field guided only by their personal views." By what, then, should judges be guided? Rehnquist opined, "It is impossible to build sound constitutional doctrine upon a mistaken understanding of constitutional history."

Justice Harry Blackmun is a likely candidate for consideration as a judicial activist. In 1972, he dissented in *Furman v. Georgia,* which declared the capital punishment laws of a number of states to be unconstitutional. Blackmun specifically rejected the majority opinion on the ground that it was an exercise in judicial activism. However, in subsequent cases Blackmun himself came out against the constitutionality of the death penalty. And Blackmun also was the author of the majority opinion in *Roe v. Wade,* the highly contentious 1973 abortion rights case, which has often been characterized by its opponents as a prime example of judicial activism.

Judicial restraint is the opposite of judicial activism and refers to the doctrine that the judiciary should show due deference to the elected branches of government and, in particular, should be slow to strike down laws as unconstitutional. Judicial restraint is a judicially conservative doctrine and is often associated with political conservatives as well. Chief Justice Roberts, a conservative, has identified himself with judicial restraint, saying, "Judges are like umpires. Umpires don't make the rules; they apply them."

Judicial restraint can also restrict the *scope* of the subject matter that the high court is prepared to accept as falling within its purview. For example, in 1964 Justice John M. Harlan II attacked what he called

> *a current mistaken view of the Constitution and the constitutional function of this court. This view, in short, is that every major social ill in this country can find its cure in some constitutional principle and that this court should take the lead in promoting reform when other branches of government fail to act. The Constitution is not a panacea for every blot upon the public welfare nor should this court, ordained as a judicial body, be thought of as a general haven of reform movements.*

Harlan is generally regarded as a conservative. But liberals also lay claim to judicial restraint. For example, Justice John Paul Stevens, who served from 1975 to 2010 and was widely regarded as a liberal justice, also claimed to be an adherent of judicial restraint. In 1983, he declared that a policy of judicial restraint "enables this Court to make its most effective contribution to our federal system of government."

IN THIS CHAPTER

» **Explaining what impeachment is (and isn't)**

» **Following the impeachment process through Congress**

» **Clarifying some misconceptions about impeachment**

» **Exploring historic cases**

» **Removing state officials**

Chapter **13**

You're Fired! Investigating the Impeachment Process

The key to democracy is people power. And the most important power the people have is to hire and fire their own government. This is normally done by means of elections, but there is a problem here: Presidential elections are held only every four years. Does this mean that a president can't be fired between elections? No. The Framers of the Constitution took care of that. They wrote into the Constitution an alternative way of getting rid of a president: impeachment.

This chapter looks at what impeachment is, who can be impeached, and how the process works. I also discuss another method for removing an unwanted politician from office: recalling a state governor.

There's Nothing Peachy about Impeachment

Election campaigns have something of a carnival atmosphere about them, accompanied as they are by hoopla, wild rallies, and raucous music. Impeachment has its own brand of exuberance but more in the nature of a lynching. A president who fails to be reelected is just a loser in the high-stakes game of politics and can come back to run again. (Grover Cleveland did so successfully in 1892.) But a president who lost his job as a result of impeachment would be finished. He would probably be barred from running for any federal office again, and his name would be mud forever. That has never happened, but there have been a couple of near misses.

Impeachment is nothing like an election; it's really a trial. Most people think of impeachment as a peculiar form of torture reserved for presidents. Not so. The Constitution says that impeachment can be used to remove the President, Vice President, or any other "civil Officers of the United States." (Note that members of the armed services can't be impeached. However, they can be removed by court martial.)

Only two Presidents have been impeached, and both were acquitted. These were Andrew Johnson in 1868 and Bill Clinton in 1998/99. (I devote a section to each later in this chapter.) Many people think that Richard Nixon was impeached too, but he wasn't. He jumped before he could be pushed; he was the only President in history to resign. (More on this topic later in the chapter as well.) Another 15 federal office-holders have been impeached, 8 of them successfully. Most recently, two Federal District Court Judges were impeached, one in 2009 and the other in 2010. The former resigned; the latter was removed from office.

"High Crimes and Misdemeanors": What Impeachment Is and Isn't

The Constitution is a pretty short document, yet it contains no fewer than seven mentions of impeachment. Article II, Section 4 states:

> The President, Vice President and all civil Officers of the United States, shall be removed from Office on Impeachment for, and Conviction of, Treason, Bribery, or other High Crimes and Misdemeanors.

Following are a few other mentions of impeachment:

>> Article I, Section 2, Clause 5: "The House of Representatives . . . shall have the sole Power of Impeachment."

>> Article I, Section 3, Clause 6: "The Senate shall have the sole Power to try all Impeachments. When sitting for that Purpose, they shall be on Oath or Affirmation. When the President of the United States is tried, the Chief Justice shall preside: And no Person shall be convicted without the Concurrence of two thirds of the Members present."

>> Article I, Section 3, Clause 7: "Judgment in Cases of Impeachment shall not extend further than to removal from Office, and disqualification to hold and enjoy any Office of honor, Trust or Profit under the United States: but the Party convicted shall nevertheless be liable and subject to Indictment, Trial, Judgment and Punishment, according to Law."

Defining impeachment

Despite the impressive rolling phrases, these provisions raise more questions than they answer. For example,

>> Is impeachment a purely political offense?

>> Can you be impeached for something that isn't a crime?

>> If you're impeached for something that *is* a crime, and then you're prosecuted for that crime, isn't that double jeopardy?

Congress has never tried to second-guess the Framers of the Constitution by defining impeachment — not officially, anyway. But maybe Congressman (later President) Gerald Ford's 1970 definition isn't so far from the mark (and he wasn't walking and chewing gum when he delivered this pearl of wisdom):

> *What, then, is an impeachable offense? The only honest answer is that an impeachable offense is whatever a majority of the House of Representatives considers it to be at a given moment in history; conviction results from whatever offense or offenses two-thirds of the other body [i.e., the Senate] considers to be sufficiently serious to require removal of the accused from office. . . . There are few fixed principles among the handful of precedents.*

Can you be impeached for something that isn't a crime at all?

Not one of the 11 articles of impeachment his accusers hurled at Andrew Johnson amounted to a crime under the ordinary law. But that doesn't necessarily mean that Johnson's enemies were wrong; the Constitution itself seems to support the view that "high crimes and misdemeanors" don't necessarily have to be crimes in the ordinary sense.

To arrive at this conclusion, we need to consider what the Constitution has to say about the punishment for impeachable offenses. Article I, Section 3, Clause 7 says that the only punishment for impeachment is removal from office and disqualification to hold office in the future. That's a pretty stiff penalty in anybody's language, but it's not the end of the story. The same clause says that even if you've been convicted on impeachment, you will still "be liable and subject to Indictment, Trial, Judgment, and Punishment, according to Law."

In other words, if the offense that leads to impeachment also involves breaking a law, the person under the microscope can be both impeached and prosecuted. After being impeached, tried, found guilty, and deprived of office (by Congress), that person can still be hauled up before a judge and jury and maybe do some jail time.

How many times can someone be punished for the same thing? After all, being punished twice for the same thing just isn't allowed — that's called *double jeopardy* and is strictly forbidden by the Fifth Amendment (see Chapter 17).

REMEMBER

The point is that being impeached is *not* the same thing as being punished under the law. That's why double jeopardy doesn't apply. With this understanding in mind, we can deduce that the Framers of the Constitution distinguished between impeachable offenses and illegal behaviors. It's certainly possible that one action can be both impeachable and illegal, but it's also possible that an action can be impeachable without being illegal.

What would qualify someone for impeachment without being illegal? See the sections on Andrew Johnson and Bill Clinton later in this chapter for the two prime examples in U.S. history. And consider what Alexander Hamilton wrote about impeachment in the *Federalist Papers*, an influential series of 85 articles written by Hamilton, James Madison, and John Jay in 1787 and 1788 advocating the ratification of the newly drafted Constitution:

> *The subjects of its jurisdiction are those offenses which proceed from the misconduct of public men, or, in other words, from the abuse or violation of some public trust. They are of a nature which may with peculiar propriety be denominated POLITICAL, as they relate chiefly to injuries done immediately to the society itself.*

Not bad for a description written before the Constitution even came into effect!

Explaining the Impeachment Process

The Constitution says that "The House of Representatives shall have the sole Power of Impeachment." But it doesn't specify how the House shall use that power. Does that mean that the procedure is fluid and can change any time the House likes? Yes and no.

On the one hand, the basic procedure is hundreds of years older than the U.S. Constitution. The House's role derives from that of the British House of Commons, which used to prosecute impeachments before the House of Lords, and the Lords' function as a trial jury has come down to the U.S. Senate. On the other hand, both the House of Representatives and the Senate have their own detailed "Rules of Procedure and Practice," which change from time to time. The Senate revised its rules in 1974 after Watergate. The current version of the Senate rules dates from 1986.

Playing grand jury and prosecutor: The role of the House

Any member of the House can propose an impeachment resolution, and in fact the initial complaint can even come from outside Congress. President Clinton's impeachment, for example, was set in motion by Independent Counsel Ken Starr, who dumped 36 boxes of evidence on the House, together with a 453-page report citing 11 possible impeachable offenses the President allegedly committed.

As with most things in the House, the Rules Committee gets to see any impeachment proposal first. From there, the proposal generally goes to the House Judiciary Committee, which may conduct its own hearings. (I explain these committees in Chapter 11.)

In the Clinton impeachment, the full House voted 258–176 to authorize a full impeachment inquiry. The Judiciary Committee then began holding televised hearings. The committee drafted four articles of impeachment, all of which it approved essentially along party lines. The first three articles alleged perjury and obstruction of justice in regard to Paula Jones, a woman who had accused the President of sexual harassment, and in connection with his relationship with intern Monica Lewinsky. The fourth and last article of impeachment alleged that Clinton had "misused and abused his office by making perjurious, false and misleading statements to Congress."

The next stage is for the articles of impeachment to return to the full House for a debate, possibly in closed session, followed by a vote on whether to impeach or not to impeach. In the Clinton case, the House passed two of the four articles. (The fourth article was rejected by a whopping 285–148 vote.)

The impeachment process doesn't end here — the Senate must then try the case and decide whether to convict, as I explain in the next section. However, if the House approves one or more articles of impeachment, the person is officially "impeached."

REMEMBER

The role of the House in impeachments is as the prosecutor. At first it acts as a grand jury, deciding whether the case should go to trial. Then, if it decides that the case should move forward, the House appoints managers to act as prosecuting counsel at the trial. (In the Clinton impeachment, 13 Republican members of the House Judiciary Committee served as managers under the chairmanship of Representative Henry Hyde of Illinois.)

Trying the articles of impeachment: The role of the Senate

REMEMBER

After passing the House, an impeachment is ready for trial by the Senate. The Senate acts as the trial jury but, unlike a jury, has the freedom to ask questions and debate the issues. The Senate hears all the legal arguments and evidence and then decides the outcome by a roll-call vote. A simple majority vote can't convict; the Constitution states that a two-thirds vote is required.

The trial process can take weeks or even months. Andrew Johnson's trial in 1868 took almost three months, but Clinton's in 1999 took only about five weeks. In the Clinton case, no live witnesses were called, but videotape evidence was presented. In both the Johnson and Clinton trials there was a majority vote for impeachment, but both of them got off — Johnson by a single vote — because the prosecutors failed to convince a two-thirds majority, as is needed for conviction.

The Framers of the Constitution were careful to appoint the Chief Justice of the U.S. Supreme Court to preside over an impeachment when the President is on trial. The Vice President, who is the president of the Senate, presides over all other impeachment trials of lesser officials. (In practice, the *president pro tempore* — the highest-ranking senator — or a deputy will often preside.) The Vice President couldn't very well be allowed to preside over the impeachment trial of the President because he'd have a conflict of interest: The conviction of the President would turn the presidency over to the Vice President!

Understanding the Implications of Impeachment

Impeachment is one of the sexiest aspects of the Constitution. It's a fun thing — except of course for the person being impeached. And when it happens to a president, everybody has an opinion. But there are a lot of misconceptions about it too.

Impeaching isn't the same as convicting

The words "impeach" and "impeachment" sound pretty bad. When we hear "A.B. was impeached," this seems to imply that he was found guilty of something. In fact, all it means is that A.B. was formally charged and tried. It says nothing about the outcome, which would either be a *conviction* (a guilty verdict) or an *acquittal* (a not guilty verdict).

REMEMBER

It's quite correct to say that Andrew Johnson and Bill Clinton were impeached, though both were acquitted. That's why the Constitution uses the clumsy phrase "impeachment for, and conviction of . . ." — because impeachment and conviction are two different things.

Keeping Congress out of the fray

According to the Constitution, any "civil officer of the United States" can be impeached. But what exactly is a civil officer? Does the term include members of Congress? This question was put to the test early in U.S. history.

In 1797, the House of Representatives impeached Senator William Blount of Tennessee. The Senate decided that it didn't have the right under the Constitution to try him. The arguments by which it reached that conclusion were far from clear, but the gist may have been that senators are not regarded as "civil officers of the United States" who alone are subject to impeachment.

An important practical consideration was the fact that the Senate had already expelled Blount for being guilty of a "high misdemeanor" inconsistent with his duty as a senator. (This decision was based on Blount's involvement in a military conspiracy to take Florida and Louisiana from Spain and hand them over to Britain.)

So does this mean that a person can escape impeachment if he is no longer a "civil officer" at the time? The punishment laid down for impeachment by Article I, Section 3, Clause 7 is not only removal from office but also "disqualification to hold and enjoy any Office of honor, Trust or Profit under the United States." This language seems to indicate that even somebody who is no longer in office can be impeached because, if found guilty, he can still be disqualified from holding office in the future. But in practice, after a person has jumped ship, it is most unlikely that he will still be pursued for impeachment. (Richard Nixon is a good example of this fact, as I discuss in a sidebar in this chapter.)

No member of Congress has been impeached since Blount, and it's unlikely that any ever will be.

Impeaching for poor private conduct

The Constitution doesn't specify whether someone can be impeached only for acts carried out in his or her official capacity. In 1881, a Minnesota judge was removed from office in a state impeachment for being found guilty of "frequenting bawdy houses and consorting with harlots." The question of whether private conduct can be the basis of an impeachment is still very much a live issue, as President Clinton's case proves.

The Constitution allows for impeachment in cases of treason and bribery, which seems clear enough. But it also allows impeachment for "High Crimes and Misdemeanors" — a strange combination. "High Crimes" sounds solemn and serious, but "Misdemeanors" usually refers to pretty insignificant offenses like jaywalking. Presumably, we need to read this phrase to mean "High Crimes and *High* Misdemeanors." But a "High Misdemeanor" sounds like a contradiction in terms, something like "grand jaywalking" or "aggravated jaywalking." Or maybe "Misdemeanor" here refers to something that is not really a crime at all but essentially means "misconduct."

TECHNICAL STUFF

The phrase "High Crimes and Misdemeanors" found its way into the Constitution as the result of compromise. George Mason, one of the delegates to the Constitutional Convention, wanted to include "maladministration" as a ground for impeachment, but James Madison felt that this word was too vague. Mason then came up with "High Crimes and Misdemeanors" to cover what he called "attempts to subvert the Constitution."

"High Crimes and Misdemeanors," then, seems to be a formula to represent political rather than purely legal offenses. This interpretation agrees with Alexander Hamilton's view of impeachment that I quote earlier in the chapter. Andrew Johnson's impeachment falls into this category. As I explain in a moment, his real crime was that he wasn't Abraham Lincoln, and he opposed everything (except the Union) that Lincoln stood for.

Ducking impeachment with a pardon?

Article II, Section 2 of the Constitution gives the President a general "Power to grant Reprieves and Pardons for Offences against the United States, except in Cases of Impeachment." This wording is another recognition of the special (political) nature of impeachment.

Didn't Richard Nixon get a presidential pardon from his successor, Gerald Ford? Yes. But keep in mind that Nixon wasn't impeached; he quit. The pardon protected Nixon from any criminal charges or civil lawsuits in the ordinary courts but ostensibly had nothing to do with impeachment. Had Nixon not resigned, he would have been impeached, and, if found guilty by the Senate, would not only have been removed from office but would also still have been exposed to criminal prosecution in court. His resignation immunized him against impeachment but did not give him any protection against a potential criminal prosecution.

At the time of this writing, President Trump appears to be attempting to protect himself against both possible impeachment and prosecution — but without resigning. On July 21, 2017, Trump tweeted on Twitter that "all agree the U.S. President has the complete power to pardon" anyone, even including himself. This is almost certainly incorrect. One of the most ancient and fundamental principles of natural justice is that "nobody ought to be a judge in his own case." The exercise of a pardoning power is clearly akin to that of a judge. So it is most unlikely that Donald Trump could possibly pardon himself, though he certainly could pardon anyone else.

But, in any case, can someone be pardoned if he has not been convicted of any crime — and has not even been charged with any crime? That was actually the position with Nixon. When he resigned, impeachment looked inevitable, but it had not yet happened. Nixon's pardon by Gerald Ford, his successor in the White House, was quickly branded by hostile commentators as a "corrupt bargain." To reassure himself that he had done the right thing, Ford used to carry around in his wallet an extract from the Supreme Court judgment in the case of *Burdick v. United States* (1915), which suggested that acceptance of a pardon amounted to an admission of guilt. *Burdick* didn't actually say that, and Nixon never confessed. On the contrary, on August 17, 1973, Nixon (in)famously declared on television: "People have got to know whether or not their President is a crook. Well, I'm not a crook."

It's still not clear whether a sitting President can be indicted on criminal charges while in office. But the position in regard to civil suits was clarified in *Nixon v. Fitzgerald* (1982), a case which had nothing to do with Watergate and was decided long after Nixon's resignation. By a 5–4 decision, the U.S. Supreme Court ruled that the President is entitled to absolute immunity from liability in a civil suit based on any official act of his performed while in office. The same is not true for civil liability for acts done before taking office. This was made clear by a unanimous U.S. Supreme Court in *Clinton v. Jones* (1997), a case Paula Jones brought against President Clinton during his presidency, alleging sexual harassment while Clinton was governor of Arkansas. Justice John Paul Stevens, writing for the Court, held that the doctrine of the separation of powers did not mean that federal courts should defer private lawsuits against a sitting President until after he had served his term.

Tracking Impeachment in Action

Impeachment is a British invention, but it hasn't been used there for more than two centuries because it was perceived as essentially political. Plus, it was very time-consuming. The celebrated trial of Warren Hastings on corruption charges lasted seven years (from 1788 to 1795), took up 145 sittings of the House of Lords, and resulted in a unanimous acquittal on all charges!

A look at Johnson, Nixon, and Clinton

IN MY
OPINION

Similar issues hover over U.S. impeachments. Andrew Johnson's impeachment in 1868 was clearly politically motivated. Johnson was Vice President under Abraham Lincoln and succeeded him as President after his assassination in 1865. The real problem was that, while Lincoln was a Republican, Johnson was a Southern Democrat — which is precisely why he was chosen as Lincoln's running mate in the 1864 election. For, though Johnson had a visceral hatred of the Republican Party and all it stood for, he was a passionate supporter of the Union, so his presence on the Republican ticket helped Lincoln to convey a message of national unity and win reelection. After Johnson was installed as President, his more moderate approach to the defeated South brought him into conflict with the Republican-controlled Congress, which is what led to his impeachment. But, after a trial before the Senate lasting almost three months, Johnson was saved from removal from office by just one vote and went on to serve out the rest of his term.

Some people are under the impression that Richard Nixon was impeached. He wasn't. Instead, he resigned — the only U.S. President ever to do so. His problem arose out of the Watergate crisis — sparked off by a break-in at the offices of the Democratic National Committee in the Watergate Building in Washington, D.C., in June 1972. To this day it's still not known whether Nixon was privy to this burglary, but the question was whether he was involved in the cover-up. This opened up a can of worms — or, to be more precise, hundreds of cans of audiotapes containing voice-activated recordings of all conversations that had taken place in the

Oval Office throughout the Nixon presidency. Nixon's refusal, based on "executive privilege," to hand the tapes over to the special prosecutor appointed by the Senate led the House of Representatives to start moving toward impeachment. But Nixon preferred to jump rather than wait to be pushed, and he resigned. The whole Watergate fiasco seems to have been motivated by Nixon's paranoid fear that his enemies were plotting his overthrow — the rash act of an over-cautious man. In the event, he won reelection in 1972 by a landslide, carrying every state except Massachusetts.

Though Nixon ducked impeachment, Bill Clinton was impeached, but, like Andrew Johnson, the only other president to be impeached, he was acquitted. Clinton's impeachment in 1998/99 arose out of his sexual exploits, or, to be more precise, untruthful evidence that he gave before a special prosecutor's grand jury in regard to them. Clinton's sexual exploits and his alleged perjury should have been dealt with through the ordinary courts. Impeachment is a valuable constitutional tool and should not be misused. After being acquitted in his impeachment trial (see Figure 13-1) before the Senate, President Clinton served out the rest of his second term and left office with a 65 percent approval rating — the highest of any retiring President since Dwight D. Eisenhower.

FIGURE 13-1:
President Bill Clinton, one of only two presidents impeached to date. He was found "not guilty" by the Senate by 55 to 45 votes on the charge of perjury and by 50 to 50 votes on obstruction of justice. A two-thirds "guilty" verdict, 67 votes, would have been needed to remove him from office.

Source: Official White House photograph

COURTING JUSTICE FOR SUPREME COURT JUSTICES

Richard Nixon was not the only public figure who jumped before he could be pushed. Justice Abe Fortas, appointed to the Supreme Court bench by President Lyndon Johnson, was hounded by the media after accepting $20,000 for becoming a consultant to a charitable foundation headed up by a former client. Johnson, himself embattled over Vietnam, had already announced that he would not be seeking reelection. As a lame-duck President, he could do nothing to help his longtime friend. In 1969, with the threat of impeachment hanging over his head, Fortas resigned from the Supreme Court in disgrace.

Several Supreme Court justices have been confronted with calls for their impeachment, notably Chief Justice Earl Warren and Justice William O. Douglas. In Douglas's case, a resolution calling for his impeachment was sponsored by 110 congressmen and introduced into the House of Representatives in 1970 by (future President) Gerald Ford. But that is as far as it got. The only Supreme Court justice who was ever actually impeached was Samuel Chase, back in 1805 — and he was acquitted.

Judging the judges

Thomas Jefferson called impeachment a "scarecrow" because the threat of impeachment is often enough to deter an official from pursuing an unacceptable course of conduct. But in some cases the threat of impeachment isn't enough: It's necessary to initiate an impeachment prosecution. Judges are the officials who are most likely to face impeachment proceedings. A total of 14 federal judges have been impeached, and 7 of them were found guilty and removed from office.

The most recent of these cases was Judge Walter Nixon (no relation to the former President), who was impeached in 1989 for committing perjury before a grand jury. The Senate convicted him and removed him from office. This impeachment, which was based on perjury, served as a precedent for impeaching President Clinton.

Removing State Officials from Office

Impeachment is not confined to federal officials. It applies equally to state officials in 49 of the 50 states. The one exception is Oregon, where "public officers" charged with "incompetence, corruption, malfeasance, or delinquency in office" are tried in the ordinary courts, which have the power to strip them of their office as well as to punish them in other ways. In the remaining 49 states, impeachment is a possibility, though the form it takes may differ slightly from the federal model.

TECHNICAL STUFF

Many state constitutions mirror the language of the U.S. Constitution, but the language is varied. There is a procession of "malfeasance," "malpractice," "misconduct," and even the vague term opposed by James Madison, "maladministration." Four states cite "moral turpitude" or "moral turpitude in office" as grounds for impeachment. (Had this language been in the U.S. Constitution, would President Clinton have been fired?)

Impeaching governors

Governors are the equivalent of the President at the state level, so they are liable to impeachment. Twelve state governors have been impeached over the years. Eight were convicted and removed from office, and one resigned.

In 2008, Governor Eliot Spitzer of New York resigned in the face of impeachment threats arising out of a scandal involving a prostitute. In 2009, Governor Rod Blagojevich of Illinois was impeached for allegedly trying to sell the Senate seat vacated by President Obama. His whirlwind impeachment trial before the Illinois State Senate ended with a unanimous 59–0 vote against him. He was immediately removed from office and disqualified from ever again holding any "office of honor or trust" in Illinois. Blagojevich's impeachment conviction did not exempt him from facing criminal charges in a regular criminal court.

Total recall, or terminating a governor

Some states have devised an even more ingenious way of ridding themselves of elected public officials between elections: *recall.* The best-known example of a recall occurred in California in 2003, when Governor Gray Davis, who had been reelected for a second term only the previous year, was recalled and replaced by Arnold Schwarzenegger.

TECHNICAL STUFF

Recall has been available to Californians since 1911. To set the process in motion requires the signatures of 12 percent of the number of votes cast in the previous election. In the 2003 case, this meant that the signatures of 897,158 registered California voters were needed!

A recall election ballot has two parts:

>> In the first part you vote "Yes" or "No" to recall the incumbent.

>> If "Yes" wins, there is a second round, in which you select the replacement candidate of your choice.

It's pretty easy to get on the ballot. All you need is 65 nomination signatures and a $3,500 filing fee.

In the 2003 California recall ballot, there was a 55.3 percent vote to recall Gray Davis, with Arnie taking 48.7 percent of the vote in part two, a remarkable feat considering that there were no fewer than 131 candidates on the ballot, 41 of them Republicans!

Without a superstar candidate to galvanize public support, recall elections are clearly not the easiest way to remove a governor from office, but they are an interesting safety valve. Above all, they are a form of direct democracy.

4

Guaranteeing Important Rights: The Bill of Rights

Gain knowledge about your constitutional rights.

Speak up! Find out about your right to freedom of speech as well as religion and assembly.

Find out about the right to bear arms and prohibiting unreasonable search and seizure.

Uncover what "Pleading the Fifth" is really all about.

Understand your right to a fair trial and a trial by jury plus the regulation of cruel and unusual punishment.

Note the Ninth Amendment — a guide on how to interpret the Constitution — and tackle the Tenth Amendment — described by Thomas Jefferson as "the foundation of the Constitution."

IN THIS CHAPTER

» **Examining the text of the First Amendment**

» **Establishing freedom of religion**

» **Safeguarding freedom of speech responsibly**

» **Protecting national secrets**

» **Assuring freedom of assembly and association**

Chapter **14**

The First Amendment: Freedom of Religion, Speech, and Assembly

The First Amendment forms part of the *Bill of Rights* — the name we give to the first ten amendments. The First Amendment is arguably the most important part not only of the Bill of Rights but also of the Constitution as a whole because it guarantees some pretty fundamental rights:

>> Freedom of religion and belief

>> Freedom of speech

>> Freedom of the press

>> Freedom of assembly and association

>> Freedom to petition the government

In this chapter, I explain each of these rights and how they've been interpreted through the years.

Considering the Amendment's Wording

Here's what the First Amendment says:

Congress shall make no law respecting an establishment of religion, or prohibiting the free exercise thereof; or abridging the freedom of speech, or of the press; or the right of the people peaceably to assemble, and to petition the Government for a redress of grievances.

Prohibiting Congress from taking away rights

Notice the unusual wording. The whole amendment is governed by the opening phrase "Congress shall make no law . . ." No other amendment starts that way. How come the First Amendment differs from all the other amendments in this important respect?

REMEMBER

The answer is that in this amendment the Framers were not granting new rights to the people. They assumed that those rights already existed. The amendment was clearly designed to stop Congress from taking away rights that already existed.

Applying the amendment to the states

The opening word of the First Amendment makes it clear that the amendment applies only to Congress, which is part of the federal government. There is no indication that it applies to the states. Should we conclude that the First Amendment doesn't apply to the states? You may assume that's the simple, logical conclusion. But the U.S. Supreme Court in its wisdom has decided otherwise.

As I explain in Chapter 17, the high court has expanded its interpretation of the famous Due Process Clause in the Fourteenth Amendment to incorporate much of the Bill of Rights — including the First Amendment — and apply it to the states. In other words, the high court has ruled that based on the Fourteenth Amendment, states must adhere to much of the Bill of Rights, just as the federal government does.

REMEMBER

The First Amendment is considered *completely incorporated.* That means all the rights spelled out in the amendment must apply at the state level, as well as at the federal level.

Separating Church and State

The first two clauses of the First Amendment are about religion. The first of these clauses — *Congress shall make no law respecting an establishment of religion* — is commonly referred to as the Establishment Clause. Let's break down the wording of this clause:

>> **Congress shall make no law:** The word *shall,* even in more modern legal documents, means "must." So "Congress shall make no law respecting an establishment of religion" means "Congress must not make any law about the establishment of religion."

>> **establishment:** In England there was (and still is) an established religion and state church, known as the Church of England. Opposition to this state church was one of the most important motivating forces leading the early settlers to leave England and come to America. A number of the colonies replaced the Church of England with their own favored brand of Protestantism, and this situation continued after independence. The intention of the Establishment Clause was to prevent Congress from establishing a national church — and also to stop Congress from interfering with existing state establishments. The only high court justice who ever showed any sign of understanding this important latter point was the much underrated Justice Potter Stewart (the judicial hero of Justice John Paul Stevens).

>> **respecting:** The phrase "respecting an establishment of religion" just means "about an establishment of religion."

If the Establishment Clause was intended to prevent the establishment of *any* official church at either the national or state level, why didn't it say so? The Establishment Clause raises more questions than it answers. Here are some of those questions:

CONTROVERSY

>> **Is it okay for a state to authorize the recitation of a voluntary, nondenominational prayer at the start of each school day?** The prayer in question, introduced by the school district of New Hyde Park, New York, read as follows: *Almighty God, we acknowledge our dependence upon Thee, and we beg Thy blessings upon us, our parents, our teachers, and our Country.* In the 1962 case *Engel v. Vitale,* the high court ruled that the use of the prayer

"breaches the constitutional wall of separation between Church and State." Justice Potter Stewart, in his lone dissent, made some trenchant points against this ruling, notably:

- The majority placed too much reliance on the phrase "wall of separation between Church and State," quoted from a letter written by Thomas Jefferson in 1802 — "a phrase nowhere to be found in the Constitution."

- Both houses of Congress open their daily sessions with prayer.

- The President's oath of office ends with "so help me God" (added to the official wording in the Constitution by George Washington and every one of his successors).

- The National Anthem, "The Star-Spangled Banner," contains the verse "And this be our motto 'In God is our Trust.'"

- "Since 1865, the words 'IN GOD WE TRUST' have been impressed on our coins."

- Since 1954, the Pledge of Allegiance to the Flag has contained the words "one nation *under God* . . ." (Several so-far indecisive legal challenges have been launched against this wording.)

- The Supreme Court itself starts each day with the invocation by the court crier, "God save the United States and this Honorable Court."

>> **Is it okay for a state to provide tuition vouchers for use in public or private schools, including religiously affiliated schools?** In the 2002 case of *Zelman v. Simmons-Harris,* the majority on the Court said yes — provided the vouchers went to parents and not to the schools, and provided the parents had a choice of nonreligious as well as religious schools.

>> **Is it okay for the Ten Commandments to be displayed in a courthouse?** In 2003, the Chief Justice of Alabama, Roy Moore, was fired for refusing to remove a granite monument of the Ten Commandments from the central rotunda of the Alabama Judicial Building. Moore's removal from office followed a ruling by a federal district court declaring that the monument violated the Establishment Clause of the First Amendment and was therefore unconstitutional. In 2005, the U.S. Supreme Court decided in a 5–4 split that displaying the Ten Commandments on a Kentucky courthouse wall violated the First Amendment's requirement of separation between church and state. But a display of the Ten Commandments on the grounds of the Texas State Capitol in Austin, Texas, was held by the same margin to be permissible!

TESTING, TESTING

The high court has formulated the *Lemon* test for legislation concerned with religious matters — named for the 1971 case *Lemon v. Kurtzman,* in which a legal challenge was mounted against Pennsylvania and Rhode Island statutes providing state aid to church-related schools. Chief Justice Warren Burger, writing for the majority, set out the test in these terms:

- *First, the statute must have a secular legislative purpose;*

- *Second, its principal or primary effect must be one that neither advances nor inhibits religion;*

- *Finally, the statute must not foster "an excessive government entanglement with religion."*

In *Lee v. Weisman,* heard in 1992, the high court supplemented the *Lemon* test with Justice Anthony Kennedy's "coercion test," which ruled as unconstitutional the giving of a nonsectarian benediction by a clergyman at a public school graduation ceremony — on the dubious basis that this religious feature placed the graduating students under subtle religious "coercion."

Justice Sandra Day O'Connor's "endorsement test" makes it even easier for a law or government action to "run afoul" of the Establishment Clause. This test asks whether the government action in question "conveys a message of endorsement or disapproval" of religion — either of which is unconstitutional.

Assuring the Free Exercise of Religion

The second clause of the First Amendment says that [*Congress shall make no law*] *prohibiting the free exercise [of religion].* This clause is known as the Free Exercise Clause.

Looking at belief and practice

In the 1879 case of *Reynolds v. United States,* the Supreme Court divided the exercise of religion into two parts: belief or opinion on the one hand and, on the other hand, practice. The Court ruled that the law can't interfere with "mere religious beliefs and opinions," but it may interfere with religious practices.

The *Reynolds* case was about polygamy, as practiced at that time by some Mormons. Could religion be a defense to illegal actions? No, said Chief Justice Morrison Waite, writing for the court; otherwise, even religiously based human sacrifice would have to be allowed.

The most recent major Supreme Court case under the Free Exercise Clause of the First Amendment is *Trinity Lutheran Church of Columbia v. Comer* (2017), which was decided by a majority of 7 to 2, with Chief Justice Roberts writing for the majority. The Constitution of Missouri (in common with over 30 other state constitutions) stipulates that "no money shall ever be taken from the public treasury, directly or indirectly, in aid of any church, sect or denomination of religion." On this basis the church in question was denied a grant for rubberizing the playground of its preschool and daycare, which had an open admissions policy. "The consequence is, in all likelihood, a few extra scraped knees," wrote Chief Justice Roberts. "But the exclusion of Trinity Lutheran from a public benefit for which it is otherwise qualified, solely because it is a church, is odious to our Constitution all the same, and cannot stand." Six justices concurred with the Chief Justice in the judgment, including the liberal justices Kagan (who joined Roberts's opinion in full) and Breyer (who concurred only in the judgment). The conservative justices Thomas and Gorsuch joined the Chief Justice's opinion but did not agree with his restricting his decision only to playground resurfacing. Justice Sotomayor, joined by Justice Ginsburg, sounded the dissent, opining that the majority reasoning "weakens this country's longstanding commitment to a separation of church and state beneficial to both. . ... The Court today profoundly changes that relationship by holding, for the first time, that the Constitution requires the government to provide public funds directly to a church."

Adopting a strict scrutiny test

In the 1963 case *Sherbert v. Verner,* the Supreme Court adopted a *strict scrutiny* test to determine whether a person's rights under the Free Exercise Clause have been violated. Adell Sherbert was a Seventh Day Adventist who was fired from her job because she refused to work on Saturdays. She couldn't find another job, so she applied for unemployment compensation. But her unemployment claim was denied by the Employment Security Commission, by a South Carolina trial court, and by the South Carolina Supreme Court. Sherbert's claim for unemployment compensation eventually reached the U.S. Supreme Court.

The high court established the following criteria for the *Sherbert* test, as it was quickly dubbed:

>> **Whether the plaintiff's religious belief was sincere:** Adell Sherbert's religious sincerity was not in doubt.

>> **Whether the government action imposed a "substantial burden" on the plaintiff's ability freely to exercise her religion:** The Supreme Court found that this requirement had been met in the Sherbert case.

If these two criteria are satisfied, then the government has to prove

>> **That there was "a compelling state interest" justifying the government's action:** In the *Sherbert* case, no compelling state interest was found that denied Adell Sherbert unemployment compensation.

>> **That it could not have pursued its compelling interest in a way that did not infringe on the plaintiff's freedom of religion:** In the *Sherbert* case, this point didn't arise.

So Adell Sherbert won her case in the Supreme Court — and in the process established a sensible *strict scrutiny* test that protected the free exercise of religion of others.

However, in 1990 the Supreme Court abandoned the need for strict scrutiny in *Employment Division v. Smith.* This change meant that freedom of religion was no longer accorded the same protection as under the *Sherbert* test. To restore the extremely popular *Sherbert* test, in 1993 Congress passed the Religious Freedom Restoration Act (RFRA) with overwhelming bipartisan support.

CONTROVERSY

But RFRA put the high court's nose out of joint because it looked as though Congress was not just *enforcing* the Constitution but *interpreting* it — a privilege that the Court had long ago arrogated to itself (see Chapter 12). In the words of Justice Anthony Kennedy, writing for the majority on the court in *City of Boerne v. Flores* (1997), "Congress does not enforce a constitutional right by changing what the right is." Come again? Wasn't it the Supreme Court that changed the test in the first place — and, in so doing, changed the right also? But, though the RFRA was held to be unconstitutional as applied to the states, it continues to be valid as applied to the federal government, as was confirmed in *Gonzales v. O Centro Espirita Beneficente União do Vegetal* (2006) and *Burwell v. Hobby Lobby Stores* (2014). In the meantime, 20 individual states enacted their own Religious Freedom Restoration Acts applicable to state governments and municipalities.

Guaranteeing Freedom of Expression

After religion, the First Amendment turns to freedom of expression. Here are the relevant words:

Congress shall make no law . . . abridging the freedom of speech, or of the press.

FLAG BURNING: PROTECTING UNSPOKEN SPEECH

In the 1989 case of *Texas v. Johnson,* a 5–4 majority on the Court characterized flag burning as protected "speech" under the First Amendment. Interestingly, the conservative Chief Justice William Rehnquist and the liberal Justice John Paul Stevens both strongly dissented for different reasons. Stevens highlighted the illogicality of the majority ruling by pointing out that if a protestor had "chosen to spray-paint his message of dissatisfaction on the façade of the Lincoln Memorial, there would be no question about the power of the Government to prohibit his means of expression."

This provision looks pretty straightforward. But let's look at it as little more closely:

REMEMBER

>> The whole provision is couched in negative terms and is governed by the words "Congress shall make no law." Why? Because the First Amendment is not *granting* any new rights. It's only *guaranteeing* rights that already existed.

>> The right to freedom of speech already existed in colonial times — but subject to certain exceptions, notably defamation and obscenity.

>> The amendment draws a distinction between freedom of speech and freedom of the press. But doesn't the term "freedom of speech" cover freedom of the press? Sure, but press freedom was considered important enough to deserve separate protection.

>> However, press freedom can also sometimes actually conflict with individual freedom of speech. A good example of this occurred in the run-up to the 2008 presidential election, when *The New York Times* refused to print an op-ed piece by John McCain responding to one by Barack Obama.

Denying protection to speech creating a "clear and present danger"

Congress has passed a number of laws that prohibit certain types of expression, particularly in regard to revolutionary speeches or writings. And the high court has addressed many questions relating to such types of expression. Here are a few:

>> **Can speech lose its First Amendment protection if it creates a "clear and present danger"?** The court answered yes (until 1969 — see the last bullet of this list). Charles Schenck, a Socialist, published a leaflet urging young men to

refuse to serve in World War I if drafted. In *Schenck v. United States,* heard in 1919, the high court rejected Schenck's claim that his publication was protected by the First Amendment. Justice Oliver Wendell Holmes, writing for a unanimous court, held that the leaflets created a "clear and present danger" that draftees would refuse to serve in the armed forces, which was a "substantive evil" that the government had the right to prevent. Holmes based this doctrine on a shaky parallel: "The most stringent protection of free speech would not protect a man in falsely shouting fire in a theatre and causing a panic."

>> **How clear and how present does the "clear and present danger" have to be?** According to the Supreme Court, not very clear and not very present. In *Gitlow v. New York,* decided in 1925, the majority on the Court greatly widened the "clear and present danger" test, upholding Benjamin Gitlow's New York conviction for advocating the violent overthrow of the government. Holmes, the originator of the "clear and present danger" test, dissented. He held that the publication of Gitlow's revolutionary writings did not create any such danger, as his views were shared by only a small minority of people — and Gitlow was only calling for a revolution at some "indefinite time in the future."

>> **Is the "clear and present danger" test still in force?** No. The high court unanimously replaced it, in the 1969 case of *Brandenburg v. Ohio,* with a new, more liberal test, allowing First Amendment protection even to advocacy of the use of force — "except where such advocacy is directed to inciting or producing imminent lawless action and is likely to incite or produce such action."

Allowing obscenity to be seen?

Are pornography and obscene publications protected under the First Amendment?

Justice Thurgood Marshall, writing for the Court in the 1964 case *Stanley v. Georgia,* famously held that "If the First Amendment means anything, it means that a State has no business telling a man, sitting alone in his own house, what books he may read or what films he may watch."

REMEMBER

In a nutshell, here's where the Court stands on protections related to obscene materials: The possession of obscene material is protected under the First Amendment. The sale and distribution of obscene material, on the other hand, does not enjoy First Amendment protection (although the American Civil Liberties Union [ACLU] successfully challenged parts of the Communications Decency Act of 1996 that made it a crime to use the Internet to send or display to anyone under the age of 18 any communication that is "patently offensive, obscene or indecent").

The possession protection does not extend to child pornography. The law on child pornography has been tightened through the years, including with the PROTECT Act of 2003. (PROTECT is an acronym for Prosecutorial Remedies and Other Tools to end the Exploitation of Children Today.) The constitutionality of this act was unsuccessfully challenged in the 2008 case of *United States v. Williams*.

This whole discussion begs the question, what is the definition of obscenity? The high court had a major problem with this question until, in 1973, it hit upon a definition that is still generally accepted. This definition, formulated in the case of *Miller v. California*, restricts the label *obscene* to

> *works which, taken as a whole, appeal to the prurient interest in sex, which portray sexual conduct in a patently offensive way, and which, taken as a whole, do not have serious literary, artistic, political, or scientific value.*

What a mouthful!

Using and abusing the right to freedom of the press

In the early days of the United States, anybody could set up a printing press in a back room of his or her house. The Framers regarded press freedom as something very precious because it gave the little person a voice against big government.

In the early 20th century, the state of Minnesota challenged freedom of the press with a state law that provided for the gagging of any "malicious, scandalous and defamatory newspaper, magazine or other periodical." *The Saturday Press*, a particularly scurrilous rag, was prosecuted under this law. But, in the 1931 case of *Near v. Minnesota*, the U.S. Supreme Court struck down the state law as unconstitutional. Chief Justice Charles Evans Hughes, writing for the majority, held that "Liberty of speech and of the press, is not an absolute right, and the State may punish its abuse" — but only after publication, not before.

The high court gave a great boost to press freedom in the landmark 1964 case of *New York Times Co. v. Sullivan*. Sullivan was a police chief in Montgomery, Alabama. *The New York Times* ran an advertisement that Sullivan claimed defamed him. An Alabama court awarded Sullivan damages of $500,000. The U.S. Supreme Court took this money away from him and created a new rule applicable to public officials bringing a defamation or libel suit concerning their official conduct. To win a libel suit, a public official needs to prove not only that the words he objects to are untrue but that they also involve *actual malice* — meaning that the person who published those words knew that they were false or didn't care whether they were true or false.

What if the published falsehood is deliberate but intended to be satirical? The well-known 1988 case of *Hustler Magazine v. Falwell* concerned a spoof interview with the Rev. Jerry Falwell in which Falwell "admitted" that his "first time" was drunken incest with his mother in an outhouse. Falwell was awarded $150,000 for emotional distress. But the high court found in favor of the magazine because the purported claims contained in the offending article were so extreme that nobody could be expected to take them seriously.

CONTROVERSY

In 1971, *The New York Times* led another notable, but somewhat dubious, triumph for press freedom. The case centered on the Pentagon Papers — a 14,000-page top-secret government report about the handling of the Vietnam War. The report was leaked to *The New York Times* by Daniel Ellsberg, who was involved in a study of the documents originally commissioned by Defense Secretary Robert McNamara. The *Times* at once began publishing excerpts from these top-secret documents in serialized form.

The majority on the high court found in favor of the newspaper's right to publish the excerpts, arguing that except when the nation was actually at war, the First Amendment guarantee of freedom of speech is absolute. In the words of Justice William Brennan:

> *The entire thrust of the Government's claim has been that publication of the material sought to be enjoined "could," or "might," or "may" prejudice the national interest in various ways. But the First Amendment tolerates absolutely no prior judicial restraints of the press predicated upon surmise or conjecture that untoward consequences may result.*

Chief Justice Warren Burger dissented, describing the published information as "purloined documents." Justice Harry Blackmun, who also dissented, concluded that publication of the Pentagon Papers "could clearly result in great harm to the nation." Blackmun set the First Amendment against the background of the Constitution as a whole:

> *The First Amendment, after all, is only one part of an entire Constitution. Article II of the great document vests in the Executive Branch primary power over the conduct of foreign affairs, and places in that branch responsibility for the Nation's safety.*

Letting money talk

In the landmark case of *Citizens United v. Federal Election Commission* (2010), the Supreme Court ruled by 5 votes to 4 that uncapped expenditure on political election campaigns by corporations, labor unions, and other associations amounts to protected speech under the First Amendment. For a fuller discussion of this important decision, see Chapter 23.

Leaking Classified Information

Does the First Amendment protect the publication of illegally obtained classified documents? No, although supporters of the self-styled "whistleblowers" involved generally defend their actions as revelations in the public interest.

U.S. Private First Class Bradley Manning (now known as Chelsea Manning) uploaded more than 700,000 secret U.S. files to WikiLeaks, an international organization that publishes secret and classified information and news leaks. Manning was arrested in 2010, pleaded guilty to 10 of 22 charges and was found guilty at a court-martial held in 2013 on most of the remaining charges, including 5 counts of espionage and theft of documents and 1 count of "wantonly [causing] to be published on the internet intelligence belonging to the U.S. government, having knowledge that intelligence published on the internet is accessible to the enemy." Manning was acquitted of "aiding the enemy." Manning apologized to the court, saying: "I am sorry that my actions hurt people. I'm sorry that they hurt the United States, I am sorry for the unintended consequences of my actions. When I made these decisions I believed I was going to help people, not hurt people." Manning was sentenced to 35 years in prison and a dishonorable discharge from the army. In January 2017, President Obama commuted all but 4 months of Manning's remaining sentence, remarking that the original 35-year sentence was "very disproportionate relative to what other leakers have received."

WikiLeaks' founder and director, Julian Assange, was reported in 2010 to be under active criminal investigation by the U.S. Justice Department, possibly with a view to prosecution under the Espionage Act of 1917, which prohibits the unauthorized retention or transmission of defense-related documents. A federal grand jury was evidently empaneled in Alexandria, Virginia, to investigate Assange and others. And in April 2017, Attorney General Jeff Sessions told CNN: "We are already stepping up our efforts against all leaks, and whenever a case can be made we will seek to put some people in jail." However, Assange is still in the Ecuadorian embassy in London, where he was given asylum in 2012.

Edward Snowden, who leaked thousands of classified National Security Agency documents to the press, was granted temporary asylum in Russia. In 2013, the U.S. Justice Department unsealed charges against him of theft of government property and violation of the Espionage Act of 1917. In July 2015, in response to a petition with over 167,000 signatures calling for a pardon for Snowden, the White House responded that "Mr. Snowden's dangerous decision to steal and disclose classified information had severe consequences for the security of our country and the people who work day in day out to protect it. . . .. He should come home to the United States, and be judged by a jury of his peers."

Having Your Cake . . .

A highly controversial case before the Supreme Court at the time of this writing combines issues under both main limbs of the First Amendment: *Masterpiece Cakeshop v. Colorado Civil Rights Commission*. A Christian bakery owner refused on religious grounds to make a wedding cake for a gay couple who were already legally married in Massachusetts. That was in 2012, before Colorado recognized same-sex marriage (in 2014) and before the U.S. Supreme Court ruled in favor of same-sex marriage in 2015. The gay couple got their cake made by another bakery, but then filed a complaint with the Colorado Civil Rights Commission — and won. The U.S. Supreme Court agreed to review that decision. The Court heard oral arguments on December 5, 2017, with a decision expected in June 2018. The question before the Court is whether the first instance decision obliging the baker to make cakes celebrating gay weddings violates the Free Speech or Free Exercise of religion clause of the First Amendment.

Protecting the Right to Assemble and Petition

The right to march to Washington, D.C., and make your feelings known to the government is still an important one, but probably less important than it was in the early days of the nation, before the rise of the party system, before radio, before television, and before the Internet.

The connection between the right to assemble and the right to petition can easily be seen, and so can the connection between the right to assemble and the right to free association — which has been interpreted to allow membership of labor unions and other associations.

United States v. Cruikshank, decided in 1875, is one of the few leading cases on this aspect of the First Amendment. An armed white mob clashed with a large gathering of African Americans at the courthouse in Colfax, Louisiana, at the time of a gubernatorial election. Some whites were charged under a Louisiana law that made it a felony for two or more persons to "combine, conspire, and confederate together, with the unlawful purpose of depriving United States citizens of African descent" of their civil rights. The U.S. Supreme Court threw out the indictments for vagueness. But the most important part of the ruling in *Cruikshank* was to refuse to apply the First Amendment to the states. In other words, the high court did not regard the First Amendment as "incorporated" by the Fourteenth Amendment's Due Process Clause. The Court held that the First Amendment applied only to the national government.

However, the U.S. Supreme Court now regards the whole of the First Amendment as "incorporated" — including the right to petition and freedom of assembly. So the states are now subordinate to the feds in regard to these rights also.

In the 1937 decision in *De Jonge v. Oregon*, a unanimous U.S. Supreme Court overturned the conviction of a Communist leader for addressing a meeting allegedly advocating "criminal syndicalism and sabotage." The high court declared the interpretation of the Oregon law by the Oregon Supreme Court to be "repugnant" to the First Amendment as incorporated into the Due Process Clause of the Fourteenth Amendment.

CONTROVERSY

National Socialist Party of America v. Village of Skokie is an interesting and highly controversial 1978 case illustrating the conflicting forces at work. A neo-Nazi group wanted to stage a march through the village of Skokie, Illinois, a largely Jewish area. The local authorities wanted to keep the neo-Nazis out. The Illinois Supreme Court, upheld by the U.S. Supreme Court, refused to ban the march. The Illinois Supreme Court even specifically refused to ban the display of the swastika emblem — using the rather dubious parallel of permission given to war protesters in another case to wear black armbands. In the end, the neo-Nazis didn't march through Skokie, but they had won a legal victory without doing so.

Surprisingly perhaps, the neo-Nazis had the backing of the generally left-leaning American Civil Liberties Union (ACLU), whose stated mission is "to defend and preserve the individual rights and liberties guaranteed to every person in this country by the Constitution and laws of the United States." In 2011 the ACLU filed an amicus brief in support of Pastor Terry Jones's plan to hold a demonstration "protesting Sharia and Jihad" in front of the Islamic Center in Dearborn, Michigan — while at the same time making it clear that the ACLU "vehemently disagrees with the content of Pastor Jones's speech." In 2012 the ACLU of Eastern Missouri filed a federal lawsuit against the City of Cape Girardeau on behalf of the right of the Traditionalist American Knights of the Ku Klux Klan (TAK) to place handbills on the windshields of parked cars. And in August 2017, the ACLU supported the alt-right's application to hold a rally in Charlottesville, Virginia, to protest against the planned removal of a statue of Confederate General Robert E. Lee, which is arguably a violation of a state law protecting war memorials. The ensuing violence resulted in the death of Heather Heyer and indirectly in the deaths of two state troopers whose helicopter unaccountably fell from the sky and burst into flames while circling the rally and demonstrations. At the time of this writing, a lawsuit brought by a group of plaintiffs including a Confederate heritage group is still going ahead in accordance with a ruling by Charlottesville Circuit Court Judge Richard Moore.

Chapter **15**

The Second Amendment: Bearing Arms

The Second Amendment is one of the shortest — and one of the most controversial — of all the amendments. Here's how the amendment reads, according to the handwritten version of the Bill of Rights now hanging in the U.S. National Archives in Washington, D.C. (as painstakingly inked on parchment by congressional clerk William Lambert back in 1789):

> *A well regulated Militia, being necessary to the security of a free State, the right of the people to keep and bear Arms, shall not be infringed.*

But the version of the amendment that was actually passed by Congress and ratified by the states is worded this way:

> *A well regulated militia being necessary to the security of a free State, the right of the people to keep and bear arms shall not be infringed.*

This version looks more modern. The difference between the two versions is two extra commas in the Lambert version: one after "Militia" and another after "Arms." Do the commas really matter? Probably not. Punctuation was more arbitrary 200 years ago than it is today. A comma could just indicate a pause without any grammatical significance.

But the interpretation of this single sentence — with or without the two extra commas — is the focus of heated debate. In this chapter, I introduce the arguments surrounding this amendment and explain the impact of a recent Supreme Court decision about gun rights.

Debating Interpretation: Individual versus State Rights

Two main schools of thought do battle over the Second Amendment: the individual (or personal) rights school of thought and the states' (or collective) rights school of thought. In a nutshell, here's how the two differ:

CONTROVERSY

>> **Individual rights:** The individual rights school interprets the amendment as giving people the right to buy guns and use them for sport, self-protection, or any other lawful purpose. This school believes that every person has the same right, not just members of the military, the National Guard, or any other kind of militia.

>> **States' rights:** This school sees the amendment as giving states the right to establish militias like the National Guard but not giving any rights to individuals.

A range of intermediate views exists, of course, which fall somewhere between these two schools of thought. For example, some people believe that the amendment

>> Restricts the right to possess firearms to members of some sort of militia but allows such members to use their arms for their own personal protection as well as for national defense

>> Allows any law-abiding and responsible citizen to possess firearms after undergoing a background check

>> Grants individual citizens the right to have firearms for their personal use, provided the firearms are of a standard military type

If you pay any attention to politics, you probably realize that people who define themselves as conservative tend to fall on one side of the debate between individual and states' rights, and people who call themselves liberal often fall on the other side. In case you opt not to pay attention to politics at all (which means you probably get less heartburn than the rest of us), here's the general breakdown:

>> **Conservatives:** Broadly speaking, conservatives favor the right of U.S. citizens to arm themselves if they so wish. Conservatives tend to oppose placing restrictions on the purchase or possession of guns because they assume that criminals can gain access to firearms anyway. By clearing away legal restrictions, they argue, the law favors law-abiding citizens over the criminal element.

>> **Liberals:** Liberals tend to fall into the states' rights camp. Many liberals fear the possibility of individuals taking the law into their own hands and are more inclined to support restrictions on buying and carrying guns.

REMEMBER

Obviously, these are generalizations, and you probably wouldn't have too much trouble finding exceptions to the rule. In general, these political views are something of a paradox, because in most other respects, conservatives tend to champion states' rights while liberals tend to oppose them. However, while the normal dichotomy is between states' rights and the rights of the federal government, when it comes to gun rights, the dichotomy is between states' rights and individual rights.

Breaking Down the Amendment's Clauses

Why, exactly, do people debate the Second Amendment so heatedly? After all, the entire Second Amendment is contained in a single sentence. The problem is that the two halves of that sentence seem to point in opposite directions:

>> The first half — *A well regulated Militia, being necessary to the security of a free State* — appears to place an emphasis on collective rights and obligations.

>> The second half — *the right of the people to keep and bear Arms, shall not be infringed* — places the emphasis on individual rights.

To understand the true meaning of the Second Amendment, we must take both its clauses into account. But the two schools of thought on this amendment each emphasize one clause at the expense of the other. The individual rights school emphasizes the second clause, while the states' rights school concentrates on the first.

In terms of English grammar, the second half of the amendment is the main clause, while the first half is a subordinate clause. This structure seems to support the individual rights interpretation, but nothing about this amendment is quite clear-cut. As I show in the next section, states' rights supporters have a different way of interpreting the sentence structure.

Understanding the states' rights interpretation

The Second Amendment is the only part of the U.S. Bill of Rights that has a preamble or prefatory clause. I have enough faith in the amendment's authors to believe that the sentence structure is not accidental, but what does the first clause tell us?

Finding meaning in "Militia"

To get an answer, consider that the word *militia* also appears in Article I, Section 8 and Article II, Section 2 of the Constitution and in the Fifth Amendment. (See the nearby sidebar "'Militia' in other parts of the Constitution.") I believe that the word *militia* means the same thing in all these passages.

The Framers of the Constitution had markedly different feelings about armies than about militias. The Framers didn't trust standing armies, which you can see from the fact that Article I, Section 8 of the Constitution prohibits Congress from financing an army for more than two years at a time. The function of keeping order and even of repelling invasions is entrusted to the "Militia" rather than the army.

Moreover, although the President is designated as Commander in Chief of the militia as well as of the army and navy (in Article II, Section 2), that chain of command applies only when the militia is "called into the actual Service of the United States." Under normal circumstances, the militia is under the control of the individual states, not of the federal government. President Thomas Jefferson explained this fact in a letter to Destutt de Tracy in 1811, in which Jefferson writes that the governor of each state is "constitutionally the commander of the militia of the State."

Jefferson was very concerned that the young Republic should have an efficient and effective militia. He referred to it frequently in his annual messages to Congress. For example, in 1808 he said:

> *For a people who are free, and who mean to remain so, a well-organized and armed militia is their best security. It is, therefore, incumbent on us, at every meeting to revise the condition of the militia, and to ask ourselves if it is prepared to repel a powerful enemy at every point of our territories exposed to invasion.*

REMEMBER

Why the sharp contrast between the attitude toward militias and toward armies? Keep in mind that in the 18th century, police as we know them did not exist, so law and order had to be kept by soldiers. But if those soldiers were formed into a standing (permanent) army, the executive government would have tremendous power. A standing army owed its loyalty to the government, and in Europe, governments had often used their troops as a repressive police force. Militias, by contrast, were the citizenry under arms (and generally carried their own arms).

By the time the Second Amendment was ratified in 1791, the original part of the Constitution had been in force for about three years. It would have been strange, therefore, if "the well regulated Militia" of the Second Amendment referred to anything other than the type of militia that had been given such prominence elsewhere in the Constitution.

Its presence in the Constitution has invested the term *militia* with a certain sanctity. Not surprisingly, a number of self-proclaimed militias exist in the United States, some of which are really no more than vigilante groups. By using this label, they wrap themselves in the flag and claim a specially protected status. But are they entitled to it? Not unless they are militias in the sense intended by the Second Amendment.

"MILITIA" IN OTHER PARTS OF THE CONSTITUTION

TECHNICAL STUFF

The term *militia* appears in several places in the Constitution. Its usage in other passages helps us determine how the Framers intended it to be interpreted in the Second Amendment.

Article I, Section 8 of the Constitution contains two clauses dealing with the militia and one dealing with armies. It gives power to Congress

To raise and support Armies, but no Appropriation of Money to that use shall be for a longer Term than two Years;

To provide for calling forth the Militia to execute the Laws of the Union, suppress Insurrections and repel Invasions;

To provide for organizing, arming, and disciplining, the Militia, and for governing such Part of them as may be employed in the Service of the United States, reserving to the States respectively, the Appointment of the Officers, and the Authority of training the Militia according to the discipline prescribed by Congress.

Article II deals with the presidency. Section 2 starts:

The President shall be Commander in Chief of the Army and Navy of the United States, and of the Militia of the several States, when called into the actual Service of the United States.

The Fifth Amendment says that nobody is to be charged with "a capital, or otherwise infamous crime" unless indicted by a grand jury "except in cases arising in the land or naval forces, or in the Militia, when in actual service in time of War or public danger."

Interpreting the second clause
with states' rights in mind

The states' righters like the first clause of the amendment better than the second, but they can't get away from the fact that the second clause is the main clause. So how do they interpret it — in particular the words "the right of the people to keep and bear Arms"?

They start by recognizing that a militia is made up of ordinary citizens under arms that they provide for themselves. They then focus on the word "bear."

In 1840, the Tennessee Supreme Court in *Aymette v. The State* was adamant that the word "bear" had a distinctly military connotation:

> *The words 'bear arms' have reference to their military use, and were not employed to mean wearing them about the person as part of the dress.*

> *A man in the pursuit of deer, elk, and buffaloes might carry his rifle every day for forty years, and yet it would never be said of him that he had borne arms; much less could it be said that a private citizen bears arms because he has a dirk or pistol concealed under his clothes, or a spear in a cane.*

This passage was fully endorsed by the Ninth Circuit Court of Appeals in *Silveira v. Lockyer* in 2002.

Explaining "the right of the people"

Now that we have a sense of how states' rights advocates interpret the two clauses of the Second Amendment, let's turn our attention to the individual rights school of thought. To start, keep in mind that individual rights advocates focus on the second half of the amendment, which is the main clause: *the right of the people to keep and bear Arms, shall not be infringed.*

The Second Amendment is not the only one to contain the phrase "the right of the people." This same expression also appears in the First and Fourth amendments (see Chapters 14 and 16), where it clearly refers to individual rights.

If the Second Amendment gives rights to individuals, what exactly are those rights and what lawful restrictions can be placed on them? For example, does the right apply to any kind of firearm, or are there some justifiable restrictions? As I show later in this chapter, the U.S. Supreme Court in *United States v. Miller* recognized the right as being a personal or individual one but held that it had to be exercised in accordance with "the security of a free State."

REMEMBER

What are the nature and scope of the rights claimed by pro-gun advocates? Most of them insist that the purpose of the Second Amendment was not to grant any new rights but to preserve and guarantee rights that were already in existence. Some take the view that these rights are absolute, or unlimited. They're afraid of the "slippery slope" — the danger that apparently minor restrictions are likely to lead to the eventual disappearance of gun rights altogether.

Others are prepared to accept restrictions on the purchase of certain types of firearms, such as automatic and semiautomatic weapons, and don't object to background checks before buying a gun. Sportsmen are sometimes prepared to accept a ban on handguns, as long as they can still buy shotguns and hunting rifles. But gun rights activists reject this approach as defeatist and insist that the amendment doesn't protect only hunting but is intended primarily for self-defense.

Upholding Individual Rights: *D.C. v. Heller*

In 2008, in the case *District of Columbia v. Heller*, the Supreme Court for the first time actually decided on the meaning of the Second Amendment. The Court was finally able to get its teeth into this important question because of a challenge to a Washington, D.C., law.

The law in question totally banned the possession of handguns in the home. It also made it a crime to carry any unregistered firearm and required any lawful firearm in the home to be bound by a trigger-lock.

CONTROVERSY

Those opposed to the D.C. law portrayed it as completely preventing homeowners and other residents from defending themselves against intruders. The law banned handguns, the firearm of choice for home protection, and disabled all other firearms by insisting that they have a trigger-lock on.

The question before the high court was therefore quite simple: Was the D.C. law in keeping with the Second Amendment, or did it violate rights under that amendment?

To answer that question, it was necessary for the Court to interpret the meaning of the amendment. As I explain earlier in the chapter, there are two main interpretations of the Second Amendment: the individual rights interpretation and the states' rights interpretation.

In its ruling, the Supreme Court divided along traditional lines, with two of the court's big hitters slugging it out:

» The heavyweight conservative standard-bearer Justice Antonin Scalia (see Figure 15-1) did battle in favor of individual rights.

» The agile 88-year-old liberal Justice John Paul Stevens gave as good as he got on the states' rights side.

FIGURE 15-1:
President Reagan with Antonin Scalia after nominating Scalia to the Supreme Court in 1986. Scalia would write for the majority in the landmark gun-rights case, *District of Columbia v. Heller* (2008), among many other high-profile cases.

Source: Bill Fitz-Patrick, White House Photographer

REMEMBER

Stevens emphasized the first clause of the amendment, while Scalia argued that the second clause was the really important one. Scalia won a narrow but decisive 5–4 victory. So it's official: You *do* have an individual constitutional right to own and use a gun.

Concentrating on the D.C. law's ban on handguns and its requirement that licensed firearms in the home be kept inoperable at all times, the majority ruled that "This makes it impossible for citizens to use firearms for the core lawful purpose of self-defense and is hence unconstitutional." The court therefore struck the D.C. law down as unconstitutional.

The minority on the court sought to uphold the D.C. law, relying on the fact that *some* regulation of the possession and use of firearms had always been allowed and the D.C. law's restrictions did not go beyond proper limits.

Justice Stephen Breyer, in an additional dissent, opined:

The protection the Amendment provides is not absolute. The Amendment permits government to regulate the interests that it serves. . .. The majority's view cannot be correct unless it can show that the District's regulation is unreasonable or inappropriate in Second Amendment terms. This the majority cannot do.

But even Justice Scalia, writing for the majority, freely admitted that the right is not unlimited. It is not "a right to keep and carry any weapon whatsoever in any manner whatsoever and for whatever purpose."

Scalia identified the following as lawful restrictions on individual gun rights:

» "prohibitions on carrying concealed weapons"

» "prohibitions on the possession of firearms by felons and the mentally ill"

» "laws forbidding the carrying of firearms in sensitive places such as schools and government buildings"

» "laws imposing conditions and qualifications on the commercial sale of arms"

» Prohibitions on "the carrying of 'dangerous and unusual weapons.'"

Considering the Continuation of the Debate

Heller is a landmark decision, but it has certainly not ended the debate. On the day after *Heller* was published, the National Rifle Association filed no fewer than five lawsuits challenging local gun laws. Among these was *Guy Montag Doe v. San Francisco Housing Authority* challenging the city's ban on guns in public housing. The case was settled on January 14, 2009, allowing residents of the San Francisco Housing Authority to possess firearms within their apartment building.

McDonald v. City of Chicago (2010) is the most important Supreme Court decision since *Heller*, dealing with the question whether the gun rights allowed by *Heller* applied to the states as well. In particular, the case challenged Chicago's handgun ban, which had been in place since 1982. One *amicus brief* (legal argument filed by a non-party) in favor of the petitioner was signed by a record number of 58 U.S. senators and 251 representatives. In addition, 32 states also filed amicus briefs. By five votes to four, the Supreme Court ruled that the right recognized by *Heller* is applicable to the states through the Due Process Clause.

The petitioner in *McDonald* asked the Court not only to incorporate gun rights into state law but to go further and overturn the Slaughter-House Cases (1873), which would have had the result of making the whole Bill of Rights binding on the states. The Supreme Court in *McDonald* was not prepared to go this far, but it did hold that self-defense, which it identified as the central component of the Second Amendment, is a basic right.

In *People v. Aguilar* (2013), the Illinois Supreme Court applied *McDonald* to strike down a state law titled the Aggravated Unlawful Use of a Weapon, under which it was a felony to carry a loaded gun. However, the court upheld another Illinois statute that made it illegal for anyone under the age of 18 to possess a firearm.

Clarifying the results

The U.S. Supreme Court clarified *Heller* and *McDonald* in *Caetano v. Massachusetts* (2016), in which possession of a stun gun was approved on the ground that:

>> "The Second Amendment right is fully applicable to the States."

>> "The Second Amendment extends, prima facie (at first sight), to all instruments that constitute bearable arms, even those that were not in existence at the time of the founding."

>> The protection is not restricted to "only those weapons useful in warfare."

In 2008, after the *Heller* decision had been handed down, the Council of the District of Columbia repealed its handgun ban but enacted a new handgun registration ordinance that made it legal for a lawfully registered handgun to be carried in the home but not outside the home. In 2014, this law was held to be unconstitutional. In response to this decision, D.C. adopted a new law allowing carry permits for outside the home only if there was "good reason," defined as "special need." On July 25, 2017, the U.S. Court of Appeals for the District of Columbia Circuit ruled on the constitutionality of the new "special needs" ordinance in two cases: *Wrenn v. District of Columbia* and *Matthew Grace and Pink Pistols v. District of Columbia*. The majority on the court held that "the right to keep and bear Arms" includes the right to bear arms outside the home, leaving it to the legislature to decide whether to require that arms be carried openly rather than concealed.

There is still plenty of scope for debate on the Second Amendment. For example, in the 2016 presidential election, Hillary Clinton promised if elected to repeal the Protection of Lawful Commerce in Arms Act of 2005, which prevents anyone from suing a gun dealer because of the "misuse" of a gun. However, firearms manufacturers and dealers are potentially liable for defective products, breach of contract, criminal misconduct, and also negligence if they have reason to know that a gun is intended for use in a crime. In October 2015, a jury ordered a gun shop in Wisconsin to pay almost $6 million to two police officers who had been shot by firearms purchased from this gun shop. In 2016, a Missouri gun store settled for $2.2 million for "negligent entrustment" after selling a gun to a schizophrenic woman who used the gun to kill her father — after the store had been warned by the woman's parents and asked not to sell her a firearm.

Continuing debate

CONTROVERSY

There is ongoing controversy about the need for and efficacy of background checks, and the extent of such checks. Mandatory federal background checks coupled with a five-day waiting period were introduced by the so-called Brady Bill of 1993, named for James Brady, President Reagan's press secretary, who was seriously injured during the attempted assassination of the President in 1981. The NRA challenged the law in *Printz v. United States* (1997), in which the U.S. Supreme Court held that the act's interim provision mandating all local sheriffs to conduct background checks was unconstitutional as a violation of the Tenth Amendment.

To sidestep the constitutional problems of the Brady Bill, the FBI in 1998 launched the National Instant Criminal Background Check System (NICS), which quickly determines whether a prospective firearms buyer's name and year of birth match those of someone who is prohibited from purchasing firearms. This system does not, however, apply to purchases from a private person or at a gun show.

A 2016 article in *The Lancet,* a well-known medical journal, concluded that: "Projected federal-level implementation of universal background checks for firearm purchase could reduce national firearm mortality from 10.35 to 4.46 deaths per 100,000 people, background checks for ammunition purchase could reduce it to 1.99 per 100,000, and firearm identification to 1.81 per 100,000." However impressive these figures may appear to be, they are essentially an opinion. And it is noteworthy that most gun show sales involve licensed dealers who are already required to conduct background checks under federal law.

Chapter **16**

The Third and Fourth Amendments: Protecting Citizens from Government Forces

The Third and Fourth amendments (which are part of the *Bill of Rights* — the first ten amendments that were all ratified together in 1791) both safeguard people against intrusion. In brief, the Third Amendment prohibits the quartering of soldiers in your house without your consent. The Fourth Amendment prohibits "unreasonable searches and seizures" of "persons, houses, papers, and effects."

Keeping the Feds Out of Your House

Before the American Revolution, a rumor spread among the colonists that the British government was about to force homeowners to accommodate troops free of charge in their homes. This fear was the product of a mistaken reading of the Quartering Acts of 1765 and 1774, which in fact allowed the British colonial authorities to quarter troops only in "uninhabited houses, outhouses, barns, or other buildings." Despite this restriction, the 1774 act was soon labeled by the colonists as one of the "Intolerable Acts."

During the course of the Revolutionary War, both sides in fact quartered troops in private homes. The Framers of the Constitution believed that quartering troops in private homes was an evil — but recognized that in times of war it was a necessary evil. So, in drafting the Third Amendment, they drew a clear distinction between war and peace.

IN MY OPINION

The Third Amendment is a bit of a Cinderella. It hasn't had the attention lavished on so many other parts of the Constitution. The U.S. Supreme Court has never had to interpret it, and the amendment has been the direct subject of litigation in a federal court only once since it was ratified in 1791. But I think this is a blessing in disguise, because when the courts get their teeth into any part of the Constitution, they tend to make a meal of it — and sometimes one that is not too appetizing!

The Third Amendment is neither long nor complicated. Here's what it says:

> *No Soldier shall, in time of peace be quartered in any house, without the consent of the Owner, nor in time of war, but in a manner to be prescribed by law.*

This wording looks pretty straightforward, but there's always room for debate about the meaning of any part of the Constitution. The potentially controversial terms here are as follows:

>> **Soldier:** This word evokes multiple questions:

- Does this word include National Guardsmen, who are under state control? Yes. This was decided by the Second Circuit Court of Appeals in the 1982 case of *Engblom v. Carey*. The court based this decision on the controversial *incorporation* doctrine — the belief that most of the rights in the Bill of Rights are applicable to the states (as well as to the federal government) as a result of being incorporated into the Due Process Clause of the Fourteenth Amendment. I discuss this thorny problem in the later section "Rewriting the Fourth Amendment," as well as in Chapter 17.

- Could this word include nonmilitary government agents, like maybe a police SWAT team snooping on a neighboring house? Hard to say. This practice is sometimes employed, but I don't know of any legal complaints about it.

>> **quartered:** In colonial times, courts often ordered felons to be "hanged, drawn and quartered" — meaning that, after being cut down, the felon's body was cut in four. So, does the Third Amendment mean that you mustn't cut a

soldier's body in four? Ummm, probably not. Quartering means the same as *billeting,* which means that the homeowner has to provide the soldier with free board and lodging.

>> **in time of peace . . . in time of war:** Troops were quartered in private homes in the War of 1812 — a formal war declared by Congress — without any legal provision for it. In the Civil War — an undeclared war — the U.S. government quartered troops in both "rebel" and Union states without any legal authority. But what about times when the United States is fighting an undeclared war purely on foreign soil — like the Korean War, the Vietnam War, or the war in Iraq? Do these actions entitle the government to quarter troops in private homes in the United States? Possibly — but then such quartering must be done "in a manner . . . prescribed by law."

PUTTING THE THIRD AMENDMENT IN PERSPECTIVE

Your doorbell rings. You open the door to a troop of smartly uniformed GIs. Their sergeant hands you an official-looking document identifying your home as their billet for an indefinite stay.

How do you react to this prospect? With enthusiasm? With resignation? With horror? Most homeowners would probably be less than enthusiastic about this scenario — and this reaction is reflected in the Third Amendment.

But what is the legal basis for the Third Amendment? Its legal foundation goes all the way back to the old English legal maxim "An Englishman's home is his castle," which traditionally gave homeowners extensive rights to protect their property against intruders — even to the point of being allowed to kill such intruders with impunity. In England this protection has now largely been lost — but it still survives in the United States.

The position in U.S. law generally is that if someone tries to break into your house and you have a reasonable fear that there's a present or immediate danger that the assailant intends to commit a felony or to attack you or your family, then the law allows you to kill the intruder to stop him from entering your house.

This legal rule is based on property rights rather than on any right of privacy. But the concept of privacy actually grew largely out of property rights. In the case of *Griswold v. Connecticut* (1965), which first established a constitutional right to privacy, Justice William O. Douglas, writing for the majority, identified the Third Amendment as creating a "zone of privacy."

- » **in any house:** *House* must be understood as covering any form of residential accommodation, including an apartment, a condominium, or possibly even a dorm-style room — which was the form of residential accommodation at issue in the *Engblom* case.

- » **Owner:** The court in *Engblom* rejected a narrow view of this term in favor of a broad interpretation covering anyone "who owns or lawfully possesses or controls property."

- » **but in a manner to be prescribed by law:** *But* means "except." So, this phrase means that in wartime, no quartering is allowed except in ways laid down by law. What sort of law does this refer to? Although the reference is vague, this presumably refers to legislation passed by Congress.

REMEMBER

A restatement of the Third Amendment would read something like this:

In peacetime, neither the federal government nor any state is permitted to billet troops in any residence without the consent of the owner, tenant, or lawful occupant. In wartime, the federal government and the states may not billet troops in private residences except in ways permitted by an Act of Congress.

Keeping the Government Off Your Back

The Fourth Amendment reads as follows:

The right of the people to be secure in their persons, houses, papers, and effects, against unreasonable searches and seizures, shall not be violated, and no Warrants shall issue, but upon probable cause, supported by Oath or affirmation, and particularly describing the place to be searched, and the persons or things to be seized.

A careful reading reveals that the amendment is in two parts:

- » "unreasonable searches and seizures" are prohibited.

- » Valid warrants require "probable cause," as well as a precise description of "the place to be searched, and the person or things to be seized."

REMEMBER

What's the connection between these two parts? Although the two halves of the amendment are linked by the word "and," there's a logical gap between them. Does the amendment say that a warrant is needed for a search to be lawful? Not really — although it's often taken for granted that the amendment does require a warrant for a search and seizure to be lawful.

Unlike the Third Amendment, the Fourth Amendment is often applied and interpreted. It's most often called into question in criminal cases involving searches of property that result in seizure of evidence that is later intended to be used at trial against a criminal defendant. It has become particularly relevant to issues of national cyber security.

Prohibiting "unreasonable searches and seizures"

At the time of this writing, there's no more topical issue than terrorism, in response to which the executive branch has employed additional powers, some of which have been attacked by critics as violating the Fourth Amendment's prohibition of "unreasonable searches and seizures."

Responding to terrorism

In response to terrorist acts, several orders have been introduced, including:

>> **National emergency:** Immediately after the 9/11 terrorist outrage, President George W. Bush declared a national emergency by Proclamation 7463 of September 14, 2001. This state of national emergency continued for the rest of President Bush's two terms — and was renewed annually by President Obama right through both his terms. President Trump extended it yet further, so that it is still in force at the time of this writing. But what exactly does a state of national emergency mean? In short, it gives the President extraordinary powers — to seize property, call up the National Guard, and hire and fire members of the military at will. It's governed by the National Emergencies Act of 1976, which requires both houses of Congress to meet within six months of an emergency to vote it up or down. That has never happened.

>> **War on terror:** In September 2001, Congress passed a resolution authorizing the President to wage a "war on terror." In accordance with this, in 2002, President Bush signed an unpublicized order authorizing the National Security Agency (NSA) to monitor without warrants the international phone calls and emails of hundreds, or even thousands, of people living in the United States to discover links to foreign terrorist organizations. The NSA has normally done its best to keep out of the public eye — to the point that it earned the nickname "No Such Agency."

>> **Search without a court order:** The USA Patriot Act (an acronym for "Uniting and Strengthening America by Providing Appropriate Tools Required to Intercept and Obstruct Terrorism Act"), signed into law on October 26, 2001, allowed the Federal Bureau of Investigation (FBI) to search telephone, email, and financial records without a court order. In 2011, three key provisions of the act were extended for four years by the PATRIOT Sunsets Extension Act.

Looking at metadata

In the meantime, on April 25, 2013, the U.S. Foreign Intelligence Surveillance Court (FISC), commonly referred to as the FISA Court, issued a secret order requiring Verizon Business Network Services to provide the NSA with a daily feed of all call detail records, for domestic as well as foreign calls.

In June 2013, this secret order was leaked to the press by Edward Snowden, a former employee of an NSA contractor and self-styled "whistleblower," together with thousands of classified NSA documents. In a 2014 NBC interview, Snowden opined that the Fourth Amendment "as it was written no longer exists . . . All of your private records, all of your private communications, all of your transactions, all of your associations, who you talk to, who you love, what you buy, what you read, all of these things can be seized and then held by the government and then searched later for any reason, hardly with[out] any justification, without any reason, without any real oversight, without any real accountability for those who do wrong."

REMEMBER

Snowden's quote paints a frightening picture of "Big Brother" looking over the shoulder of every law-abiding member of society. But upon closer examination, even this lurid description contains some concessions. For example, the phrase "and then searched later" is a tacit admission that what the government "seizes" and "holds" is not data, but only *metadata* — lists of numbers contacting one another, together with the date, time, and duration of the calls, but not the content of the conversations themselves. To be able to read the content, the government needs a federal court order. The same applies to the NSA's mass surveillance on the Internet, which again produces not data but metadata. Metadata can be defined as data about data. As an aid to identifying terrorists, collecting metadata is only the first step. It can't usually be used in litigation.

Findings by the courts

The court decisions on mass surveillance have gone both ways.

VIOLATING THE FOURTH AMENDMENT

In December 2013, U.S. District Judge Richard Leon, in a case called *Klayman v. Obama*, described the NSA's mass collection of metadata of Americans' phone records as "almost-Orwellian" and ruled that the program "likely" violated the Fourth Amendment's prohibition of "unreasonable searches and seizures." The judge accepted the plaintiffs' claim that unless they were given "injunctive relief" (that is, a court order stopping the NSA's collection of their personal phone metadata), they would suffer "irreparable harm." The judge went on: "The Government responds that the public's interest in combating terrorism is of paramount importance — a proposition that I accept without question. But the

Government offers no real explanation as to how granting relief to these plaintiffs would be detrimental to that interest . . . . This case is yet the latest chapter in the Judiciary's continuing challenge to balance the national security interests of the United States with the individual liberties of our citizens."

The judge granted the request for an injunction to stop the NSA from collecting phone metadata on the plaintiffs, but "in light of the significant national security interest at stake and the novelty of the constitutional issues, I will stay my order pending appeal."

Despite his opposition to the government program, the judge quoted a government spokesperson's justification of the program: "According to the declaration submitted by NSA Director of Signals Intelligence Directorate (SID) Teresa H. Shea, the data collected as part of the Bulk Telephony Metadata Program — had it been in place at that time — would have allowed the NSA to determine that a September 11 hijacker living in the United States had contacted a known al Qaeda safe house in Yemen."

UPHOLDING THE FOURTH AMENDMENT

On the other hand, the U.S. District Court for the Southern District of New York in *ACLU v. Clapper*, decided just ten days after *Klayman*, held that there was no infringement of Fourth Amendment rights. The ruling, by Judge William Pauley, a Clinton appointee, was based squarely on *Smith v. Maryland* (1979), the latest U.S. Supreme Court decision in this area, which held that phone users have "no expectation of privacy" for information that they provide to phone companies, as all the metadata collected by the NSA is voluntarily revealed by users to phone companies. Judge Pauley accepted the government's claim that the program had successfully blocked several planned terrorist attacks, and his judgment contained several interesting observations, including the following:

>> "Fifteen different FISC judges have found the metadata collection program lawful a total of thirty-five times since May 2006."

>> "The right to be free from searches and seizures is fundamental, but not absolute. As Justice Jackson famously observed: 'The Bill of Rights is not a suicide pact.' *Terminiello v. City of Chicago* (1949)."

>> "Every day, people voluntarily surrender personal and seemingly private information to transnational corporations, which exploit that data for profit. Few think twice about it, even though it is far more intrusive than bulk telephony metadata collection."

>> "There is no evidence that the Government has used any of the bulk telephony metadata it collected for any purpose other than investigating and disrupting terrorist attacks."

» Describing the program as a "vital tool," Judge Pauley added: "The bulk telephony metadata collection program is subject to executive and congressional oversight, as well as continual monitoring by a dedicated group of judges who serve on the Foreign Intelligence Surveillance Court (FISC)."

» "Like [sic] the 9/11 Commission observed: The choice between liberty and security is a false one, as nothing is more apt to imperil civil liberties than the success of a terrorist attack on American soil."

» Judge Pauley concluded: "For all these reasons, the NSA's bulk telephony metadata collection program is lawful."

However, this eminently sensible and carefully reasoned decision was reversed on appeal by the Second U.S. Circuit Court of Appeals in Manhattan, which on May 7, 2015, held that "the telephone metadata program exceeds the scope of what Congress has authorized and therefore violates [Section 215 of the Patriot Act]." The court did not rule on the constitutionality of the bulk surveillance and declined to halt the program. Noting the pending expiration of relevant parts of the Patriot Act, notably Section 215, it was held that it would be "prudent" to give Congress a chance to decide the matter in view of the national interests at stake.

Parts of the Patriot Act, which had expired at midnight on May 31, 2015, were restored by the U.S.A. Freedom Act passed two days later. Section 215 of the Patriot Act was restored in amended form to stop the NSA from continuing its mass collection of phone metadata, which would now be retained by the phone companies, with the NSA needing to obtain a federal court order to obtain actual data about targeted individuals.

REMEMBER

It's extremely important to distinguish the metadata collected by the NSA from the digital contents of a cellphone. In *Riley v. California* (2014), a unanimous U.S. Supreme Court held that the search and seizure of the digital contents of a cellphone without a warrant is unconstitutional. I discuss this landmark decision in Chapter 23.

Excluding evidence

English common law didn't concern itself with *how* evidence was obtained. Even if evidence was stolen, it was still admissible in court. U.S. law followed suit until 1914, when the Supreme Court ruled that evidence obtained illegally — in particular, contrary to the Fourth Amendment — could not be used.

The Supreme Court first adopted this *exclusionary rule* in the case of *Weeks v. United States.* Missouri police and a federal marshal entered Fremont Weeks's house in his absence and seized a lot of stuff — including some candy! The candy wasn't the problem. The search turned up evidence that Weeks had been sending lottery tickets through the mail — a federal offense. Neither the police nor the federal marshal had a warrant, so the search and seizure was held to be a violation of the Fourth Amendment — and the evidence derived from it was excluded.

The exclusionary rule makes sense because if police know that they can use evidence even if it has been obtained by illegal search and seizure, they can simply ignore the Fourth Amendment. On the other hand, strict enforcement of the exclusionary rule in the 1970s and 1980s wrapped criminal defendants in a protective cocoon and made it harder to get convictions.

It's important to realize that the exclusionary rule doesn't appear anywhere in the U.S. Constitution but is a purely judge-made rule. Justice Benjamin Cardozo, generally thought of as a liberal judge, opposed the rule. In a 1926 New York case, before his elevation to the Supreme Court, Cardozo sarcastically characterized the exclusionary rule as one in which "The criminal is to go free because the constable has blundered."

President Ronald Reagan had a similar take on the rule. Addressing a police convention in 1981, he attacked the exclusionary rule, which is based on the "absurd proposition that a law enforcement error, no matter how technical, can be used to justify throwing out an entire case," even when the defendant was plainly guilty of a serious criminal offense.

An extension of the exclusionary rule may also exclude evidence indirectly obtained with the use of illegally obtained information. The evidence obtained in this situation is called "the fruit of the poisonous tree." This doctrine goes back to the U.S. Supreme Court decision in *Silverthorne Lumber Co. v. United States* (1920). Justice Oliver Wendell Holmes, Jr., for the majority, wrote that allowing evidence which had been gathered as an indirect result of an unconstitutional search and seizure "reduces the Fourth Amendment to a form of words." Chief Justice Edward D. White and Justice Mahlon Pitney dissented. This extension of the exclusionary rule has remained controversial ever since, and its scope is not always clear.

In the 1980 case of *United States v. Crews*, three women were robbed in a women's restroom by a 16-year-old boy. The robber's description was circulated, and he was picked up by police ostensibly for truancy. He was later charged with armed robbery. His victims identified him in a court-ordered lineup. But his lawyers argued that the identification evidence should be excluded as "fruit of the poisonous tree" because it derived from the initial arrest, for which there was no probable cause. The District of Columbia Court of Appeals bought this argument. But a unanimous U.S. Supreme Court disagreed and allowed the identification evidence to stand. Justice William Brennan, writing for the Court, made the point that the identification evidence was independent of the original truancy arrest.

The U.S. Supreme Court recognizes that the exclusionary rule is "a judicially created remedy designed to safeguard Fourth Amendment rights generally through its deterrent effect, rather than a personal constitutional right of the party aggrieved." On this basis, the Court has carved out more and more exceptions to the exclusionary rule. Here are some of these exceptions:

>> **The exclusionary rule doesn't apply to evidence before a grand jury.** The Supreme Court decided this in *United States v. Calandra* in 1974.

>> **When law enforcement can enter premises without a warrant.** "Exigent circumstances" allow law enforcement to enter premises without a warrant where there is imminent danger to life or serious damage to property, to prevent the escape of a suspect, "or some other consequence improperly frustrating legitimate law enforcement efforts" (*U.S. v. McConney*, 9th Circuit, 1984).

>> **Evidence unlawfully obtained by a private person is admissible.** The Fourth Amendment affords protection only against government agents.

>> **Evidence obtained illegally is admissible if it would have been found legally anyway.** Here's an example of this exception to the exclusionary rule: On Christmas Eve 1968, Robert Anthony Williams abducted and murdered a 10-year-old girl. He confessed to the police and pointed out to them where he had hidden the body. Because the police had agreed not to question Williams until his attorney was present, the finding of the body was technically a violation of Williams's Fourth Amendment rights. A strict application of the exclusionary rule would have made the body and the autopsy inadmissible at Williams's trial — as a result of which, a brutal killer would probably have walked. Fortunately, however, the Supreme Court decided in *Nix v. Williams* in 1984 that this evidence was admissible because the police would inevitably have found the body anyway.

>> **Evidence obtained from an independent legal source is admissible.** This exception to the exclusionary rule is similar to the previous exception. Here's an example: Police followed suspects into an apartment without a warrant. One of the suspects was found to be in possession of cocaine and was immediately arrested. Two officers remained in the apartment until a search warrant was issued — 19 hours later! *After* getting the warrant, the officers found cocaine and records of drug dealing. The case reached the Supreme Court in 1984 under the name of *Segura v. United States.* The Court ruled that "whether the initial entry was illegal or not is irrelevant to the admissibility of the evidence, and exclusion of the evidence is not warranted as 'fruit of the poisonous tree'." The court reached this eminently sensible decision only by the narrowest of margins, 5 votes to 4.

»» Good faith is an exception to an unduly strict interpretation of the rules.
A literal application of the exclusionary rule can easily result in injustice by giving undue protection to criminal defendants. The good faith exception is a welcome commonsense counterblast to the exclusionary rule — which, it must always be remembered, is just a judge-made rule anyway. A good example of this exception is the 1984 case of *United States v. Leon.* After an anonymous tip, the police placed Alberto Leon under surveillance. On this basis, the police got a warrant from a judge to search Leon's house. They found large quantities of illegal drugs there, and Leon was charged. His lawyers objected that the information on which the search warrant was based was too vague, so the warrant should be set aside and the evidence obtained under the warrant should be excluded. But the Supreme Court ruled that, even if the police should not have been given a search warrant, they acted in good faith, so the evidence obtained under the warrant was admissible in court. In the words of Justice Byron White, writing for the majority, "Indiscriminate application of the exclusionary rule may well generate disrespect for the law and administration of justice."

Rewriting the Fourth Amendment

The Fourth Amendment applies only to government searches and seizures. But which government? Does the amendment apply only to the feds, or to the states as well?

The Sixth, Tenth, and Eleventh amendments specifically mention the states — but not the Fourth. Was James Madison, who drafted the whole of the Bills of Rights (see Figure 16-1), such a sloppy thinker as to assume that the Fourth Amendment applied to the states without bothering to say so in so many words? No way!

So how come the Supreme Court now says that the Fourth Amendment — and most of the rest of the Bill of Rights too — binds the states as well as the feds? This ruling is based on the Due Process Clause of the Fourteenth Amendment, which reads as follows:

> *nor shall any State deprive any person of life, liberty, or property, without due process of law.*

This clause sure binds the states. But can the little phrase "without due process of law" really burden the states with the obligations of much of the rest of the Bill of Rights?

FIGURE 16-1:
James Madison,
fourth President
and author of
the Bill of Rights.
You would never
guess from this
portrait that
he stood only
5 ft. 4 in. tall.

Source: Portrait by John Vanderlyn

**IN MY
OPINION**

This question opens up a huge can of worms labeled the *doctrine of incorporation*, which can be blamed on the vague wording of the Due Process Clause. For a full discussion of this controversial doctrine, see Chapter 17. The draftsmen of the Fourteenth Amendment, which was ratified in 1868, weren't in the same ballpark — or even in the same league — as James Madison. But could even these little league draftsmen have been *that* dumb that they just assumed they'd incorporated the bulk of the Bill of Rights in one vague five-word clause? Most unlikely.

The thinking behind the draftsmen of the Fourteenth can be seen from the so-called *Blaine Amendment.* In 1875 — just seven years after the ratification of the Fourteenth Amendment — James G. Blaine, a leading politician who had been a member of Congress during the passing of the Fourteenth Amendment, proposed a constitutional amendment that passed the House of Representatives but was four votes shy of the necessary two-thirds majority in the Senate.

The Blaine Amendment read:

> *No State shall make any law respecting an establishment of religion . . .*

REMEMBER

Familiar? Sure. The wording is lifted straight from the First Amendment but applies specifically to the states. This wording can mean only one thing: that Blaine and the majority of Congress did not think that the First Amendment already applied to the states through the Fourteenth Amendment.

Despite this evidence, in 1949 the Supreme Court decided in *Wolf v. Colorado* that the Fourth Amendment was incorporated into the Due Process Clause of the Fourteenth Amendment and that the Fourth Amendment therefore applied to the states as well as to the federal government — but that the exclusionary rule did not apply to the states. So, the states were bound by the Fourth Amendment, but any evidence found by state police in violation of the Fourth could still be used in court!

In 1961, the high court abandoned this position for a more extreme but more logical position in *Mapp v. Ohio,* which brought the states' obligations under the Fourth Amendment into line with the feds' obligations. The Court ruled that "all evidence obtained by searches and seizures in violation of the Constitution is, by [the Fourth Amendment] inadmissible in a state court."

This decision was one of many made by the Supreme Court under Chief Justice Earl Warren that favored criminal defendants. Although the wording of this ruling looks clear enough, it presented the Court with the problem of how and when to exclude evidence in individual cases. I discuss the exceptions to the exclusionary rule earlier in this chapter.

Defining "probable cause"

The concept of probable cause holds the key to the second part of the Fourth Amendment, which says that "no Warrants shall issue, but upon probable cause."

The word *but* here means "except." *Warrant* refers to a legal document issued by a judge or magistrate authorizing law enforcement officers to do something that would otherwise be against the law — in particular, to search and seize evidence for use in a criminal prosecution.

So this clause means that a valid warrant needs to be based on probable cause. But what is the meaning of *probable cause?* In 1878, the Supreme Court defined it like this:

> *If the facts and circumstances before the officer are such as to warrant a man of prudence and caution in believing that the offense has been committed, it is sufficient.*

But, "good faith on the part of the arresting officer is not enough" to constitute probable cause:

> *If subjective good faith alone were the test, the protections of the Fourth Amendment would evaporate, and the people would be 'secure in their persons, houses, papers, and effects,' only in the discretion of the police.*

The case of *Illinois v. Gates,* heard by the Supreme Court in 1983, is a good example of the commonsense approach now adopted by the Court on the question of probable cause. The police received an anonymous tip accusing a husband and wife of interstate drug trafficking. After finding that the couple's movements conformed to the pattern described in the anonymous letter, the police got a search warrant and found drugs and weapons in the couple's car and house. The couple challenged the legality of the search on the ground that the anonymous letter couldn't constitute probable cause. However, the high court ruled that the question of probable cause could not be reduced to a formula but depended on "the totality of the circumstances" — and in this case, the anonymous tip-off plus police corroboration of some of its details did amount to probable cause. Justice William Rehnquist put the whole question in context by remarking that "[t]he most basic function of any government [is] to provide for the security of the individual and of his property."

Forbidding police fishing expeditions

The second half of the Fourth Amendment reads as follows:

> *no Warrants shall issue, but upon probable cause, supported by Oath or affirmation, and particularly describing the place to be searched, and the persons or things to be seized.*

Why are there such detailed requirements for a valid warrant? To answer this question, we have to go back to colonial times.

In 1765, Lord Camden, Chief Justice of the Court of Common Pleas in England, handed down a historic decision against the British Government known as *Entick v. Carrington.* Three government agents had entered the house of John Entick, a radical journalist, armed with a "general warrant" issued by the Secretary of State allowing the agents to search through all of Entick's papers and possessions. The agents spent several hours doing just that.

Lord Camden's judgment was in strong terms. Here is an extract from it:

> *The great end for which men entered into society, was to secure their property . . . By the laws of England, every invasion of private property, be it ever so minute, is a trespass.*

From that time onward, general warrants were banned — and couldn't be issued by the government itself anyway. To conduct a lawful search and seizure, the government had to get a warrant from a judge on the basis of a sworn statement specifying the place that was to be searched and the persons or things to be seized.

The Fourth Amendment essentially repeats these requirements, as a safeguard of the liberty of the individual against the government. But too literal an application of these provisions can hinder law enforcement. So it's fortunate that in recent years, the U.S. Supreme Court has relaxed the rigor of its application of these requirements.

For example, in the 1987 case of *Maryland v. Garrison*, police intending to search an apartment occupied by the McWebbs had a warrant specifying "third floor apartment." In fact, there were two apartments on the third floor, although the police didn't realize this fact at the time. The police accidentally entered the wrong apartment — and found drugs and cash. They arrested the occupant, Mr. Garrison, who objected that the warrant wasn't valid.

The Supreme Court rejected this contention and held that the search and seizure were lawful. In the words of Justice John Paul Stevens, writing for the majority:

> *There is no question that the warrant was valid and was supported by probable cause . . . Prior to the officers' discovery of the factual mistake, they perceived McWebb's apartment and the third-floor premises as one and the same; therefore their execution of the warrant reasonably included the entire third floor. Under either interpretation of the warrant, the officers' conduct was consistent with a reasonable effort to ascertain and identify the place intended to be searched within the meaning of the Fourth Amendment.*

Searching people or premises without a warrant?

The Fourth Amendment says that a warrant is required for a lawful search and seizure to take place — or does it? The two halves of the amendment are linked by the word *and*, but not by any clear, logical connection.

In certain circumstances, the Supreme Court is prepared to allow evidence in on the basis of probable cause alone — even in the absence of a warrant. *Terry v. Ohio,* heard by the Supreme Court in 1968, is a good example of this approach. A very experienced police officer observed two men walking up and down past a store window and stopping to look into the same window no fewer than 24 times in the space of a few minutes. The officer suspected the men of "casing a job, a stickup." He stopped the men, patted them down, and found a concealed revolver on each of them. The question before the Supreme Court was whether the revolver found on one of the men was admissible in evidence against him — because the police officer who arrested him did not have a warrant. The high court held that the evidence of the revolver was admissible in court because the men's suspicious behavior constituted probable cause, and in the circumstances no warrant was needed.

Can the police ever search premises without a warrant? Yes. In 1999, in *Flippo v. West Virginia,* the Supreme Court ruled that "police may make warrantless entries on to premises if they reasonably believe a person is in need of immediate aid and may make prompt warrantless searches of a homicide scene for possible other victims or a killer on the premises." But the Court rejected a general "murder scene exception" allowing the police to conduct a warrantless search of premises just because a homicide had been committed there.

The high court case of *Hudson v. Michigan* (2006) is the latest Supreme Court consideration of the so-called "knock and announce" requirement of police officers to give residents an opportunity to open the door prior to a search. This requirement is not contained in the U.S. Constitution itself, but it's codified in the United States Code governing Fourth Amendment searches by the feds. Most states have codified the rule into their own statutes. In *Hudson,* six Detroit police officers armed with a search warrant entered Hudson's home through the unlocked front door "three to five seconds" after calling out "police, search warrant." The State of Michigan conceded that this amounted to a breach of the knock-and-announce rule. But the question before the Supreme Court was whether the evidence found in such circumstances should be excluded. Justice Antonin Scalia, writing for the majority of 5 to 4, held that violation of the knock-and-announce rule alone was not enough to suppress evidence.

The Supreme Court by a majority of 5 to 3 limited the scope of the exclusionary rule in *Utah v. Strieff* (2016). Police, suspecting Edward Strieff of a drug offense, stopped him on the street. Finding an outstanding arrest warrant against him for a traffic violation, officers conducted a search incidental to his arrest and found drug paraphernalia and methamphetamine. The prosecution admitted that the stop was unlawful but successfully argued that the evidence seized during the detention should not be excluded. Strieff pleaded guilty to the drugs charges but appealed against the court's decision to admit the evidence. In the Supreme Court, Justice Clarence Thomas, writing for the majority (comprising not only the "conservative" members of the court but also Justice Kennedy and the usually "liberal" Justice Breyer), held that the evidence was admissible because "the discovery of a valid arrest warrant was a sufficient intervening event to break the causal chain between the unlawful stop and the discovery of drug-related evidence on Strieff's person." Justice Sonia Sotomayor, in her dissenting opinion, argued that the evidence should have been excluded and that "unlawful police stops corrode all our civil liberties and threaten all our lives." A less extreme dissent was expressed by Justice Kagan (joined by Justice Ginsburg), in which she contended that the majority decision "creates unfortunate incentives for the police."

IN THIS CHAPTER

» Avoiding self-incrimination

» Indicting suspects with a grand jury

» Banning double jeopardy

» Disentangling due process

» Understanding the incorporation doctrine

» Seizing private property for public use

Chapter **17**

Taking the Fifth — and a Bit of the Fourteenth

The Fifth Amendment, ratified in 1791, is one of the meatiest of all the articles of the Constitution, and one of the most controversial. It deals with some heavy-hitting issues:

» The so-called "Great Right" against self-incrimination

» The role of the grand jury

» Double jeopardy

» Due process

» Eminent domain

Due process is picked up in the Fourteenth Amendment, ratified in 1868. For that reason, I tackle part of the Fourteenth in this chapter as well. (I give the rest of the Fourteenth Amendment its due in Chapter 21.) But first we need to give our rapt attention to the Fifth.

Invoking the "Great Right" against Self-Incrimination

If you watch movies or TV shows, you've heard of the Fifth Amendment. (If you don't watch movies or TV shows, I'm guessing you're better read and more muscular than the rest of us.) "I'll take da Fift(h)" is the gangster's stock in trade. Why? Because the Fifth Amendment doesn't allow anyone to be "compelled in any criminal case to be a witness against himself."

REMEMBER

This is the "Great Right" that gives protection against self-incrimination. If you're asked a question in court (or in some other formal proceeding) and your reply could amount to an admission of a crime on your part, you can refuse to answer.

Normally, you have to answer any question that you're asked in court, and lying under oath can expose you to the serious charge of perjury. The Fifth Amendment gives you a way out under certain circumstances. The formal way of invoking the Fifth is by saying, "I refuse to answer the question on the ground that it might incriminate me." A witness may claim this privilege in criminal cases as well as civil cases — if the witness is afraid that his answer is likely to expose him to a criminal charge.

Some lawyers advise their clients to take the Fifth even if they're innocent. However, there is a catch: Taking the Fifth is often interpreted as an admission of guilt. For example, the label *Fifth Amendment Communists* was attached to people who refused to answer questions before the House Un-American Activities Committee just after World War II. In *Baxter v. Palmigiano* (1976), a unanimous Supreme Court held that adverse inferences could be drawn against parties to civil suits who took the Fifth in response to "probative evidence offered against them."

CONTROVERSY

The Fifth Amendment, like the rest of the Bill of Rights, was originally taken to apply only to federal law. To what extent it now applies to state law (if at all) has been the subject of heated debate. I present the basics of this debate in a section later in the chapter called "Agonizing over Due Process."

THE MIRANDA WARNING

The Fifth Amendment clearly states that you can't be forced to give evidence against yourself. But if you choose to answer an incriminating question, you must accept the consequences. Do you have to be warned about this fact in advance? Not in a court of law. But in 1966, the U.S. Supreme Court decided that you do have to be warned if you are being questioned by police. The case in question was *Miranda v. Arizona,* and the statement a police officer must make to a suspect is the well-known Miranda warning:

> *You have the right to remain silent. Anything you say may be used against you in a court of law. You have the right to an attorney. If you cannot afford an attorney, one will be provided for you.*

The wording varies slightly from state to state, but unless you're cautioned in proper form, any statement you make to the police should be thrown out by the court.

Not everyone has been thrilled by this requirement. In 2000, Chief Justice William Rehnquist stated the problem with the Miranda warning this way: "Statements which may be by no means involuntary, made by a defendant who is aware of his 'rights,' may nonetheless be excluded and a guilty defendant go free as a result."

In 1968, Congress passed a law seeking to reverse the worst excesses of the Miranda rule. If a confession was voluntary, said Congress, it should be allowed as evidence even if no Miranda warning was given. But in 2000, *Dickerson v. U.S.* set the congressional law aside and put the Miranda rule back in the driving seat. The argument was that the Miranda rule had become part of the Constitution, and the law that Congress passed was therefore unconstitutional.

I would argue (as others, like Justice Antonin Scalia, have done) that the Miranda rule isn't part of the Constitution; it's simply *based* on the Constitution. But for now, the Miranda warning is required prior to any police interrogation.

Peeking Behind the Closed Doors of the Grand Jury

The opening clause of the Fifth Amendment actually isn't related to self-incrimination. Instead, it deals with the grand jury system. It reads, in part:

> *No person shall be held to answer for a capital, or otherwise infamous crime, unless on a presentment or indictment of a Grand Jury . . .*

The words "infamous crime" have been interpreted to mean that a grand jury is required only for felonies — not for misdemeanors.

The grand jury is a wonderful American institution. Like so many others, it long predates the U.S. Constitution. Its origins lie in the earliest days of English Common Law, even before the Norman Conquest of 1066. By 1368, grand juries had taken on something very like their modern American form, but they were abolished in England in 1933.

The grand jury gets its name from its size. A regular trial jury usually has 12 members, but grand juries are generally bigger. Federal grand juries range from 16 to 23 members. However, the real difference between a grand jury and a regular jury is not size but function. Regular juries are *trial* juries. In criminal cases they decide whether the defendant is guilty or not guilty. Grand juries are not trial juries. They come in at a much earlier stage to decide whether a suspect should be indicted with a crime at all.

It's worth noting that although this part of the Fifth Amendment applies only to federal law, all the states have provisions for grand juries. However, their use is obligatory in only 22 states. The alternative to a grand jury is an adversarial preliminary hearing before a trial court judge.

Deciding whether to indict

The chief function of a grand jury is to decide whether to bring criminal charges against a suspect. In the federal courts (and in many states), nobody can be charged with a felony unless a grand jury has decided to indict that person. (However, in certain states it's possible for the district attorney to file what's called an *information* or *accusation* as an alternative to a grand jury indictment. This step is followed by a preliminary hearing before a judge at which the defendant can be represented by counsel.)

REMEMBER

Grand juries generally do the prosecutor's bidding. Sol Wachtler, former Chief Judge of New York, said in 1985 that a prosecutor could get a grand jury to indict a ham sandwich! A grand jury is very much the prosecutor's show, and its proceedings are secret. No judge is present. The prosecutor presides and can call witnesses, forcing them to come by serving them with a subpoena. Here are some other ways a grand jury hearing differs from a regular trial:

>> The normal rules of evidence are relaxed. For example, the usually strict "exclusionary rule," which makes any evidence inadmissible if it's obtained

by an "unreasonable search and seizure," doesn't apply. (See Chapter 16 for more about this rule.) The practical effect of this is that a prosecutor can use evidence to secure a grand jury indictment that later may not be admissible at the trial on the same charges.

» Suspects aren't allowed to call witnesses or cross-examine prosecution witnesses, but a suspect can be called to testify.

» A suspect or a witness before a grand jury can have a lawyer, but the lawyer can't be inside the jury room! However, generally the suspect or witness is free to leave the proceedings to consult with counsel.

» A grand jury witness is normally given a warning against self-incrimination, but if the warning isn't given and the witness lies under oath, the witness can still be prosecuted for perjury. As Justice William Brennan noted in *U.S. v. Mandujano* (1976), "Our legal system provides methods for challenging the Government's right to ask questions — lying is not one of them."

» In *Branzburg v. Hayes* (1972), a 5–4 majority of the Supreme Court decided that a journalist summoned to testify before a grand jury could not use the First Amendment's protection of press freedom as a defense, provided the government could "convincingly show a substantial relation between the information sought and a subject of overriding and compelling state interest." Does this ruling apply to testimony at a trial as well? So far, surprisingly, this has never been tested in the U.S. Supreme Court.

Victimizing suspects or protecting victims?

The grand jury system has been criticized as unfair to defendants and suspects. After all, they can't be represented by counsel, can't call witnesses, and can't cross-examine prosecution witnesses. Some critics don't like the ease with which prosecutions can be achieved as a result. They particularly don't like the control that prosecutors usually have over grand juries.

There's no doubt that the grand jury process is one-sided. But many people see the grand jury system as acting in the interests of victims of crime, providing a small but essential counterbalance to the elaborate apparatus of protection surrounding criminal suspects and defendants. (For a taste of this apparatus, see the sidebar "The Miranda warning" earlier in this chapter.)

Avoiding Double Jeopardy

I'm not talking about the game show here. *Double jeopardy* means being tried twice for the same crime, and the second clause of the Fifth Amendment forbids it:

> *nor shall any person be subject for the same offence to be twice put in jeopardy of life or limb.*

As with the rest of the Bill of Rights, the ban on double jeopardy originally applied only to federal courts. But in 1969, the U.S. Supreme Court "incorporated" this guarantee into the Due Process Clause of the Fourteenth Amendment, making it applicable to state courts too. (To get a sense of the debate behind this decision, see the upcoming section in this chapter headed "Agonizing over Due Process.")

Applying the principle

Protection against double jeopardy is way older than the U.S. Constitution; it can be traced back to ancient Greece and Rome. There are three practical applications of the principle:

REMEMBER

>> If you're *acquitted* (found not guilty) of a crime, you can't be put on trial for it again. This is by far the most important aspect of the principle, which is confined to criminal cases.

>> You can't be tried again for a crime of which you have been convicted.

>> If you've already been punished for committing a certain crime, you can't be given a second punishment for that same offense.

Mistrials are an exception. A *mistrial* occurs when the judge cancels the trial — usually for some procedural reason — before the jury has returned a verdict. If a mistrial occurs, a retrial can be ordered. Another exception is when the original trial is a *nullity* — for example, if a defendant bribes the judge or members of the jury to achieve an acquittal. This offense makes the trial a nullity, or a non-trial. It's as if the original trial never took place.

Allowing for an end to litigation

It seems only fair that after you've faced the music and the music has finally stopped, that should be the end of the matter. Especially if you've been acquitted, it would seem wrong for the same crime to hang over your head for the rest of your life.

However, some arguments against this principle carry weight. Say you've been tried and acquitted of a particular crime and new evidence later comes to light pointing to your guilt. Wouldn't it be fair to your victim for you to be hauled before the court again?

It may not seem fair in every instance, but there's an ancient principle of law going back to Roman times that "it's in the public interest for there to be an end to litigation." In other words, it's not good to keep flogging a dead horse. Doing so would result in an intolerable situation for successful defendants, who would have all their old charges hanging over them indefinitely, or until the statute of limitations ran out. (Or until they were retried and convicted.)

REMEMBER

Because of this ancient principle, repackaged in the Fifth Amendment, if someone literally gets away with murder, there's nothing to stop that person from crowing about it. Oh, except that the victim's family can take him or her to the cleaners in a civil wrongful death suit. This situation is not considered to be double jeopardy because the parties aren't the same as in a criminal prosecution and the standard of proof is different.

Let me explain: A criminal case is brought by the prosecution against a named defendant. In federal cases the prosecutor is the United States, and in state criminal cases the prosecutor is the state (often designated "The People" or sometimes "The Commonwealth"). The burden of proof is on the prosecution, and the standard of proof is "beyond a reasonable doubt," which is a very high standard indeed.

In a civil suit, the case is brought by the victim or the victim's family, which bears the burden of proof but on a much lower standard. The burden of proof is to demonstrate that a "preponderance of the evidence" indicates the defendant did the deed, which just means that it's more likely than not.

O.J. Simpson provides us with probably the best-known example of the difference between the two types of cases. Simpson was found not guilty of murder in a criminal trial but was later found liable for the death of his ex-wife Nicole Brown Simpson and Ron Goldman in a civil wrongful death suit.

Jeopardizing "life or limb"

The Fifth Amendment clause on double jeopardy talks about being "put in jeopardy of life or limb." What's with this "life or limb" business? You may interpret that to mean that double jeopardy applies only to really serious crimes. "Life" refers to the death penalty. But "limb" refers to old-fashioned punishments such as the *stocks* — a wooden frame used to torture and humiliate criminals found guilty of even quite minor offenses. So double jeopardy covers misdemeanors as well as felonies.

In general, what this clause means is that you can't be tried twice for the same offense, no matter whether you were found guilty or acquitted the first time around.

Agonizing over Due Process

If the courts have made a meal of double jeopardy, they have made a gargantuan, indigestible, multi-course banquet of due process. The Fifth Amendment wording goes like this:

No person shall be . . . deprived of life, liberty, or property, without due process of law.

This wording was picked up in the Fourteenth Amendment, ratified in 1868 during the Reconstruction period just after the Civil War:

nor shall any State deprive any person of life, liberty, or property, without due process of law.

Why was it necessary for due process to be repeated in the Fourteenth Amendment when it was already included in the Fifth Amendment? The Fifth deals with federal law, and the Fourteenth with the states. Other than that difference, the Due Process clauses in the two amendments are practically identical.

Trying to define the term

What does *due process* mean, anyway? In 1884, the Supreme Court defined due process really broadly. Ready for a mouthful?

[A]ny legal proceeding enforced by public authority, whether sanctioned by age and custom, or newly devised in the discretion of the legislative power, in furtherance of the general public good, which regards and preserves these principles of liberty and justice, must be held to be due process of law.

REMEMBER

Let me help you out: *Due process* is really just an old-fashioned way of saying "proper procedure." The Due Process clauses in both amendments originally meant no more and no less than this: You can't be executed, imprisoned, or fined, or have your property confiscated, except after a fair trial conducted according to proper legal procedure. As Supreme Court Justice Felix Frankfurter put it: "The history of American freedom is, in no small measure, the history of procedure."

The next question is, what exactly is proper legal procedure? In 1914, the U.S. Supreme Court gave a short answer to this important question: "The fundamental requisite of due process of law is the opportunity to be heard." This explanation may seem too narrow, but it happens to be one of the two principles of natural justice that have come down to us from antiquity (the other being the rule against bias, which is covered by the Sixth Amendment). *Natural justice* is a philosophy that says that God or nature has laid down certain moral standards that form the basis of civilized society. Thomas Jefferson was strongly influenced by this philosophy. This influence is clear in the Declaration of Independence, of which Jefferson was the main author. (I discuss the Declaration of Independence in Chapter 2.)

Triggering due process

Two important questions emerge:

>> What's needed to trigger a due process claim?

>> How much due process is actually due?

Let's consider an example. A security guard in Cleveland wrote on his job application that he'd never been convicted of a felony. He got the job. But it turned out that he'd been convicted of grand larceny, which sure is a felony. (The guard claimed he thought it was only a misdemeanor!) He was fired without being given an opportunity to explain or defend himself.

In 1985, the U.S. Supreme Court heard the case, known as *Cleveland Board of Education v. Loudermill*. It concluded that, because this man's employment could be terminated only "for cause," this meant that it was a property right within the Fourteenth Amendment, which triggered due process. But the extent of due process due to him was only the right to be heard before dismissal — not anything more. What does this example mean? Essentially two things:

>> The word "property" in the Due Process clauses of the Fifth and Fourteenth amendments has a very broad meaning. It can even include possession of a job.

>> There's a whole range of due process rights. The issue is decided on a case-by-case basis, which makes sense but which also makes it difficult to predict what a court will decide in any particular situation.

At the beginning of this section I asked, "What's needed to trigger a due process claim?" Back in 1855, the U.S. Supreme Court said that in order to determine whether a process is due process or not, the court must "examine the Constitution itself, to see whether this process be in conflict with any of its provisions." An unfair trial, for example, is always contrary to due process. In addition, there are some rights that don't appear to be connected with due process but are now regarded by the U.S. Supreme Court as protected by due process:

>> Privacy

>> Contraception

>> Abortion

>> Same-sex marriage

These all belong to *substantive due process,* which I discuss next.

Wrestling with substantive due process

Due process is about procedure, right? Right. But a significant body of judicial opinion indicates that it can also be about the substance of a law. The doctrine of *substantive due process,* which emerged as early as the mid-19th century, says that due process is not just about *how* something should be done but also *what* should be done.

Substantive due process has undergone some important changes. Justice Hugo Black, who always opposed substantive due process of any kind, particularly criticized the old-style approach to due process. In Black's words, this approach "authorizes courts to hold laws unconstitutional when they believe the legislature has acted unwisely. . .." In other words, the courts gave themselves the right to second-guess Congress. If the Supreme Court thought Congress had passed a law that the Court didn't agree with, the Court declared that law unconstitutional. Black opposed this approach because he believed it was unconstitutional for the courts to "substitute their social and economic beliefs for the judgment of legislative bodies, who are elected to pass laws."

REMEMBER

Substantive due process greatly expanded the power of the courts — especially the U.S. Supreme Court. The doctrine gave the courts the power to examine not only the procedure used to enforce a law but also the actual content of the law.

Noting some famous early cases

Possibly the earliest use of substantive due process was in the notorious *Dred Scott* case in 1856. Dred Scott was a slave who had moved with his master to various free states and territories. At that time, certain states were designated as slave states and others as free. Dred Scott claimed that after he'd breathed the free air of Illinois, he became a free man and couldn't then be reduced to slavery again on return to a slave state. The Supreme Court rejected this claim, saying that the Fifth Amendment's Due Process Clause protected a slave owner from being deprived of his property — including his slaves — just because he'd brought it into a free state.

The 1905 case *Lochner v. New York* put substantive due process on the map. In those days, journeymen bakers worked very long hours in unhygienic conditions, often in basements. New York State passed the Bakeshop Act of 1895 limiting work to a maximum of 10 hours a day or 60 hours per week. Joseph Lochner owned a small bakery and was fined $50 because one of his employees had worked more than 60 hours in a particular week.

After losing two appeals before the New York courts, Lochner took his case to the U.S. Supreme Court. He argued successfully that the Bakeshop Act was contrary to the Due Process Clause of the Fourteenth Amendment because it infringed on Lochner's "liberty of contract." The Bakeshop Act was struck down as unconstitutional. This is an example of substantive due process because it addresses the fact that certain rights we hold can't be taken away from us — in this case, Lochner's right to enter into contracts with his employees.

Lochner gave its name to an era because for the next 32 years, a conservative brand of substantive due process dominated the Supreme Court. State laws setting minimum wages, banning child labor, or regulating the banking, insurance, or transportation industries were declared unconstitutional on the basis of substantive due process.

Threatening the New Deal

This trend reached a climax during Franklin Delano Roosevelt's New Deal. In a radio fireside chat, FDR said that the Constitution was "so simple and practical that it can always meet extraordinary needs." But the President hadn't reckoned with the Supreme Court. After initially accepting some New Deal legislation, the Court struck down the provisions of Roosevelt's economic recovery program one by one. The cases threatened doom for the New Deal, which had been endorsed by an unprecedented proportion of the popular vote in the 1932 election.

FDR wasn't about to allow a bunch of unelected judges to trample the New Deal. He condemned the Court for reverting to "the horse-and-buggy definition of interstate commerce" and came up with a novel plan to counter the judges. Cleverly using the Constitution against the Court itself, he proposed to increase the size of the Supreme Court — which was not fixed by the Constitution — by adding one new justice (up to a maximum of six) for every justice over the age of 70, plus up to 44 new lower court judges.

FDR was met with a barrage of criticism for this bold plan. Even the liberal justices on the Supreme Court, who mostly supported the New Deal, were up in arms. But the mere announcement of the proposal was enough to achieve the desired effect. Swing-vote Justice Owen Roberts went over to the President's side in what was quickly labeled as "The Switch in Time that Saved Nine" (that is, the existing size of the Supreme Court). In 1937, the Court upheld a Washington state minimum wage law that was practically identical to one declared unconstitutional just a year before. The Court similarly upheld the constitutionality of the National Labor Relations Board Act, which created an agency charged with investigating claims of unfair labor practices.

The conservative economic phase of substantive due process was over.

Reemerging in recent decades

In 1965, a new-style substantive due process doctrine appeared thanks to *Griswold v. Connecticut.* The question before the U.S. Supreme Court was the constitutionality of an "uncommonly silly law" (as Justice Potter Stewart called it) banning contraceptives. The Court held that it was unconstitutional. Justice William O. Douglas wrote that though the law in question didn't exactly breach any express right in the Bill of Rights, it offended against a right of privacy.

But Justice John Marshall Harlan put the matter firmly on the basis of the Due Process Clause of the Fourteenth Amendment. He wrote:

> *In my view, the proper constitutional inquiry in this case is whether this Connecticut statute infringes the Due Process Clause of the Fourteenth Amendment . . . I believe that it does.*

Justice Hugo Black disagreed with Harlan's broad application of the Fourteenth Amendment, arguing that even if the Supreme Court believes that certain laws are "unreasonable, unwise, arbitrary, capricious or irrational," the Court shouldn't have such broad authority to strike down those laws. Otherwise, the Court would have too much power, which would "jeopardize the separation of governmental powers that the Framers set up and . . . threaten to take away much of the power of States to govern themselves. . .."

Despite Black's dissent, the new-style substantive due process doctrine continued to gain ground, most notably in *Roe v. Wade* (1973), which struck down two anti-abortion state laws. The argument put forward by Justice Harry Blackmun, writing for the majority, was that a woman's right to choose is based on her right of privacy, which in turn is based on the Due Process Clause of the Fourteenth Amendment.

Continuing to stoke controversy

More recently, some Supreme Court justices, notably Antonin Scalia and Clarence Thomas, argued against substantive due process, which Scalia called an oxymoron. In 1994, he wrote that "the Due Process Clause guarantees no substantive rights, but only (as it says) process."

The accepted position is probably still that expressed by Chief Justice William Rehnquist in 1997: acceptance of substantive due process within closely defined limits. But I have no doubt that the Court will continue to wrestle with the issue of whether the Constitution permits courts to create or take away rights under the auspices of substantive due process.

Opening Up the Incorporation Debate

Before the ratification of the Fourteenth Amendment, the U.S. Supreme Court understood that the Bill of Rights applied only to federal law and not to the states. But the Fourteenth Amendment changed that understanding for some people, and it opened a can of worms that clogged the legal system for quite some time.

Does the Bill of Rights apply to the states?

Supreme Court Justice Hugo Black, who served on the Court from 1937 to 1971, argued that the first section of the Fourteenth Amendment — the section that deals with due process — *incorporates* the bulk of the first eight amendments to the Constitution, making all those guarantees of the Bill of Rights binding on the states as well as on the federal government. In other words, because the Fourteenth Amendment mentions due process as a protection under state law, it also provides protection under state law for freedom of speech and the right to bear arms; against unwarranted search and seizure, self-incrimination, and double jeopardy; and for all the other provisions included in the Bill of Rights.

Black prided himself on taking every word of the Constitution at face value. "The Constitution is my legal bible," he would say, referring to the well-thumbed copy that he kept on him at all times. "I cherish every word of it from the first to the last."

IN MY OPINION

But here's the flaw with Black's argument: The Fifth Amendment guarantees due process as one of several separate rights. Nothing in the Fifth Amendment suggests that due process encompasses all the other rights contained in that amendment, let alone in the whole of the Bill of Rights. So why should due process in the Fourteenth Amendment be any different?

If due process in the Fifth Amendment had an all-embracing nature, this fact would surely have been indicated by the wording. Instead, it's listed as one of several guarantees, each on the same level as the others.

If the Framers of the Fourteenth Amendment had wanted to incorporate all the Bill of Rights guarantees, they could easily have listed them or otherwise indicated that those rights were to be applicable to the states as well as to the federal government. Instead, the Due Process Clause of the Fifth Amendment is the only provision in the Bill of Rights repeated in the Fourteenth Amendment.

There's a rule of interpretation that lawyers use, known in Latin as *expressio unius est exclusio alterius,* or "the expression of one thing amounts to the exclusion of another." When a kid asks, "Mommy, can I have some cake?" and the reply comes back "You may have a cookie," this means not only what it says *(expressio unius)* but also that the kid is not allowed any cake *(exclusio alterius).* In the Constitution, the specific mention of due process in the Fourteenth Amendment amounts to an exclusion of all the other guarantees referred to in the Bill of Rights.

Watching selective incorporation in action

The Supreme Court didn't buy Justice Black's *total incorporation* approach to due process. Instead, it adopted the slightly less extreme doctrine of *selective incorporation.* The Supreme Court considered the merits of a variety of cases that dealt with whether the Fourteenth Amendment made the entire Bill of Rights applicable under state law, and it made decisions on a case-by-case basis.

The result is that the Court gradually broadened its interpretation of the Fourteenth Amendment until the bulk of the guarantees of the Bill of Rights were accepted as being binding on the states as well as the federal government.

It's commonly said that essentially the whole of the Bill of Rights is now incorporated against the states. However, that's not the case. The true position is much messier. Some amendments in the Bill of Rights are recognized by the high court as completely incorporated, others as partly incorporated, and others again as not incorporated at all. This patchwork is in itself a strong argument against the whole incorporation doctrine. If the drafters of the Fourteenth Amendment really intended their Due Process Clause to have such an uneven effect on the Bill of Rights, how could they have expected that intention to be understood from a reading of the amendment? There's absolutely no indication in the text of the Fourteenth Amendment of any incorporation whatsoever. So why should we not just accept that as being the true position?

Here's a breakdown of the parts of the Bill of Rights that the high court now recognizes as incorporated:

>> **First Amendment:** Completely incorporated; see Chapter 14.

>> **Second Amendment:** Not recognized as incorporated. However, the 2008 Supreme Court ruling in *D.C. v. Heller* has made the question of the incorporation of this amendment a live issue, and several applications have been filed in federal court to get the Second Amendment incorporated. See Chapter 15 for more.

>> **Third Amendment:** Not recognized as incorporated. The high court has never considered the possible incorporation of this amendment. But in the 1982 case of *Engblom v. Carey,* the U.S. Court of Appeals for the Second Circuit accepted that this amendment applied to the states. See Chapter 16.

>> **Fourth Amendment:** Completely incorporated; see Chapter 16.

>> **Fifth Amendment:** Completely incorporated, except for the right to Indictment by a grand jury, as decided by the high court in 1884 in *Hurtado v. California.* Justice Stanley Matthews, writing for the majority, pointed out that, as the Fifth Amendment contains both a right to due process and a right to grand jury indictment, the one can't be included in the other. So the absence of any mention of grand juries in the Fourteenth Amendment must mean that that right doesn't apply to the states.

>> **Sixth Amendment:** Completely incorporated; see Chapter 18.

>> **Seventh Amendment:** Not recognized as incorporated. This amendment guarantees the right to jury trial in civil suits. In the 1974 case of *Curtis v. Loether,* a civil rights case, the high court specifically refused to rule on whether the Seventh Amendment was incorporated, especially in civil rights cases. See Chapter 18.

>> **Eighth Amendment:** The prohibition against "cruel and unusual punishments" is recognized by the high court as incorporated. However, the high court has never ruled on whether the prohibitions of "excessive bail" and "excessive fines" are incorporated. See Chapter 18.

>> **Ninth and Tenth amendments:** Not incorporated. It's commonly assumed that, although these two amendments form part of the Bill of Rights, they don't specifically confer any rights. For a discussion of these amendments, see Chapter 19.

Note: Those parts of the Bill of Rights that aren't regarded as incorporated apply only to federal law. But some of them do apply to the states anyway — by virtue of state law. Prohibition of excessive bail is an example of this, as it's found in every state constitution.

THE BLAINE AMENDMENT: A COMPELLING ARGUMENT AGAINST INCORPORATION

The Framers of the Fourteenth Amendment didn't understand it as incorporating the bulk of the Bill of Rights. How do we know this? James G. Blaine proposed a new amendment to the Constitution mirroring the first clause of the First Amendment but applying it to the states. Instead of starting "Congress shall make no law . . .," the Blaine Amendment began, "No State shall make any law respecting an establishment of religion . . . ."

Blaine proposed his new amendment in 1875 — just seven years after the ratification of the Fourteenth Amendment. If Blaine's proposed amendment was already sitting inside the Fourteenth Amendment, there would have been no need for Blaine to propose it. Was Blaine just plain ignorant of the Fourteenth Amendment? No, sirree. He was one of the most influential members of the House of Representatives, one of the Framers of the Fourteenth Amendment, and then Speaker! He wouldn't have gone to all the trouble of putting the Establishment Clause of the First Amendment (the first clause, which refers to "an establishment of religion") into a new amendment applicable to the states if the First Amendment already applied to the states by "incorporation." This is perhaps the strongest argument against the whole incorporation theory.

TECHNICAL STUFF

What about *reverse incorporation*? Some commentators have suggested that the Equal Protection Clause of the Fourteenth Amendment, which applies specifically to the states, should be read as applying also to the federal government through incorporation into the Due Process Clause of the Fifth Amendment. Whew! That's not the law at present, and the U.S. Supreme Court has never ruled on it.

Taking Private Property

The last part of the Fifth Amendment hasn't clogged the courts to quite the extent due process has done, but it has generated its share of heated controversy. It reads as follows:

nor shall private property be taken for public use, without just compensation.

Recognizing eminent domain

This clause is intended to offer protection to property owners, but it also recognizes the absolute right of the government to take private property. This had been the case for hundreds of years under English law, and earlier under Roman law. In the words of the famous Dutch jurist Hugo Grotius, written in 1625, "the property of subjects is under the eminent domain of the state." That's why U.S. law uses the term *eminent domain* to refer to the right of the government to take private property.

CONTROVERSY

The taking of private property can only be "for public use," and the definition of this phrase has been highly controversial. At first it was narrowly defined, referring to use by the public, as for example, the taking of someone's home to build or widen a roadway. But the U.S. Supreme Court has broadened the definition considerably. See Figure 17-1.

FIGURE 17-1:
Thomas Jefferson, who was to become the third president, opposed the whole idea that the government can take away private property.

Source: Official presidential portrait of Thomas Jefferson by Rembrandt Peale, 1800

Losing protection

In 1954, the Supreme Court heard a case about a department store that the District of Columbia wanted to take possession of and hand over to a private agency for redevelopment for private use. Because the private agency was redeveloping a larger area surrounding the department store with the intention of removing slum properties, the Court refused to interfere with the redevelopment project. The justices argued that the project had to be looked at as a whole. If the success of the larger project depended on clearing a non-slum property such as the department store, that was an acceptable casualty.

In *Kelo v. City of New London* (2005), the U.S. Supreme Court went even further. It ruled that local governments could take private homes and businesses against the wishes of their owners and hand the property over to private developers of shopping malls and hotel complexes. Writing for the liberal majority, Justice John Paul Stevens held that local officials knew better than federal judges what was good for their communities. He also recognized that the states could, if they wished, pass laws granting property owners more rights than under the U.S. Constitution.

The conservative members of the court, and swing-voter Justice Sandra Day O'Connor, registered a strong dissent. "Any property may now be taken for the benefit of another private party," wrote O'Connor, "but the fallout from this decision will not be random. The beneficiaries are likely to be those citizens with disproportionate influence and power in the political process, including large corporations and development firms."

The 2005 decision was greeted with dismay across the nation, and in 2006 no fewer than 34 states adopted some form of eminent domain reform to minimize the effects of the judgment. In the same year, President George W. Bush issued an executive order requiring the federal government to restrict its taking of private property to "public use" with "just compensation" for the "purpose of benefiting the general public" and specifically "not for the purpose of advancing the economic interest of private parties to be given ownership or use of the property taken." But the effect of this order is minimal, as eminent domain is more often invoked by state and local authorities than by the federal government.

Chapter **18**

Regulating Crime and Punishment: The Sixth through Eighth Amendments

The Sixth through Eighth amendments of the Constitution are part of the Bill of Rights, the unofficial name that belongs to the first ten amendments, collectively, which were all ratified together on December 15, 1791.

Amendments six through eight don't have the glamour or pizzazz of the First Amendment, the Fifth, or even the Fourteenth. But amendments six through eight are still pretty important. Here's a brief summary:

» The Sixth Amendment guarantees a fair trial to defendants in a criminal prosecution, including the right to a jury trial and the assistance of counsel.

» The Seventh Amendment guarantees the right to trial by jury in civil trials.

>> The Eighth Amendment is best known for banning "cruel and unusual punishments."

I discuss all three amendments in this chapter.

Outlining Defendants' Rights in Criminal Prosecutions: The Sixth Amendment

The Sixth Amendment is quite a mouthful (see the Appendix). It contains no fewer than eight rights applicable to "all criminal prosecutions." Here are the rights that this article guarantees to a defendant in a criminal prosecution:

>> The right to a speedy trial

>> The right to a public trial

>> The right to a trial by an impartial jury from the district where the crime was committed

>> The right to be informed of the nature of the accusation

>> The right to be informed of the cause of the accusation

>> The right to be confronted with the witnesses against him

>> The right to compel the attendance of witnesses in his favor

>> The right to be represented by counsel

This list of rights looks pretty comprehensive, but it raises quite a few questions, including these:

>> Do these eight rights really apply to "all criminal prosecutions," as the Sixth Amendment says? Do they apply to prosecutions for misdemeanors as well as to felonies, and to state and federal prosecutions alike?

>> How speedy must a speedy trial be?

>> Why is a public trial necessary?

>> What exactly is meant by "an impartial jury," and how can it be guaranteed?

>> What exactly is meant by the "cause of the accusation"?

>> Why is it a right for a defendant to be confronted by the witnesses against him?

>> How can witnesses be compelled to attend?

>> Is the right to be represented by counsel a general right? What if the defendant can't afford it? And what if a defendant wants to defend himself? Does he have the right to do so?

I tackle each of these questions in turn.

Having the same rights in a state and federal trial

The opening words of the Sixth Amendment state categorically that all the rights guaranteed in that amendment apply "[i]n all criminal prosecutions." But is that really true?

The Bill of Rights originally applied only to federal law, but the U.S. Supreme Court has gradually incorporated more and more of its provisions into the Due Process Clause of the Fourteenth Amendment, which applies to the states. I discuss the whole incorporation debate in Chapter 17.

REMEMBER

As of now, the whole of the Sixth Amendment is accepted as incorporated in this way. So the rights listed in the Sixth Amendment do apply to state prosecutions as well as to federal prosecutions (with some exceptions). The crucial case in applying the amendment to state prosecutions was *Duncan v. Louisiana,* decided by the U.S. Supreme Court in 1968.

The Supreme Court ruled that the right to trial by jury in criminal cases is fundamental and central to the American concept of justice. So the right to a jury trial applies to the states as well as to federal courts — except for "petty crimes" whose maximum possible punishment is a $500 fine and six months of jail time.

How speedy is a speedy trial?

"Justice delayed is justice denied." This old saying puts the importance of a speedy trial in a nutshell. Delaying a trial means that the accusation hangs over the defendant until the case comes to court. In the meantime, witnesses' memories can become increasingly unreliable, and some witnesses may disappear or even die.

If a guilty defendant has posted bail, he can commit more crimes during a long wait for his trial. So the right to a speedy trial isn't only in the interest of defendants; it also protects society. And if a defendant can't make bail, he has to sit in jail until his trial; a long wait is unfair to him and adds to the overcrowding of the prisons.

In 1972, the U.S. Supreme Court identified four factors that must be tested to decide whether there has been a violation of the right to a speedy trial:

>> **The length of the delay:** The Court held that a delay of a year or more from the date of arrest can usually be presumed to violate the defendant's right to a speedy trial, but the Court declined to set any definite limit. The Court held instead that this issue has to be decided on a case-by-case basis.

>> **The reason for the delay:** Here, the Court proposed a sliding scale. "A deliberate attempt to delay the trial in order to hamper the defense should be weighted heavily against the government," it determined. At the other extreme, "a valid reason, such as a missing witness, should serve to justify appropriate delay."

>> **The defendant's assertion of his right to a speedy trial:** Does a defendant lose his right to a speedy trial if he doesn't assert this right? No, but "failure to assert the right will make it difficult for a defendant to prove that he was denied a speedy trial."

>> **Prejudice to the defendant:** The Court identified three factors that would likely prejudice (or harm) the interests of the defendant, including "oppressive pretrial incarceration" and "the possibility that the defense will be impaired."

Appreciating the need for a public trial

"Justice must not only be done but must be seen to be done." It would be hard to disagree with this old saying. If you don't know what went on in a trial, how can you be sure that it was fair?

U.S. courtrooms have always been open to the public, and now many trials are even televised, which may not always be a good thing. For example, O.J. Simpson's murder trial in 1995 turned into a media circus. But whether a trial should be televised or not is a different question from whether it should be open to the public.

REMEMBER

Is a trial behind closed doors ever justified? If the evidence is so sensitive that it would be dangerous for the evidence to be published, yes. Also, if one of the parties files a motion of *closure* (meaning the trial should be conducted in private), the judge has to decide whether to grant the motion. Closure may be allowed in cases involving organized crime or rape and is routinely ordered in juvenile cases.

It's important to realize that the question of public trials affects rights not only under the Sixth Amendment but may also implicate First Amendment rights of freedom of speech and freedom of the press. I discuss the First Amendment in Chapter 14.

Guaranteeing trial by jury

Trial by jury is an important constitutional right that can be traced back to Magna Carta in 1215 (see Chapter 2).

REMEMBER

Courts have always treated petty offenses as an exception to the right to trial by jury. *Petty offenses* are those that carry a sentence of not more than six months in jail or a fine of not more than $500, or both.

What if a defendant is charged at the same trial with a number of petty offenses, so that his total jail time could exceed six months? In 1996, the U.S. Supreme Court said that a trial for multiple petty offenses would not trigger the right to a jury trial.

Selecting an impartial jury

The Sixth Amendment says that criminal defendants have the right to trial by "an impartial jury." But is this really a right that defendants are likely to claim? Aren't they more likely to want juries that are favorably disposed toward them — just as prosecutors prefer juries that are more likely to convict? Of course. Maybe the Framers were a bit naïve in this respect.

But, whether defendants want an impartial jury or not, the system is set up to deliver impartial juries, although it clearly doesn't always succeed in doing so. The states compile lists of people who are eligible for jury service. A jury pool or a jury in waiting is summoned. The actual group of 12 jurors is selected from these potential jurors. The prosecution and the defense can challenge these potential jurors *for cause*, and both sides can also exercise a fixed number of *peremptory challenges*:

>> **Challenge for cause:** Any potential juror can be challenged "for cause." Examples of "cause" are bias against one party, acquaintance with a party or lawyer, and inability to serve as a juror. The judge and attorneys ask potential jurors a number of questions to find out more about them and whether there is some reason they should not serve on the jury. (*The Simpsons* poked fun at jury selection when Homer Simpson explained how he got out of jury duty: "The trick is to say you're prejudiced against all races.")

>> **Peremptory challenge:** Both parties also have the right to have a predetermined number of individual jurors excluded from the jury without "cause." This is called a *peremptory challenge* and can generally be freely exercised by a lawyer. However, in 1986, in *Batson v. Kentucky,* the Supreme Court decided that a peremptory challenge couldn't be used to exclude jurors solely on grounds of race. In other words, a lawyer can't "stack" the jury with members of a certain race. Chief Justice Warren Burger dissented, arguing that the

majority decision effectively abolished peremptory challenge, "a procedure which has been part of the common law for many centuries and part of our jury system for nearly 200 years."

So important is jury selection that lawyers increasingly hire jury consultants in high profile or high stakes cases. A jury consultant can charge hundreds of thousands of dollars to pick the right jury for the side that has hired him or her. An apparently innocuous question put to prospective jurors can pay dividends to the perceptive analyst. Prospective jurors may be asked, "Who is your favorite person?" If your answer is Cher, according to jury consultant Howard Varinsky, "It says you're not very bright." Does that mean that such a person shouldn't be selected for the jury? Not at all. Says Varinsky: If the case involves complex information that is unfavorable to your side, a juror who doesn't understand the information could be a plus. This statement echoes the cynical comment made by the humorist Dave Barry: "If you are accused of a crime, you have the right to a trial before a jury of people too stupid to get out of jury duty."

Recognizing the importance of juries

You should never underestimate the importance of jury trials in the whole constitutional framework. The role of the jury is as the *finder of fact*. The judge advises the jury on the law that should be applied to those facts. But the jury's verdict decides whether the defendant is guilty or not guilty.

The power of juries has increased in recent years. For example, in *Ring v. Arizona*, heard in 2002, the U.S. Supreme Court ruled that only a jury was allowed to determine whether there were aggravating factors necessary for imposing the death penalty. This decision struck down the rule in Arizona and some other states that allowed judges to make this determination.

Juries aren't usually informed of another power that they have long had: *jury nullification*. The judge is supposed to instruct the jury on the law, and the jury is supposed to accept the judge's instructions. But in practice juries have long reserved the right to ignore the law and to act according to their consciences. This is called jury nullification. During Prohibition, for example, juries often refused to convict defendants charged under the alcohol control laws. This resistance may well have contributed to the repeal of Prohibition by the Twenty-First Amendment.

Most judges aren't too happy about jury nullification. In a 1988 case, a judge who was asked by the jury about jury nullification replied, "There is no such thing as valid jury nullification." In 1997, the Second Circuit held that a juror who intended to nullify the law could be dismissed from the jury panel. But perhaps the last word should go to Supreme Court Justice Antonin Scalia, who described juries as "the spinal column of American democracy."

Being "informed of the nature and cause of the accusation"

A fair criminal justice system must let an accused person know exactly what charges he or she is facing. An indictment is normally based on a *statute* — a law passed by Congress or a state legislature. It is essential in the interests of justice that the statute is clear. If it isn't clear, it can be declared void for uncertainty or void for vagueness, and therefore unconstitutional. The tests for vagueness include the following:

>> Is it clear which persons fall within the scope of the statute?

>> Does the statute alert those persons who are subject to it?

>> Are there safeguards against the arbitrary or discriminatory application of this statute?

>> What conduct does the statute prohibit?

>> What punishment does the statute impose?

But clarity in the law itself isn't enough. The indictment may have to go beyond the words of the statute and "must descend to particulars," as the U.S. Supreme Court held in *United States v. Cruikshank* in 1875.

Confronting adverse witnesses

Why does the Sixth Amendment guarantee the right of criminal defendants to confront the witnesses giving evidence against them? The alternative would be to allow witnesses' statements to go unchallenged, which isn't fair unless the statement is uncontroversial and is accepted by both sides.

The principle that criminal defendants must be allowed to confront their accusers dates back to the revulsion at the way Sir Walter Raleigh was treated in his treason trial in 1603. Raleigh wasn't allowed to question the witnesses against him, whose signed statements had been extracted under torture.

REMEMBER

The right to cross-examine your accusers is important for several reasons:

>> It enables skillful counsel to confront witnesses with inconsistencies in their evidence.

>> It may even result in a witness being caught in a lie.

>> It gives the jury a view of the *demeanor* of the witness — including the witness's body language, which can be revealing.

Child witnesses or other vulnerable witnesses may be allowed to give their evidence in the judge's chambers without being cross-examined. This situation is the main exception to the rule stated in the Sixth Amendment.

Compelling witnesses to attend

If a witness supports your case, that witness will surely be only too happy to come to court to give evidence in your favor, right? Unfortunately not. Too many people are afraid of appearing in court, or just can't be bothered. So it's necessary to be able to compel them to attend. This is done by serving such a witness with a *subpoena* — a formal document issued by the court ordering the witness to appear in court to give evidence at a certain time and place. The reason this procedure is called a *subpoena* — from the Latin, meaning "subject to penalty" — is that a witness who disobeys the order may be found guilty of a contempt of court, for which the penalty can be jail.

Demanding the right to counsel

The Sixth Amendment says that "In all criminal prosecutions, the accused shall . . . have the Assistance of Counsel for his defence." In 1968, the U.S. Supreme Court decided that the whole of the Sixth Amendment was incorporated into the Due Process Clause of the Fourteenth Amendment. In other words, all the rights enumerated in the Sixth Amendment apply to the states as well as to federal courts.

However, the courts haven't always recognized the right to counsel. In *Betts v. Brady,* the Supreme Court decided in 1942 that criminal defendants in state courts couldn't claim legal representation unless there were "special circumstances" in their cases — for example, if they were facing the death penalty.

Betts is one of the best-known Supreme Court cases that have been overruled by a later Supreme Court decision. This overruling happened in the landmark case *Gideon v. Wainwright,* heard by the Supreme Court in 1963. The story of Gideon's case was graphically told in the book *Gideon's Trumpet,* by Anthony Lewis, which became the basis of a movie. Gideon's moving petition to the Supreme Court was neatly handwritten and couched in legal terminology that Gideon had meticulously researched in the prison library. A unanimous Supreme Court held that the right to counsel in the Sixth Amendment was indeed incorporated into the Due Process Clause of the Fourteenth Amendment and did therefore apply to criminal trials in state courts as well as in federal court.

In an equally famous case, *Miranda v. Arizona,* heard in 1966, the U.S. Supreme Court went further, holding that "The right to have counsel present at the interrogation is indispensable to the protection of the Fifth Amendment privilege" against self-incrimination. As a result of this holding, the right to counsel at public expense is now incorporated into the Miranda warning that police officers routinely give to suspects:

> *You have the right to remain silent . . . You have the right to speak to an attorney, and to have an attorney present during any questioning. If you cannot afford a lawyer, one will be provided for you at government expense.*

But what if a criminal defendant doesn't want legal representation? In 1975 the U.S. Supreme Court held that it is in keeping with the Sixth Amendment for a defendant to represent himself: "A knowing and intelligent waiver" of the right to counsel "must be honored out of that respect for the individual, which is the life-blood of the law."

However, in *Martinez v. Court of Appeals of California*, decided in 2000, the U.S. Supreme Court denied the right of a criminal defendant to conduct his own appeal against a conviction. The Court held that the Sixth Amendment right to represent yourself applies to trials but not to appeals.

IN MY OPINION

It's hard to understand the justification for making this distinction. The Sixth Amendment guarantees *rights*, but in *Martinez* the Supreme Court appears to have treated a *right* as if it were an *obligation*. This is a serious logical error. If you're playing *Who Wants to Be a Millionaire?* you have the *right* to phone a friend; you don't have an *obligation* to do so.

REMEMBER

Since the *Gideon* decision, the system of public defenders has been greatly expanded in every state to cater to criminal defendants who can't afford to pay for legal representation. There's a certain amount of controversy surrounding public defenders, who are sometimes thought to be too inclined to encourage their clients to plead guilty.

Guaranteeing Jury Trials in Civil Suits: The Seventh Amendment

The Seventh Amendment preserves an old right of trial by jury in certain civil suits. Here's what the amendment says:

> *In Suits at common law, where the value in controversy shall exceed twenty dollars, the right of trial by jury shall be preserved, and no fact tried by a jury, shall be otherwise re-examined in any Court of the United States, than according to the rules of the common law.*

The right to trial by jury in civil suits long predates the U.S. Constitution. It existed in English law from time immemorial, but it has been largely abolished there. Thanks to the Seventh Amendment, jury trials in civil lawsuits are still alive and well in the United States.

REMEMBER

The Seventh Amendment right doesn't extend to state courts because the U.S. Supreme Court doesn't regard the Seventh Amendment as incorporated into the Fourteenth Amendment by the Due Process Clause (see Chapter 17). However, most states have provisions for civil jury trials in their individual constitutions, so civil juries are alive and well in state courts too.

What's with the emphasis on the common law in the Seventh Amendment? When this amendment was ratified in 1791, English law drew a distinction between *common law* and *equity*. Not only were the two types of law distinct, but there were separate law courts for each:

>> Common law courts tried cases involving contract, tort, and many other types of lawsuits.

>> Disputes involving wills, trusts, and real estate went to the courts of equity.

In the common law courts, jury trials were the norm, but in the courts of equity, all trials were *bench trials* — heard by a judge sitting alone.

This pattern existed not only in England but also in the 13 American colonies, and it's reflected in the Seventh Amendment. Because jury trials were found only in common law suits, not in equity, the amendment preserves and perpetuates this distinction.

TECHNICAL
STUFF

This tradition sometimes results in tedious arguments. For example, in *Chauffeurs, Teamsters & Helpers Local No. 391 v. Terry,* heard in 1990, the U.S. Supreme Court had to decide whether a labor dispute would have been a suit "at common law" back in 1791. Justice William Brennan held that many of the legal rights available today can't easily be classified in terms of the categories of English law of 200 years ago, and that modern U.S. judges aren't qualified to analyze the law in those terms. The right to trial by jury, he added, was too important to depend on such "needless and intractable excursions into increasingly unfamiliar territory."

Prohibiting "Cruel and Unusual Punishments": The Eighth Amendment

The Eighth Amendment is best known for banning "cruel and unusual punishments," but it also contains prohibitions against excessive bail and excessive fines. Here's the entire wording of the Eighth Amendment:

Excessive bail shall not be required, nor excessive fines imposed, nor cruel and unusual punishments inflicted.

Banning excessive bail

After someone has been arrested and booked on suspicion of committing a crime, he or she appears before a judge for *arraignment.* The judge hears the charges and asks the accused person to enter a plea. If the plea is "not guilty," a court date is set for the trial. But that date may be months or even years away. So the court has to decide whether to keep the accused person, or *defendant*, in jail or to allow him or her to go free until the trial date.

The bail system is intended to give a defendant an incentive to appear in court as required and not to skip town before the trial date. A defendant facing a murder charge is likely to be given bail of at least $500,000. But in order to *post bail*, it's usually necessary to pay only 10 percent of the bail amount upfront. If the defend- ant duly shows up in court, the amount paid is refunded. (However, if a bail bondsman is used to post bail, he retains the 10 percent of the bail amount paid to him as his fee.) If the defendant fails to appear in court, the whole amount of the bail has to be paid to the court.

The words "Excessive bail shall not be required" were lifted directly from the Virginia Constitution, which in turn comes straight from the English Bill of Rights of 1688. This formulation raises some questions:

>> How much is "[e]xcessive"? You know from the news that celebrities and rich defendants are often required to pay very high amounts of bail, sometimes running into hundreds of thousands of dollars or even more. So, does the appropriate level of bail depend on the seriousness of the charge or on the resources of the accused person? The level of bail set should be just enough to ensure that the defendant in question won't skip town before his trial, but this amount isn't easy to assess. If a defendant believes that he has been asked to post too much bail, he can apply to the court for a reduction.

>> Does the Eighth Amendment mean that criminal defendants must always be given the opportunity to post bail? No. Where a defendant is facing a very serious charge like murder, bail can be denied. At the same time that Congress debated the Eighth Amendment, it also considered the Judiciary Act, which defined which offenses were bailable and which were not bailable. As so often is the case, the words of the Constitution have to be read in conjunc- tion with other legislation.

>> Does the Eighth Amendment allow "preventive detention" without bail? The U.S. Supreme Court answered yes to this question in *United States v. Salerno* in

1987. The Court was deciding on the constitutionality of the Bail Reform Act of 1984. This law allows a federal court to detain an arrestee pending trial if the government shows that no release conditions "will reasonably assure the safety of any other person and the community." This provision goes way beyond any previous law that allowed denial of bail. Anthony Salerno was alleged to be a mafia boss, but the 1984 law is tailor-made for use against suspected terrorists. In the words of Chief Justice William Rehnquist, here are some factors that have to be considered in deciding whether to deny bail to an arrestee:

- "The nature and seriousness of the charges,

- The substantiality of the Government's evidence against the arrestee,

- The arrestee's background and characteristics, and

- The nature and seriousness of the danger posed by the suspect's release."

Removing excessive fines

The U.S. Supreme Court has generally taken a narrow view of the meaning of the word *fines*. In 1989, the Court adopted the definition of *fines* that was current when the Eighth Amendment was ratified in 1791: "The word 'fine' was understood to mean a payment to a sovereign [government] as punishment for some offense . . . The Excessive Fines Clause was intended to limit only those fines directly imposed by, and payable to, the government." But how much is excessive? In *U.S. v. Bajakajian* (1998), the Supreme Court ruled by 5 votes to 4 that confiscation of $357,144 was excessive. U.S. Customs caught Mr. Bajakajian trying to leave the United States with this sum of money without declaring it, though the law requires any amount over $10,000 to be declared. Justice Clarence Thomas, writing for the majority, held that "such a forfeiture would be grossly disproportionate to his offense." The case produced an unusual lineup, with the liberal Justice Stevens agreeing with the conservative Thomas, while the conservative Chief Justice Rehnquist and Justice Scalia dissented. Another point of interest is the fact that this is the only case to date when the Supreme Court found a fine unconstitutional under the Eighth Amendment.

TECHNICAL
STUFF

In 1993 the Supreme Court decided that an order for forfeiture of property could be considered a fine under the Eighth Amendment, though it declined to determine how much forfeiture would amount to an excessive fine.

Barring "cruel and unusual punishments"

The ban on the infliction of "cruel and unusual punishments" is one of the best-known provisions of the Constitution. This prohibition applies to state law as well as to federal law because the U.S. Supreme Court accepts it as incorporated by the Due Process Clause of the Fourteenth Amendment (see Chapter 17). But what exactly is meant by this memorable phrase?

Understanding the importance of "and"

Does the word *and* have any significance? Does "cruel *and* unusual punishments" have a different meaning from "cruel *or* unusual punishments"? The answer is yes. On this basis, the *three strikes laws* have been upheld: laws that allow courts to impose an extra-long jail sentence on anyone convicted of three felonies. This type of punishment sure was unusual, but it was held not to be cruel.

However, some three-strike cases make for worrying reading, like the 2003 California case *Lockyer v. Andrade.* The theft of five videotapes was classified as a felony and, because the offender had a few prior convictions, he was sentenced to jail for 50 years to life. The U.S. Supreme Court ruled that this sentence did not amount to cruel and unusual punishment.

Identifying some completely forbidden punishments

Here are some punishments that are completely forbidden:

>> **Torture:** This term presumably includes the use of those old-time favorites, the pillory, the rack, the stocks, and cutting off ears and limbs. The exact meaning of the prohibition on cruel and unusual punishments has been debated since the days of the Framers. In 1789, representative Samuel Livermore said, "It is sometimes necessary to hang a man, villains often deserve whipping, and perhaps having their ears cut off; but are we in the future to be prevented from inflicting these punishments because they are cruel?" Except in regard to hanging, the answer was yes. In 1878, the U.S. Supreme Court in *Wilkerson v. Utah* ruled that all punishments "of unnecessary cruelty" were forbidden by the Eighth Amendment.

Until the 9/11 terrorist outrage, torture did not figure prominently in U.S. politics or law. However, in August 2002 the "Torture Memos," signed by Assistant Attorney General Bybee, advised the President, the CIA and the Department of Defense that enhanced interrogation techniques, including waterboarding, which had previously been regarded as torture, might be legally permissible under presidential authority during the "War on Terror" launched by President George W. Bush shortly after the 9/11 attacks. *Waterboarding* entails covering a person's face with a cloth over which water is poured, causing a gag reflex and giving the person concerned the sensation of drowning. In reaction against the "Torture Memos," in 2008 both houses of

Congress approved a bill banning waterboarding and other harsh interrogation methods, but President Bush vetoed this bill, citing the waterboarding ban as his reason for the veto. However, on January 22, 2009, the newly inaugurated President Obama signed an executive order requiring both U.S. military and all government agencies to use the Army Field Manual as the guide to interrogation techniques. The Manual banned waterboarding among other interrogation techniques such as hooding and the application of electric shocks. In 2015, Congress incorporated that ban into law in the National Defense Authorization Act. So, does waterboarding constitute torture? There is still no agreement on this, but it is now illegal under U.S. law.

» **Canceling the citizenship of a U.S. citizen:** Albert Trop, a native-born U.S. citizen, escaped from an army stockade while serving in the U.S. Army in World War II. He was court-martialed, sentenced to three years at hard labor, and received a dishonorable discharge.

Later, Trop applied for a passport and was denied on the grounds that his army desertion had stripped him of U.S. citizenship. In 1958, the U.S. Supreme Court branded this refusal "cruel and unusual punishment." Chief Justice Earl Warren, writing for the majority, held that "denationalization" is "the total destruction of the individual's status in society." Pointing out that desertion from the army can be punishable by death, Justice Felix Frankfurter hit back in his dissent: Can it "be seriously urged that loss of citizenship is a fate worse than death?"

» **Punishing someone for suffering from an illness:** Drug addiction, for example, is an illness and shouldn't be criminalized; the Supreme Court said so in *Robinson v. California* in 1962. But this decision put the Court on a slippery slope, as the 1968 case of *Powell v. Texas* illustrates. In that case the majority of the Court ruled that criminalizing public drunkenness didn't amount to cruel and unusual punishment. Where to draw the line? Justice Abe Fortas suggested this test: "Criminal penalties may not be inflicted upon a person for being in a condition he is powerless to change." On this basis, Fortas dissented in favor of the drunk in *Powell.* But is an alcoholic really powerless to change his condition? Alcoholics Anonymous might dissent from Abe Fortas!

» **Punishments that are cruel and unusual because they're excessive:** Can a punishment be held to be cruel and unusual purely because it's regarded as excessive? Yes. This doctrine was first adopted by the U.S. Supreme Court back in 1910. In *Coker v. Georgia,* heard in 1977, the Court held that the death penalty for the rape of an adult female was excessive and amounted to cruel and unusual punishment.

Debating the death penalty

When the Bill of Rights was ratified in 1791, capital punishment was commonplace and taken for granted. Nobody then thought that the death penalty could constitute "cruel and unusual punishment." The Fifth Amendment refers to capital punishment no fewer than three times:

>> *No person shall be held to answer for a capital, or otherwise infamous crime . . .* A capital crime means one that carries the death penalty.

>> *nor shall any person be subject to the same offences to be twice put in jeopardy of life or limb.* The word *life* here refers again to the death penalty.

>> *Nor be deprived of life, liberty or property, without due process of law.* Yep, the good ole Due Process Clause itself takes it for granted that you can be executed by due process.

The Due Process Clause of the Fourteenth Amendment, ratified in 1868, similarly shows that capital punishment was still perfectly acceptable then:

> *nor shall any State deprive any person of life, liberty or property, without due process of law.*

How could a state deprive anyone of his or her life by due process of law if the death penalty was unconstitutional? Obviously, it would be impossible.

In the case of *Wilkerson v. Utah*, heard in 1878, the U.S. Supreme Court made it clear that certain modes of execution did amount to cruel and unusual punishments, but others didn't. Burning people alive at the stake, drawing and quartering, and disemboweling were all unconstitutional as cruel and unusual punishments. But death by firing squad — the form of execution used in Utah — was constitutionally acceptable.

The first real challenge to the death penalty as such occurred in *Furman v. Georgia*, heard by the U.S. Supreme Court in 1972 together with two other death penalty cases. By 5 votes to 4 the court overturned all three capital sentences. Only two justices (William Brennan and Thurgood Marshall) actually went so far as to declare that the death penalty by its very nature constituted cruel and unusual punishment (see Figure 18-1). Three justices concurred in overturning the particular sentences under review but stopped well short of condemning capital punishment as being invariably and inescapably unconstitutional. Instead they focused on the arbitrariness and capriciousness with which the death penalty was imposed, especially as it tended to fall disproportionately on African Americans.

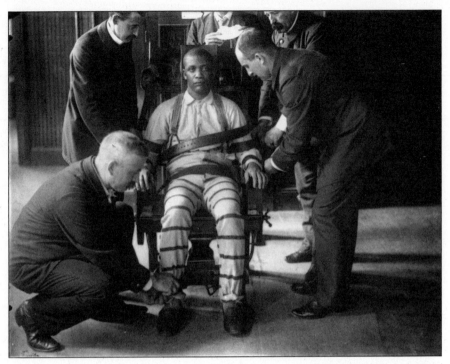

Source: George Eastman House, by Nesnad

Only four years later the U.S. Supreme Court changed its position on capital punishment. The key case was *Gregg v. Georgia*, which was heard in 1976 together with four other cases.

REMEMBER

The majority of the court held that

>> The death penalty for murder does not in itself violate the Eighth and Fourteenth amendments.

>> Capital punishment for murder can't be unconstitutional because it was accepted by the Framers of the Constitution and has been accepted by the U.S. Supreme Court for 200 years.

>> Retribution and deterrence are relevant considerations for sentencing.

>> Capital punishment for murder is not disproportionate to the severity of the crime.

In recent years, Congress and 36 states have enacted new statutes providing for the death penalty. This fact seems to show that the death penalty isn't contrary to contemporary standards of decency.

In 2008, the high court heard a landmark case on capital punishment called *Baze v. Rees.* The question before the court was whether execution by lethal injection constituted "cruel and unusual punishment." In a 7–2 decision, the Court ruled that lethal injection — or, to be more precise, execution by means of the particular cocktail of lethal drugs administered by injection under Kentucky law — is not unconstitutional. In the curious case of *Glossip v. Gross* (2015), by a 5–4 majority, the Supreme Court reaffirmed its decision that lethal injection, specifically with the use of midazolam, is constitutional, with the strange rider that condemned prisoners could challenge their method of execution only if they could come up with a known and available alternative method! For more on this case, see Chapter 23.

Justice Antonin Scalia, in his concurring opinion, concluded with this line:

> *I take no position on the desirability of the death penalty, except to say . . . that it is preeminently not a matter to be resolved here. And especially when it is explicitly permitted by the Constitution.*

Scalia here drew an important logical distinction that Justices William Brennan and Thurgood Marshall in the 1970s failed to make: namely, the distinction between what the Constitution says and what we would like the Constitution to say. Scalia recognized that there are some strong arguments against the death penalty but that it would be wrong of the Court even to get involved in that debate because that would lead to judges amending the Constitution, which is not permitted. The only way that the death penalty could be made unconstitutional would be by means of a proper constitutional amendment proposed and ratified by the procedure laid down in Article V of the Constitution. There doesn't appear to be nearly enough public support for such an amendment, and neither of the main political parties is proposing it. However, American public opinion is evidently gradually shifting away from the death penalty. A 2016 Gallup poll showed capital punishment supported by 60 percent of Americans surveyed, down from 64 percent in 2010 and 68 percent in 2001.

Chapter **19**

Analyzing an "Inkblot" and a "Truism": The Ninth and Tenth Amendments

The Ninth and Tenth amendments are both really important parts of the Bill of Rights. Unlike the first eight amendments, neither the Ninth Amendment nor the Tenth Amendment contains actual concrete rights. Both amendments appear vague, which is why so many people have failed to recognize their importance.

The Ninth Amendment gives guidance on how to interpret the Constitution and makes it clear that rights that are not mentioned in the Constitution belong to the American people. But Judge Robert Bork described this amendment as "a meaningless inkblot," and other influential commentators have been hardly less flattering (see Figure 19-1).

Thomas Jefferson called the Tenth Amendment "the foundation of the Constitution," but the U.S. Supreme Court hasn't always recognized its importance.

FIGURE 19-1:
Robert Bork, unsuccessfully named to the Supreme Court by President Reagan, famously likened the Ninth Amendment to an "inkblot."

In 1931, the Court commented that this amendment "added nothing to the Constitution as originally ratified." However, in recent years the Court has started to give the Tenth Amendment the respect that it deserves.

Reading the Constitution: The Ninth Amendment

The Ninth Amendment is probably the most misunderstood part of the Constitution. It's hard to understand why so many people have made such heavy weather of this fairly straightforward, single-sentence provision:

> *The enumeration in the Constitution, of certain rights, shall not be construed to deny or disparage others retained by the people.*

Let me put this amendment in plain English. It may help if I expand it slightly:

>> The U.S. Constitution confers or guarantees a number of individual rights.

>> But those are not the only rights that individuals possess.

>> The rights that are not mentioned in the Constitution belonged to the people before there was a United States of America.

>> And those rights still belong to the people.

>> The fact that the Constitution doesn't mention those rights doesn't cancel or detract from them.

>> The Constitution must not be construed, or interpreted, in a way that deprives the people of those retained rights.

So, what exactly are these rights "retained by the people"? The word *retained* indicates that the people had these rights before. But when? Clearly, before the U.S. Constitution was ratified. In short, these rights derive from English common law, going back at least 600 years before the United States came into existence.

REMEMBER

The Constitution confers or guarantees *positive rights*, but the common law works *negatively*. Under the common law, anything that is not prohibited — usually by statute — is allowed.

In drafting the Ninth Amendment, James Madison was anxious to make it clear that the fact that the Constitution contained *some* rights didn't mean that these were the *only* rights people had. He also wanted to make it quite clear that the rights not mentioned in the Constitution didn't somehow fall to the new U.S. government but remained where they had always been — in the hands of the people.

There are hundreds, probably thousands, of these rights "retained by the people." Here are just a few examples:

>> **The right to pick your nose in public:** It's not a very nice thing to do, but as long as there is no law against it, you have the right to do it. In a recent poll, the majority of Americans admitted that they did exercise this right!

>> **The right to kill bugs:** Certain religions regard the killing of any living thing as a heinous sin, but it's not a crime under U.S. law — not yet anyway!

>> **The right to engage in lesbian sex:** Unlike male homosexual activity, which used to be a criminal offense, sex between women was never a crime under U.S. law. Does this mean that you always had a right to engage in lesbian sex? Yes, but it was a bit difficult for about half the population!

IS THE NINTH AMENDMENT AN INKBLOT?

IN MY OPINION

It's quite alarming to see how many eminent jurists have totally misunderstood the Ninth Amendment:

- Judge Robert Bork described the amendment as "a meaningless inkblot." The meaning of the Ninth Amendment, said Bork during his abortive Supreme Court confirmation hearing, is as indecipherable as it would have been had the text been obscured by an inkblot.

- In *Griswold v. Connecticut,* heard by the U.S. Supreme Court in 1965, Justice Arthur Goldberg opined that the Ninth Amendment did not constitute "an independent source of rights protected from infringement by either the States or the Federal Government."

- In *Roe v. Wade,* decided in 1972, Justice William O. Douglas wrote, "The Ninth Amendment obviously does not create federally enforceable rights."

- Professor Laurence Tribe wrote that "The Ninth Amendment is not a source of rights as such; it is simply a rule about how to read the Constitution."

- In *Troxel v. Granville,* Justice Antonin Scalia wrote in 2000: "The Constitution's refusal to 'deny or disparage' other rights is far removed from affirming any one of them, and even farther removed from authorizing judges to identify what they might be, and to enforce the judges' list against laws duly enacted by the people."

Am I right in saying that all these characterizations of the Ninth Amendment are wrong? I believe so. Here's why:

- The Ninth Amendment is at pains to emphasize that the pre-Constitution rights that the people possessed are still there. So how can that mean that the amendment doesn't "affirm" those rights? It can't.

- Can retained rights be claimed in a court of law? Sure. For example, if you're charged with possession of an illegal drug, you can't be convicted if you show that what looked like cocaine was actually a bag of salt. You must assert your right to be in possession of salt. Is there such a right? Of course. It's one of the innumerable retained rights. How do you know you have that right? Because there's no law against being in possession of a bag of salt.

- Does the Ninth Amendment tell us how to read the Constitution? Yes, it does. It tells us that we must not construe (interpret) the Constitution to "deny or disparage" — to negate or downplay — the rights retained by the people. So, the Ninth Amendment tells us how to read the Constitution, but it does much more than that. It tells us that the rights stated in the Constitution are not the only rights enjoyed by the people. There are plenty more, and you must not interpret the Constitution in a way that interferes with those rights.

Considering the Tenth Amendment

The Tenth Amendment packs some pretty powerful punches. It tackles these topics:

>> Federalism

>> States' rights

>> People power

The Tenth Amendment also provides guidance on how to read the Constitution. This amendment views the Constitution not as the sole source of legal power in the nation, but as only one of three sources, the other two being the states and the people.

Analyzing the wording

Here's what the Tenth Amendment says in its entirety:

> *The powers not delegated to the United States by the Constitution, nor prohibited by it to the States, are reserved for the States respectively, or to the people.*

What does this amendment mean? The key word here is "delegated." To *delegate* a power means to hand it down to somebody else. For example, your boss at work may delegate to you the power to purchase stationery.

REMEMBER

The Tenth Amendment looks at the political structure of the nation this way:

>> In the beginning, all power belonged to the people.

>> After the Declaration of Independence, the people delegated some of their power to the states.

>> When the states ratified the U.S. Constitution, they delegated some of their power to the federal government.

>> The federal government doesn't possess any powers that are not specifically delegated to it by the Constitution.

>> All powers not delegated to the federal government continue to be "reserved" to the states or to the people.

Balancing power between federal and state governments

Sharing power between the federal government and the states is what federalism is all about, and the United States has a federal form of government (see Chapter 7).

The Tenth Amendment makes it clear that power originates with the states and the people — not with the federal government. In the words of James Madison, the author of the Bill of Rights (including the Tenth Amendment):

> The powers delegated by the proposed Constitution to the federal government are few and defined. Those which are to remain in the State governments are numerous and indefinite. This division of authority was adopted by the Framers to ensure protection of our fundamental liberties.

Does this explanation mean that state law is higher than federal law? No. That would be too easy. The U.S. Constitution is supreme, but its scope is limited.

REMEMBER

The more complicated reality is this:

>> The U.S. Constitution is the highest law in the nation, and any law that conflicts with it is treated as void, or as if it had never existed in the first place. (I discuss the legal status of the Constitution in Chapter 3.)

>> The U.S. Constitution delegates certain powers to the federal government, including the President and the Congress.

>> The federal government has no right to exercise any powers that are not mentioned in the Constitution (known as *unenumerated* powers).

>> In the interests of the liberty of the people, the constitutional powers of the federal government must be strictly interpreted by the courts.

>> All powers other than those delegated by the Constitution to the federal government belong to the states or to the people.

This explanation raises further questions. Here are a few:

>> Exactly which powers have been delegated to the federal government?

>> What is meant by "powers prohibited by [the Constitution] to the States"?

>> What is the split between the powers that are reserved to the states and the powers that are reserved to the people?

I address each of these questions in turn.

Determining the limits of federal power

The Constitution sets out the powers of the federal government, but the precise nature and scope of these powers are open to interpretation. This fact creates a serious problem because neither the courts nor the government stick to the same interpretation all the time. Let me illustrate this problem with a couple of examples.

The Alien and Sedition Acts

The Alien and Sedition Acts of 1798 made the offense of seditious libel a federal crime. *Seditious libel* means writing words intended to subvert the government. This legislation attempted to silence critics of the administration of President John Adams. These laws greatly expanded the power of Congress and came close to claiming that Congress had a power to enforce the *common law* — the case law hammered out by the courts over centuries.

The problem with this view was that the Constitution didn't give Congress any such power. So the Alien and Sedition Acts were clearly in violation of the Tenth Amendment, which restricts the power of the federal government to powers specifically *delegated* to it by the Constitution.

Thomas Jefferson beat the incumbent, John Adams, in the 1800 presidential race. Jefferson then denounced the Alien and Sedition Acts as unconstitutional and void, and he pardoned everyone who had been convicted under them. (The Alien and Sedition Acts in their original form contained four laws. None of these laws has been tested in the courts, and only one of them — the Alien Enemies Act — still survives.)

The Violence Against Women Act

The U.S. Supreme Court under William Rehnquist — who served as Chief Justice from 1986 to 2005 — returned to a more traditional, conservative approach to the Constitution, which some people have named the "Federalism Revolution" or "the New Federalism."

The Rehnquist Court enforced the Tenth Amendment by taking a narrow view of federal power and even striking down parts of some federal laws as unconstitutional because they didn't conform to the principles of that amendment. One such law was the Violence Against Women Act of 1994.

A freshman at Virginia Tech, Christy Brzonkala, claimed that she'd been raped by two members of the school's football team. A Virginia grand jury was unable to find enough evidence to charge either man with any crime. So Brzonkala filed suit in federal court under the Violence Against Women Act (VAWA), passed by

Congress and signed into law by President Bill Clinton in 1994. The act allowed women to file a civil suit in federal court for rape and sexual harassment.

Brzonkala's case reached the U.S. Supreme Court in 2000. The Court ruled as unconstitutional the part of VAWA that allowed women to file suit in federal court. Here's how the Supreme Court reached this conclusion:

» Civil suits for sexual assault and harassment fall under the jurisdiction of the state courts.

» Federal courts can hear cases only on issues specifically enumerated in the Constitution or on issues concerned with interstate commerce. (I deal with interstate commerce in Chapter 9.)

» Sexual assault and harassment are not enumerated in the Constitution and have nothing to do with interstate commerce.

» Therefore, the part of VAWA allowing women to file suit in federal court for sexual assaults and harassment is unconstitutional.

President Clinton must have regretted signing VAWA into law, because Paula Jones used that very law against him just a year later! Clinton paid Paula Jones $850,000 to make her VAWA lawsuit go away.

Puzzling over "prohibited" powers

The Tenth Amendment is only one sentence long, but one phrase is slightly puzzling. Let me quote the amendment again and put the phrase in bold:

> The powers not delegated to the United States by the Constitution, **nor prohibited by it to the States,** are reserved for the States respectively, or to the people.

Recognizing states' limits

The amendment classifies powers like this:

» Powers delegated by the Constitution to the federal government

» **Powers prohibited by the Constitution to the states**

» Powers reserved to the states

» Powers reserved to the people

The second category refers to Article I, Section 10 of the Constitution. The list of prohibited powers is a long one, including the power

>> To make treaties with foreign powers

>> To coin money

>> To "grant any Title of Nobility"

>> To impose import duties

>> To "engage in War, unless actually invaded, or in such imminent Danger as will not admit of delay"

These powers all belong to nations, so it's easy to see why they are denied to individual states. Most of these powers are granted to Congress by Article I, Section 8 of the Constitution. (However, the power to grant titles of nobility is specifically denied to the federal government by Article I, Section 9. The Constitution therefore makes it clear that no U.S. institution, either federal or state, has the power to grant titles of nobility. The United States is a republic, and any formal gradations in society just don't belong.)

Probably the most interesting power is the last one I've listed: the power to engage in war. Do the states really have this power? Article I, Section 10 of the Constitution essentially says "yes, but only in exceptional circumstances." It's easy enough to see whether a state has been invaded, but who decides whether a state is threatened by "imminent Danger"? Presumably the state governor and legislature. But the precise interpretation of this provision has never been tested in the courts.

Dragging in the Fourteenth Amendment

Does Article I, Section 10 contain the only restrictions on state power in the Constitution? No. The Fourteenth Amendment also contains major restrictions on the power of the states. When the Tenth Amendment was ratified in 1791, nobody could have anticipated the Fourteenth Amendment, which was a product of the Civil War and became part of the Constitution only in 1868.

But we must read the Tenth Amendment in the light of the Fourteenth Amendment, Section 1, which says:

> No State shall make or enforce any law which shall abridge the privileges or immunities of citizens of the United States; nor shall any State deprive any person of life, liberty, or property, without due process of law; nor deny to any person within its jurisdiction the equal protection of the laws.

These words come from a completely different world than the one that produced the Tenth Amendment. The Tenth Amendment is anxious to emphasize the limitations on federal power, but the Fourteenth Amendment sharply restricts the power of the states. Does the Fourteenth Amendment modify the Tenth Amendment? Yes, undoubtedly. But if the Tenth Amendment has to be read in the light of the Fourteenth, doesn't that interpretation nullify the whole purpose of the Tenth Amendment? The answer to this question depends on how broadly or narrowly you interpret the Fourteenth Amendment. If the Fourteenth Amendment is given a broad interpretation, it seriously diminishes the power of the states, and that sure knocks a dent in the Tenth Amendment. A narrow interpretation of the Fourteenth Amendment is more in keeping with the spirit of the Tenth Amendment. I deal with the Due Process Clause of the Fourteenth Amendment in Chapter 17 and with the rest of that amendment in Chapter 21.

Disentangling states' rights from individual rights

The Tenth Amendment says that any powers not delegated to the federal government are reserved to the states or to the people. But what happens if there's a conflict between the interests of a state and the interests of the people? This situation has arisen quite a few times, and the result is not always easy to predict. The important but now overruled case of *Lochner v. New York* (1905) is a good example.

In 1896, New York State passed a law setting a maximum of 60 hours of work per week in bakeries. Joseph Lochner owned a bakery in Utica, New York. He required his employees to work for more than 60 hours a week. He was charged, convicted, and fined for breaking this state law. Lochner unsuccessfully appealed his conviction to the highest court in New York State.

He then took his case to the U.S. Supreme Court, which heard it in 1905 under the name of *Lochner v. New York.* Lochner's appeal was based on the Fourteenth Amendment, and I discuss this aspect of the case in Chapter 17. But the case is also relevant to an understanding of the Tenth Amendment.

Arguing for individual liberty

Four potentially conflicting forces were involved in this case:

» The federal government — particularly the U.S. Supreme Court

» New York State

» Bakery owners

» Bakery workers

Lochner said that his employees had freely entered into a contractual agreement to work more than 60 hours a week. Lochner's lawyers argued that the New York State law limiting working hours was contrary to *freedom of contract* and therefore infringed on individual liberty.

New York State claimed that the law about working hours in bakeries was necessary to protect the health of bakery employees.

The high court agreed with Lochner and overturned his conviction under the New York law. The Supreme Court called the New York law an "unreasonable, unnecessary and arbitrary interference with the right and liberty of the individual to contract."

Analyzing the Supreme Court decision

Was the *Lochner* case really a victory for people power, as the Supreme Court claimed? Probably not. Lochner himself wanted his employees to work long hours. His employees agreed to do so. But was their agreement truly free? Did they really want to put in as many paid hours of work as possible? Or did they agree to the contract because that was the only way they could keep their jobs? It's impossible to tell.

The majority decision in the *Lochner* case was savaged by Justice Oliver Wendell Holmes, Jr., who in his dissent accused the majority of *judicial activism* — making law rather than interpreting it, as they were supposed to do. Holmes said that the majority decision was based on "an economic theory which a large part of the country does not entertain . . . But a constitution is not intended to embody a particular economic theory."

IN MY OPINION

Let's look at this case from the point of view of the Tenth Amendment. The Tenth Amendment says that the federal government — including the U.S. Supreme Court — is not entitled to exercise any power that is not delegated to it by the Constitution. In my opinion, the Supreme Court had no right to overturn the New York law in the first place. By doing so the Court overstepped its constitutional role.

Next, let me look at the New York law. Did the state have the right under its "police powers," as it claimed, to pass a law limiting working hours in bakeries? Note that the term *police powers* is used here in a very broad sense, meaning the power of the state to regulate behavior in the interests of public welfare, security, or morality. So the answer must be yes: The state was right in claiming that the health of the workers was in danger.

Does this conclusion infringe on the rights of the people? No, because freedom of contract is fine in general, but it's not a sacred principle. And in the *Lochner* case it's doubtful that the workers did freely agree to the long working hours that Joseph Lochner required.

In 1937, the Supreme Court rejected the approach that it had taken in *Lochner*, and *Lochner* is no longer an authority followed by the courts. However, *Lochner* is useful in helping to understand the competing interests involved in some legal disputes.

Giving the Tenth Amendment its due

The U.S. Supreme Court once characterized the Tenth Amendment as a mere "truism," just stating the obvious without adding anything new. I don't agree. On the contrary, I think the Tenth Amendment is crucial.

The Tenth Amendment provides a checklist on how to read and interpret the Constitution. Here's how it guides us to determine the constitutionality of a law:

>> **For federal laws:** What part of the Constitution gives Congress the power to pass this law? If there's no such justification, the law is unconstitutional.

>> **For state laws:** Does this law belong to one of the areas prohibited to the states by the U.S. Constitution? If it does, it's unconstitutional. If not, the next question is: Have the people delegated to the state — for example, by means of the state constitution — the power to make this law? If so, the law is okay. If not, the law is void.

5

Addressing Liberties and Modifying the Government: More Amendments

IN THIS PART . . .

Further check out Amendments of the Constitution — Eleventh through the Twenty-Seventh.

Look at the abolition of slavery.

Find out about equal protection.

Discover what's new with the Constitution.

Chapter **20**

States' Rights, Elections, and Slavery: The Eleventh through Thirteenth Amendments

The Eleventh, Twelfth, and Thirteenth amendments are very different from one another, but they all share something in common: Each was introduced to get the Constitution out of some deep doo-doo. Here's a rundown of the amendments with the problem that each was intended to solve:

» **Eleventh Amendment:** This amendment was introduced to overrule the Supreme Court decision in the case of *Chisholm v. Georgia,* which was viewed by many as an attack on states' rights.

» **Twelfth Amendment:** This amendment was an emergency measure to prevent the mess of the 1800 presidential election from recurring.

» **Thirteenth Amendment:** This amendment abolished slavery, which had divided the nation and dragged it into a ruinous civil war.

I discuss each in turn in this chapter.

The Eleventh Amendment: Asserting State Sovereign Immunity?

The Eleventh Amendment, ratified in 1795, contains only 43 words, but it has been interpreted in at least four different ways. Here's what the amendment says:

> The judicial power of the United States shall not be construed to extend to any suit in law or equity, commenced or prosecuted against one of the United States by Citizens of another State, or by Citizens or Subjects of any Foreign State.

Overruling the Supreme Court

The Eleventh Amendment was passed to overturn the Supreme Court ruling in the 1793 case of *Chisholm v. Georgia*. Alexander Chisholm of South Carolina filed suit against the State of Georgia for breach of contract, seeking payment for goods supplied to Georgia during the War of Independence.

Georgia refused to play ball, saying that Chisholm couldn't sue a state without its consent because it possessed sovereign immunity from suit. The Supreme Court didn't like this argument — not surprisingly, because it cut the Court's power. The Court found in favor of Chisholm and ruled that Article III, Section 2 of the Constitution took away the states' sovereign immunity because in the list of cases that could be heard by the U.S. Supreme Court, that section included "Controversies . . . between a State and Citizens of another State."

However, such was the outcry against this decision that two days after the Supreme Court handed down its decision in *Chisholm*, a senator put a proposal before Congress that was to become the Eleventh Amendment. The intention of the amendment was never a secret: It was passed to stop a federal lawsuit from being brought against a state without its consent. But is that really what the Eleventh Amendment says?

Interpreting the Eleventh Amendment

There are four main interpretations of the Eleventh Amendment:

>> The simplest and most straightforward interpretation of the amendment reads it as saying that nobody can sue a state in federal court without the consent of the state concerned.

>> The second interpretation reads the amendment as permitting a state to be sued by a citizen of another state or of a foreign country, but not by a citizen

of the state itself. According to this reading, the State of Utah can't be sued in federal court by a resident of Utah itself, but Utah can be sued by a resident of Nebraska or by a citizen of Outer Mongolia.

» The third interpretation is exactly the opposite, excluding only lawsuits against a state by a citizen of a different state.

» The fourth interpretation is broader. It says that in general, federal courts can't hear cases against states without their consent, but Congress can take away a state's sovereign immunity. If Congress does so, that state is no longer protected against suits in federal court.

Cutting across these four different interpretations are four recognized exceptions to the ban on lawsuits against states:

» A lawsuit can always be brought in federal court against a state's subdivisions, such as counties, cities, and municipalities.

» A state can always consent to a lawsuit being brought against it in federal court.

» Congress can *abrogate* — or remove — a state's immunity from suit in federal court, provided Congress's intention to abrogate a state's immunity is "unmistakably clear." However, in the 1996 case of *Seminole Tribe v. Florida*, the Supreme Court ruled that the Commerce Clause in Article I, Section 8 of the Constitution doesn't give Congress the power to abrogate a state's immunity from suit in federal court. This ruling calls into question the power of federal courts to hear lawsuits against states to enforce congressional legislation under the Commerce Clause relating to environmental law, bankruptcy, or intellectual property, to name but three major areas of commercial law.

» If a state violates federal law, the state itself can't be sued in federal court — but a federal court can order state *officials* in their own name to comply with federal law. The Supreme Court decided this in the controversial 1908 case *Ex parte Young*. This ruling was based on the fiction that a state official enforcing an unconstitutional state law is a private person — while still remaining a state agent when it comes to remedying the unconstitutional law! For example, in the 1993 ruling in *Martin v. Voinovich*, the high court ordered the governor of Ohio to construct housing for handicapped people to comply with the Americans with Disabilities Act.

REMEMBER

The question that lies at the heart of the Eleventh Amendment is whether the individual states can still be regarded as possessing *sovereignty*: complete legal independence. This certainly was the position for the first decade of independence under the Articles of Confederation. But did this position continue under the U.S. Constitution, which was ratified in 1788? In short, are, say, Maine, Ohio, Kentucky, and Texas as independent of one another and of the U.S. federal government as, say, France, India, Brazil, and Australia are of one another? Clearly not, but they obviously have a high degree of autonomy nevertheless. If the states were indeed sovereign states in the fullest sense, immunity from suit would follow. Because they don't have full sovereignty, their immunity from suit is also only partial.

In general, conservative justices on the Supreme Court have favored state immunity from suit, while liberal justices have tended to favor curtailing such immunity. The high watermark of state immunity was reached in *Alden v. Maine* (1999), in which a 5–4 conservative majority ruled that Congress doesn't have the authority under Article 1 of the Constitution to abrogate state immunity from suit either in federal or state court. However, in *Central Virginia Community College v. Katz*, which, significantly, was decided in 2006 after the death of Chief Justice Rehnquist, a liberal-led majority of five ruled that Congress could abrogate state immunity under the Bankruptcy Clause of Article 1 of the Constitution.

The technical-sounding arguments marshaled on both sides in Eleventh Amendment cases mask a clash between two fundamental principles: the principle of sovereign immunity on the one hand, and on the other the principle that "where there is a right there must be a remedy." The liberal position is particularly strong when, as in *Alden*, the scope of state sovereign immunity is so broad as to deprive of any possibility of redress an individual wanting to sue a state.

Cleaning Up the Framers' Political Mess: The Twelfth Amendment

The mess that the Twelfth Amendment was intended to clean up reflects the Framers' naïve innocence in the dirty world of politics.

The Twelfth Amendment introduced the system of presidential elections that is still in force today — at least in theory. It was intended as an emergency fix for the 1804 presidential election after the two previous elections, held in 1796 and 1800, had gone badly wrong.

Electing the President: The original rules

You can find the original arrangements for presidential elections in the unamended text of Article II, Section 1 of the Constitution. The arrangements were as follows:

>> Each state legislature appointed as many electors for that state as there were senators plus representatives from that state combined. Let's take a

hypothetical state with 12 representatives in the House of Representatives. This state would also have had two senators (because every state is entitled to two senators). So, the total number of electors for that state would have been 14.

» The electors of each state met separately.

» Each elector had two votes without differentiating between President and Vice President.

» The candidate with the most votes (provided they amounted to more than 50 percent of the total) became the President, and the runner-up became the Vice President.

» If no candidate obtained more than 50 percent of the votes, the presidential election was thrown into the House of Representatives, and the Senate picked the Vice President.

These original rules omitted all mention of political parties. The whole arrangement was undemocratic because the Framers didn't trust the ordinary people to pick the President. Their naïve idea was that the electors would choose the best candidate to be the President and the second-best candidate to be the Vice President.

Not surprisingly, the whole of this arrangement came unstuck as soon as it was put into practice in the first real contested presidential election in 1796.

Understanding politics 1796 style

In the 1796 presidential election, John Adams and Thomas Jefferson, the two main opposing candidates for President, ended up as President and Vice President, respectively. It's just as if Hillary Clinton had become Donald Trump's Veep!

John Adams, a Federalist, got 71 electoral votes — more than 50 percent of the total — and Thomas Jefferson, a Republican or Democratic-Republican, received 68 electoral votes. Although Jefferson and Adams didn't see eye-to-eye politically, Jefferson was sworn in as Adams's Vice President. What a mess! But worse was to follow.

Tying and vying with your running mate: The 1800 election

The 1800 election was a rematch between Adams and his own Vice President, Jefferson. To avoid a repetition of the same problem as in 1796, the political parties each nominated two candidates, one intended to run for President and the other for Vice President. The Federalist ticket of John Adams and Charles Pinckney was confronted by the Democratic-Republican ticket of Thomas Jefferson and Aaron Burr.

Jefferson and Burr won with 73 electoral votes each. It was well understood that Jefferson was the party's presidential candidate and Burr his running mate, but the Constitution drew no distinction between candidates for the two offices. Each elector just had two equal votes.

Because neither Jefferson nor Burr had a majority, the choice of President was left to the House of Representatives. Here the contest was no longer between Jefferson and Adams but between Jefferson and his own running mate, Aaron Burr!

After 36 ballots and a lot of horse-trading, Jefferson was elected President and Burr Vice President.

This chaotic election made an amendment to the Constitution a pressing necessity, and the Twelfth Amendment was duly ratified on June 15, 1804, less than five months before that year's presidential election.

Preventing future chaos

The Twelfth Amendment has stood the test of time, even though it still doesn't mention political parties. It indirectly recognizes the existence of parties by providing that electors cast a separate vote for President and Vice President.

So, it's no longer a problem if a party's vice-presidential candidate gets the same number of electoral votes as that party's candidate for President — which indeed is what normally happens.

CONTROVERSY

Some people criticize the entire Electoral College system as laid down in the Constitution and the Twelfth Amendment, labeling it undemocratic. I discuss the Electoral College in depth in Chapter 10 and explain why the Framers opted for this method of election instead of relying on the popular vote.

Removing the Blot of Slavery: The Thirteenth Amendment

"All men are created equal," proclaims the Declaration of Independence, written by Thomas Jefferson — a lifelong slave owner. How can slavery be lawful in a nation based on equality? This conundrum took a civil war to sort out.

Although the words *slave* and *slavery* don't appear in the original unamended Constitution, slavery was legally established in a number of states, particularly in the South. And there are indirect allusions to slavery in the text of the Constitution. For example, Article I, Section 9, Clause 1 refers to "the Importation of . . . Persons" — clearly a reference to the slave trade. And Article I, Section 2 allowed slaves to be counted as three-fifths of free persons when calculating state populations for purposes of representation in the House of Representatives — an ironic rule, considering that slaves didn't have the right to vote!

Tracking the debate on slavery

As the United States expanded in the first decades after independence, the question of slavery reared its ugly head at every turn. It eventually reached the U.S. Supreme Court in 1857 in the now-notorious case of *Dred Scott v. Sandford*. Dred Scott was a slave whose master was an army doctor who kept moving around, taking Scott with him. Scott was born into slavery in Virginia, a slave state, but lived for a time in Illinois, a free state, and also in the Wisconsin Territory, where slavery was prohibited under the Missouri Compromise, passed by Congress and signed into law by President James Monroe in 1820. Scott claimed that his residence in a free state and a free territory had emancipated him from slavery. The U.S. Supreme Court roundly rejected this argument. Chief Justice Roger Taney, writing for the majority, ruled that the Fifth Amendment prohibited the federal government from depriving anybody of property — including slaves — "without due process of law." The Missouri Compromise of 1820, he held, was therefore unconstitutional. In Taney's words, "An act of Congress which deprives a citizen of the United States of his liberty or property merely because he came himself or brought his property into a particular Territory of the United States, and who had committed no offence against the laws, could hardly be dignified with the name of due process of law." On this basis, the Court decided by a 6–2 vote that Scott was still a slave and, moreover, that no African American, whether slave or free, could ever become a U.S. citizen.

By denying the power of Congress to prohibit slavery in the territories, the Supreme Court incensed antislavery opinion throughout the nation. The widening rift between the free North and the slave-owning South led to increasing talk in the South about secession from the Union.

For the election of 1860, the recently formed Republican Party adopted a platform that opposed the spread of slavery to the territories but did not propose to abolish slavery in those states where it already existed. The Republican presidential candidate, Abraham Lincoln, was a moderate Republican. Lincoln regarded slavery as immoral, but he accepted that it was recognized by the Constitution.

Sliding into secession

The 1860 election revealed just how divided the nation was (see Figure 20-1). Lincoln won handily in the North, while incumbent Vice President John C. Breckinridge swept the South. Lincoln's name didn't even appear on the ballot in nine southern states. Lincoln won less than 40 percent of the popular vote nationwide, but this translated into just under 60 percent of the electoral votes, which put him into the White House.

FIGURE 20-1:
A cartoon showing Abraham Lincoln depending partly on the slavery issue in the 1860 presidential election.

Source: Louis Maurer, 1832–1932

Although Lincoln wasn't an abolitionist, the South assumed that he was, and he refused to promise not to abolish slavery altogether. Seven southern states seceded from the Union even before Lincoln was inaugurated on March 4, 1861.

In a last-ditch attempt to placate the South and bring the seceding states back into the Union, lame-duck President James Buchanan asked Congress to propose an "explanatory amendment" to the Constitution based on the *Dred Scott* decision of the Supreme Court.

A special committee of the House of Representatives under Thomas Corwin of Ohio, a Republican, quickly produced a draft. On March 2, 1861 — with just two days of Buchanan's presidency left — Congress passed the proposed amendment with the requisite two-thirds majority in both houses. President Buchanan signed it enthusiastically, although the President's approval is not needed for amendments.

Considering the Corwin amendment

The *Corwin amendment*, as it's usually called, reads as follows:

> *No amendment shall be made to the Constitution which will authorize or give to Congress the power to abolish or interfere, within any state, with the domestic institutions thereof, including that of persons held to labor or service by the laws of said state.*

Despite the absence of the word *slave* or *slavery*, there was no mistaking the meaning of this proposed amendment. It clearly guaranteed the preservation of slavery in all already-existing slave states without, however, dealing with the vexed question of slavery in the territories or new states.

It's significant that this proposed amendment was able to command such widespread support in Congress at a time when many southern members had withdrawn. This means that an amendment guaranteeing the permanent existence of slavery in the established slave states had substantial support among the politicians representing the free states of the North.

Amazingly, two days later, on March 4, 1861, the newly elected President Lincoln also gave the proposed amendment his grudging blessing in his first inaugural address.

The proposed amendment was then sent on its way to obtain the ratification of the states. It was validly ratified by Ohio and Maryland and invalidly by Illinois (by a constitutional convention that just happened to be in session at the time). But Buchanan's and Corwin's frantic efforts to avert a civil war came too late. By the time the proposed amendment passed Congress, seven states had not only seceded but already established a breakaway government under the title of the Confederate States of America, or the *Confederacy*, as it's commonly known.

Jefferson Davis, who became the president of the Confederacy, was a U.S. senator from Mississippi from 1857 to 1861. After Mississippi seceded in January 1861 — against Davis's advice — he withdrew from the Senate. In his farewell address, he identified the reason for the secession of the South as the Republican Party's failure "to recognize our domestic institutions [slavery] which preexisted the formation of the Union — our property, which was guarded by the Constitution."

REMEMBER

Recognition of slavery where it was already legally established was precisely what the Corwin amendment sought to achieve. The Buchanan-Corwin initiative wasn't the first time that such a solution had been proposed. But it was the first time that it had reached the stage of being adopted by Congress for ratification as a constitutional amendment.

President Buchanan deplored the secession, saying, "The South has no right to secede, but I have no power to prevent them." Prevention is better than cure, but a cure was at hand — military action. Buchanan regarded that cure as worse than the disease, but it was eagerly embraced by his successor, Lincoln, who was determined to bring the seceding states to heel. With a full-scale civil war raging as of April 1861, the Corwin amendment was quickly forgotten.

Could the ratification of the Corwin amendment have prevented the bloody carnage that followed Lincoln's inauguration? Or was Lincoln's famous earlier remark more accurate? — that "A house divided against itself cannot stand. I believe this government cannot endure, permanently half slave and half free."

Graduating from emancipation to abolition

The Civil War raged from 1861 to 1865. In the early stages, Lincoln didn't allow his generals to free slaves in captured territories, and he even reversed their emancipation proclamations. For example, when General John Frémont freed all slaves in Missouri, Lincoln canceled the general's proclamation and relieved him of his command.

In 1862, in response to a call by a newspaper editor for the total abolition of slavery, Lincoln wrote, "My paramount object in this struggle is to save the Union, and is not either to save or destroy slavery. If I could save the Union without saving any slave I would do it, and if I could save it by freeing all the slaves I would do it."

Lincoln had long been an advocate of sending freed slaves to colonize Liberia, in West Africa. As President he also championed a succession of schemes of black colonization in Panama and off the coast of Haiti.

Lincoln took the view that the Constitution didn't give a peacetime President the power to abolish slavery. However, a mass rally of abolitionists in Chicago held in September 1862 calling for an immediate end to slavery placed the President under pressure.

Later the same month, Lincoln issued his Emancipation Proclamation as a wartime measure. It freed the slaves living in those states of the Confederacy that had not returned to Union control by January 1, 1863. However, it didn't have any effect on the slaves in border states that had remained loyal to the Union. Remarkably, the Proclamation also favored the idea of encouraging African Americans to leave the country and establish settlements elsewhere in the Americas or in Africa.

The radical Republicans, hard-line abolitionists, pressed for the immediate and complete abolition of slavery throughout the nation. They thought Lincoln was pussyfooting around the issue of slavery. So in May 1864 they nominated General John Frémont — the radical abolitionist who had had a run-in with Lincoln earlier in the war and had actually been the first presidential candidate of the newly formed Republican Party in 1856 — to run against Lincoln for President.

Introducing an entirely different thirteenth amendment

In the meantime, the strongly Republican Senate spearheaded the introduction of a very different thirteenth amendment — one abolishing slavery altogether. This was to become the actual Thirteenth Amendment and is still part of the Constitution today. Section 1 reads as follows:

> *Neither slavery nor involuntary servitude, except as a punishment for crime whereof the party shall have been duly convicted, shall exist within the United States, or any place subject to their jurisdiction.*

This amendment was proposed in 1864 while the Civil War was still raging and the slave-owning states of the South still formed part of the breakaway Confederacy. So, an amendment abolishing slavery might have been expected to enjoy widespread support in Congress, from which the Confederate states were excluded.

But in fact, abolition was by no means universally popular in the North. For example, Francis Hughes, an influential Pennsylvania Democrat, warned that abolition would flood the state with freed slaves. In the 1862 midterm elections to the House of Representatives, the Republican Party had lost 22 seats, leaving them with only 86 seats out of a total of 185, or just over 46 percent of the seats.

So, although the proposed amendment easily passed the Senate — whose members in those days were not directly elected but appointed by their state legislatures — it was initially rejected by the House of Representatives, which it passed only nine months later, on January 31, 1865.

By this time Lincoln felt much more secure after comfortably winning a second term as President. Congress had taken the initiative over abolition, so Lincoln — always a cautious politician — could now safely come out in its favor. He followed President Buchanan's example (in regard to the Corwin amendment) by writing by hand on the Joint Resolution of Congress passing the proposed new amendment, "Approved February 1, 1865 — Abraham Lincoln."

The proposal was quickly ratified by the free states in the North but was rejected by slave states that had remained loyal to the Union, including New Jersey (which had only a handful of slaves), Delaware, and Kentucky. Nevertheless, by the time the Civil War ended in April 1865, no fewer than 20 states had ratified the proposed amendment — out of a requisite 27, three-fourths of the 36 states then in existence.

The last seven states to complete the ratification process included some southern states under Union occupation. Ratification was completed with the ratification by the occupied state of Georgia on December 6, 1865. By contrast, Mississippi, another Confederate state, which still had its own elected (Democratic Party) governor at the same time, rejected the amendment on December 5, 1865 — and ratified it only on March 16, 1995!

REMEMBER

The importance of the slavery issue in the history of the United States can't be exaggerated. It has generated — and still generates — strong emotions. To put the whole subject in perspective, it may be helpful to read two very different accounts of what slavery was like. First, there's Kenneth M. Stampp's classic negative portrayal of slavery in his 1956 book *The Peculiar Institution: Slavery in the Ante-Bellum South.* A very different view of slavery emerges from a 1974 two-volume blockbuster by the Nobel laureate Robert W. Fogel together with Stanley L. Engerman called *Time on the Cross: The Economics of American Negro Slavery.* This radical revisionist work, based on detailed economic data, concluded that the material conditions of slaves compared favorably with those of free industrial workers in the North. The book was countered in turn by a number of publications, notably Herbert Gutman's *Slavery and the Numbers Game* (1975) and the later book by Peter Kolchin titled *American Slavery 1619-1877,* published in 1993.

JUSTIFYING THE DRAFT?

Is conscription, Selective Service, or the draft prohibited by the Thirteenth Amendment as a form of "involuntary servitude"? The Supreme Court in *Arver v. United States,* heard in 1918 during World War I, ruled that performance of a citizen's "supreme and noble duty of contributing to the defense of the rights and honor of the nation, as the result of a war declared by the great representative body of the people" couldn't possibly "be said to be the imposition of involuntary servitude in violation of the prohibitions of the Thirteenth Amendment."

That decision specifically refers to wars declared by Congress. But what about wars not officially declared by Congress? After all, the United States has not issued any formal declaration of war since World War II. Does the 1918 ruling mean that the draft is legal only for wars formally declared by Congress? Probably not, but this question remains open. For more on the President's war powers, see Chapter 10.

The draft was replaced in 1973 by all-volunteer U.S. armed forces, but it's still obligatory for all male U.S. citizens and resident non-citizens aged between 18 and 25 to register with the Selective Service System within 30 days of their 18th birthday. This requirement has been (so far unsuccessfully) challenged in court, not under the Thirteenth Amendment but on the basis that it discriminates against males in violation of the Equal Protection Clause of the Fourteenth Amendment. For more on this, see Chapter 21.

Chapter **21**

The Fourteenth Amendment: Ensuring Equal Protection

The Fourteenth Amendment, ratified in 1868, is one of the most important — and one of the most controversial — parts of the Constitution. It's a meaty amendment, dealing with some pretty weighty topics. These include:

» The definition of citizenship

» The obligation of the states to uphold the privileges and immunities of United States citizens

» Due process

» The obligation of the states not to deny "the equal protection of the laws"

» How representation in Congress is calculated

» Disqualification from holding office

» Denial of any obligation to compensate former slave owners for the emancipation of their slaves

With the exception of due process, which I discuss in Chapter 17, you can sink your teeth into all these topics in this chapter. I hope you're hungry!

Defining Citizenship

The first clause of Section 1 of the Fourteenth Amendment defines citizenship:

All persons born or naturalized in the United States, and subject to the jurisdiction thereof, are citizens of the United States and of the State wherein they reside.

This definition looks pretty straightforward, but it isn't. Here's why:

>> United States citizenship is based on *birthright* rather than on the "right of blood." Birthright citizenship means that citizenship depends on *where* a person is born rather than *who* his or her parents are. The U.S. Supreme Court confirmed the birthright basis of U.S. citizenship in 1898. This ruling was made in the case of Wong Kim Ark, who was born in the United States to Chinese noncitizen parents. The Court decided that he was a U.S. citizen even though his parents were not.

Chief Justice Melville Fuller in his dissenting opinion in Wong's case put his finger on a problem with the birthright rule: "It is unreasonable to conclude that 'natural-born citizen' applied to everybody born within the geographical tract known as the United States, irrespective of circumstances; and that the children of foreigners, happening to be born to them while passing through the country . . . were eligible to the presidency, while children of our citizens, born abroad, were not."

>> The definition of citizenship in the Fourteenth Amendment is very different from what it would have been at the time when the Bill of Rights was ratified in 1791. Back then, not everybody who was born in the United States "and subject to the jurisdiction thereof" was a citizen because slaves weren't recognized as citizens even though most of them had been born in the United States. In *Dred Scott v. Sandford* (1857), the Supreme Court ruled that African Americans had never been and could never become citizens of the United States. The prime purpose of the Fourteenth Amendment was to reverse this decision and to make it clear that former slaves, who had been emancipated by the Thirteenth Amendment, enjoyed the full rights of citizenship.

>> This definition of citizenship contains a twofold test. To be a citizen you have to be "born or naturalized in the United States" *and* "subject to the jurisdiction thereof." Let's see how that pans out in practice:

- The children of U.S. citizens are automatically citizens if they are born in the United States.

- Laws passed by Congress have also given automatic U.S. citizenship to children born outside the United States, provided at least one of their parents is a U.S. citizen — even if they are born out of wedlock. (Precise conditions vary according to the dates of birth of the children concerned.)

- Any child under 18 who has been adopted by a U.S. citizen gets citizenship immediately on arrival in the United States under the Child Citizenship Act of 2000.

- The children of aliens who are lawfully in the United States are automatically U.S. citizens — provided the children are born in the United States.

CONTROVERSY

- What about the children of illegal aliens? This is a highly controversial issue. The Supreme Court's decision in *Wong Kim Ark* (1898) is generally interpreted as meaning that all children born in the United States are U.S. citizens, regardless of their parents' legal status. But there's a good deal of opposition to this kind of "birthright" citizenship, as it's called, and several abortive bills have been introduced in Congress in the hope of reinterpreting the Fourteenth Amendment in order to end it.

- Opponents of "birthright" citizenship focus on the words "subject to the jurisdiction thereof" in Section 1 of the Fourteenth Amendment. This provision is usually interpreted as excluding only the children of foreign diplomats from becoming U.S. citizens, if they are born in the United States, but not the children of illegal immigrants. Professor John C. Eastman, an opponent of "birthright" citizenship, argues that the phrase "subject to the jurisdiction thereof" has to be interpreted in the light of the Civil Rights Act of 1866, which Section 1 of the Fourteenth Amendment was intended to codify. That act reads as follows: "All persons born in the United States, and not subject to any foreign power . . . are hereby declared to be citizens of the United States." Senator Jacob Howard, one of the movers of the citizenship clause of the amendment on the floor of the Senate, explained it as excluding "persons born in the United States who are foreigners, aliens, or who belong to the families of ambassadors or foreign ministers." Similarly, Michigan Chief Justice Thomas Cooley's influential treatise, *The General Principles of Constitutional Law in America,* published in 1880, explained the phrase "subject to the jurisdiction" of the United States to mean "full and complete jurisdiction, to which citizens are generally subject, and not any qualified and partial jurisdiction, such as may consist with allegiance to some other government."

> The point made here is that illegal immigrants remain citizens of other countries, to which they still owe allegiance while living in the United States. The counter-argument to that is that an illegal immigrant is subject to the jurisdiction of the United States just as much as a legal immigrant and, unlike foreign diplomats, has no immunity from the laws of the United States.

Whichever view one takes, the children of illegal immigrants born in the U.S. will continue to enjoy "birthright" citizenship until or unless the Supreme Court rules against that interpretation or unless the Constitution is amended accordingly. It's important to stress that the question of "birthright" citizenship is quite separate from the issue of "Dreamers," children of undocumented immigrants who were not born in the U.S. but arrived in the U.S. under 16 years old and have lived in the U.S. since June 15, 2007. Dreamers were protected against deportation by DACA, or the Deferred Action for Childhood Arrivals, an executive program initiated by President Obama in 2012, which was blocked by the U.S. Supreme Court in a one-line decision by an equally divided Court in *United States v. Texas* (2016).

Can a U.S. citizen be stripped of his or her citizenship? In a rare show of unanimity, the Supreme Court ruled in *Maslenjak v. United States* (2017) that a naturalized U.S. citizen can be stripped of his or her citizenship for making a false statement — but only in very limited circumstances. "We hold," said Justice Elena Kagan, writing for the Court, "that the government must establish that an illegal act by the defendant played some role in her acquisition of citizenship."

What about citizens by birth who are guilty of disloyalty? Can they be stripped of their citizenship on the ground that they have rejected the jurisdiction of the United States? No. In 2004, the U.S. Supreme Court heard a case involving Yaser Hamdi. Hamdi was allegedly fighting on the side of the Taliban when he was captured in Afghanistan in 2001. Could the U.S. government hold him in Guantanamo Bay and deny him due process as an "illegal enemy combatant"? No, said the Supreme Court, because he was a U.S. citizen. He was born in the United States and raised in Saudi Arabia, of which he was also a citizen. Faced with a judicial brick wall, the U.S. government made a deal with Hamdi. In return for his release, Hamdi gave up his U.S. citizenship and promised to live permanently in Saudi Arabia.

Understanding States' Obligations

The Bill of Rights contains a lot of rights enjoyed by the people against the government. But which government is that — the federal government, state governments, or both? This important question is not directly answered in the Bill of Rights. The U.S. Supreme Court confronted it only in 1833, in the case of *Barron v. Baltimore*.

The Court's answer was clear: The Bill of Rights binds only the federal government, not the states. In the words of Chief Justice John Marshall, "The question thus presented is, we think, of great importance, but not of much difficulty." He explained that the U.S. Constitution is concerned only with the federal government and not with the individual states, each of which has its own constitution.

This restrictive reading of the Constitution prevailed right up until the ratification of the Fourteenth Amendment in 1868. The wording of the Fourteenth Amendment makes it quite clear that it applies just as much to the states as to the federal government. Allow me to pick out references to the states to demonstrate:

> All persons born or naturalized in the United States, and subject to the jurisdiction thereof, are citizens of the United States and of the State wherein they reside. No State shall make or enforce any law which shall abridge the privileges or immunities of citizens of the United States; nor shall any State deprive any person of life, liberty, or property, without due process of law; nor deny to any person within its jurisdiction the equal protection of the laws.

Let's look more closely at the obligations of states contained in this section.

Disentangling state citizenship

> All persons born or naturalized in the United States, and subject to the jurisdiction thereof, are citizens of the United States and of the State wherein they reside.

Okay, so all U.S. citizens are also citizens "of the State wherein they reside." Generations ago, that may have seemed simple enough, but these days, few people live their entire lives in the states in which they're born. If you are born in Arizona, go to college in Indiana, and then move to Hawaii, of which state are you a citizen? All of them, at different times. You can get a driver's license in whichever state you move to, vote in that state's elections, and enjoy all the rights of state citizenship as if you were born and raised there.

Analyzing "privileges or immunities"

Look again at the opening of the second clause of Section 1 of the Fourteenth Amendment:

> No State shall make or enforce any law which shall abridge the privileges or immunities of citizens of the United States . . .

What exactly does it mean?

>> To *abridge* means to shorten, restrict, limit, or reduce.

>> A *privilege* is a right that's enjoyed only by some people. The privileges referred to in the Fourteenth Amendment are specifically the privileges enjoyed only by U.S. citizens.

>> *Immunities* are really the flip side of privileges. Privileges are positive, immunities negative. Nowadays, the word *immunity* is most often used in reference to disease. But in the Constitution, *immunity* means a special negative right enjoyed by U.S. citizens, such as the right not to be deported to a foreign country.

>> The first *shall* means "must" and the second one "will."

Let me rewrite the whole clause in modern English. Here goes:

No state is allowed to make or enforce any law that reduces the special positive and negative rights of citizens of the United States.

But what exactly are these special positive and negative rights?

Dredging the past for "privileges or immunities"

The answer to this question lies in the history of the phrase "privileges or immunities." The "privileges or immunities" clause of the Fourteenth Amendment clearly echoes the first clause of Section 2 of Article IV of the Constitution, which reads:

The Citizens of each State shall be entitled to all Privileges and Immunities of Citizens in the several States.

This wording in turn can be traced back hundreds of years to English common law.

The phrase crystallized in a wonderful judgment given in 1823 by George Washington's nephew, Justice Bushrod Washington, in *Corfield v. Coryell.* Congress cited this decision when it adopted the "privileges or immunities" clause of the Fourteenth Amendment.

Justice Washington stressed that the phrase "Privileges and Immunities" in Article IV of the Constitution doesn't refer to *all* the privileges and immunities enjoyed by citizens, but only to "those privileges and immunities which are, in their nature, fundamental." If this is the meaning of "Privileges and Immunities" in Article IV, it must also be the meaning of the phrase in the Fourteenth Amendment, which intentionally echoes it. (The only reason for the switch from "and" to "or" is that the phrase in Article IV is positive, and the phrase in the Fourteenth Amendment is negative. Check it out.)

Listening to George Washington's favorite nephew

Here are some of the privileges and immunities that Bushrod Washington identified:

>> "Protection by the government"

>> The enjoyment of life, liberty, and property

>> "The right of a citizen of one state to pass through, or to reside in any other state"

>> The right "to claim the benefit of the writ of habeas corpus"

>> The right "to institute and maintain actions of any kind in the courts of the state"

>> The right "to take, hold and dispose of property, either real or personal"

>> The right to vote

Achieving "Equal Justice Under Law" — Or Not

Equality is one of the big principles of the American Revolution, but more in theory than in practice. The Declaration of Independence proclaims "all men are created equal," but Thomas Jefferson, who drafted the Declaration, was a slave owner.

You may have seen the words "Equal Justice Under Law" emblazoned above the entrance to the U.S. Supreme Court Building. (Surprisingly enough, this slogan was coined not by any Supreme Court justice, but by the architects of the building!) The concept encapsulated in this memorable phrase is a close cousin to the Equal Protection Clause of the Fourteenth Amendment:

> *nor [shall any State] deny to any person within its jurisdiction the equal protection of the laws.*

As is so often the case, this clause raises more questions than it answers. In the following sections, I address some of the topics that are — or could be, if challenged in court — affected by the Equal Protection Clause.

Age discrimination

A 1984 federal law called the National Minimum Drinking Age Act indicates that federal revenue will be withheld from states that allow people under the age of 21 to buy alcohol. Even so, each state technically still has the right to decide the legal drinking age within its borders. Most states set that age at 21 (although some states sidestep the issue somewhat by forbidding the purchase — but not the consumption — of alcohol by people under age 21).

You can vote when you turn 18, so why do you have to wait another three years before you can drink? Is it in accordance with "equal protection of the laws" to allow 21-year-olds to drink but not 18-year-olds? No, but most people would probably regard this kind of discrimination as justified.

South Dakota, which allowed 19-year-olds to buy beer containing up to 3.2 percent alcohol, challenged the 1984 federal law in the U.S. Supreme Court. The challenge was based not on the Fourteenth Amendment but on the Twenty-First Amendment, which gives the states control over liquor (see Chapter 22). South Dakota's challenge failed, and the 1984 federal law was upheld. Would a challenge based on the Fourteenth Amendment have been more likely to succeed? Probably not, mainly because of the problem of drunk driving among young drivers.

Capital punishment

What about executing juveniles or those that are developmentally disabled? Is it right to treat them the same as everybody else? Is that the type of "equal protection" the Fourteenth Amendment refers to?

The U.S. Supreme Court has come out against the execution of anyone who fits in either of these categories. In the case of *Roper v. Simmons*, which was heard in 2005, the Court ruled that a 17-year-old murderer could not be executed, even though

>> He broke into his victim's house, tied her hands, and blindfolded her.

>> He then drove her to a state park and threw her off a railroad bridge while she was still alive, all for the theft of $6!

>> He had planned his actions carefully.

>> He videotaped a reenactment of events afterward.

>> He boasted about his actions.

>> He confessed to the killing.

Did this killer deserve to be spared the death penalty just because he was a few months shy of his 18th birthday? The Missouri jury that sentenced him to death sure didn't think so. This is a case where most people might agree that equal justice was called for. However, the case wasn't fought on that basis at all, but simply under the Eighth Amendment's prohibition of "cruel and unusual punishments," which I discuss in Chapter 18.

Racial segregation

In the well-known case of *Plessy v. Ferguson,* decided in 1896, the U.S. Supreme Court ruled in favor of a Louisiana law requiring racial segregation on the railroad. The Court held that this law didn't violate the Equal Protection Clause of the Fourteenth Amendment. The Equal Protection Clause, said the Court, was concerned with equality in civil rights, not in social arrangements. The Louisiana law, it held, satisfied the test of reasonableness and was based on "the established usages, customs and traditions of the people."

However, in 1954, in *Brown v. Board of Education,* the U.S. Supreme Court signaled a fundamental change of mind. The Court, speaking through Chief Justice Earl Warren, proclaimed that

> *in the field of public education the doctrine of 'separate but equal' has no place. Separate educational facilities are inherently unequal. Therefore, we hold that the plaintiffs and others similarly situated . . . are, by reason of the segregation complained of, deprived of the equal protection of the laws guaranteed by the Fourteenth Amendment.*

I discuss this important case in Chapter 23.

School busing

Does the ban on segregation entitle the courts to enforce mixed schools? In 1971, the U.S. Supreme Court ordered the integration of all 105 schools in Charlotte-Mecklenburg, North Carolina, by busing students to different schools. The intention was to achieve the same whites-to-blacks ratio in the schools as in the population of the area as a whole. The Supreme Court based its unanimous decision specifically on the Equal Protection Clause of the Fourteenth Amendment.

But this important decision backfired. The Supreme Court believed that forced integration would lead to greater equality in the education offered to members of different ethnic groups — and to an improvement in the educational levels attained by minority students. Yet a 1992 Harvard University study found that black and Hispanic students lacked "even modest overall improvement" as a result of busing.

CONTROVERSY

Here are some other bad effects of busing:

>> Some students were spending as much as three hours a day on the bus! As a result, less time was available for sports and other extracurricular activities.

>> Busing sometimes transported kids to dangerous neighborhoods.

>> Kids were often bused from integrated schools to less integrated schools.

>> "White flight" to the suburbs occurred at least partly in response to forced integration. Another response to busing was for white parents to send their children to private or parochial schools.

>> The result was that inner city public schools became largely made up of minorities — exactly the opposite of the intention behind busing. Today, Boston public schools are 75 percent African American and Hispanic, even though Boston's black and Hispanic populations together represent less than 40 percent of the city's total population. Similar examples abound. Private schools sprang up in Pasadena, California — 48 at the last count — where white kids now make up only 15 percent of the public school population.

Since 1971, the U.S. Supreme Court has gradually pulled away from the extreme interpretation of the Equal Protection Clause that led to forced busing. In *Milliken v. Bradley,* heard in 1974, the Supreme Court banned forced busing across district lines unless a number of school districts had engaged in deliberate segregation. In *Board of Education of Oklahoma City v. Dowell,* decided in 1991, the Supreme Court recognized that the existence of single-race schools didn't necessarily amount to a violation of the Equal Protection Clause.

In two cases decided together in 2007, the Supreme Court finally almost reversed its 1971 interpretation of the Equal Protection Clause. The two cases in question were *Parents Involved in Community Schools v. Seattle School District No. 1* and *Meredith v. Jefferson County Board of Education.* The Supreme Court rejected the use of race as the sole basis for assigning students to schools. This turned the 1971 interpretation of the Equal Protection Clause on its head. In the words of Chief Justice John Roberts, "The way to stop discrimination on the basis of race is to stop discriminating on the basis of race" — an important recognition that discrimination in favor of minorities is racial discrimination nevertheless.

Affirmative action

A related topic is whether the Equal Protection Clause supports affirmative action. In *Grutter v. Bollinger,* heard in 2003, the U.S. Supreme Court upheld the University of Michigan Law School's affirmative action admissions policy. Justice Sandra Day

O'Connor, writing for the majority, held that there was "a compelling interest in obtaining the educational benefits that flow from a diverse student body." Justice Clarence Thomas (see Figure 21-1), in a strongly worded dissent, labeled the law school's admissions policy as racial discrimination and "a practice that can only weaken the principle of equality embodied in the Declaration of Independence and the Equal Protection Clause." By contrast, in *Gratz v. Bollinger,* decided on the same day, the University of Michigan undergraduate affirmative action admissions program was held to be a "disguised quota" system, and therefore unconstitutional in accordance with the ruling in the leading 1978 case, *Regents of the University of California v. Bakke.* For more on both *Bollinger* cases, see Chapter 23.

FIGURE 21-1:
Associate Justice Clarence Thomas, appointed in 1991, opposes affirmative action on the basis that it's just another form of racial discrimination, and stated "under our Constitution, the government may not make distinctions on the basis of race."

Source: Steve Petteway, Collection of the Supreme Court of the United States

In the wake of the two Bollinger decisions, in 2006 Michigan voters approved a proposal amending the state's constitution to make affirmative action illegal in public employment, public education, and for public contracting purposes (unless mandated by federal law or to obtain federal funding). This amendment to the Michigan constitution banning affirmative action was held by the Supreme Court not to be unconstitutional in *Schuette v. Coalition to Defend Affirmative Action* (2014).

Gerrymandering

Gerrymandering refers to redrawing the boundaries of a voting district to favor one political party. The word is the dubious legacy of Massachusetts Governor Elbridge Gerry, whose 1812 redistricting map showed an elongated voting district that resembled a salamander. *Gerry* plus *salamander* produced the new word *gerrymander*.

Obviously, gerrymandering has been practiced for a long time, but is it legal, or does it violate the Equal Protection Clause?

In the Supreme Court case of *Vieth v. Jubelirer* (2004), the outcome was essentially a cop-out, with a plurality holding that gerrymandering claims were non-justiciable (not capable of being heard by a court of law) because, in the words of Justice Scalia, there was "a lack of judicially discoverable and manageable standards for resolving the question."

In 2006, the League of United Latin American Citizens challenged the recent redistricting of Texas on the ground that it diluted the Latino vote and amounted to an unconstitutional gerrymander, contrary to the Equal Protection Clause. The Supreme Court ruled that the redistricting of one Texas voting district, Congressional District 23, violated section 2 of the Voting Rights Act of 1965, but that the other newly created districts complained about were kosher. Justices Stevens and Breyer dissented, wanting to declare the whole of Texas's 2003 redistricting plan a violation of the Equal Protection Clause on the ground that the Republicans had created "their own impermissible stranglehold on political power."

Gill v. Whitford is due to be heard by the Supreme Court in June 2018. This is another case alleging unconstitutional partisan gerrymandering by Republicans, this time in Wisconsin.

In *Bethune-Hill v. Virginia State Board of Elections* (2017), the Supreme Court held that a U.S. District Court had applied an incorrect legal standard in ruling that race didn't predominate in 11 of the 12 voting districts complained of by a number of Virginia voters as "unconstitutional racial gerrymandering."

On a related point, in *Evenwel v. Abbott* (2016), the Supreme Court ruled that the one person, one vote principle under the Equal Protection Clause of the Fourteenth Amendment allows states to continue to use the total population, not just the total voter-eligible population as urged by Sue Evenwel, in drawing their legislative voting districts. Evenwel's objection to the current system was that it diluted citizens' votes in a number of urban districts by including large numbers of non-voting non-citizens.

THE COURTS' STANDARD OF SCRUTINY

What standard of scrutiny should the courts apply in lawsuits brought under the Equal Protection Clause? The U.S. Supreme Court has identified three levels of scrutiny:

- **Strict scrutiny,** applicable to cases involving race, religion, voting rights, and other rights regarded as fundamental. The test here is that a challenged law or decision is unconstitutional unless it's "narrowly tailored" to serve a "compelling government interest."

- **Heightened or intermediate scrutiny,** applicable to cases involving sex or gender. The test here is that a challenged law must be "substantially related" to an "important government interest." The U.S. Supreme Court first applied this standard in 1976 in the case of *Craig v. Boren.* This case mounted a challenge of an Oklahoma law that permitted the sale of low-alcohol beer to females over the age of 18 but to males only over the age of 21. The Supreme Court held that the Oklahoma law didn't pass the requisite test, contravened the Equal Protection Clause, and was therefore unconstitutional.

- **Rational basis scrutiny,** applicable to all other cases. The test here is that a challenged law must be "reasonably related" to a "legitimate government interest." The Supreme Court applied this level of scrutiny to a proposed amendment to the constitution of Colorado. The proposed amendment banned the passing of any state law that accorded homosexuals or bisexuals "minority status, quota preferences, protected status or a claim of discrimination." The case in question was *Romer v. Evans,* decided in 1996. The Supreme Court ruled that the proposed amendment was unconstitutional. The majority on the Court claimed not to be applying strict scrutiny or even heightened scrutiny, on the ground that the proposed amendment didn't even come up to the much lower standard of being "reasonably related" to "a legitimate government interest."

The outcome of a case can easily depend on the level of scrutiny that the Court decides to apply to it. The stricter the scrutiny, the harder it is for the law or decision under review to pass muster.

A 1996 case involving the Virginia Military Institute (VMI) provides a good illustration of this important point. VMI, a state military college, had an all-male admissions policy. This policy was challenged in the U.S. Supreme Court under the Equal Protection Clause. The majority on the Court held that the school's admissions policy violated the Equal Protection Clause because the school failed to show "exceedingly persuasive justification" for that policy. Justice Antonin Scalia pointed out in his dissent that this test was essentially one of strict scrutiny, which was far too high. The appropriate standard was that of intermediate scrutiny or even just that of a rational-basis review.

Disqualifying Confederates from Office

Section 3 of the Fourteenth Amendment bars from public office anyone in public office before the Civil War who then supported the Confederacy. This section was aimed at the leading figures in the Confederacy, most of whom had held public office in the pre-war United States.

After the war, Jefferson Davis, the first and only President of the Confederacy, was elected to the U.S. Senate again by the state legislature of Mississippi, but this provision in the Fourteenth Amendment prevented him from taking his seat.

The section ends with a clause of remarkable foresight, allowing Congress to lift the service ban on a particular individual by a two-thirds majority vote in both houses. In 1978, Congress applied this provision and lifted the ban posthumously on Jefferson Davis and the Confederate commander, General Robert E. Lee. This tolerant spirit has been conspicuous by its absence in the recent wave of acts of protest against statues of Confederate leaders. "Many of those tearing down Confederate and other statues," warned the leading liberal lawyer Alan Dershowitz on August 22, 2017, "are trying to take America down with them."

Repudiating Confederate Debts

Section 4 of the Fourteenth Amendment is in two parts. The first part proclaims: "The validity of the public debt of the United States . . . shall not be questioned." This provision is hard to understand in isolation, but it becomes clear when you read the second part. This part repudiates all Confederate debts and makes it clear that the United States would not pay compensation to slave owners for the loss of their slaves.

Empowering Congress

The fifth and last section of the Fourteenth Amendment is brief:

The Congress shall have power to enforce, by appropriate legislation, the provisions of this article.

The same wording is also found at the end of the Thirteenth, Fifteenth, Nineteenth, Twenty-Third, Twenty-Fourth, and Twenty-Sixth amendments.

You may wonder why Congress needs to be given this power. Does the amendment not speak for itself? None of the first ten amendments contains any such provision, so why do so many later amendments need it?

The answer is that this provision was first used just after the Civil War, which gave the federal government much more power than before. The Civil War also resulted in great distrust between different sectors of U.S. society.

In *City of Boerne v. Flores* (1997), the Supreme Court not only struck down an Act of Congress but also introduced a new test for deciding whether Congress had exceeded its powers under Section 5 of the Fourteenth Amendment. The act in question was the Religious Freedom Restoration Act (RFRA) of 1993, and the new test was the "congruence and proportionality" test. Congressional power under the section is now subject to two conditions: "there must be a congruence [equivalence] between the means used and the ends to be achieved," and the legislation must not be out of proportion to these ends. So, in what respect did the RFRA fall foul of this new test? In short, by overriding a local zoning ordinance. But, by making up a new test like this and then proceeding to use it to strike down a law passed (in the case of the RFRA) by a near-unanimous Congress, wasn't the Supreme Court usurping the role of Congress to make law? Go figure! An interesting sidelight on the *Boerne* case is the exceptional makeup of the six-strong majority on the Court: Anthony Kennedy joined by three conservative justices, plus liberal justices Stevens and Ginsburg, with liberal justices Souter and Breyer dissenting — an indication perhaps that conservative justices aren't always as wedded to judicial restraint as they like to claim!

Chapter **22**

Starts, Stops, and Clarifications: Amendments since 1870

The U.S. Constitution is more than 200 years old, but it hasn't remained the same over that long period. Here are the stages in its development:

» 1788 — The original Constitution is ratified, which is made up of all those heavy articles about what Congress, the President, and the Supreme Court can and can't do.

» 1791 — Ratification of the first ten amendments, or the Bill of Rights, takes place.

» 1865 — The end of the Civil War ushers in some pretty important amendments prohibiting discrimination on grounds of race and dictating to the states.

» 1870 to the present — A grab bag of 13 diverse amendments have been passed, most of which are not very well known.

I deal with the 13 latest amendments in this chapter. I take them one by one.

Removing Race Qualifications for Voting: The Fifteenth Amendment

The Fifteenth Amendment is the last of three amendments introduced in the wake of the Civil War. The Thirteenth Amendment abolished slavery. The Fourteenth Amendment went further and declared that "all persons born or naturalized in the United States . . . are citizens of the United States and of the State wherein they reside."

Didn't this provision automatically take care of voting rights? No, because the states each had their own rules governing voting rights. So citizenship alone didn't guarantee the right to vote. Hence the need for the Fifteenth Amendment, ratified in 1870, the main part of which reads as follows:

> The right of citizens of the United States to vote shall not be denied or abridged by the United States or by any State on account of race, color, or previous condition of servitude.

The meaning of this provision is self-explanatory: Racial voting qualifications are no longer allowed. But is this all that the amendment means?

Some people, including some who are regarded as constitutional law experts, have suggested that the Fifteenth Amendment contains a "cluster" of rights that go way beyond the simple right to vote in elections. Where do these people get this idea from? Their argument runs along these lines:

>> The Fifteenth Amendment confers the right to vote.

>> But the right to vote isn't confined to voting in elections.

>> Congressmen and other legislators also have the right to vote — for or against bills.

>> So the Fifteenth Amendment must include the right to run for election to Congress and state legislatures.

IN MY OPINION

Is this argument correct? No. It's one of many examples of trying to change the Constitution by reading stuff into it that isn't actually there. Here's why the argument that I've just summarized is wrong:

>> The original draft of the Fifteenth Amendment presented to Congress contained the right to run for election as well as the right to vote. The right to run for election was dropped from the final version.

>> The reason for this change was that this amendment was difficult enough to pass in its cut-down form. In 1868, 11 of the then 21 northern states denied blacks the right to vote. New York withdrew its ratification of the Fifteenth Amendment and then re-ratified it as power shifted in that state. Delaware ratified it only in 1901, Oregon in 1959, California in 1962, Maryland in 1973, Kentucky in 1976, and Tennessee in 1997.

>> Does the right to vote in elections automatically include the right to run for election? No. Check out the Twenty-Sixth Amendment, whose wording mirrors that of the Fifteenth Amendment in extending the right to vote to all U.S. citizens "who are eighteen years of age or older." Does this amendment give 18-year-olds the right to run for Congress? Not at all. You've got to be at least 25 to run for the House of Representatives, and there are a couple of other requirements too, as laid down by Article I, Section 2 of the Constitution.

The meaning of the Fifteenth Amendment isn't a problem. But the amendment does have two other major problems:

>> Was the Fifteenth Amendment validly ratified?

- It was proposed in 1869 by a Congress from which the 11 former break-away Confederate states were excluded.

- Ten of these southern states ratified it only because the First Reconstruction Act of March 2, 1867 — passed over the veto of President Andrew Johnson — gave all adult black males in those states the right to vote as a precondition of readmission of those states into the Union.

REMEMBER

>> Did the Fifteenth Amendment have any effect in practice? In the North, yes. But in the border states, and in the South after 1876, blacks tended to be excluded from the vote by the imposition of literacy tests and poll taxes. Literacy tests were finally outlawed by the Voting Rights Act of 1965, and poll taxes were eventually declared unconstitutional by the U.S. Supreme Court in 1966.

After the end of Reconstruction in 1877, the Republican Party in the South collapsed. The Democratic Party controlled the "solid South," as it came to be known, until the 1960s. So, the really important election in the southern states was not the general election but the Democratic primary. Here's what a Texas statute said that was still in force in 1924: "In no event shall a negro be eligible to participate in a Democratic party primary election held in the State of Texas." The U.S. Supreme Court declared this particular law unconstitutional, but it wasn't until 1944 that all-white primaries were completely banned.

Letting Uncle Sam Raid Your Piggy Bank: The Sixteenth Amendment

Can Uncle Sam legally tax you on your income? You may resent this government power, but it is kosher. However, that hasn't always been the case. Income tax is a *direct* tax because it's paid directly to the government. But it was unknown in the early days of the Republic. The earliest form of direct tax was a *capitation tax* — or poll tax — a flat tax of the same amount payable by everybody regardless of wealth or earnings.

Article I, Section 9 contains this little tidbit about direct taxes:

> *No Capitation, or other direct, Tax shall be laid, unless in Proportion to the Census or Enumeration herein before directed to be taken.*

A capitation tax is of course automatically in proportion to population — but income tax normally varies according to income, which prevents it from being proportional to population.

Income tax was first introduced in 1861 to pay for the Civil War. It was abolished in 1872, and when the government tried to reintroduce it in 1894 it was immediately challenged. In 1895 the U.S. Supreme Court declared income tax unconstitutional.

However, most politicians recognized the need for income tax. In the presidential election of 1912, all three main candidates — incumbent President William H. Taft, former President Theodore Roosevelt, and the winner, Woodrow Wilson — supported the legalization of income tax. The Sixteenth Amendment, which was ratified in 1913, was introduced precisely to achieve that objective. Here's what it says:

> *The Congress shall have power to lay and collect taxes on incomes, from whatever source derived, without apportionment among the several States, and without regard to any census or enumeration.*

Electing the Senate: The Seventeenth Amendment

The Framers of the Constitution didn't trust the people. Under the original, unamended Constitution, the House of Representatives was the only directly elected body. Article I, Section 3 provided that

The Senate of the United States shall be composed of two Senators from each State, chosen by the Legislature thereof . . .

The Senate was intended to balance the House in two ways:

» By favoring the smaller states — because each state regardless of size is entitled to two senators. California, with its population of almost 40 million, has two senators, and Wyoming, with just over half a million, also has two senators.

» By being *selected* by the state legislatures rather than directly *elected* by the people.

U.S. senators were originally seen as ambassadors of their states. The states kept their senators on a tight rein and even instructed them how to vote on particular issues — something that never happened with members of the House, who were not chosen by state legislatures. Because of the close relationship between senators and their states, a U.S. senator is formally described as "senator *from* XYZ state." For example, Marco Rubio is "the junior Senator *from* Florida." This style, using *from* rather than *of*, also serves to distinguish U.S. senators from state senators. What's with the *senior* and *junior* label? It doesn't denote status but simply indicates which senator was elected first in date. So, at the time of this writing, the senior senator from Florida is Bill Nelson, who was elected in 2001, while Marco Rubio, elected in 2011, is the junior senator.

The system of state-appointed senators worked smoothly at first, but in the run-up to the Civil War, difficulties started appearing, and in the late 19th century, deadlocks were commonplace. Between 1893 and 1902, popular pressure mounted for the Senate to be directly elected. By 1913, such was the pressure on Congress that only one more state was needed to call a national constitutional convention.

The prospect of a national convention has always terrified Congress, because once a convention was summoned there was no guarantee that it would limit itself to considering the one amendment that had brought it into existence. It could well become a loose cannon, destroying the whole carefully crafted fabric of the Constitution. The prospect of a national convention quickly galvanized Congress into action in 1913, and what became the Seventeenth Amendment was soon ratified, providing for the direct election of senators by the people of each state.

The Seventeenth Amendment also makes provision for the filling of a vacant Senate seat when a senator dies or resigns for any reason. In most states, the governor calls a "special election" and in the meantime appoints someone (usually of the same party as the previous incumbent) to fill the vacancy.

Outlawing Liquor: The Eighteenth Amendment

The Eighteenth Amendment, ratified in 1919, banned the manufacture, sale, transportation, import, or export of all "intoxicating liquors," which were defined by a companion Act of Congress as any beverage containing over 0.5 percent alcohol.

The evils of alcohol had been preached since early colonial days, and Massachusetts banned the sale of "strong liquor" in 1657. However, the temperance movement really came into its own after the Civil War. The Prohibition Party was founded in 1869, and in 1873 the influential Women's Christian Temperance Union came into existence.

Although only one congressman and one governor were ever elected on the Prohibition Party ticket, the party managed to get liquor banned in many cities and a number of states. During World War I, the pressure on lawmakers by the prohibition lobby was so great that Congress proposed the Eighteenth Amendment in 1917, and it was ratified in 1919. Two states, Connecticut and Rhode Island, rejected the amendment and never ratified it.

IN MY
OPINION

The Eighteenth Amendment is an excellent example of just how impossible it is to change human nature by legislation — and how disastrous it is even to try. As a direct result of prohibition, illegal, or *bootleg*, liquor became available in *speakeasies*: illicit, disguised bars. Prohibition was the best thing that ever happened to the Mafia, which took full advantage of it.

Giving Women the Vote: The Nineteenth Amendment

Did women first get the right to vote in the United States as a result of the ratification of the Nineteenth Amendment in 1920? Yes and no. The Nineteenth Amendment gave the right to vote to all women in the nation over the age of 21. However, women had the vote in New Jersey between 1776 and 1807. Wyoming Territory gave women the vote in 1869. Colorado followed suit in 1893, and Utah in 1896.

The drive for votes for women across the nation began in earnest with the formation of the National Woman Suffrage Association in 1869. This organization lobbied every Congress between 1869 and 1919. In 1915, a woman's suffrage bill was brought before the House of Representatives but was defeated by 174 to 204 votes.

In 1918, President Woodrow Wilson put his weight behind an amendment extending the vote to women. On January 10, 1918, a bill proposing this amendment passed the House with just one vote more than the two-thirds required. In the Senate, the proposed amendment lost out by two votes in September 1918. When it was presented to the Senate again in February 1919, it was only one vote short of the requisite two-thirds majority.

President Wilson was anxious to get the amendment passed in time for the election of 1920, in which he was planning to run for a third term. He called a special session of Congress to consider the proposed amendment. This time it passed the House with 42 votes to spare, and the Senate also accepted it with a victorious margin of 2 votes.

The amendment was quickly ratified by the three-fourths of the states required by the Constitution, but a few states held out. The last states to ratify it were eight southern states. Mississippi ratified it only in 1984.

The wording of the Nineteenth Amendment was borrowed from the Fifteenth Amendment. Here's the main part of the amendment:

> The right of citizens of the United States to vote shall not be denied or abridged by the United States or by any State on account of sex.

Moving Out of the Horse and Buggy Age: The Twentieth Amendment

In the time of George Washington, travel was slow and roads were bad. So the Founders allowed a period of four months between the presidential election and the inauguration. The original, unamended Constitution fixed March 4 as the date when all presidential and congressional terms started. This arrangement meant that, when there was a change of President, the nation had to endure a four-month period of a lame-duck administration.

The Twentieth Amendment fixed a much earlier date, January 20, for presidential inaugurations, and January 3 for the start of congressional terms.

The amendment also dealt with a couple of other questions, notably: What happens if a President-elect dies before taking office? Answer: The Vice President-elect becomes President. Surprisingly, the Twentieth Amendment didn't address the more basic question: If the President dies in office and is succeeded by the Vice President, does the Vice President become President or only Acting President? This issue was left to be dealt with by the Twenty-Fifth Amendment.

The Twentieth Amendment met with very little opposition. It was passed by Congress on March 2, 1932, and was finally ratified on January 23, 1933. The first presidential term it applied to was when Franklin D. Roosevelt succeeded himself as President on January 20, 1937.

Repealing Prohibition: The Twenty-First Amendment

The Eighteenth Amendment introducing Prohibition is the only amendment ever to have been repealed. This was done by the Twenty-First Amendment just under 14 years after Prohibition had been introduced.

What happened in that short time to turn opinion so completely around? In fact, local politicians hadn't really changed their minds because many of them either owed the Prohibition lobby favors or else were afraid of the influence wielded by that lobby in their localities.

But Prohibition had never been that popular among ordinary Americans. After Prohibition ushered in an orgy of crime, Congress was determined to end Prohibition, and it used the nation's deep-seated dislike of Prohibition to achieve this end. So, after handily passing the proposed Twenty-First Amendment, Congress stipulated that ratification was to be effected not by the state legislatures but by the alternative method laid down in Article V of the Constitution — by special conventions in the individual states. The Twenty-First Amendment is the only amendment ever ratified this way.

South Carolina rejected the Twenty-First Amendment, and the voters of North Carolina refused even to call a convention to consider it. But all the other states held conventions that duly accepted the amendment, which was ratified in December 1933.

REMEMBER

It's important to realize, however, that the Twenty-First Amendment doesn't just repeal the Eighteenth Amendment. It does so in Section 1, but it then goes on to provide that

> The transportation or importation into any State, Territory, or possession of the United States for delivery or use therein of intoxicating liquors, in violation of the laws thereof, is hereby prohibited.

This section enabled any state that wanted to remain "dry" to do so. Mississippi was the last state to remain dry, which it was until 1966, and Kansas banned public bars until 1987. There are still over 500 dry municipalities in the nation because many states have delegated the power to ban alcohol to local authorities.

Taking George Washington's Lead: The Twenty-Second Amendment

Article II, Section 1 of the original, unamended Constitution set the President's term of office at four years, but it didn't place any limit on the number of times that a President could be reelected.

George Washington was elected President without any opposition in 1788 and again in 1792. He would undoubtedly have been reelected without any problem in 1796 as well, but he decided that he'd had enough. So he delivered his famous Farewell Address — not a live speech, incidentally, but an open letter to the nation carried by many newspapers — and retired to Mount Vernon to dedicate himself to farming and to the construction of a large whiskey distillery.

As two terms were good enough for the Father of the Nation, that should be enough for anybody. Thomas Jefferson, James Madison, and James Monroe — all of whom were two-term presidents — respected Washington's example and didn't attempt to run for a third term. They effectively established a convention that was followed, sometimes reluctantly, until Franklin Delano Roosevelt decided to run for a third term in 1940.

Roosevelt, ever the wily politician, employed a ruse to get over the two-term tradition. First, he switched the 1940 Democratic Party Convention to Chicago, which was controlled by a tightly organized Democratic Party machine — which of course also controlled the public address system in the convention hall. Then FDR disarmed his opponents by announcing that he would not run unless drafted, and that the delegates were free to vote for whomever they liked. Dead on cue, the loudspeakers in the hall screamed: "We want Roosevelt . . . The world wants Roosevelt!" The delegates joined in the manufactured frenzy and nominated Roosevelt by 946 votes to 147. After that, winning the general election was a walk in the park. And, having shattered the two-term mold, Roosevelt had no trouble getting nominated for a fourth term, which he again easily won, though with a reduced majority. He died less than three months after his fourth inauguration.

When the Republicans swept Congress in the 1946 midterm elections, they were determined to prevent any future president from emulating Roosevelt's successful flouting of the two-term limit. They recognized that to achieve this aim they needed a constitutional amendment. So in March 1947, Congress passed a proposal to enforce the two-term limit. The proposal became the Twenty-Second Amendment, which was finally ratified in February 1951. Only two states rejected it: Oklahoma and Massachusetts.

The main part of the Twenty-Second Amendment reads as follows:

No person shall be elected to the office of the President more than twice, and no person who has held the office of President, or acted as President, for more than two years of a term to which some other person was elected President shall be elected to the office of the President more than once.

REMEMBER

Here's what it means:

>> You can't be elected to more than two presidential terms — regardless of whether they are consecutive or not.

>> If you have succeeded to the presidency on the death, removal, or resignation of the President and have served *more than two years* of that President's term, you can't be elected President yourself more than once.

>> If you have succeeded to the presidency on the death, removal, or resignation of the President and have served *two years or less* of that President's term, you can be elected President yourself a maximum of two times.

>> If you have been filling in for an indisposed President only as Acting President, you can be elected President yourself for a maximum of two terms, unless you have been Acting President for more than two years, in which case you can't be elected President yourself more than once.

One thing that the Twenty-Second Amendment doesn't do is to place any term limit on the vice presidency. No, sirree! You can be elected Veep as many times as you like — or rather, as many times as the voters like.

Repeal of the Twenty-Second Amendment has been suggested several times, notably in the 1980s in order to "win one more for the Gipper" (Ronald Reagan) and again in the 1990s to elect Bill Clinton to a third term. Those moves came to nothing.

Enfranchising the Nation's Capital: The Twenty-Third Amendment

When the Constitution was ratified in its original form in 1788, New York City was the nation's capital. But the so-called "District Clause" in Article I, Section 8 of the Constitution made provision for a purpose-built new capital, which was to be under the exclusive authority of Congress. Washington, D.C., became the nation's capital and the seat of the federal government on December 1, 1800 — on land ceded by Virginia and Maryland.

William Henry Harrison, the short-lived ninth President who died on April 4, 1841, just one month into his term of office, championed the cause of the inhabitants of the nation's capital in his long inaugural address. He described them as being "deprived of many important political privileges," adding, "The people of the District of Columbia are not the subjects of the people of the States, but free American citizens."

By 1960, when the District of Columbia had a bigger population than 13 of the 50 states, Congress proposed the Twenty-Third Amendment giving the District of Columbia three electoral votes in presidential elections — the same number as the smallest states, whose entitlement is calculated by adding their two senators to their single representative in the House. The amendment was ratified in 1961 and was first applied in the 1964 presidential election.

REMEMBER

In regard to presidential elections, therefore, the District is now treated as if it were a state. It's important to realize, however, that the amendment does *not* make the District a state.

The District has no representation in the U.S. Senate, but since 1971 it has sent a *delegate* to the House of Representatives. Until 1993, the delegate from the District, in common with the delegates from the U.S. territories, didn't have voting rights. That changed in 1993, but voting rights (except in committees) were lost again two years later after the Republicans gained control of the House. In 2007, the House gave the D.C. delegate the right to vote in the Committee of the Whole, which considers amendments — subject to the proviso that if the delegate's vote tips the balance, the vote is taken again without the delegate's participation.

Proposed amendments to make the District a state (possibly under the title of "New Columbia," which makes it sound like an encyclopedia), or at least to give it proper representation in Congress, have all failed. Any such amendment would have the effect of repealing the "District Clause" in Article I of the Constitution, which places Washington, D.C., under congressional authority. The real reason for opposition to congressional representation for D.C. is political — because the District is solidly Democratic.

Banning Tax Barriers to Voting:
The Twenty-Fourth Amendment

After the end of Reconstruction in the South in 1877, barriers were erected to reduce the number of blacks registering as voters. The two most common ways of discouraging voting were literacy tests and taxation, especially the poll tax. No fewer than 11 southern states introduced a poll tax requirement for voting. This was a simple tax of a fixed sum to be paid by everybody, regardless of race, color, earnings, or wealth.

REMEMBER

In what way was the poll tax disadvantageous to blacks? Proof that you had paid your poll tax was often made a condition of voting in an election. But some southern states had a "grandfather clause" that allowed you to vote regardless of whether you'd paid your poll tax or not — provided your grandfather had voted at a named date before the abolition of slavery. This type of clause placed blacks and poor whites at a disadvantage as compared with property-owning white men.

Objections to the poll tax came mainly from blacks. And in 1962, Congress proposed the Twenty-Fourth Amendment to make it unlawful to make the right to vote conditional on the payment of the poll tax or any other tax. The amendment was finally ratified on January 23, 1964, but several southern states never ratified it.

The main part of the Twenty-Fourth Amendment reads as follows:

> The right of citizens of the United States to vote in any primary or other election for President or Vice President, for electors for President or Vice President, or for Senator or Representative in Congress, shall not be denied or abridged by the United States or any State by reason of failure to pay any poll tax or other tax.

The wording of the amendment makes sure it covers all bases — but only in respect to federal elections. It doesn't cover state elections at all.

So it was left to the U.S. Supreme Court to ban the use of poll taxes as a condition for voting in state elections. It did so in the 1966 case *Harper v. Virginia Board of Elections*. Justice William O. Douglas, writing for the majority, ruled as follows:

> We conclude that a State violates the Equal Protection Clause of the Fourteenth Amendment whenever it makes the affluence of the voter or payment of any fee an electoral standard. Voter qualifications have no relation to wealth nor to paying or not paying this or any other tax.

Hugo Black, one of the three dissenting justices, stressed that the majority decision "is to no extent based on a finding that the Virginia law as written or as applied is being used as a device or mechanism to deny Negro citizens of Virginia the right to vote on account of their color."

Justice Black then rounded on the majority for departing without good reason from the unanimous decision in *Breedlove v. Suttles* (1937), which upheld the constitutionality of a poll tax as a qualification for voting in state elections — and for amending the Constitution, which the court is not allowed to do under Article V.

Succeeding to the Presidency: The Twenty-Fifth Amendment

The Twenty-Fifth Amendment, ratified in 1967, made some arrangements about the presidency and vice presidency, most of which ought to have been tackled much earlier.

Succeeding as President or Acting President?

When the President dies, resigns, or is removed from office, does the Vice President become President or only Acting President?

By 1967, this question had long been settled in practice. When President William Henry Harrison died on April 4, 1841, just one month after his inauguration, he was succeeded by Vice President John Tyler (see Figure 22-1). But was Tyler then President or only Acting President? Article II, Section 1, Clause 6 of the Constitution was ambiguous. Tyler, a southern Democrat in a Whig administration, was surrounded by enemies who did not want him to be the President but only Acting President — the Vice President acting as President. Tyler himself was equally adamant that he was the President, and he managed to get Congress to agree.

Tyler struck a blow not only for himself but also for all subsequent Vice Presidents succeeding to the presidency, all of whom were recognized as Presidents and not just as Acting Presidents.

The Twenty-Fifth Amendment belatedly endorsed Tyler's position — luckily, otherwise we'd have to renumber all the Presidents since 1841 and disqualify a few of them. Section 1 of the amendment provides in clear and simple terms that

> *In case of the removal of the President from office or of his death or resignation, the Vice President shall become President.*

FIGURE 22-1:
John Tyler, President 1841–1845. Vice President Tyler succeeded William Henry Harrison, who died a month after his inauguration. By refusing to accept that he was only "Acting President," Tyler settled the position for the future, which was finally formalized by the Twenty-Fifth Amendment, ratified in 1967.

Source: Engraved portrait of Tyler as President by the Bureau of Engraving & Printing (BEP)

Replacing the Veep

The next question that the Twenty-Fifth Amendment addresses was completely neglected for 180 years: Who takes over as Vice President when the Vice President becomes the President — or when the Veep simply drops dead (which has also happened)?

The answer to this question until the Twenty-Fifth Amendment came along was: nobody. That's right. The Constitution previously just allowed the vice presidency to remain vacant. Was that a problem? Not really, because since 1792, there has been a Presidential Succession Act laying down a long and detailed line of succession to the presidency.

But now Section 2 of the Twenty-Fifth Amendment provides for the appointment of a new Vice President when the vice presidency falls vacant. Here's what it says:

> *Whenever there is a vacancy in the office of the Vice President, the President shall nominate a Vice President who shall take office upon confirmation by a majority vote of both Houses of Congress.*

This provision has been used twice. The first time was when President Richard Nixon picked Congressman Gerald Ford to succeed Spiro Agnew when Agnew resigned as Vice President in 1973. Then, when Ford became President on Nixon's resignation in 1974, Ford appointed former New York Governor Nelson Rockefeller as Vice President.

Acting as President

Sections 3 and 4 of the Twenty-Fifth Amendment deal with another neglected (but this time very real) problem — arrangements for when the President is incapacitated. These sections provide that, when that situation occurs, the Vice President becomes Acting President.

Amazingly, the presidency lasted for 180 years without any such provision in place — although there was clearly a need for it. For example, in 1881, President James Garfield lingered for 80 days before dying from an assassin's bullet, during which time he was unable to attend to affairs of state. President Woodrow Wilson's incapacity from a stroke was kept even from his Vice President and Cabinet — by his wife, who was the effective President for the last year and a half of his second term.

Section 3 provides for the situation when the President himself recognizes his incapacity, which was done once by President Ronald Reagan and twice by President George W. Bush. On all three occasions, the transfer of power to the Vice President as Acting President lasted a very short time.

Section 4, which has never been used, deals with the much trickier situation when the Vice President and Cabinet decide that the President is "unable to discharge the powers and duties of his office." This provision is potentially dangerous, as it could be used as a political weapon against a President who is disliked by his Vice President and a majority of his Cabinet — which is not at all impossible.

Lowering the Voting Age: The Twenty-Sixth Amendment

The voting age was 21 until the ratification of the Twenty-Sixth Amendment in 1971, which lowered it to 18. What was the justification for this change?

REMEMBER

The Vietnam War was probably the main reason for lowering the voting age. Young men became liable for the draft at age 18. "Old enough to fight, old enough to vote" was a slogan that became popular during that time.

In 1970, Congress passed a law lowering the minimum voting age to 18 for all elections, state and federal alike. The state of Oregon challenged the law's constitutionality. In *Oregon v. Mitchell,* the U.S. Supreme Court ruled that Congress could set the voting age for federal elections but not for state and local elections.

This ruling was impractical. States wanting to leave the minimum voting age at 21 would have had to establish two voters' rolls, one for federal elections and the other for state and local elections.

Congress therefore decided to short-circuit the Court ruling by amending the Constitution. The result was the Twenty-Sixth Amendment, which was ratified on July 1, 1971.

The wording of the amendment is copied from that of the Fifteenth and Nineteenth amendments. The main part of it reads as follows:

> *The right of citizens of the United States, who are eighteen years of age or older, to vote shall not be denied or abridged by the United States or by any State on account of age.*

The amendment was ratified in record time — just over three months from passing Congress to ratification by three-fourths of the states. The reason for this enthusiasm on the part of the states was no doubt because it saved the states from the muddle that would have resulted from an attempt to implement the Supreme Court ruling in *Oregon v. Mitchell.*

Limiting Congressional Pay Raises: The Twenty-Seventh Amendment

A fun amendment at last! The Twenty-Seventh Amendment is of interest less for what it says than for the way it was ratified. It was proposed by Congress in 1789 but was ratified only in 1992, more than 200 years later. The unratified and completely forgotten amendment was "discovered" by Gregory Watson, a sophomore at the University of Texas, Austin, in 1982. Watson's paper advocating ratification of the forgotten amendment was awarded a C. Stung into action, Watson started on a frenzied letter-writing campaign to lawmakers around the country that eventually resulted in ratification in 1992.

The Twenty-Seventh Amendment reads as follows:

> *No law varying the compensation for the services of the Senators and Representatives shall take effect, until an election of Representatives shall have intervened.*

This seems to be saying that if members of Congress vote themselves a pay raise, the new salaries can't come into effect until after a congressional election. This looks good because voters would be unimpressed by senators and representatives who'd voted themselves more money — so members of Congress would be less likely to do so, in case the voters turned them out in the intervening election.

However, Congress has gotten around this sensible provision by voting themselves annual *cost-of-living adjustments*, or COLAs — which go well beyond paying for the occasional soda! The U.S. Court of Appeals for the District of Columbia ruled in 2001 that COLAs are not repugnant to the Twenty-Seventh Amendment. The U.S. Supreme Court has yet to pronounce on this question. Watch this space.

6

The Part of Tens

Gain insight on ten landmark Supreme Court cases, including *Brown v. Board of Education* on public school segregation and the *Roe v. Wade* case on a woman's right to an abortion.

Meet ten influential Supreme Court Justices, including John Marshall, who made the Supreme Court the powerful player that it is today, and Thurgood Marshall (no relation), the first African-American justice to sit on the Court.

Check out two sides of five Constitutional conundrums, including whether the Electoral College system should be abolished and whether the President is too powerful.

Chapter **23**

Ten Landmark Constitutional Cases

The best-known Supreme Court decisions have effectively changed the Constitution and expanded the power of the Court in the process. But are these decisions necessarily good? No, because the Constitution doesn't actually give the Court the power to encroach on the authority of Congress or the President. Some Supreme Court justices have recognized this problem. In the words of Justice Oliver Wendell Holmes, an advocate of judicial restraint, "I do not think the United States would come to an end if we lost our power to declare an Act of Congress void."

Marbury v. Madison (1803)

Marbury v. Madison established the U.S. Supreme Court's right of *judicial review* — the power to strike down a law as unconstitutional. As I explain in Chapter 12, William Marbury was appointed a Justice of the Peace by outgoing President John Adams. But the new Secretary of State, James Madison, refused to deliver

Marbury's commission — the formal document of appointment. Marbury asked the U.S. Supreme Court to order Madison to hand him his commission.

Chief Justice John Marshall (see Figure 23-1), writing for the Court, held that

>> Madison's refusal to deliver the commission to Marbury was unlawful. *This is undoubtedly correct.*

>> But the Supreme Court did not have the power to make such an order. *This is not actually correct.*

>> Because the law that purportedly gave the Supreme Court this power was itself invalid. *This is also probably wrong.*

>> And the Supreme Court had the power to strike down invalid laws. *Yeah? The Constitution sure doesn't say so, although Alexander Hamilton in the influential* Federalist Papers, *written in 1788, assumed that the Court had this power.*

This judgment is an excellent example of Marshall's "twistifications" (Thomas Jefferson's term). Note that Marshall should have recused himself from hearing the case anyway because the whole case arose out of the failure of President John Adams's Secretary of State to give Marbury his commission. And who was that Secretary of State? Why, none other than John Marshall himself!

FIGURE 23-1:
Chief Justice John Marshall, best known for his leading opinion in *Marbury v. Madison* (1803).

Source: Henry Inman — Virginia Memory

Here's what Jefferson said about Marshall's new doctrine of judicial review: "The opinion which gives to the judges the right to decide what laws are constitutional and what not . . . would make the Judiciary a despotic branch."

Brown v. Board of Education (1954)

In *Brown v. Board of Education*, a unanimous Supreme Court outlawed racial segregation in public schools throughout the United States. In so doing, the Court declared 17 state laws unconstitutional, including some from northern states. The Court also overturned its own 1896 ruling in *Plessy v. Ferguson* that had approved the "separate but equal" formula, which had said that it was okay to provide separate facilities for the different races as long as those facilities were equal.

In *Brown*, Chief Justice Earl Warren crafted a short opinion that commanded unanimous support. Here are the main points he made:

>> The history of the Fourteenth Amendment with respect to segregated schools was "inconclusive." *Not at all! The Fourteenth Amendment, ratified in 1868, gives Congress the power to enforce it. Congress exercised this power by enacting several laws. But none of these laws says anything about segregation in education — which must mean that Congress did not then regard segregated schools as being a violation of the Fourteenth Amendment.*

>> "We cannot turn the clock back to 1868 when the Amendment was adopted." *Warren wasn't interested in finding out the meaning of the amendment in 1868 — or even the intention of its Framers. He adopted the "living Constitution" approach, enabling him to interpret the amendment any way he liked.*

>> "Segregation of white and colored children in public schools has a detrimental effect upon the colored children." *And years of forced integration by busing didn't really help.*

>> "We conclude that in the field of public education the doctrine of 'separate but equal' has no place. Separate educational facilities are inherently unequal." *True. Yet the long-term effect of heavy-handed judicial intervention has been "white flight" to the suburbs, a huge increase in the number of white kids in private education, and a serious decline in the standards of the predominantly black inner city schools.*

Grutter v. Bollinger and *Gratz v. Bollinger* (2003)

These two affirmative action cases, both brought against the University of Michigan, were decided by the U.S. Supreme Court on the same day, with opposite outcomes. The Court upheld the use of race as an admissions factor while condemning the use of a quota system. So the affirmative action but non-quota-based admissions policy in force in the Law School was upheld, while the "points" system applied for undergraduate admissions was condemned.

In *Grutter v. Bollinger,* by a majority of 5 votes to 4, the Supreme Court held that "strict scrutiny must be applied to any admissions program using racial categories or classifications." On this basis, the Court upheld the affirmative action policy of the University of Michigan Law School in admitting a "critical mass" of minority students, but added: "We expect that 25 years from now, the use of racial preferences will no longer be necessary to further the interest approved today." The case was brought by Barbara Grutter, a 43-year-old white Michigan resident who had been denied admission to the Law School in favor of minority students. Her surprise turned to "dismay" when she read a Detroit newspaper article indicating that minorities admitted to the university had lower test scores and grades than admitted whites. Justice Sandra Day O'Connor, writing for the majority, held that the U.S. Constitution "does not prohibit the law school's narrowly tailored use of race in admissions decisions to further a compelling interest in obtaining the educational benefits that flow from a diverse student body." The university's policy carefully avoided using any quotas, and all applicants were given the same "individualized" and "holistic" review.

Chief Justice Rehnquist, joined by Justices Scalia, Kennedy, and Thomas, dissented, claiming that the Law School's admissions policy was actually a "disguised quota" system, which was unconstitutional because the Court had condemned quotas in the well-known *Bakke* case in 1978. Justice Scalia similarly called the Law School's admissions policy "a sham to cover a scheme of racially proportionate admissions." He stated emphatically: "The Constitution proscribes government discrimination on the basis of race, and state-provided education is no exception."

By contrast with *Grutter,* in *Gratz v. Bollinger* a 6–3 majority of the Supreme Court struck down as unconstitutional Michigan's points-based undergraduate admissions policy, under which minority ethnic groups were given an automatic 20-point bonus, with 100 points needed for admission. This, according to Chief Justice Rehnquist, writing for the majority, "operated as the functional equivalent of a quota running afoul" of the condemnation of quotas, as decided in *Bakke.* Was this system really that different from the more carefully crafted admissions policy applied in the Law School? Two of the justices who approved of the admissions policy for freshman undergraduates as well as the one for the Law School made a surprising concession. These were Justice David Souter and Justice Ruth Bader Ginsburg, who were in the majority in *Grutter* and in the minority in *Gratz*. Souter admitted that the undergraduate "college simply does by a numbered scale what the law school accomplishers in its 'holistic' review." Ginsburg made a similar admission, writing that "institutions of higher education may resort to camouflage" and to "winks, nods and disguises." But, instead of making these two liberal justices reject both the naked quota system and the disguised quota system, this realization had the opposite effect of making them approve of both, on the assumption that they were in some sense fairer than a colorblind, pure merit-based system.

These two Michigan cases aren't the most recent high court decisions on affirmative action, but at the time of this writing, they're still the gold standard against which such issues are measured. The long saga of *Fisher v. University of Texas* reached the U.S. Supreme Court twice, *Fisher I* in 2013 and *Fisher II* in 2016. In the first *Fisher* case, Justice Clarence Thomas characterized the University of Texas's admissions policy as a form of racial discrimination, adding that "a State's use of race in higher education admissions decisions is categorically prohibited by the Equal Protection Clause." Calling for *Grutter* to be overruled, Thomas held that: "Racial discrimination is never benign . . . The University's professed good intentions cannot excuse its outright racial discrimination any more than such intentions justified the now denounced arguments of slaveholders and segregationists . . . There can be no doubt that the University's discrimination injures white and Asian applicants who are denied admission because of their race. But I believe the injury to those admitted under the University's discriminatory admissions program is even more harmful. Blacks and Hispanics admitted to the University as a result of racial discrimination are, on average, far less prepared than their white and Asian classmates . . . Tellingly, neither the University nor any of the 73 *amici* briefs in support of racial discrimination has presented a shred of evidence that black and Hispanic students are able to close this substantial gap during their time at the University . . . Furthermore, the University's discrimination does nothing to increase the number of blacks and Hispanics who have access to a college education generally . . . The University admits minorities who otherwise would have attended less selective colleges where they would have been more evenly matched . . . Although cloaked in good intentions, the University's racial tinkering harms the very people it claims to be helping."

During oral arguments in *Fisher II*, Justice Scalia made very much the same point as the one by Justice Thomas in *Fisher* I. Scalia's remark led to an outcry from the University of Texas's African-American students and on Twitter, but before the final decision was handed down, Scalia died, on February 13, 2016. As Justice Kagan had recused herself because of her earlier involvement with the case as solicitor general, the case was decided by only seven justices: three liberals, three conservatives, and Justice Anthony Kennedy, who sided with the liberals and wrote the majority opinion, which held that: "The race-conscious admissions program in use at the time of [Abigail Fisher's] application is lawful under the Equal Protection Clause." It found the university's admissions policy similar to that approved in *Grutter*.

CONTROVERSY

The debate on affirmative action is still ongoing and shows no sign of ending any time soon. The old issue of racial quotas has now raised its head once more. This time it's about negative quotas, which are arguably even worse than positive quotas. Both are discriminatory and are disallowed under *Gratz*. The current issue concerns an allegation of the use of racial quotas to reduce the number of Asian-American students. A coalition of 64 Asian-American groups filed a complaint against Harvard University with the U.S. Departments of Education and Justice in 2015, alleging that "for Asian-American students to gain admission, they have to have SAT scores 140 points higher than white students, 270 points higher than Hispanic students, and 450 points higher than African-American students." A nonprofit organization known as Students for Fair Admissions has filed a lawsuit on the same basis against Harvard. In August 2017, at President Trump's prompting, it was revealed that the Department of Justice was seeking lawyers to work "investigations and possible litigation related to intentional race-based discrimination in college and university admissions."

Kelo v. City of New London (2005)

Susette Kelo lost her lovely old house. The City of New London, Connecticut, had condemned her home and 114 other lots in a working-class neighborhood in the interests of "economic development." However, the beneficiaries of this program weren't the public at large, but Pfizer, the pharmaceutical giant, and a property development corporation — a private entity.

Does the "takings clause" in the Fifth Amendment of the Constitution entitle a city to take property from private citizens for the benefit of other private citizens and corporations? By a 5–4 majority, the high court said yes, even though the Constitution says that private property can be taken only for "public use."

It's significant that in this case, the four liberal justices on the Court (plus swing-vote Justice Anthony Kennedy) supported heavy-handed local government power against the interests of poor property owners. On the other hand, the conservative minority stood up for the rights of the individual. In her dissent, Justice Sandra Day O'Connor cited a 1798 opinion condemning "a law that takes property from A. and gives it to B." as "against all reason and justice."

Clinton v. Jones (1997)

This case is the flip side of *Nixon v. Fitzgerald.* In that case, the high court ruled that the President is totally immune from civil suits for anything he does in his official capacity. In this later case, a unanimous high court held that the President is *not* immune from suit for anything that he did *before* he became president — and that such private lawsuits can go ahead even while the President is still in office. What about civil lawsuits arising out of private acts that the President commits while in office? Can a sitting President be sued for these too? Yes, apparently so.

The case arose out of a civil suit brought against President Bill Clinton by Paula Jones, who accused Clinton of sexual harassment while he was Governor of Arkansas. The case led indirectly to Clinton's impeachment. Clinton survived the impeachment process and was acquitted, which enabled him to serve out the rest of his second term. He left office in 2001 with (according to Gallup) an approval rating of 65 percent — up from the 50 percent average approval rating during his first term.

Roe v. Wade (1973)

This case has become the litmus test for confirmation to the U.S. Supreme Court bench. No judge who comes out openly against *Roe* is likely to be confirmed. In *Roe* the Supreme Court ruled 7–2 that women have the right to an abortion, at least during the first trimester of pregnancy. The Court characterized abortion as a "fundamental" constitutional right, which means that any law aiming to restrict it is subject to the standard of *strict scrutiny*. In *Planned Parenthood v. Casey* (1982), the high court modified *Roe* by giving the state the right to regulate an abortion even in the first trimester as long as that regulation doesn't pose an "undue burden" on the woman's fundamental right to an abortion. One such "undue burden" identified in Casey was any requirement for the woman to notify her husband. A Texas law that placed certain restrictions on abortion clinics in the state was struck down by the Supreme Court 5–3 as placing an "undue burden" on abortion rights in *Whole Woman's Health v. Hellerstedt* (2016). In *Stormans Inc v. Wiesman* (2016), a 5-justice majority on the Court refused to hear a challenge to a Washington state law making it illegal for pharmacists to refuse to dispense contraceptive drugs. In a dissent, Justice Alito, joined by Chief Justice Roberts and Justice Thomas, wrote: "This case is an ominous sign . . . If this is a sign of how religious liberty claims will be treated in the years ahead, those who value religious freedom have cause for great concern."

Roe v. Wade is as controversial as it is important. I discuss the main issues that it raises in Chapter 5.

Citizens United v. Federal Election Commission (FEC) (2010)

This highly controversial case is important for two reasons: first, because of its effect on elections, and secondly, because it struck down a major bipartisan Act of Congress, which had been essentially upheld by the Supreme Court itself.

The conservative nonprofit organization Citizens United wanted to run TV commercials to promote its film *Hillary: The Movie* in the run-up to the 2008 Democratic presidential primary elections. This would have been illegal under the Bipartisan Campaign Reform Act, generally known as the McCain–Feingold Act, of 2002, which prohibited the broadcast of "electioneering communications" paid for by corporations in the 30 days before a presidential primary and in the 60 days before a general election.

In the Supreme Court, Justice Kennedy wrote the majority opinion in favor of Citizens United, striking down the prohibition in McCain–Feingold of independent expenditure by corporations and labor unions as a violation of the First Amendment's protection of free speech. Kennedy wrote: "If the First Amendment has any force, it prohibits Congress from fining or jailing citizens, or associations of citizens, for simply engaging in political speech." The majority ruling also overruled provisions in earlier Supreme Court decisions which allowed restrictions on corporate spending on election campaigns, including *Austin v. Michigan Chamber of Commerce* (1990) and *McConnell v. FEC* (2003).

In a strong dissenting opinion, Justice John Paul Stevens, joined by liberal Justices Ginsburg, Breyer, and Sotomayor, argued that the majority ruling "threatens to undermine the integrity of elected institutions across the Nation . . . A democracy cannot function effectively when its constituent members believe laws are being bought and sold." This ties in with Senator McCain's remark in his 2002 book with the curious title *Worth the Fighting For:* "Money does buy access in Washington, and access increases influence that often results in benefiting the few at the expense of the many."

The most worrying perceived result of the *Citizens United* decision was the rise of "super PACs," or "political action committees," which do not themselves contribute to political candidates or parties but can accept unlimited contributions from individuals, corporations, and labor unions. In fact, it was the decision by the U.S. Court of Appeals for the District of Columbia in *SpeechNOW.org v. FEC* (2010) that allowed the creation of super PACs. In a 9–0 decision, the D.C. Circuit Court held that on the basis of *Citizens United,* a nonprofit organization like SpeechNOW, which itself made only "independent expenditures," could not be subject to any contribution limits. "Independent expenditure" means money spent advocating for the election of a particular candidate but without consultation, cooperation, or any "material" involvement with that candidate.

Citizens United also means that the laws of 24 states prohibiting or limiting "independent expenditures" by corporations and labor unions are under threat. And in *McCutcheon v. FEC* (2014), the U.S. Supreme Court swept away the previous prohibition on individuals contributing more than $48,600 combined to all federal candidates and more than $74,600 combined to all parties and super PACs. But an individual's contributions to an individual politician's campaign are still capped at $2,700 per election. In the words of Chief Justice Roberts, writing for the majority: "The government may no more restrict how many candidates or causes a donor may support than it may tell a newspaper how many candidates it may endorse." Justice Breyer, writing for the dissenting minority, argued that the decision "creates a loophole that will allow a single individual to contribute millions of dollars to a political party or to a candidate's campaign." Whoever is right, election campaigns are now more awash with money than ever before.

The whole new approach to campaign finance rests on the definition of contributions to political campaigns as protected speech under the First Amendment. Though Chief Justice Roberts was one of the chief protagonists of this approach, he was also concerned about the way *Citizens United* struck down much of the McCain–Feingold Act and overruled some recent Supreme Court decisions to boot — in contradiction to Roberts's stated commitment to judicial restraint and *stare decisis,* or fidelity to precedent. So the Chief Justice, joined by Justice Alito, wrote a separate concurrence to address this important problem. "There is a difference between judicial restraint and judicial abdication," wrote Roberts. He quoted Justice Oliver Wendell Holmes in remarking that "Judging the constitutionality of an Act of Congress is 'the gravest and most delicate duty that this Court is called upon to perform.'" But he did not really justify the complete redefinition of "political speech" in *Citizens United.* His justification of the majority's departure from precedent was more persuasive. If *stare decisis* were an "inexorable command," he explained, "segregation would be legal, minimum wage laws would be unconstitutional, and the Government could wiretap ordinary criminal suspects without first obtaining warrants."

REMEMBER

Citizens United remains a radical and highly controversial reinterpretation of the free speech clause of the First Amendment, with a major effect on elections.

Obergefell v. Hodges (2015)

This landmark 5–4 U.S. Supreme Court decision legalized same-sex marriage throughout the United States and its possessions and territories. It marked the culmination of a long battle fought out in a number of states, 37 of which, plus the District of Columbia, had legalized gay marriage prior to the ruling and 13 of which had banned it. The majority opinion, penned by Justice Anthony Kennedy, held that state laws banning same-sex marriage were a violation of the Equal Protection Clause and the Due Process Clause of the Fourteenth Amendment. Kennedy concluded, referring to the petitioners: "They ask for equal dignity in the eyes of the law. The Constitution grants them that right."

Chief Justice Roberts and Justices Scalia, Thomas, and Alito put in a strong dissent. Justice Scalia attacked the thinking, analysis, and legal reasoning of the majority, which he likened to "the mystical aphorisms of the fortune cookie." Justice Alito wrote: "Neither petitioners nor the majority cites a single case or other legal source providing any basis for such a constitutional right [as that of same-sex marriage]. None exists, and that is enough to foreclose their claim." Chief Justice Roberts specifically attacked what he called the 5-justice majority's "extravagant conception of judicial supremacy." He added: "Allowing unelected federal judges to select which unenumerated rights rank as 'fundamental' — and to strike down state laws on the basis of that determination — raises obvious concerns about the judicial role." Referring to the Founders' struggle "for the precious right to govern themselves," he added: "They would never have imagined yielding that right on a question of social policy to unaccountable and unelected judges . . . The Court's accumulation of power does not occur in a vacuum. It comes at the expense of the people." The Chief Justice concluded his vigorous dissent by sounding a warning that the legalization of same-sex marriage could endanger religious liberty: "Many good and decent people oppose same-sex marriage as a tenet of faith, and their freedom to exercise religion is — unlike the right imagined by the majority — actually spelled out in the Constitution."

Glossip v. Gross (2015)

This was a U.S. Supreme Court 5–4 decision upholding the constitutionality under the Eighth Amendment of lethal injection by a three-drug protocol including midazolam as an acceptable form of execution. The Court also, rather strangely, held that death-row prisoners could challenge their method of execution only if they came up with an alternative method! — what may be characterized as a "pick your poison" ruling. An unusual feature of this case was that the condemned man, Richard Glossip, was convicted of first-degree murder even though he didn't kill anyone himself but was found guilty of hiring someone else to commit the murder for him, which was done by beating the victim to death with a baseball bat. Another unusual feature of the case is the fact that there wasn't much evidence against Glossip other than the testimony of the actual killer, Justin Sneed, who was given life imprisonment without parole in return for confessing and pointing the finger at Glossip. Sneed's own grown daughter wrote to the Oklahoma Pardon and Parole Board that, based on her many communications with her father, she "strongly believes" that Glossip was innocent, adding: "For a couple of years now, my father has been talking to me about recanting his original testimony. I feel his conscious [sic] is getting to him." This letter arrived too late for it to be considered by the board. But Glossip, who has never stopped proclaiming his innocence, turned down a plea bargain under which he would have been sentenced to life *with* parole.

However, the Supreme Court wasn't concerned with the curious facts of the case, only with the question of a constitutionally acceptable form of lethal injection. Justice Breyer, who is opposed to capital punishment of any kind, claimed that "this country has fallen short of the aspiration that capital punishment be reserved for the 'worst of the worst.'" Justice Clarence Thomas, concurring with the majority, rejected Justice Breyer's whole argument and recited a catalog of gruesome murders whose perpetrators had been granted a stay of execution by the Supreme Court itself. Thomas concluded his opinion with this powerful, down-to-earth observation: "To the extent that we are ill at ease with these disparate outcomes, it seems to me that the best solution is for the Court to stop making up Eighth Amendment claims in its ceaseless quest to end the death penalty through undemocratic means." This is a salutary reminder that, as the death penalty is implicitly approved by the Constitution, it would be undemocratic for the Court to abolish it — something that can only be done by the process of amendment, involving a vote in Congress followed by ratification by the states.

Justice Alito, for the majority, wrote that "because it is settled that capital punishment is constitutional, 'it necessarily follows that there must be a [constitutional] means of carrying it out.' And because some risk of pain is inherent in any method of execution, we have held that the Constitution does not require the avoidance of all risk of pain . . . Holding that the Eighth Amendment demands the elimination of essentially all risk of pain would effectively outlaw the death penalty altogether."

So far, so good. Capital punishment is currently legal in 31 states. But in May 2016, the giant pharmaceutical company Pfizer announced that its drugs could no longer be used in lethal injections. Pfizer is the last big-name pharmaceutical company to withdraw its products from the death penalty industry, placing a question mark over the future of lethal injection. Maybe other states will consider following the example of Utah, which has now relegalized its traditional method of execution by firing squad.

Riley v. California (2014)

This case is remarkable for several reasons, not least because the U.S. Supreme Court decision was unanimous, ruling that trawling through the digital contents of a cellphone without a warrant is unconstitutional as a violation of the Fourth Amendment. The case arose out of an incident in 2009 in which David Leon Riley was pulled over in his Lexus by a San Diego police officer for expired registration tags. During the stop the officer also found that Riley had a suspended driver's license. Two loaded handguns were subsequently discovered hidden in the car that matched the firearms used in a recent gangland murder of which Riley had been a suspect.

On the basis of all this information, Riley was placed under arrest, and a search of his cellphone without a warrant yielded evidence of Riley's membership of the "Bloods" gang, contacts, text messages, and photographs, including one of a red Oldsmobile (his gang's color) also owned by Riley, which was the vehicle involved in the gangland shooting. Riley was then charged in connection with the gang shooting. Riley's application to exclude the cellphone evidence from his trial was denied, and he was convicted of attempted murder and sentenced to 15 years to life in prison. The California Court of Appeal upheld his conviction and sentence, and the California Supreme Court found the seizure of Riley's cellphone kosher because it occurred during a "search incident to arrest."

A unanimous Supreme Court — a rare phenomenon indeed — disagreed. Chief Justice John Roberts, writing for the Court, waxed lyrical in defense of individual liberty in the digital age: "Modern cellphones are not just another technological convenience. With all they contain and all they may reveal, they hold for many Americans 'the privacies of life.' The fact that technology now allows an individual to carry such information in his hand does not make the information any less worthy of the protection for which the Founders fought."

Justice Alito, while concurring in the holding of the Court, raised some commonsense concerns about possible anomalies: "It would be very unfortunate if privacy protection in the 21st century were left primarily to the federal courts using the blunt instrument of the Fourth Amendment. Legislatures, elected by the people, are in a better position than we are to assess and respond to the changes that have already occurred and those that almost certainly will take place in the future."

"Won battle, lost war" is how the *San Diego Union-Tribune* put it, because, despite his victory in the Supreme Court, David Riley was ordered to stay in jail to serve out the rest of his sentence of 15 years to life. The reason was that Riley's conviction didn't depend on the erroneous admission into evidence of the digital contents of his cellphone.

How, if at all, does the Supreme Court's decision in *Riley* impact the issue of the National Security Agency's bulk collection of metadata, which was not mentioned in *Riley*? The key lies in the term *metadata*, which doesn't give any information about the contents of the calls. So *Riley* has no direct bearing on the NSA cases, which I discuss in Chapter 16.

Chapter **24**

Ten Influential Supreme Court Justices

The U.S. Supreme Court has experienced an exponential increase in power and influence since it opened for business in 1789. In the early days, the Court didn't even have a building to call its own, and it was unsure of the extent of its powers. John Jay, the first Chief Justice, lamented that the Court lacked "the energy, weight, and dignity which are essential to its affording due support to the national government."

REMEMBER

That all changed with the appointment of John Marshall as Chief Justice in 1801. Marshall started the transformation that has made the Court probably the most important branch of government.

But is the expansion of the Court's power necessarily a good thing? The other two branches of government — Congress and the President — are popularly elected. By contrast, the Court is made up of unelected justices appointed "during good Behaviour," meaning essentially for life. This arrangement protects the independence of the judiciary. Alexander Hamilton remarked in the *Federalist Papers*, written in 1788 (before the Constitution came into force), that this security of tenure was "the best expedient which can be devised in any government, to secure a steady, upright, and impartial administration of the laws." But Hamilton completely underestimated the future power of the judiciary, which he described as "beyond comparison the weakest of the three departments of power," because it "has no influence over either the sword or the purse . . . It may truly be said to have neither FORCE nor WILL, but merely judgment."

But appointment for life enables the judiciary to butt into areas reserved to the other two branches of government — particularly by *making* law rather than merely *interpreting* it, as judges are supposed to do.

Among the ten most influential Supreme Court justices that I introduce in this chapter, I include some judicial activists and some practitioners of judicial restraint. (Keep in mind that no judge ever labels *himself* a judicial activist. That label yells that the judge in question habitually exceeds the proper powers of a judge or justice.)

John Marshall

John Marshall was the longest serving Chief Justice in U.S. history, holding office from 1801 until his death in 1835. He was also the most influential Supreme Court justice.

As a person, Marshall was easygoing, affable, friendly, and unassuming. Even Marshall's political enemies liked him — except Thomas Jefferson, who was actually a distant cousin of his. Jefferson realized that Marshall's bland exterior concealed a wily nature and a crafty mind. "You must never give him an affirmative answer," said Jefferson, "or you will be forced to grant his conclusion. Why, if he were to ask me if it were daylight or not, I'd reply, 'Sir, I don't know, I can't tell.'"

Some of Marshall's "twistifications of the law" (Jefferson's phrase) occurred in the following leading cases:

>> *Marbury v. Madison:* This case established the right of the Supreme Court to declare Acts of Congress unconstitutional and therefore void. I discuss this landmark case in Chapter 23.

>> *Fletcher v. Peck:* This was the first case in which the Supreme Court struck down a state law as unconstitutional — while upholding a corrupt contract.

>> *McCulloch v. Maryland:* This case established the supremacy of federal law over state law.

>> *Cohens v. Virginia:* This case established the power of the Supreme Court to hear all cases involving constitutional issues.

>> *Gibbons v. Ogden:* In this case, the Supreme Court held that the Commerce Clause in the U.S. Constitution gave Congress a power overriding state law. I deal with the sticky subject of the Commerce Clause in Chapter 9. Read it at your peril!

John Marshall wrote the opinion of the Supreme Court in all these cases, and in 519 of the 1,106 opinions filed by the Court during his tenure.

Marshall had the mind of a lawyer but the heart of a politician. His judicial decisions were heavily influenced by his political views, which

>> Favored a strong federal government over states' rights

>> Promoted the power of the Supreme Court over that of Congress and the Presidency

>> Advanced commercial and industrial interests over rural and agrarian concerns

Oliver Wendell Holmes, Jr.

Oliver Wendell Holmes, Jr., who was an associate justice from 1902 to 1932, is still probably the most oft-quoted Supreme Court justice of all time.

A strong believer in freedom of speech, Holmes nevertheless upheld the conviction of a socialist for exhorting draftees in World War I to oppose the draft. Holmes found that the words used created "a clear and present danger that they will bring about the substantive evils that Congress has a right to prevent." Holmes added that "The most stringent protection of free speech would not protect a man in falsely shouting fire in a theatre and causing panic."

Holmes is less well known for his practice of judicial restraint — his reluctance to interfere with laws passed by elected legislatures. But sometimes he went too far in this direction, as when he upheld Virginia's compulsory sterilization law with the flippant remark, "Three generations of imbeciles are enough."

Hugo Black

Hugo Lafayette Black sat as an associate justice of the U.S. Supreme Court from 1937 to 1971, a period of 34 years, making him one of the longest serving members in the history of the Court. He was also one of its most influential members, though his name is hardly remembered today.

Black was a bundle of contradictions. Starting out as a member of the Ku Klux Klan and as a senator from Alabama who led a filibuster to defeat an anti-lynching bill, he was also a staunch supporter of President Franklin Roosevelt's New Deal and, as a judge, came to be regarded as an extreme liberal — though coupled with a belief in textualism and judicial restraint.

Though a strong supporter of civil rights and desegregation, Black tended to uphold law and order over civil rights activism such as sit-ins, demonstrations, and protest marches. He was quoted as coming out in 1968 against "special privileges under the law" for African Americans — a rare recognition by a judge of the distinction between rights and privileges.

Black's textualist approach to the Constitution was most in evidence in regard to the First Amendment. He rejected as unconstitutional any curtailment of freedom of speech on any ground at all, including obscenity and even national security. He even regarded the law of defamation as an unconstitutional abridgement of freedom of speech. However, he didn't accept that flag-burning was speech, and in *Street v. New York* (1969), he accordingly was prepared to uphold a state law that made the deliberate burning of the American flag a criminal offense.

Justice Black regarded as his most significant opinion his dissent in *Adamson v. California* (1947). The issue in that case was whether the Fifth Amendment freedom against self-incrimination applied to the states as well as to federal courts. A 5–4 majority of the Supreme Court said no. Black disagreed, arguing for the "incorporation" of the first eight amendments of the Bill of Rights, meaning that the states should be bound by them. Black's view was essentially gradually accepted by the Supreme Court. The only provisions in the first eight amendments that are not now expressly recognized as incorporated are the Fifth Amendment provision of indictment by a grand jury and the Seventh Amendment right to a jury trial in civil lawsuits.

Earl Warren

President Dwight Eisenhower was looking for a conservative Chief Justice when he nominated Earl Warren to fill that seat in 1953. Warren soon turned out to be a liberal activist who hugely expanded the power of the Court. Eisenhower regretted his choice, remarking that his nomination of Warren "was the biggest damned-fool mistake I ever made."

A typical example of Warren's views is the opinion that he wrote in a 1967 ruling that a member of the Communist Party could not be barred from working in a defense establishment — even though there was a federal law against it. Two justices dissented, noting that "Nothing in the Constitution requires this result."

Warren is best known for his opinion in *Brown v. Board of Education,* striking down state laws that established segregated public schools. Referring specifically to this decision, former Supreme Court Justice James F. Byrnes said, "The Court did not interpret the Constitution — the Court amended it." In *Miranda v. Arizona,* decided in 1966, Warren's opinion commanded only a 5–4 majority. But this was yet another landmark decision that cast a long shadow. The ruling in this case introduced the familiar Miranda warning that you've heard so many times on TV and in the movies: "You have the right to remain silent. . .." Three dissenting justices maintained that the majority decision "represents poor constitutional law and entails harmful consequences for the country at large."

Thurgood Marshall

Thurgood Marshall was the first African American to sit on the Court, serving for 24 years, from 1967 until 1991. A straight line can be drawn from Marshall's appointment in 1967 to the election of another African American lawyer as the first black President in 2008. It's hard to envision the election of President Barack Obama without the long struggle for black civil rights so successfully waged by Thurgood Marshall.

REMEMBER

As chief counsel for the National Association for the Advancement of Colored People (NAACP) between 1940 and 1961, Marshall argued 32 cases before the Supreme Court — of which he won no fewer than 29! The best-known of his victories was the earth-shattering 1954 case of *Brown v. Board of Education,* which forever consigned the doctrine of "separate but equal" to the trash can of history.

Marshall's time on the Court was marked by his championing of liberal causes, most of which are less fashionable today. Here's a bird's-eye view of two of Marshall's key issues:

>> **Death penalty:** Marshall and his close ally Justice William Brennan consistently held that the death penalty always amounted to "cruel and unusual punishment" prohibited by the Eight Amendment. Their stance caused the death penalty to be suspended between 1972 and 1976. Since 1976, the majority on the Court has rejected the view that capital punishment is automatically unconstitutional. At the time of this writing, capital punishment is permitted in 31 states.

>> **Affirmative action:** Allan Bakke, a white man, was twice rejected for admission to medical school by the University of California (UC) Davis. Bakke's qualifications were superior to those of 16 minority students who were admitted under the university's affirmative action program. Bakke claimed

that he was the victim of racial discrimination. When Bakke's case reached the Supreme Court in 1978, the majority on the Court held that race could be taken into account together with other factors in determining admissions to a university, but that a fixed quota system such as the one operated by UC Davis was unconstitutional.

Marshall robustly dissented from this conclusion. He came out strongly in support of the university's affirmative action program favoring the admission of minorities. Marshall didn't even mention Bakke's claim that he was the victim of racial discrimination himself. Today, 40 years later, Bakke is still authoritative.

John Paul Stevens

John Paul Stevens, nominated by President Gerald Ford, served as an associate justice of the U.S. Supreme Court for over 34 years, from 1975 until 2010, retiring at the age of 90. He's generally considered to have been a liberal judge, although even as late as 2007 he was still describing himself as a judicial conservative.

Starting out as a strong critic of affirmative action, his attitude toward affirmative action changed over time, and he ended up supporting the University of Michigan Law School's affirmative action program in *Grutter v. Bollinger* (2003). However, in *Crawford v. Marion County Election Board* (2008), he wrote the winning plurality opinion in support of an Indiana law requiring photo ID for voting. In so doing he was supported by the conservatives on the Court, while three liberal justices dissented. Stevens wrote: "Because Indiana's cards are free, the inconvenience of going to the Bureau of Motor Vehicles, gathering required documents, and posing for a photograph does not qualify as a substantial burden on most voters' right to vote, or represent a significant increase over the usual burdens of voting."

In *Texas v. Johnson* (1989), as a proud World War II veteran, Stevens strongly dissented from the majority view that flag-burning was "protected speech" under the First Amendment, adding: "The case has nothing to do with 'disagreeable ideas.' It involves disagreeable conduct that, in my opinion, diminishes the value of an important national asset."

Stevens was a consistent advocate of gun control. In *Printz v. United States* (1997), he was a member of the minority on the Court that supported the provision in the Brady Act commanding local chief law enforcement officers to conduct background checks. This also tied in with his general opposition to the so-called "new federalism," which he saw as curtailing the power of Congress. His support for gun control culminated in his strong dissent in *District of Columbia v. Heller* (2008), in which he characterized the majority opinion as "a strained and unpersuasive reading" of the Second Amendment, which caused a dramatic upheaval in the law.

Stevens also adopted a strong liberal position in *Citizens United v. Federal Election Commission* (2010), in which he led a four-strong liberal dissent, showing the strength of his disagreement by reading part of his 90-page opinion from the bench. The majority ruling gave a green light to unrestricted spending on election campaigns by corporations and labor unions. Stevens concluded his dissent with these words: "While American democracy is imperfect, few outside the majority of this Court would have thought its flaws included a dearth of corporate money in politics."

In *Bush v. Gore* (2000), Stevens dissented strongly from the majority opinion, which put George W. Bush into the White House. Stevens concluded his dissent with these words: "Although we may never know with complete certainty the identity of the winner of this year's Presidential election, the identity of the loser is perfectly clear. It is the Nation's confidence in the judge as an impartial guardian of the rule of law."

In 2014 Stevens published a book titled *Six Amendments: How and Why We Should Change the Constitution.* His chief motivation for writing the book was his objection to changes made to the Constitution by unelected judges, usurping the proper democratic process for amending the Constitution as laid down in the Constitution itself. Or, in Stevens's own words: In the previous 40 years, "rules crafted by a slim majority of the members of the Supreme Court have had such a profound and unfortunate impact on our basic law that resort to the process of amendment is warranted." Stevens's confidence "that the soundness of each of my proposals will become more and more evident, and that ultimately each will be adopted" is probably misplaced optimism, but only time will tell.

Sandra Day O'Connor

Sandra Day O'Connor was the first woman ever to sit on the U.S. Supreme Court, which she did from 1981 to 2006. This fact alone earned her a place in history. But she deserves to be remembered for her opinions too — and for her tactics, which gave her added influence as the swing vote in a number of leading cases.

O'Connor adopted a case-by-case approach to her work on the Court, which enabled her to switch sides when it suited her. For example, she was on different sides in two cases decided in 2003 about the affirmative action admissions policy of the University of Michigan Law School. The Court decided both cases by a 5–4 majority — and O'Connor was in the majority both times!

Among her many skillful tightrope acts was her opinion in *Webster v. Reproductive Health Services,* a case on abortion. She was careful to oppose overturning *Roe v. Wade* while effectively cutting back on it. As was so often the case, she managed to be the swing vote in a 5–4 majority decision.

Antonin Scalia

Antonin Scalia served as an associate justice of the Supreme Court for nearly 30 years, from 1986 until his sudden and unexpected death in 2016. In regard to constitutional interpretation, Scalia was an *originalist* — believing that the Constitution means what it meant to the Framers. And when it came to statutory interpretation, he described himself as a *textualist*, meaning, as he put it, that "it is the law that governs, not the intent of the lawgiver." And: "A text should not be construed strictly, and it should not be construed leniently; it should be construed reasonably, to contain all that it fairly means."

Scalia's textualism is well illustrated by his dissent in *Smith v. U.S.* (1993). When John Angus Smith offered to trade an automatic weapon to an undercover police officer in return for cocaine, he was convicted and sentenced to a more severe penalty on the ground that he had made "use" of a firearm "during and in relation to" a drug offense. By 7 votes to 2, the Court upheld the imposition of the heavier penalty in this case. Scalia dissented, on the ground that Smith had not made "use" of the gun in the way that the law envisioned. Here's how he explained his position: "When someone asks 'Do you use a cane?' he is not inquiring whether you have your grandfather's silver handled walking stick on display in the hall; he wants to know whether you walk with a cane. Similarly, to speak of 'using a firearm' is to speak of using it for its distinctive purpose, i.e. as a weapon." Scalia was joined in his dissent, for quite different reasons, by the liberal Justice John Paul Stevens.

This was not the only occasion on which his textualism resulted in Scalia having a strange bedfellow, with whom, as a political conservative, he would normally have had little in common. Another such example was *Hamdi v. Rumsfeld* (2004), in which he was again allied with liberal Justice John Paul Stevens, this time in taking an uncompromising stand against the U.S. government. In *Texas v. Johnson* (1989), Scalia's textualism made him join the liberals on the Court in ruling that flag-burning was protected speech under the First Amendment. Scalia's vote tipped the balance in favor of this liberal view, while the generally liberal Stevens dissented for patriotic reasons.

But more often than not, Scalia's conservatism dovetailed with his originalism. "The Supreme Court of the United States has descended from the disciplined legal reasoning of John Marshall and Joseph Story to the mystical aphorisms of the fortune cookie." In his opposition to gay marriage and to benefits for same-sex couples, Scalia remarked in a 2013 speech: "It's not up to the courts to invent new minorities that get special protections." His last controversial remark occurred in *Fisher II v. University of Texas* (2016), in which he supported the view that "it does not benefit African-Americans to get them into the University of Texas, where they do not do well, as opposed to having them go to a less-advanced school, a slower-track school where they do well."

Scalia's originalism also tied in well with his belief in judicial restraint, and in particular, his belief that changes to the law should be made not by judges but by lawmakers. As he put it in a 2011 interview in regard to the possibility of outlawing sexual discrimination: "If the current society wants to outlaw discrimination by sex, hey we have things called legislatures, and they enact things called laws."

Scalia's inflexibility and doctrinaire, even pedantic, approach to the law limited his influence on his fellow justices — except in one respect. Scalia early on started subjecting counsel to the third degree with quick-fire questions. This novel approach soon caught on among new appointees to the Court (except for Justice Clarence Thomas, who until Scalia's death generally maintained a stony silence throughout oral arguments).

Anthony Kennedy

Associate Justice Anthony Kennedy has arguably been far more influential than President John Kennedy or any member of his family, to which Justice Kennedy is not related. Kennedy, nominated by Ronald Reagan in 1988, has now sat on the Supreme Court for 30 years. Between 1992 and 2005, while the conservative William Rehnquist was Chief Justice, Kennedy kept to a conservative line. However, after Rehnquist's death Kennedy became more eclectic, often emerging as the decisive swing vote with the influential right to craft the majority opinion.

Among the areas of law where Kennedy cast the swing vote and wrote the majority opinion are the following:

>> **Same-sex marriage:** Kennedy wrote the majority 5 to 4 decision in the landmark case of *Obergefell v. Hodges* (2015), which ruled that marriage is a fundamental right guaranteed to same-sex couples by both the Due Process Clause and Equal Protection Clause of the Fourteenth Amendment.

- **Capital punishment:** In *Kennedy v. Louisiana* (2008), the Supreme Court ruled by 5 votes to 4 that, in the words of Justice Kennedy, writing for the majority: "The death penalty should not be expanded to instances where the victim's life was not taken."

- **Habeas corpus:** Kennedy wrote the 5–4 majority opinion in *Boumediene v. Bush* (2008), which decided that foreign terrorist suspects held at Guantanamo Bay, Cuba, had the right to challenge their detention in the U.S. courts and petition for habeas corpus (which is actually not a right but a privilege).

- **Strip-search:** In *Florence v. Board of Chosen Freeholders* (2012), a 5–4 majority of the Supreme Court ruled, in an opinion penned by Justice Kennedy, that it was permissible to strip-search someone who has been arrested for any crime before admitting that person to jail, even if the offense in question was a minor one and even if there was no reasonable suspicion that the person was carrying contraband.

- **Immigration:** In *Arizona v. United States* (2012), Kennedy, writing for a 5–3 majority made up of Chief Justice Roberts together with three liberal justices, held that "Arizona may have understandable frustrations with the problems caused by illegal immigration while that process continues, but the state may not pursue polices that undermine federal law." Justice Scalia dissented, arguing that: "As a sovereign, Arizona has the inherent power to exclude persons from its territory, subject only to those limitations expressed in the Constitution or constitutionally imposed by Congress. That power to exclude has long been recognized as inherent in sovereignty."

John Roberts

Only 9 percent of those surveyed in a 1989 *Washington Post* poll could name the Chief Justice, who at that time was William Rehnquist. The current Chief Justice, John G. Roberts, Jr., (see Figure 24-1) is even less of a household name, even though he has been Chief Justice since Rehnquist's death in 2005.

Roberts's declared aim of achieving more unanimity on the Court has been notable by its absence. Unlike some of his predecessors, the Chief Justice has not proved very adept at bringing his colleagues round to his view.

Roberts is generally thought of as a judicial conservative. As he put it during his confirmation hearings: "Judges are like umpires. Umpires don't make the rules; they apply them. The role of an umpire and a judge is critical. They make sure everybody plays by the rules. But it is a limited role. Nobody ever went to a ball game to see the umpire."

FIGURE 24-1:
John G. Roberts, Jr., Chief Justice since 2005.

Despite this, Roberts has sometimes adopted a more activist role than might have been anticipated. In particular, in *National Federation of Independent Business v. Sebelius* (2012), Roberts, joined by four liberal justices, upheld the constitutionality of the individual mandate component of Obamacare, albeit on the unexpected basis that it was a tax.

However, Roberts has more often remained true to his conservative principles, as in the so-called "PICS" case, *Parents Involved in Community Schools v. Seattle School District No. 1* (2007), in which two school districts used racial classifications as the basis of student assignment. Writing for a conservative plurality of four, Roberts penned the oft-quoted words: "The way to stop discrimination on the basis of race is to stop discriminating on the basis of race."

In *Utah v. Strieff* (2016), the Chief Justice joined Justice Clarence Thomas's majority opinion limiting the scope of the Fourth Amendment's exclusionary rule. Edward Strieff had been stopped on the street by police officers lacking reasonable suspicion, but it was then discovered that Strieff had an outstanding warrant for a traffic violation. In the ensuing search Strieff was found to be in possession of illegal drugs. Writing for the majority, Thomas held that the drug evidence was admissible because "the discovery of a valid arrest warrant was a sufficient intervening event to break the causal chain between the unlawful stop and the discovery of drug-related evidence on Strieff's person." Though the majority included the liberal Justice Stephen Breyer, three other liberal justices dissented, Justice Sonia Sotomayor going so far as to claim that the majority's ruling would "corrode all our civil liberties."

Chapter **25**

Two Sides of Five Constitutional Conundrums

Dear Reader, please don't think you've been short-changed. Yes, I know that this is "The Part of Tens" and this chapter contains only five sections. But please don't go back to the bookstore — or worse, the publisher — and ask for your money back! I couldn't do justice to more than these five topics in the limited space available for this chapter. But I have given you both sides of the argument on all these highly controversial issues — and two times five equals ten!

The point of this chapter is to identify some issues that are at the forefront of debate on the Constitution. These are

» Whether the Constitution is still relevant today

» Whether presidential elections are truly democratic

» Whether the Supreme Court has too much power

» Whether the U.S. really is a democracy

» Whether the President has too much power

Is the Constitution Outdated?

The U.S. Constitution is 230 years old. If the Constitution were a person, it would be long dead — or, at the very least, extremely frail and completely out of touch with the realities of modern life! Is the Constitution any different?

Here are some arguments in favor of the view that the Constitution is outdated:

>> When the Constitution was drafted, not only were there no cheeseburgers, cellphones, or MP3 players — which some people today regard as necessities — but there also were no automobiles, airplanes, electricity, TV, or computers. It really was a totally different world.

>> Social values were way different then too: Slavery was rife, the death penalty was unquestioned, women had fewer legal rights, and gay sex was outlawed.

>> A constitution emanating from such an alien background can remain relevant only if it's constantly reinterpreted by the Supreme Court to keep abreast of changing values.

But a lot of people reject this approach. Here are some of the arguments against the view that the Constitution is outdated:

>> The core values enshrined in the Constitution are timeless and represent the underpinnings of this country as originally conceived.

>> The Constitution is a force for stability in law, government, and society.

>> Only by sticking closely to the original meaning of the Constitution can the Supreme Court achieve a uniform approach to it.

>> A proliferation of inconsistent interpretations of the Constitution could lead people to lose respect for the Supreme Court — and for the Constitution itself.

>> It's wrong for judges to second-guess the Framers of the Constitution because that would amount to changing the meaning of the Constitution.

>> The Supreme Court is not allowed to change the Constitution. That can be done only by the elaborate process of amendment as laid down in the Constitution itself.

As for "updating" the Constitution, why should a group of nine — or, all too often, five — middle-aged to positively ancient judges have the right to decide what values are kosher? Isn't that an exercise in lawmaking, or legislation, which is reserved by the Constitution to Congress, with the President's approval? And why should issues such as freedom of contract, abortion, or same-sex marriage be regarded as having anything to do with the Constitution in any event? Justice Ruth Bader Ginsburg, an ardent supporter of abortion rights for women, was nevertheless critical of the Supreme Court's 1973 decision in *Roe v. Wade*, which she labeled in a 1985 article as "heavy-handed judicial activism" that "appears to have provoked, not resolved, conflict." She added: "The political process was moving in the early 1970s, not quickly enough for the advocates of quick, complete change, but majoritarian institutions were listening and acting." By "majoritarian institutions" Ginsburg was referring to legislatures representing majority opinion. This perceptive observation was a recognition that it would have been better to wait until public opinion was firmly behind abortion rights than for the Supreme Court to create these rights without "majoritarian" backing. This ties in with developments in other countries, like Britain, for example, where abortion rights were established by legislation and never became a focus of controversy.

Should the Electoral College Be Abolished?

The Framers of the Constitution didn't trust the ordinary people. In the original, unamended Constitution, the House of Representatives was the only directly elected body. Senators were originally chosen by the state legislatures, and the President was elected by an Electoral College.

The Electoral College system is still in force for presidential elections. The rise of political parties has made the whole operation much more democratic than the Framers ever intended, but it's still not completely democratic. (See Chapter 10 for an explanation of how the system works.)

Here are some of the undemocratic features of the Electoral College system, which have resulted in calls for its abolition:

>> Although members of the Electoral College are pledged to support a particular candidate for President, there have been no fewer than 158 "faithless electors" over the years in votes for President or Vice President. Although pledged to vote for a particular candidate, these electors all cast their votes for somebody else.

In 71 of the 158 cases, the voting change made perfect sense because the pledged candidate had died before the election. But the remaining cases have been more complex. The biggest defection occurred in 1836, when all 23 of Virginia's electors who had pledged to vote for Martin Van Buren as President refused to vote for his running mate, Richard M. Johnson, because he had been living with a family slave with whom he had two daughters.

REMEMBER

>> With the exception of Maine and Nebraska, the candidate winning a plurality of the popular vote in a state carries that state and takes *all* its electoral votes. For example, in 2000, the whole election turned on a few votes in Florida. By declaring George W. Bush the winner of the popular vote in Florida, the U.S. Supreme Court gave him all 25 of Florida's then total number of electoral votes and thus handed him the presidency.

>> This winner-take-all arrangement can result in the candidate with the smaller number of popular votes becoming President. This happened in 1824, 1876, 1888, 2000, 2016, and possibly also in 1960.

>> In the event of a tie in the Electoral College, the election of the President is thrown into the House of Representatives, with each state having just a single vote — hardly a democratic solution.

On the other hand, the Electoral College also has its advantages, including the following points:

>> The Electoral College system reflects and maintains the federal structure of the nation. No state, however small, has fewer than three electoral votes — because the number of electoral votes allocated to a state is the number of representatives from that state in the House, plus two, for its two senators. This formula compensates the smaller states for their lower levels of population.

>> Although the election result is calculated by the total number of electoral votes won by each candidate across the nation, the number of *states* carried by each candidate is also important, as is the result in each particular state. Take, for example, the significance of Al Gore's failure to carry his home state, Tennessee, in the 2000 election — which cost him the election. He wouldn't have needed to carry Florida if he'd had Tennessee's 11 electoral votes under his belt.

>> The Electoral College favors the two-party system by making it harder for a third party to break through. Some people think this is a bad feature of the Electoral College system. But if the President was directly elected by popular vote, the practical result of a serious third-party challenge would likely throw the election into the House of Representatives. In both 1992 and 1996, the Reform Party candidate, Ross Perot, took enough votes to deprive either of the major party candidates of a majority of the popular vote. Without the Electoral College, both of these elections would have been decided by the House.

The main objection leveled against the Electoral College system is the winner-take-all arrangement in presidential elections — which is not a necessary part of the Electoral College system at all and is not mandated by the U.S. Constitution. This is the arrangement under which the candidate with the most votes in a particular state takes *all* the electoral votes of that state. A margin of just one in the popular vote is enough.

This was the problem in the 2000 election. The result of the voting in Florida was too close to call. The punched card ballots didn't help, with the resulting "pregnant chads" or "hanging chads" (referring to incompletely punched holes in a ballot). The Florida result was crucial to the outcome of the election. Without Florida, George Bush had 246 electoral votes to Al Gore's 266. The magic number of electoral votes needed to win the presidency was 270. Whoever polled a bigger share of the popular vote in Florida would carry that state as a whole with all its (then) 25 electoral votes. The matter ended up in the U.S. Supreme Court, which by a 5–4 majority found in favor of Bush — on the basis of a 537 vote plurality over Gore in Florida. With Florida in his column, Bush's total electoral vote jumped from 246 to 271, winning him the presidency by the skin of his teeth.

Regardless of the fact that Gore beat Bush in the national popular vote by over half a million votes, the result would have been different if, instead of winner-take-all, Florida had adopted a split-vote arrangement along the lines of Nebraska and Maine. That would obviously have had to be put in place well ahead of the 2000 election — by a law enacted by the Florida state legislature. As Bush and Gore were neck and neck in Florida, with Bush at 48.85 percent of the vote and Gore at 48.84 percent, and assuming the system in place was one that split the electoral vote in proportion to the share of the popular vote, Bush would have received 13 of Florida's (then) 25 electoral votes and Gore 12. This would have given Bush a grand total of 259 electoral votes to Gore's 278, making Gore the clear winner of the presidency.

Nebraska and Maine use a slightly more complicated version of the split-vote system, referred to as the Congressional District Method. This system has affected the total electoral vote once in each state. In 2008, John McCain won 4 of Nebraska's electoral votes and Barack Obama 1. And in 2016, Hillary Clinton won 3 of Maine's electoral votes to Donald Trump's 1.

REMEMBER

A simple split of the electoral vote in proportion to the popular vote would be by far the fairest arrangement and be perfectly in keeping with the Constitution. It could also have far-reaching effects, especially in the larger states. For example, if California with 55 electoral votes, Texas with 36, New York with 29, and Florida with 29 — or any one of them — went over to a split-vote system, that would make the election a bit more democratic. A simple calculation proves this. If, for example, presidential candidate X garners 60 percent of the vote in California and candidate Y receives 40 percent; under the present system, candidate X picks up all 55 of California's electoral votes, which may well be decisive in putting candidate X into the White House. But, it means that 40 percent of the California electorate who actually voted are effectively disfranchised, as their votes are simply ignored. But, if California had a split-vote system, candidate X would receive 33 electoral votes and candidate Y would get 22. This is much less likely to swing the whole election and is also fairer to the 40 percent who voted for Y, as their votes would now be fully in play.

Does the U.S. Supreme Court Have Too Much Power?

In *Marbury v. Madison*, decided in 1803, Chief Justice John Marshall airily declared: "It is emphatically the province and duty of the judicial department to say what the law is," and, on that basis, to decide the constitutionality of a law. Jefferson, a distant cousin of Marshall's who, however, found his repeated "twistifications" unacceptable, remarked, quite correctly: "The question whether the judges are invested with exclusive authority to decide on the constitutionality of a law has been heretofore a subject of consideration with me in the exercise of official duties. Certainly there is not a word in the Constitution which has given that power to them more than to the Executive or Legislative branches."

However, Marshall had the last word and scored a lasting victory over Jefferson in that case, which I discuss in Chapter 23. A century later, in 1907, Charles Evans Hughes, who was later to become Chief Justice, would say, "We are under a Constitution, but the Constitution is what the judges say it is." Hughes's remark was not meant as a criticism, because he went on to say, "And the judiciary is the safeguard of our liberty and property under the Constitution."

Hughes's observation is still correct, and since 1791 the Constitution has changed far more as a result of judicial interpretation than through formal amendments. Here are some major constitutional changes brought about by decisions of the U.S. Supreme Court:

>> Enforcing "freedom of contract" as a supposed constitutional principle in 1905 — and abandoning it 30 years later. The Court then went to the opposite extreme of supporting tight central government control of the economy through a broad interpretation of the Commerce Clause. In the years between 1995 and 2005, there were intermittent signs of a return to more states' rights, which came to an end with *Gonzales v. Raich* (2005), in which by a majority of 6 to 3 the Supreme Court ruled that the federal government could, under the Commerce Clause, outlaw the use of marijuana for medicinal purposes even if it never crossed state lines. I discuss the Commerce Clause in Chapter 9.

>> Outlawing segregation in public schools in the landmark case of *Brown v. Board of Education* (1954) — overruling at least three prior Supreme Court

decisions: *Plessy v. Ferguson* (1896), *Cumming v. Richmond County Board of Education* (1899), and *Berea College v. Kentucky* (1908).

>> Approving the use of busing to achieve desegregation of public schools, decided by a unanimous Supreme Court in *Swann v. Charlotte-Mecklenburg Board of Education* (1971), but restricted in *Milliken v. Bradley*, in which the Supreme Court ruled that busing should not take place across district lines unless there was legalized busing across multiple school districts.

>> Providing additional protection for criminal defendants, for example, by requiring the well-known *Miranda* warning (*Dickerson v. United States,* 2000).

>> Disapproving of the death penalty in 1972 in *Furman v. Georgia* — even though it's explicitly referred to in the Constitution. Within four years, the Supreme Court pulled back from this position in *Gregg v. Georgia* (1976). The current position is now *Baze v. Rees* (2008) and *Glossip v. Gross* (2015), allowing lethal injection with certain drugs. Capital punishment is now lawful in 31 states and under federal law.

>> Establishing the expectation of privacy as a constitutionally protected right in *Griswold v. Connecticut* (1965) on the rather shaky legal basis of "penumbras, formed by emanations" from several existing constitutional protections. (In other words, a vague peripheral product issuing from existing constitutional guarantees.)

>> Supporting a woman's right to have an abortion (within certain time constraints) in *Roe v. Wade* (1973) based on the right to privacy. The legal basis of this decision has been questioned even by liberal academics. For example, Professor Laurence Tribe of Harvard wrote in the *Harvard Law Review* that "Behind its own verbal smokescreen, the substantive judgment on which it rests is nowhere to be found."

>> Upholding affirmative action but prohibiting the use of quotas in college admissions, in *Regents of the University of California v. Bakke* (1978).

>> Invalidating laws in 48 states that prohibited the desecration of the U.S. flag, in *Texas v. Johnson* (1989). The 5–4 majority, led by liberal Justice William Brennan but also including conservative Justice Antonin Scalia, characterized flag-burning as "symbolic speech" protected under the First Amendment. (The dissenting minority included liberal Justice John Paul Stevens.)

>> Legalizing same-sex sexual activity throughout the U.S. in *Lawrence v. Texas* (2003), and invalidating sodomy laws in 14 states.

>> Allowing unlimited expenditure on political campaigns by corporations, labor unions, and other associations, in *Citizens United v. Federal Election Commission* (2010), on the basis that restricting such expenditure would be a violation of the First Amendment's guarantee of freedom of speech. The decision overturned two previous Supreme Court decisions and declared unconstitutional the main provisions of the McCain–Feingold Act of 2002.

>> Upholding the constitutionality of most of the Patient Protection and Affordable Care Act, or Obamacare, in *National Federation of Independent Business v. Sebelius* (2012). The ruling notably upheld the individual mandate to buy health insurance — on the unexpected basis of Congress's taxing power.

>> Legalizing same-sex marriage throughout the U.S. in *Obergefell v. Hodges* (2015), on the basis that marriage is a fundamental right guaranteed to same-sex couples by the Due Process Clause and the Equal Protection Clause of the Fourteenth Amendment.

Above all, most of these decisions are essentially political and rest on flimsy legal underpinnings. Justice Antonin Scalia wittily but not entirely unfairly likened the reasoning of the majority in the *Obergefell* case to "the mystical aphorisms of the fortune cookie." On the other hand, there's more than a little merit in the concluding words of Justice John Paul Stevens's 90-page dissenting opinion in *Citizens United*: "While American democracy is imperfect, few outside the majority of this Court would have thought its flaws included a dearth of corporate money in politics."

The question here is not whether you agree or disagree with any of these Supreme Court rulings, but rather whether the Court should have had the right to change the Constitution in all these different respects, bypassing the proper process of amendment as laid down by the Constitution, which does not involve the courts at all. Most of these decisions involved striking down state laws, and in some cases federal laws as well, together with earlier decisions of the Supreme Court itself.

Here are a few reasons why I think the Supreme Court should not have this kind of power:

>> Federal judges are unelected, and Supreme Court justices are practically irremovable as well, so they should not strike down laws passed by democratically elected legislatures. In the words of Chief Justice William Rehnquist, "How can government by the elected representatives of the people coexist with the power of the federal judiciary . . . to declare invalid laws duly enacted by the popular branches of government?"

>> Supreme Court decisions have no teeth. (I'm not referring here to the justices' dental health, although they are allowed to continue to sit on the bench until they drop stone dead!) The Court has no police force to ensure obedience to its decisions.

>> Judge-made law is also contrary to the fundamental constitutional principle of the separation of powers. The Supreme Court is part of the judiciary, but laws are supposed to be created only by a legislature.

>> The U.S. Supreme Court is a branch of the federal government. When it strikes down state laws, this amounts to an attack on federalism and democracy alike.

Why do some people believe it's a good idea for the high court to have such sweeping powers? The most common argument in favor of the Court's power relates to the concept of the *living Constitution*. The idea is that the Constitution needs to be constantly reinterpreted in order to reflect society's changing values and needs. But who is to decide what those values and needs are?

Since the *Bakke* case of 1978, the Supreme Court has allowed affirmative action in college admissions as long as it did not involve quotas. But according to the National Conference of State Legislatures, at the time of this writing, eight states already ban the use of race in admissions altogether at state colleges and universities: Arizona, California, Florida, Michigan, Nebraska, New Hampshire, Oklahoma, and Washington. The Michigan ban was actually an amendment to the state constitution, based on an initiative passed by a 58 percent majority. In *Schuette v. Coalition to Defend Affirmative Action* (2013), the Supreme Court ruled that such a ban on affirmative action does not violate the Equal Protection Clause of the Fourteenth Amendment. In August 2017, the Justice Department confirmed that it was examining claims of racial discrimination by Harvard University against Asian-American applicants for admission.

Is the United States a Democracy?

The word "democracy" doesn't figure in the U.S. Constitution at all. That is no accident. The Founders of the United States were mostly wealthy property owners and pillars of the community. What they wanted to establish was a "republic," not a "democracy," which was commonly identified with mob rule. John Adams, the future second President, warned: "Democracy will soon degenerate into an anarchy, such an anarchy that every man will do what is right in his own eyes and no man's life or property or reputation or liberty will be secure." James Madison, the "Father of the Constitution," who would become the nation's fourth President, described democracy as "the most vile form of government."

No wonder, therefore, that the Constitution as originally drafted was intended to keep the ordinary people at arm's length. Hence the elaborate Electoral College system for presidential elections — in which the electors were expected to have total freedom to pick whomever they liked as President and Vice President. The Senate was similarly elected indirectly — by the state legislatures. The only part of the federal government that was chosen by popular election was the House of Representatives — but until the 1830s, the right to vote in most states was restricted to white male property owners. The reason that this is not spelled out in the Constitution is simply that voting rights were set by the individual states and not on a nationwide basis.

So how did this anti-democratic and essentially aristocratic system morph into what is now claimed to be a democracy and sometimes even the world's oldest democracy? The answer is essentially universal suffrage, or one person one vote.

On the other hand, it could be argued that the fact that every U.S. citizen has the right to vote is not enough in itself to prove that the system of government really is a democracy, for the following reasons, among others:

>> In practice, voters have a choice of only two candidates for President and usually also for their U.S. senator and representative. The numerous small parties are effectively frozen out by the two-party system.

>> Although voters do also have a say in primary elections to determine who their party's nominee is to be, here too their freedom of choice is more illusory than real, because political election campaigns are hugely expensive, so that only billionaires or candidates supported by political action committees, or "super PACs," stand any real chance.

>> In the 2016 election, according to the Cook Report, only 72 of the 435 seats in the House of Representatives, or 16.5 percent, were swing seats, or seats which both parties had a genuine chance of winning. The rest were in either deep red or deep blue voting districts. The votes of minority party supporters in these districts are therefore essentially thrown away.

>> Gerrymandering, or partisan redistricting, is one reason for this, but an even more important reason for it is "self-sorting," or the growing tendency of people to prefer to live in neighborhoods of likeminded people.

>> "We the People" and even the federal government arguably have less of a say on policy matters than the U.S. Supreme Court. Examples include abortion rights, same-sex marriage, eminent domain, capital punishment, healthcare, and corporate money in politics.

Does the President Have Too Much Power?

The U.S. President is commonly said to be the most powerful person in the world. But how true is this? In a book titled *Congressional Government* written in 1885, the young Woodrow Wilson wrote: "Congress is fast becoming the governing body of the nation." This reads rather strangely today, and Wilson himself, who would become President in 1913, turned out to be a strong President. But it was Franklin Roosevelt, President from 1933 until his death in 1945, who established the so-called "imperial presidency," a label coined by historian Arthur Schlesinger in

1973 to imply that the President exceeded his proper constitutional limits. See Chapter 10 for a discussion of the presidency and Chapter 13 on impeachment.

Here I will just home in on a few controversial issues concerning the President's power:

» **Appointments:** The President appoints a huge number of office-holders. But presidential discretion in this regard is not nearly as unfettered as you may expect. Article II of the Constitution gives the President the power to appoint "principal officers" of the United States like the Secretary of State and other Cabinet secretaries, federal judges, and ambassadors. But all these appointments require the consent of the Senate. There are between 1,200 and 1,400 such positions, in addition to about 350 senior posts which don't need Senate confirmation.

One serious problem in connection with Senate confirmation used to be the use of the filibuster to hold up consideration of a nomination. A *filibuster* means the holding of the floor by one or more senators by endless talking on any subject under the sun, which requires a "cloture" (closure) motion supported by a 60-vote super-majority to stop it. In 2013, the so-called "nuclear option" was adopted to eliminate the filibuster for all presidential nominations except those to the Supreme Court. This exception was removed in 2017 to allow the confirmation of President Trump's nomination of Neil Gorsuch to the Supreme Court by a simple majority. In the event, Judge Gorsuch was confirmed by 54 votes to 45. But this would not have happened without a Republican majority in the Senate — which is what stymied Merrick Garland's nomination by Democratic President Obama, which the Republican-led Senate simply ignored for almost ten months in the hope (which was realized) of the election of a Republican President.

» **Special counsel:** The position of special counsel, special prosecutor, or independent counsel is peculiar, because though the person concerned is in the Department of Justice, which forms part of the Executive branch of government, and is therefore under the President, he or she is not appointed by the President and can't be fired directly by the President. The best-known example of this occurred when President Nixon wanted to fire Watergate special prosecutor Archibald Cox in 1973, which led to the "Saturday Night Massacre," in which both the Attorney General (who had appointed Cox) and the Deputy Attorney General chose to resign rather than fire Cox, leaving it to Solicitor General Robert Bork to do the President's bidding. In May 2017, Deputy Attorney General Rod Rosenstein appointed former FBI Director Robert Mueller (see Figure 25-1) as special counsel to investigate possible Russian interference in the 2016 election.

Source: Federal Bureau of Investigation (http://www.fbi.gov/about-us/executives)

>> **Executive orders, presidential memoranda, and proclamations:** The President's role in lawmaking is very limited, confined chiefly to approving bills passed by both houses of Congress. The President may of course also veto bills, but a veto can be overridden by a two-thirds majority of both houses. The Constitution makes lawmaking, or legislation, the preserve of Congress. Article II of the Constitution does contain a catch-all clause saying that the President "shall take Care that the Laws be faithfully executed," but it's hard to interpret this as allowing the President to legislate without Congress. Nevertheless, presidents from George Washington onward have issued orders that have the force of law: executive orders, presidential memoranda, and proclamations. Proclamations are generally concerned with ceremonial matters, though some of them, like Abraham Lincoln's Emancipation Proclamation, have packed quite a punch. Presidential memoranda usually delegate tasks to members of the Executive branch. Of the three types of presidential lawmaking, executive orders are the most important. It was by this means, for example, that, within a few days of taking office in 2017, President Trump signed into law a travel ban on the nationals of certain countries. Like any other kind of legislation, the constitutionality of executive orders can be challenged in court. So here again, presidential power is hedged about with restrictions.

Two areas of particular concern about the degree of presidential power are terrorism and war powers. Let me look briefly at these.

>> **Terrorism:** What powers does the President have to curb terrorism? Even here, presidential power is more limited than you may expect.

- Does the President have the power to detain a U.S. citizen indefinitely as an "enemy combatant"? In *Hamdi v. Rumsfeld,* decided in 2004, a majority on the Supreme Court said No.

  In the similarly named *Hamdan v. Rumsfeld,* decided in 2006, the President lost again. The question before the Supreme Court was whether it was legal for military commissions to try "enemy combatants." The majority on the Court said No. Justice Clarence Thomas, dissenting, claimed that the majority opinion "openly flouts our well-established duty to respect the Executive's judgment in matters of military operations and foreign affairs."

  President Trump's travel bans were motivated by a concern over terrorism and were titled "Protecting the Nation from Foreign Terrorist Entry into the United States."

>> **Authorization for Use of Military Force (AUMF):** This was passed by Congress on September 14, 2001, authorizing the use of force against those responsible for 9/11 or those who harbored any of them. In December 2016, the Office of the President published a brief interpreting AUMF as giving the President congressional authorization for the use of force against al-Qaeda and other Islamic militant groups. The 61-page brief asserted that AUMF covered military action in all the following theaters: Afghanistan, Iraq, Syria, Somalia, Libya, and Yemen. AUMF could also presumably be taken to cover U.S. military involvement in Niger, West Africa, where four U.S. Army Green Berets were killed in October 2017.

>> **War powers:** The Constitution gives Congress the power "To declare War," but it makes the President the Commander in Chief. Does this mean that the President's role as Commander in Chief takes effect only after Congress has made a declaration of war? If that is the right interpretation, then most presidents since World War II have acted unconstitutionally — because Congress has not made a single formal declaration of war since that time. And even the War Powers Act of 1973 would be unconstitutional because, although the act limits the President's power to wage war without the consent of Congress, it does not prohibit it. However, the War Powers Act has never been declared unconstitutional.

In October 2002, Congress passed a Joint Resolution authorizing President George W. Bush "to use the Armed Forces of the United States as he determines necessary and appropriate in order to defend the national security of the United States against the continuing threat posed by Iraq." This resolution was certainly not a declaration of war against Iraq but claimed to be based on the War Powers Act. Did this Joint Resolution authorize the President to invade Iraq? It's not clear, but the President certainly applied it in that sense.

So, does the President have too much power in regard to terrorism and war powers? As Commander in Chief he has more power in these areas than in internal affairs. But he is restricted by a Constitution that clearly was not intended to create an imperial presidency. If the Supreme Court or Congress wishes to rein the President in on the basis of a close reading of the Constitution, it would be difficult for the President to break free.

Appendix

Constitution of the United States of America

Following is the complete text of the U.S. Constitution, which was adopted by the Philadelphia Convention on September 17, 1787. It's followed by the 27 amendments that have been made to the Constitution since its ratification.

Preamble

We the People of the United States, in Order to form a more perfect Union, establish Justice, insure domestic Tranquillity, provide for the common defence, promote the general Welfare, and secure the Blessings of Liberty to ourselves and our Posterity, do ordain and establish this Constitution for the United States of America.

Articles

Article I

Section 1. All legislative Powers herein granted shall be vested in a Congress of the United States, which shall consist of a Senate and House of Representatives.

Section 2. The House of Representatives shall be composed of Members chosen every second Year by the People of the several States, and the Electors in each State shall have the Qualifications requisite for Electors of the most numerous Branch of the State Legislature.

No Person shall be a Representative who shall not have attained to the age of twenty five Years, and been seven Years a Citizen of the United States, and who shall not, when elected, be an Inhabitant of that State in which he shall be chosen.

[Representatives and direct Taxes shall be apportioned among the several States which may be included within this Union, according to their respective Numbers, which shall be determined by adding to the whole Number of free Persons, including those bound to Service for a Term of Years, and excluding Indians not taxed, three fifths of all other Persons.] *[The preceding section in square brackets was changed by Section 2 of the Fourteenth Amendment.]* The actual Enumeration shall be made within three Years after the first Meeting of the Congress of the United States, and within every subsequent Term of ten Years, in such Manner as they shall by Law direct. The Number of Representatives shall not exceed one for every thirty Thousand, but each State shall have at Least one Representative; and until such enumeration shall be made, the State of New Hampshire shall be entitled to chuse three, Massachusetts eight, Rhode-Island and Providence Plantations one, Connecticut five, New-York six, New Jersey four, Pennsylvania eight, Delaware one, Maryland six, Virginia ten, North Carolina five, South Carolina five, and Georgia three.

When vacancies happen in the Representation from any State, the Executive Authority thereof shall issue Writs of Election to fill such Vacancies.

The House of Representatives shall chuse their Speaker and other Officers; and shall have the sole Power of Impeachment.

Section 3. The Senate of the United States shall be composed of two Senators from each State, [chosen by the Legislature thereof,] *[the preceding section in square brackets was changed by the first paragraph of the Seventeenth Amendment]* for six Years; and each Senator shall have one Vote.

Immediately after they shall be assembled in Consequence of the first Election, they shall be divided as equally as may be into three Classes. The Seats of the Senators of the first Class shall be vacated at the Expiration of the second Year, of the second Class at the Expiration of the fourth Year, and of the third Class at the Expiration of the sixth Year, so that one third may be chosen every second Year; [and if Vacancies happen by Resignation, or otherwise, during the Recess of the Legislature of any State, the Executive thereof may make temporary Appointments until the next Meeting of the Legislature, which shall then fill such Vacancies.] *[The preceding section in square brackets was changed by the second paragraph of the Seventeenth Amendment.]*

No Person shall be a Senator who shall not have attained to the Age of thirty Years, and been nine Years a Citizen of the United States, and who shall not, when elected, be an Inhabitant of that State for which he shall be chosen.

The Vice President of the United States shall be President of the Senate, but shall have no Vote, unless they be equally divided.

The Senate shall chuse their other Officers, and also a President pro tempore, in the Absence of the Vice President, or when he shall exercise the Office of President of the United States.

The Senate shall have the sole Power to try all Impeachments. When sitting for that Purpose, they shall be on Oath or Affirmation. When the President of the United States is tried, the Chief Justice shall preside: And no Person shall be convicted without the Concurrence of two thirds of the Members present.

Judgment in Cases of Impeachment shall not extend further than to removal from Office, and disqualification to hold and enjoy any Office of honor, Trust or Profit under the United States: but the Party convicted shall nevertheless be liable and subject to Indictment, Trial, Judgment and Punishment, according to Law.

Section 4. The Times, Places and Manner of holding Elections for Senators and Representatives, shall be prescribed in each State by the Legislature thereof; but the Congress may at any time by Law make or alter such Regulations, except as to the Places of chusing Senators.

The Congress shall assemble at least once in every Year, and such Meeting shall [be on the first Monday in December] *[the preceding section in square brackets was changed by Section 2 of the Twentieth Amendment]*, unless they shall by Law appoint a different Day.

Section 5. Each House shall be the judge of the Elections, Returns and Qualifications of its own Members, and a Majority of each shall constitute a Quorum to do Business; but a smaller Number may adjourn from day to day, and may be authorized to compel the Attendance of absent Members, in such Manner, and under such Penalties as each House may provide.

Each House may determine the Rules of its Proceedings, punish its Members for disorderly Behaviour, and, with the Concurrence of two thirds, expel a Member.

Each House shall keep a journal of its Proceedings, and from time to time publish the same, excepting such Parts as may in their judgment require Secrecy; and the Yeas and Nays of the Members of either House on any question shall, at the Desire of one fifth of those Present, be entered on the Journal.

Neither House, during the Session of Congress, shall, without the Consent of the other, adjourn for more than three days, nor to any other Place than that in which the two Houses shall be sitting.

Section 6. The Senators and Representatives shall receive a Compensation for their Services, to be ascertained by Law, and paid out of the Treasury of the United States. They shall in all Cases, except Treason, Felony and Breach of the Peace, be privileged from Arrest during their Attendance at the Session of their respective Houses, and in going to and returning from the same; and for any Speech or Debate in either House, they shall not be questioned in any other Place.

No Senator or Representative shall, during the Time for which he was elected, be appointed to any civil Office under the Authority of the United States, which shall have been created, or the Emoluments whereof shall have been encreased during such time; and no Person holding any Office under the United States, shall be a Member of either House during his Continuance in Office.

Section 7. All Bills for raising Revenue shall originate in the House of Representatives; but the Senate may propose or concur with Amendments as on other Bills. Every Bill which shall have passed the House of Representatives and the Senate, shall, before it become a Law, be presented to the President of the United States; If he approve he shall sign it, but if not he shall return it, with his Objections to that House in which it shall have originated, who shall enter the Objections at large on their Journal, and proceed to reconsider it. If after such Reconsideration two thirds of that House shall agree to pass the Bill, it shall be sent, together with the Objections, to the other House, by which it shall likewise be reconsidered, and if approved by two thirds of that House, it shall become a Law. But in all such Cases the Votes of both Houses shall be determined by yeas and Nays, and the names of the Persons voting for and against the Bill shall be entered on the Journal of each House respectively. If any Bill shall not be returned by the President within ten Days (Sundays excepted) after it shall have been presented to him, the Same shall be a Law, in like Manner as if he had signed it, unless the Congress by their Adjournment prevent its Return, in which Case it shall not be a Law.

Every Order, Resolution, or Vote to which the Concurrence of the Senate and House of Representatives may be necessary (except on a question of Adjournment) shall be presented to the President of the United States; and before the Same shall take Effect, shall be approved by him, or being disapproved by him, shall be repassed by two thirds of the Senate and House of Representatives, according to the Rules and Limitations prescribed in the Case of a Bill.

Section 8. The Congress shall have Power To lay and collect Taxes, Duties, Imposts and Excises, to pay the Debts and provide for the common Defence and general Welfare of the United States; but all Duties, Imposts and Excises shall be uniform throughout the United States;

To borrow Money on the credit of the United States;

To regulate Commerce with foreign Nations, and among the several States, and with the Indian Tribes;

To establish an uniform Rule of Naturalization, and uniform Laws on the subject of Bankruptcies throughout the United States;

To coin Money, regulate the Value thereof, and of foreign Coin, and fix the Standard of Weights and Measures;

To provide for the Punishment of counterfeiting the Securities and current Coin of the United States;

To establish Post Offices and post Roads;

To promote the Progress of Science and useful Arts, by securing for limited Times to Authors and Inventors the exclusive Right to their respective Writings and Discoveries;

To constitute Tribunals inferior to the supreme Court;

To define and punish Piracies and Felonies committed on the high Seas, and Offences against the Law of Nations;

To declare War, grant Letters of Marque and Reprisal, and make Rules concerning Captures on Land and Water;

To raise and support Armies, but no Appropriation of Money to that Use shall be for a longer Term than two Years;

To provide and maintain a Navy;

To make Rules for the Government and Regulation of the land and naval Forces;

To provide for calling forth the Militia to execute the Laws of the Union, suppress Insurrections and repel Invasions;

To provide for organizing, arming, and disciplining, the Militia, and for governing such Part of them as may be employed in the Service of the United States, reserving to the States respectively, the Appointment of the Officers, and the Authority of training the Militia according to the discipline prescribed by Congress;

To exercise exclusive Legislation in all Cases whatsoever, over such District (not exceeding ten Miles square) as may, by Cession of particular States, and the Acceptance of Congress, become the Seat of the Government of the United States, and to exercise like Authority over all Places purchased by the Consent of the Legislature of the State in which the Same shall be, for the Erection of Forts, Magazines, Arsenals, dock-Yards, and other needful Buildings;—And

To make all Laws which shall be necessary and proper for carrying into Execution the foregoing Powers, and all other Powers vested by this Constitution in the Government of the United States, or in any Department or Officer thereof.

Section 9. The Migration or Importation of such Persons as any of the States now existing shall think proper to admit, shall not be prohibited by the Congress prior to the Year one thousand eight hundred and eight, but a Tax or duty may be imposed on such Importation, not exceeding ten dollars for each Person.

The Privilege of the Writ of Habeas Corpus shall not be suspended, unless when in Cases of Rebellion or Invasion the public Safety may require it.

No Bill of Attainder or ex post facto Law shall be passed.

[No Capitation, or other direct, Tax shall be laid, unless in Proportion to the Census or Enumeration herein before directed to be taken.] *[The preceding section in square brackets was changed by the Sixteenth Amendment.]*

No Tax or Duty shall be laid on Articles exported from any State.

No Preference shall be given by any Regulation of Commerce or Revenue to the Ports of one State over those of another; nor shall Vessels bound to, or from, one State, be obliged to enter, clear, or pay Duties in another.

No Money shall be drawn from the Treasury, but in Consequence of Appropriations made by Law; and a regular Statement and Account of the Receipts and Expenditures of all public Money shall be published from time to time.

No Title of Nobility shall be granted by the United States: And no Person holding any Office of Profit or Trust under them, shall, without the Consent of the Congress, accept of any present, Emolument, Office, or Title, of any kind whatever, from any King, Prince, or foreign State.

Section 10. No State shall enter into any Treaty, Alliance, or Confederation; grant Letters of Marque and Reprisal; coin Money; emit Bills of Credit; make any Thing but gold and silver Coin a Tender in Payment of Debts; pass any Bill of Attainder, ex post facto Law, or Law impairing the Obligation of Contracts, or grant any Title of Nobility.

No State shall, without the Consent of the Congress, lay any Imposts or Duties on Imports or Exports, except what may be absolutely necessary for executing its inspection Laws: and the net Produce of all Duties and Imposts, laid by any State on Imports or Exports, shall be for the Use of the Treasury of the United States; and all such Laws shall be subject to the Revision and Controul of the Congress.

No State shall, without the Consent of Congress, lay any Duty of Tonnage, keep Troops, or Ships of War in time of Peace, enter into any Agreement or Compact with another State, or with a foreign Power, or engage in War, unless actually invaded, or in such imminent Danger as will not admit of delay.

Article II

Section 1. The executive Power shall be vested in a President of the United States of America. He shall hold his Office during the Term of four Years, and, together with the Vice President, chosen for the same Term, be elected, as follows:

Each State shall appoint, in such Manner as the Legislature thereof may direct, a Number of Electors, equal to the whole Number of Senators and Representatives to which the State may be entitled in the Congress: but no Senator or Representative, or Person holding an Office of Trust or Profit under the United States, shall be appointed an Elector.

[The Electors shall meet in their respective States, and vote by Ballot for two Persons, of whom one at least shall not be an Inhabitant of the same State with themselves. And they shall make a List of all the Persons voted for, and of the Number of Votes for each; which List they shall sign and certify, and transmit sealed to the Seat of the Government of the United States, directed to the President of the Senate. The President of the Senate shall, in the Presence of the Senate and House of Representatives, open all the Certificates, the Votes shall then be counted. The Person having the greatest Number of Votes shall be the President, if such Number be a Majority of the whole Number of Electors appointed; and if there be more than one who have such Majority, and have an equal Number of Votes, then the House of Representatives shall immediately chuse by Ballot one of them for President; and if no Person have a Majority, then from the five highest on the list the said House shall in like Manner chuse the President. But in chusing the President, the Votes shall be taken by States, the Representation from each State having one Vote; a quorum for this Purpose shall consist of a Member or Members from two thirds of the States, and a Majority of all the States shall be necessary to a Choice. In every Case, after the Choice of the President, the Person having the greatest Number of Votes of the Electors shall be the Vice President. But if there should remain two or more who have equal Votes, the Senate shall chuse from them by Ballot the Vice President.] *[The preceding section in square brackets has been changed by the Twelfth Amendment.]*

The Congress may determine the Time of choosing the Electors, and the Day on which they shall give their Votes; which Day shall be the same throughout the United States.

No Person except a natural born Citizen, or a Citizen of the United States, at the time of the Adoption of this Constitution, shall be eligible to the Office of President; neither shall any Person be eligible to that Office who shall not have attained to the Age of thirty five Years, and been fourteen Years a Resident within the United States.

In Case of the Removal of the President from Office, or of his Death, Resignation, or Inability to discharge the Powers and Duties of the said Office, the Same shall devolve on the Vice President, and the Congress may by Law provide for the Case of Removal, Death, Resignation or Inability, both of the President and Vice President, declaring what Officer shall then act as President, and such Officer shall act accordingly, until the Disability be removed, or a President shall be elected. *[The preceding provision has been affected by the Twenty-Fifth Amendment.]*

The President shall, at stated Times, receive for his Services, a Compensation, which shall neither be encreased nor diminished during the Period for which he shall have been elected, and he shall not receive within that Period any other Emolument from the United States, or any of them.

Before he enter on the Execution of his Office, he shall take the following Oath or Affirmation: "I do solemnly swear (or affirm) that I will faithfully execute the Office of President of the United States, and will to the best of my Ability, preserve, protect and defend the Constitution of the United States."

Section 2. The President shall be Commander in Chief of the Army and Navy of the United States, and of the Militia of the several States, when called into the actual Service of the United States; he may require the Opinion, in writing, of the principal Officer in each of the executive Departments, upon any Subject relating to the Duties of their respective Offices, and he shall have Power to grant Reprieves and Pardons for Offences against the United States, except in Cases of Impeachment.

He shall have Power, by and with the Advice and Consent of the Senate, to make Treaties, provided two thirds of the Senators present concur; and he shall nominate, and by and with the Advice and Consent of the Senate, shall appoint Ambassadors, other public Ministers and Consuls, judges of the supreme Court, and all other Officers of the United States, whose Appointments are not herein otherwise provided for, and which shall be established by Law: but the Congress may by Law vest the Appointment of such inferior Officers, as they think proper, in the President alone, in the Courts of Law, or in the Heads of Departments.

The President shall have Power to fill up all Vacancies that may happen during the Recess of the Senate, by granting Commissions which shall expire at the End of their next Session.

Section 3. He shall from time to time give to the Congress Information of the State of the Union, and recommend to their Consideration such Measures as he shall judge necessary and expedient; he may, on extraordinary Occasions, convene both Houses, or either of them, and in Case of Disagreement between them, with Respect to the Time of Adjournment, he may adjourn them to such Time as he shall think proper; he shall receive Ambassadors and other public Ministers; he shall take Care that the Laws be faithfully executed, and shall Commission all the Officers of the United States.

Section 4. The President, Vice President and all civil Officers of the United States, shall be removed from Office on Impeachment for, and Conviction of, Treason, Bribery, or other high Crimes and Misdemeanors.

Article III

Section 1. The judicial Power of the United States shall be vested in one supreme Court, and in such inferior Courts as the Congress may from time to time ordain and establish. The Judges, both of the supreme and inferior Courts, shall hold their Offices during good Behaviour, and shall, at stated Times, receive for their Services a Compensation, which shall not be diminished during their Continuance in Office.

Section 2. The judicial Power shall extend to all Cases, in Law and Equity, arising under this Constitution, the Laws of the United States, and Treaties made, or which shall be made, under their Authority;—to all Cases affecting Ambassadors, other public Ministers and Consuls;—to all Cases of admiralty and maritime Jurisdiction;—to Controversies to which the United States shall be a Party;—to Controversies between two or more States;—between a State and Citizens of another State *[The Eleventh Amendment limited federal jurisdiction over civil litigation brought against a state.]*;—between Citizens of different States;—between Citizens of the same State claiming Lands under Grants of different States, and between a State, or the Citizens thereof, and foreign States, Citizens or Subjects.

In all Cases affecting Ambassadors, other public Ministers and Consuls, and those in which a State shall be Party, the supreme Court shall have original juris-diction. In all the other Cases before mentioned, the supreme Court shall have appellate Jurisdiction, both as to Law and Fact, with such Exceptions, and under such Regulations as the Congress shall make.

The Trial of all Crimes, except in Cases of Impeachment, shall be by Jury; and such Trial shall be held in the State where the said Crimes shall have been committed; but when not committed within any State, the Trial shall be at such Place or Places as the Congress may by Law have directed.

Section 3. Treason against the United States, shall consist only in levying War against them, or in adhering to their Enemies, giving them Aid and. Comfort. No Person shall be convicted of Treason unless on the Testimony of two Witnesses to the same overt Act, or on Confession in open Court.

The Congress shall have Power to declare the Punishment of Treason, but no Attainder of Treason shall work Corruption of Blood, or Forfeiture except during the Life of the Person attained.

Article IV

Section 1. Full Faith and Credit shall be given in each State to the public Acts, Records, and judicial Proceedings of every other State. And the Congress may by general Laws prescribe the Manner in which such Acts, Records and Proceedings shall be proved, and the Effect thereof.

Section 2. The Citizens of each State shall be entitled to all Privileges and Immunities of Citizens in the several States.

A Person charged in any State with Treason, Felony, or other Crime, who shall flee from Justice, and be found in another State, shall on Demand of the executive Authority of the State from which he fled, be delivered up, to be removed to the State having jurisdiction of the Crime.

[No Person held to Service or Labour in one State, under the Laws thereof, escaping into another, shall, in Consequence of any Law or Regulation therein, be discharged from such Service or Labour, but shall be delivered up on Claim of the Party to whom such Service or Labour may be due.] *[This paragraph refers to slavery and indentured servitude, abolished by the Thirteenth Amendment.]*

Section 3. New States may be admitted by the Congress into this Union; but no new State shall be formed or erected within the Jurisdiction of any other State; nor any State be formed by the Junction of two or more States, or Parts of States, without the Consent of the Legislatures of the States concerned as well as of the Congress.

The Congress shall have Power to dispose of and make all needful Rules and Regulations respecting the Territory or other Property belonging to the United States; and nothing in this Constitution shall be so construed as to Prejudice any Claims of the United States, or of any particular State.

Section 4. The United States shall guarantee to every State in this Union a Republican Form of Government, and shall protect each of them against Invasion; and on Application of the Legislature, or of the Executive (when the Legislature cannot be convened) against domestic Violence.

Article V

The Congress, whenever two thirds of both Houses shall deem it necessary, shall propose Amendments to this Constitution, or, on the Application of the Legislatures of two thirds of the several States, shall call a Convention for proposing Amendments, which, in either Case, shall be valid to all Intents and Purposes, as Part of this Constitution, when ratified by the Legislatures of three fourths of the several States, or by Conventions in three fourths thereof, as the one or the other Mode of Ratification may be proposed by the Congress; Provided that no Amendment which may be made prior to the Year One thousand eight hundred and eight shall in any Manner affect the first and fourth Clauses in the Ninth Section of the first Article; and that no State, without its Consent, shall be deprived of its equal Suffrage in the Senate.

Article VI

All Debts contracted and Engagements entered into, before the Adoption of this Constitution, shall be as valid against the United States under this Constitution, as under the Confederation.

This Constitution, and the Laws of the United States which shall be made in Pursuance thereof; and all Treaties made, or which shall be made. under the Authority of the United States, shall be the supreme Law of the Land; and the judges in every State shall be bound thereby, any Thing in the Constitution or Laws of any State to the Contrary notwithstanding.

The Senators and Representatives before mentioned, and the Members of the several State Legislatures, and all executive and judicial Officers, both of the United States and of the several States, shall be bound by Oath or Affirmation, to support this Constitution; but no religious Test shall ever be required as a Qualification to any Office or public Trust under the United States.

Article VII

The Ratification of the Conventions of nine States, shall be sufficient for the Establishment of this Constitution between the States so ratifying the Same.

Signatures

Done in Convention by the Unanimous Consent of the States present the seventeenth Day of September in the Year of our Lord one thousand seven hundred and Eighty seven and of the Independence of the United States of America the Twelfth. IN WITNESS whereof We have hereunto subscribed our Names,

George Washington,

> President and deputy from Virginia.

New Hampshire:

> John Langdon,
>
> Nicholas Gilman.

Massachusetts:

> Nathaniel Gorham,
>
> Rufus King.

Connecticut:

> William Samuel Johnson,
>
> Roger Sherman.

New York:

> Alexander Hamilton.

New Jersey:

> William Livingston,
>
> David Brearley,
>
> William Paterson,
>
> Jonathan Dayton.

Pennsylvania:

> Benjamin Franklin,
>
> Thomas Mifflin,

Robert Morris,

George Clymer,

Thomas FitzSimons,

Jared Ingersoll,

James Wilson,

Gouverneur Morris.

Delaware:

George Read,

Gunning Bedford Jr.,

John Dickinson,

Richard Bassett,

Jacob Broom.

Maryland:

James McHenry,

Daniel of St. Thomas Jenifer,

Daniel Carroll.

Virginia:

John Blair,

James Madison Jr.

North Carolina:

William Blount,

Richard Dobbs Spaight,

Hugh Williamson.

South Carolina:

John Rutledge,

Charles Cotesworth Pinckney,

Pierce Butler.

Georgia:

William Few,

Abraham Baldwin.

(Ratification of the Constitution was completed on June 21, 1788)

Amendments

The first ten amendments constitute the Bill of Rights, ratified December 15, 1791.

Amendment I

Congress shall make no law respecting an establishment of religion, or prohibiting the free exercise thereof; or abridging the freedom of speech, or of the press; or the right of the people peaceably to assemble, and to petition the Government for a redress of grievances.

Amendment II

A well regulated Militia, being necessary to the security of a free State, the right of the people to keep and bear Arms, shall not be infringed.

Amendment III

No Soldier shall, in time of peace be quartered in any house, without the consent of the Owner, nor in time of war, but in a manner to be prescribed by law.

Amendment IV

The right of the people to be secure in their persons, houses, papers, and effects, against unreasonable searches and seizures, shall not be violated, and no Warrants shall issue, but upon probable cause, supported by Oath or affirmation, and particularly describing the place to be searched, and the persons or things to be seized.

Amendment V

No person shall be held to answer for a capital, or otherwise infamous crime, unless on a presentment or indictment of a Grand Jury, except in cases arising in the land or naval forces, or in the Militia, when in actual service in time of War or public danger; nor shall any person be subject for the same offence to be twice put in jeopardy of life or limb; nor shall be compelled in any criminal case to be a witness against himself, nor be deprived of life, liberty, or property, without due process of law; nor shall private property be taken for public use, without just compensation.

Amendment VI

In all criminal prosecutions, the accused shall enjoy the right to a speedy and public trial, by an impartial jury of the State and district wherein the crime shall have been committed, which district shall have been previously ascertained by law, and to be informed of the nature and cause of the accusation; to be confronted with the witnesses against him; to have compulsory process for obtaining witnesses in his favor, and to have the Assistance of Counsel for his defence.

Amendment VII

In Suits at common law, where the value in controversy shall exceed twenty dollars, the right of trial by jury shall be preserved, and no fact tried by a jury, shall be otherwise re-examined in any Court of the United States, than according to the rules of the common law.

Amendment VIII

Excessive bail shall not be required, nor excessive fines imposed, nor cruel and unusual punishments inflicted.

Amendment IX

The enumeration in the Constitution, of certain rights, shall not be construed to deny or disparage others retained by the people.

Amendment X

The powers not delegated to the United States by the Constitution, nor prohibited by it to the States, are reserved to the States respectively, or to the people.

Amendment XI

(Ratified February 7, 1795)

The judicial power of the United States shall not be construed to extend to any suit in law or equity, commenced or prosecuted against one of the United States by Citizens of another State, or by Citizens or Subjects of any Foreign State.

Amendment XII

(Ratified June 15, 1804)

The Electors shall meet in their respective states, and vote by ballot for President and Vice-President, one of whom, at least, shall not be an inhabitant of the same state with themselves; they shall name in their ballots the person voted for as President, and in distinct ballots the person voted for as Vice-President, and they shall make distinct lists of all persons voted for as President, and of all persons voted for as Vice-President, and of the number of votes for each, which lists they shall sign and certify, and transmit sealed to the seat of the government of the United States, directed to the President of the Senate;—The President of the Senate shall, in the presence of the Senate and House of Representatives, open all the certificates and the votes shall then be counted;—The person having the greatest number of votes for President, shall be the President, if such number be a majority of the whole number of Electors appointed; and if no person have such majority, then from the persons having the highest numbers not exceeding three on the list of those voted for as President, the House of Representatives shall choose immediately, by ballot, the President. But in choosing the President, the votes shall be taken by states, the representation from each state having one vote; a quorum for this purpose shall consist of a member or members from two-thirds of the states, and a majority of all the states shall be necessary to a choice. [And if the House of Representatives shall not choose a President whenever the right of choice shall devolve upon them, before the fourth day of March next following, then the Vice-President shall act as President, as in the case of the death or other constitutional disability of the President.] *[The preceding section in square brackets was superceded by Section 3 of the Twentieth Amendment.]* The person having the greatest number of votes as Vice-President, shall be the Vice-President, if such number be a majority of the whole number of Electors appointed, and if no person have a majority, then from the two highest numbers on the list, the Senate shall choose the Vice-President; a quorum for the purpose shall consist of two-thirds of the whole number of Senators, and a majority of the whole number shall be necessary to a choice. But no person constitutionally ineligible to the office of President shall be eligible to that of Vice-President of the United States.

Amendment XIII

(Ratified December 6, 1865)

Section 1. Neither slavery nor involuntary servitude, except as a punishment for crime whereof the party shall have been duly convicted, shall exist within the United States, or any place subject to their jurisdiction.

Section 2. Congress shall have power to enforce this article by appropriate legislation.

Amendment XIV

(Ratified July 9, 1868)

Section 1. All persons born or naturalized in the United States, and subject to the jurisdiction thereof, are citizens of the United States and of the State wherein they reside. No State shall make or enforce any law which shall abridge the privileges or immunities of citizens of the United States; nor shall any State deprive any person of life, liberty, or property, without due process of law; nor deny to any person within its jurisdiction the equal protection of the laws.

Section 2. Representatives shall be apportioned among the several States according to their respective numbers, counting the whole number of persons in each State, excluding Indians not taxed. But when the right to vote at any election for the choice of electors for President and Vice President of the United States, Representatives in Congress, the Executive and Judicial officers of a State, or the members of the Legislature thereof, is denied to any of the male inhabitants of such State, being twenty-one years of age, *[see the Nineteenth and Twenty-Sixth amendments]* and citizens of the United States, or in any way abridged, except for participation in rebellion, or other crime, the basis of representation therein shall be reduced in the proportion which the number of such male citizens shall bear to the whole number of male citizens twenty-one years of age in such State.

Section 3. No person shall be a Senator or Representative in Congress, or elector of President and Vice President, or hold any office, civil or military, under the United States, or under any State, who, having previously taken an oath, as a member of Congress, or as an officer of the United States, or as a member of any State legislature, or as an executive or judicial officer of any State, to support the Constitution of the United States, shall have engaged in insurrection or rebellion against the same, or given aid or comfort to the enemies thereof. But Congress may by a vote of two-thirds of each House, remove such disability.

Section 4. The validity of the public debt of the United States, authorized by law, including debts incurred for payment of pensions and bounties for services in suppressing insurrection or rebellion, shall not be questioned. But neither the United States nor any State shall assume or pay any debt or obligation incurred in aid of insurrection or rebellion against the United States, or any claim for the loss or emancipation of any slave; but all such debts, obligations and claims shall be held illegal and void.

Section 5. The Congress shall have power to enforce, by appropriate legislation, the provisions of this article.

Amendment XV

(Ratified February 3, 1870)

Section 1. The right of citizens of the United States to vote shall not be denied or abridged by the United States or by any State on account of race, color, or previous condition of servitude.

Section 2. The Congress shall have power to enforce this article by appropriate legislation.

Amendment XVI

(Ratified February 3, 1913)

The Congress shall have power to lay and collect taxes on incomes, from whatever source derived, without apportionment among the several States, and without regard to any census or enumeration.

Amendment XVII

(Ratified April 8, 1913)

The Senate of the United States shall be composed of two Senators from each State, elected by the people thereof, for six years; and each Senator shall have one vote. The electors in each State shall have the qualifications requisite for electors of the most numerous branch of the State legislatures.

When vacancies happen in the representation of any State in the Senate, the exec-utive authority of such State shall issue writs of election to fill such vacancies: Provided, That the legislature of any State may empower the executive thereof to make temporary appointments until the people fill the vacancies by election as the legislature may direct.

This amendment shall not be so construed as to affect the election or term of any Senator chosen before it becomes valid as part of the Constitution.

Amendment XVIII

(Ratified January 16, 1919)

After one year from the ratification of this article the manufacture, sale, or transportation of intoxicating liquors within, the importation thereof into, or the exportation thereof from the United States and all territory subject to the jurisdiction thereof for beverage purposes is hereby prohibited.

The Congress and the several States shall have concurrent power to enforce this article by appropriate legislation.

This article shall be inoperative unless it shall have been ratified as an amendment to the Constitution by the legislatures of the several States, as provided in the Constitution, within seven years from the date of the submission hereof to the States by the Congress.

[The Eighteenth Amendment was repealed by Section 1 of the Twenty-First Amendment.]

Amendment XIX

(Ratified August 18, 1920)

The right of citizens of the United States to vote shall not be denied or abridged by the United States or by any State on account of sex.

Congress shall have power to enforce this article by appropriate legislation.

Amendment XX

(Ratified January 23, 1933)

Section 1. The terms of the President and Vice President shall end at noon on the 20th day of January, and the terms of Senators and Representatives at noon on the 3d day of January, of the years in which such terms would have ended if this article had not been ratified; and the terms of their successors shall then begin. Section 2. The Congress shall assemble at least once in every year, and such meeting shall begin at noon on the 3d day of January, unless they shall by law appoint a different day.

Section 2. The Congress shall assemble at least once in every year, and such meeting shall begin at noon on the 3d day of January, unless they shall by law appoint a different day.

Section 3. *[See the Twenty-Fifth Amendment.]* If, at the time fixed for the beginning of the term of the President, the President elect shall have died, the Vice President elect shall become President. If a President shall not have been chosen before the time fixed for the beginning of his term, or if the President elect shall have failed to qualified, then the Vice President elect shall act as President until a President shall have qualified; and the Congress may by law provide for the case wherein neither a President elect nor a Vice President elect shall have qualified, declaring who shall then act as President, or the manner in which one who is to act shall be selected, and such person shall act accordingly until a President or Vice President shall have qualified.

Section 4. The Congress may by law provide for the case of the death of any of the persons from whom the House of Representatives may choose a President whenever the right of choice shall have devolved upon them, and for the case of the death of any of the persons from whom the Senate may choose a Vice President whenever the right of choice shall have devolved upon them.

Section 5. Sections 1 and 2 shall take effect on the 15th day of October following the ratification of this article.

Section 6. This article shall be inoperative unless it shall have been ratified as an amendment to the Constitution by the legislatures of three-fourths of the several States within seven years from the date of its submission.

Amendment XXI

(Ratified December 5, 1933)

Section 1. The eighteenth article of amendment to the Constitution of the United States is hereby repealed.

Section 2. The transportation or importation into any State, Territory, or possession of the United States for delivery or use therein of intoxicating liquors, in violation of the laws thereof, is hereby prohibited.

Section 3. This article shall be inoperative unless it shall have been ratified as an amendment to the Constitution by conventions in the several States, as provided in the Constitution, within seven years from the date of the submission hereof to the States by the Congress.

Amendment XXII

(Ratified February 27, 1951)

Section 1. No person shall be elected to the office of the President more than twice, and no person who has held the office of President, or acted as President, for more than two years of a term to which some other person was elected President shall be elected to the office of the President more than once. But this Article shall not apply to any person holding the office of President when this Article was proposed by the Congress, and shall not prevent any person who may be holding the office of President, or acting as President, during the term within which this Article becomes operative from holding the office of President or acting as President during the remainder of such term.

Section 2. This article shall be inoperative unless it shall have been ratified as an amendment to the Constitution by the legislatures of three-fourths of the several States within seven years from the date of its submission to the States by the Congress.

Amendment XXIII

(Ratified March 29, 1961)

Section 1. The District constituting the seat of Government of the United States shall appoint in such manner as the Congress may direct:

A number of electors of President and Vice President equal to the whole number of Senators and Representatives in Congress to which the District would be entitled if it were a State, but in no event more than the least populous State; they shall be in addition to those appointed by the States, but they shall be considered, for the purposes of the election of President and Vice President, to be electors appointed by a State; and they shall meet in the District and perform such duties as provided by the twelfth article of amendment.

Section 2. The Congress shall have power to enforce this article by appropriate legislation.

Amendment XXIV

(Ratified January 23, 1964)

Section 1. The right of citizens of the United States to vote in any primary or other election for President or Vice President, for electors for President or Vice President, or for Senator or Representative in Congress, shall not be denied or abridged by the United States or any State by reason of failure to pay any poll tax or other tax.

Section 2. The Congress shall have power to enforce this article by appropriate legislation.

Amendment XXV

(Ratified February 10, 1967)

Section 1. In case of the removal of the President from office or of his death or resignation, the Vice President shall become President. Section 2. Whenever there is a vacancy in the office of the Vice President, the President shall nominate a Vice President who shall take office upon confirmation by a majority vote of both Houses of Congress.

Section 2. Whenever there is a vacancy in the office of the Vice President, the President shall nominate a Vice President who shall take office upon confirmation by a majority vote of both Houses of Congress.

Section 3. Whenever the President transmits to the President pro tempore of the Senate and the Speaker of the House of Representatives his written declaration that he is unable to discharge the powers and duties of his office, and until he transmits to them a written declaration to the contrary, such powers and duties shall be discharged by the Vice President as Acting President.

Section 4. Whenever the Vice President and a majority of either the principal officers of the executive departments or of such other body as Congress may by law provide, transmit to the President pro tempore of the Senate and the Speaker of the House of Representatives their written declaration that the President is unable to discharge the powers and duties of his office, the Vice President shall immediately assume the powers and duties of the office as Acting President.

Thereafter, when the President transmits to the President pro tempore of the Senate and the Speaker of the House of Representatives his written declaration that no inability exists, he shall resume the powers and duties of his office unless the Vice President and a majority of either the principal officers of the executive department or of such other body as Congress may by law provide, transmit within four days to the President pro tempore of the Senate and the Speaker of the House of Representatives their written declaration that the President is unable to discharge the powers and duties of his office. Thereupon Congress shall decide the issue, assembling within forty-eight hours for that purpose if not in session. If the Congress, within twenty-one days after receipt of the latter written declaration, or, if Congress is not in session, within twenty-one days after Congress is required to assemble, determines by two-thirds vote of both Houses that the President is unable to discharge the powers and duties of his office, the Vice President shall continue to discharge the same as Acting President; otherwise, the President shall resume the powers and duties of his office.

Amendment XXVI

(Ratified July 1, 1971)

Section 1. The right of citizens of the United States, who are eighteen years of age or older, to vote shall not be denied or abridged by the United States or by any State on account of age.

Section 2. The Congress shall have power to enforce this article by appropriate legislation.

Amendment XXVII

(Ratified May 7, 1992)

No law varying the compensation for the services of the Senators and Representatives shall take effect, until an election of Representatives shall have intervened.

Index

A

E

F

I

Illegal Immigration Reform and Immigrant Responsibility Act (1996), 96
Illinois, 85
Illinois v. Gates, 236
immigration, 86, 362
Immigration and Nationality Act (INA) (1952), 102
Immigration and Naturalization Service (INS), 96
immunities, 82, 103–105, 307–308
impeachment, 98, 181–194
imperial presidency, 73, 133–134, 374
INA (Immigration and Nationality Act) (1952), 102
inauguration, 70
incorporation, 75
incorporation debate, 251–254
independents, 78
indicting, 242–243
indirect democracy, 71
individual interpretation, 212–213
individual liberty, 284–285
individual mandate, 116
individual rights, 212–213, 217–219, 284–286
inkblot, 278
INS (Immigration and Naturalization Service), 96
Intelligence committee, 161
intermediate scrutiny, 315
internal conflict, 104–105
Internal Revenue Service (IRS), 95
international treaties, 51
interpretations, 212–214, 290–292
interrogation methods, 270
interstate commerce, 108, 109, 114
Intolerable Acts, 224
Iraq, 225, 377
Iraq War, 153
irreparable harm, 228
IRS (Internal Revenue Service), 95
Islamic Center, 210

J

Jackson, Andrew, 29, 69–70
Jacksonian democracy, 69

Jacobins, 69
James II, 21
jargon, 32
Jay, John, 10, 12, 184, 353
Jefferson, Thomas, 10, 21, 26, 68
Jews, 77
Johnson, Andrew, 98, 182, 190–192
Johnson, Lyndon, 94, 98, 135
Johnson, Richard M., 367
Johnson Method, 136
Joint Resolution, 158, 378
Jones, Paula, 103, 185, 190
Jones, Terry, 210
judge-made law, 59–63
judges, 13, 48, 165–168, 192
judicial activism, 179–180, 285
Judicial branch, 73, 76, 89, 137
Judicial Campaign Reform Act, 168
judicial independence without accountability, 168–170
judicial interpretation, 38, 51
judicial restraint, 180
judicial review, 49, 98, 171–176, 348
judicial system, 163–168, 170–178
Judiciary Committee, 185
judiciary's position, 99
juries, 261–262
jurisdiction, 164–165
Jurisdiction stripping, 96
jury nullification, 262
Justice Against Sponsors of Terrorism Bill (2006), 74

K

Kagan, Elena, 39, 202
Kansas v. Marsh, 177
Kelo, Susette, 20
Kelo v. City of New London, 177, 256, 344
Kennedy, Anthony, 138, 178, 317, 361–362
Kennedy, John F., 61, 85, 131
Kennedy v. Louisiana, 177, 362
Kennedy–Johnson ticket, 94
key positions, 130–131

McCain, John, 78, 104, 127, 204

McCain–Feingold Act, 62, 346, 371

McConnell v. FEC, 346

McCulloch v. Maryland, 46

McCutcheon v. FEC, 347

McDonald v. City of Chicago, 219

McGehee v. Hutchinson, 41

McNamara, Robert, 207

Medellin v. Texas, 88

Medicaid, 87

Medicare, 87

Medicare Improvements for Patients and Providers Bill (2008), 75

membership, 94, 137

memorials, 158

Meredith v. Jefferson County Board of Education, 312

metadata, 228, 230, 351

methamphetamine, 238

Mexican–American War (1846–1848), 139

Meyer v. Nebraska, 25

Migratory Bird Treaty Act (1918), 88

Military Commissions Act (MCA) (2006), 96

military conspiracy, 187

militia, 33, 141, 214–215

Miller v. California, 206

Milliken v. Bradley, 312, 371

minority rights, 11

minority students, 311

Miranda v. Arizona, 241, 264, 357

Miranda warning, 241

Missouri Compromise (1820), 295

Missouri v. Holland, 88

mistrial, 245

modern electoral system, 124–125

monarchies, absolute, 91

money, First Amendment and, 207

Monroe, James, 10

Montesquieu, Baron de, 91

Moore, Richard, 210

Moore, Roy, 200

moral turpitude, 193

moral values, 8

Mueller, Bob, 104, 105

Mueller III, Robert, 74

municipalities, 327

murder, 36, 37

Murray's Lessee v. Hoboken Land & Improvement Co., 96

N

NAACP (National Association for the Advancement of Colored People), 170, 357

NAFTA (North American Trade Agreement), 88, 137

national anthem, 25

National Archives, 18

National Association for the Advancement of Colored People (NAACP), 170, 357

national conventions, 54, 69

National Emergencies Act (1976), 227

National Federation of Independent Business v. Sebelius, 87, 363, 372

national government, 29, 79

National Guard, 33, 141, 212, 227

National Instant Criminal Background Check System (NICS), 221

National Labor Relations Board (NLRB) Act, 250

National Labor Relations Board (NLRB) v. Jones & Laughlin Steel Corporation, 113

National Minimum Drinking Age Act, 310

National Organization for Women, 170

National Rifle Association, 219

National Security Agency (NSA), 208, 226

National Security Council (NSC), 134

National Socialist Party of America v. Village of Skokie, 210

Native Americans, 44, 46, 109

natural born Citizen, 120–122

natural justice, 247

natural law, 18

natural rights, 25

nature law (law of nature), 24

navy, 214

Near v. Minnesota, 206

Nebraska congressional district method, 126–127

Necessary and Proper Clause, 46, 87

New Deal, 113, 248–250

About the Author

Photographer: Anthony Oakshett (anthony.oakshett@btinternet.com)

Dr. Michael Arnheim is an English Barrister and Sometime Fellow of St John's College, Cambridge. His active interest in the U.S. Constitution started with a comparative paper he wrote at the age of 17, for which he was awarded a special prize in the Royal Commonwealth Society Essay Competition. As a junior barrister he wrote a fortnightly column in the *Solicitors Journal*, in which he dealt with U.S. constitutional issues among others. In 1994, he was invited to edit the comparative *Common Law* volume in the prestigious *International Library of Essays in Law and Legal Theory*, published by Ashgate Dartmouth. He has also been consulted on matters involving immigration, healthcare, protectionism, states' rights, and same-sex marriage.

Dr. Arnheim is the author of numerous articles and 20 published books to date, including the following titles: *Drafting Settlements of Disputes* (Tolley, 1994), *Civil Courts Practice & Procedure Handbook* (Butterworths, 1999), *A Handbook of Human Rights Law* (Kogan Page, 2004), *Principles of the Common Law* (Duckworth, 2004), *The Problem with Human Rights Law* (Civitas, 2015), *Two Models of Government* (Imprint Academic, 2016), and *A Practical Guide to Your Human Rights and Civil Liberties* (Straightforward Publishing, 2017).

In 1985, Dr. Arnheim spent several enjoyable hours on David Brudnoy's radio talk show on WRKO in Boston, fielding calls from listeners on topical legal and political issues. More recently, he has appeared on *Sky News* television in regard to U.S. politics and elections.

Dr. Arnheim started life as a member of the "Quiz Kids" team on South African national radio. He went to university at 16, took his first degree when he was 19, received a First Class Honours degree at 20, and was awarded a master's degree (with distinction) at age 21. He then won a national scholarship to St John's College, Cambridge, where he took his PhD and was elected a Fellow of the College.

After spending several years researching and teaching Classics and Ancient History as a Fellow of St John's College, Cambridge, at the age of 31 he was appointed a full Professor and Head of the Department of Classics at his original university in South Africa. Returning to Britain, he was called to the English Bar by Lincoln's Inn in 1988.

When he is not trying cases or advising clients, Dr. Arnheim spends his time teaching, writing, and (less often than he should) swimming.

Here is a link to Dr. Arnheim's Wikipedia page:

`https://en.wikipedia.org/wiki/Michael_Arnheim`

To his *Huffington Post* blogs:

`https://www.huffingtonpost.com/author/dr-michael-arnheim`

And to his YouTube channel:

`https://www.youtube.com/channel/UCxO-xcdVI7dOg75Nwml_MLw?view_as=subscriber`

Dedication

To the memory of my beloved parents.

To my students over the years, who kept me on my toes.

And to the spirit of American liberty, in the light of Abraham Lincoln's challenge:

> *Must a government, of necessity, be too strong for the liberties of its own people, or too weak to maintain its own existence?*

Author's Acknowledgments

My classical and historical training has stood me in good stead in my practice of law, and, not least, in my study of the U.S. Constitution. Professor Theo Haarhoff taught me how difficult it sometimes is to differentiate between objective views and subjective views that mimic objectivity. Professor Hugo Jones and Professor John Crook of Cambridge University were two of the most tolerant minds that I have ever come across, but they never made the mistake of equating toleration with acceptance of all views as equally valid.

Special thanks to my editors at Wiley: Tracy Boggier, Linda Brandon, Todd Lothery, and, not least, my Technical Editor, Tom Malnati. I owe a particular debt of gratitude to Kathy Nebenhaus, Vice President and Executive Publisher at Wiley, who, beyond the call of duty, took the original edition of this book under her wing and saw it through to completion, and then arranged for me to be offered a contract for this new edition.

Thanks also to my friends Jack Ward, Shola Awoderu, Brian Abramson, and Clive Russ, and special thanks to my cousin Colonel Ralph Holstein.

As I don't have a cat, I can't blame it for clambering over the keyboard. The sole responsibility for any mistakes rests on me. The law as stated in the book is correct as of Presidents' Day, February 19, 2018.

Publisher's Acknowledgments

Acquisitions Editor: Tracy Boggier
Project Manager: Linda Brandon
Development Editor: Linda Brandon
Copy Editor: Todd Lothery
Technical Editor: Thomas Malnati

Production Editor: Siddique Shaik
Cover Photo: © James Steidl/Shutterstock

Leverage the power

Dummies is the global leader in the reference category and one of the most trusted and highly regarded brands in the world. No longer just focused on books, customers now have access to the dummies content they need in the format they want. Together we'll craft a solution that engages your customers, stands out from the competition, and helps you meet your goals.

Advertising & Sponsorships

Connect with an engaged audience on a powerful multimedia site, and position your message alongside expert how-to content. Dummies.com is a one-stop shop for free, online information and know-how curated by a team of experts.

- Targeted ads
- Video
- Email Marketing
- Microsites
- Sweepstakes sponsorship

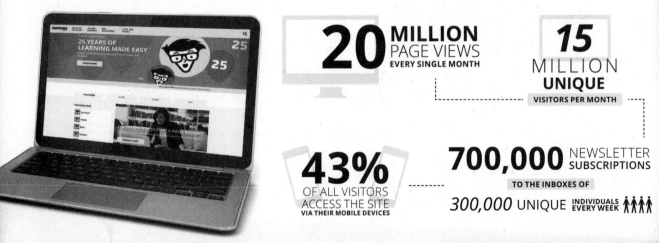

20 MILLION PAGE VIEWS EVERY SINGLE MONTH

15 MILLION UNIQUE VISITORS PER MONTH

43% OF ALL VISITORS ACCESS THE SITE VIA THEIR MOBILE DEVICES

700,000 NEWSLETTER SUBSCRIPTIONS TO THE INBOXES OF

300,000 UNIQUE INDIVIDUALS EVERY WEEK

# of dummies

Custom Publishing

Reach a global audience in any language by creating a solution that will differentiate you from competitors, amplify your message, and encourage customers to make a buying decision.

- Apps
- Books
- eBooks
- Video
- Audio
- Webinars

Brand Licensing & Content

Leverage the strength of the world's most popular reference brand to reach new audiences and channels of distribution.

For more information, visit dummies.com/biz

PERSONAL ENRICHMENT

Staying Sharp	Facebook	Guitar	Investing	Beekeeping	Digital Photography
9781119187790	9781119179030	9781119293354	9781119293347	9781119310068	9781119235606
USA $26.00	USA $21.99	USA $24.99	USA $22.99	USA $22.99	USA $24.99
CAN $31.99	CAN $25.99	CAN $29.99	CAN $27.99	CAN $27.99	CAN $29.99
UK £19.99	UK £16.99	UK £17.99	UK £16.99	UK £16.99	UK £17.99

Meditation	Pregnancy	Samsung Galaxy S7	iPhone	Crocheting	Nutrition
9781119251163	9781119235491	9781119279952	9781119283133	9781119287117	9781119130246
USA $24.99	USA $26.99	USA $24.99	USA $24.99	USA $24.99	USA $22.99
CAN $29.99	CAN $31.99	CAN $29.99	CAN $29.99	CAN $29.99	CAN $27.99
UK £17.99	UK £19.99	UK £17.99	UK £17.99	UK £16.99	UK £16.99

PROFESSIONAL DEVELOPMENT

Windows 10	AutoCAD	Excel 2016	QuickBooks 2017	macOS Sierra	LinkedIn	Windows 10 All-in-One
9781119311041	9781119255796	9781119293439	9781119281467	9781119280651	9781119251132	9781119310563
USA $24.99	USA $39.99	USA $26.99	USA $26.99	USA $29.99	USA $24.99	USA $34.00
CAN $29.99	CAN $47.99	CAN $31.99	CAN $31.99	CAN $35.99	CAN $29.99	CAN $41.99
UK £17.99	UK £27.99	UK £19.99	UK £19.99	UK £21.99	UK £17.99	UK £24.99

SharePoint 2016	Fundamental Analysis	Networking	Office 2016	Office 365	Salesforce.com	Coding
9781119181705	9781119263593	9781119257769	9781119293477	9781119265313	9781119239314	9781119293323
USA $29.99	USA $26.99	USA $29.99	USA $26.99	USA $24.99	USA $29.99	USA $29.99
CAN $35.99	CAN $31.99	CAN $35.99	CAN $31.99	CAN $29.99	CAN $35.99	CAN $35.99
UK £21.99	UK £19.99	UK £21.99	UK £19.99	UK £17.99	UK £21.99	UK £21.99

Learning Made Easy

ACADEMIC

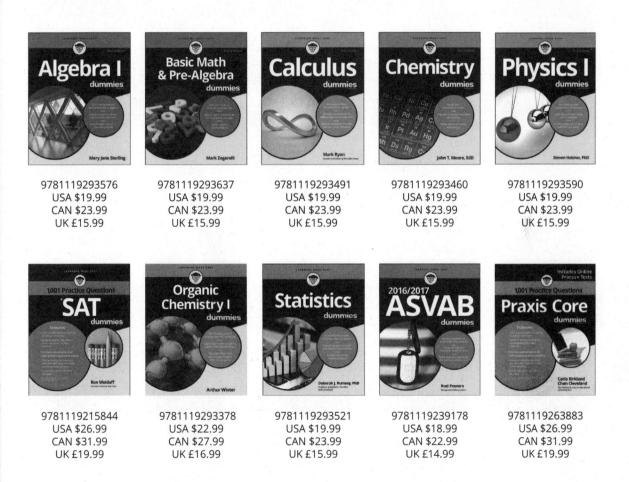

Algebra I dummies
Mary Jane Sterling
9781119293576
USA $19.99
CAN $23.99
UK £15.99

Basic Math & Pre-Algebra dummies
Mark Zegarelli
9781119293637
USA $19.99
CAN $23.99
UK £15.99

Calculus dummies
Mark Ryan
9781119293491
USA $19.99
CAN $23.99
UK £15.99

Chemistry dummies
John T. Moore, EdD
9781119293460
USA $19.99
CAN $23.99
UK £15.99

Physics I dummies
Steven Holzner, PhD
9781119293590
USA $19.99
CAN $23.99
UK £15.99

1,001 Practice Questions
SAT dummies
Ron Woldoff
9781119215844
USA $26.99
CAN $31.99
UK £19.99

Organic Chemistry I dummies
Arthur Winter
9781119293378
USA $22.99
CAN $27.99
UK £16.99

Statistics dummies
Deborah J. Rumsey, PhD
9781119293521
USA $19.99
CAN $23.99
UK £15.99

2016/2017 **ASVAB** dummies
Rod Powers
9781119239178
USA $18.99
CAN $22.99
UK £14.99

Includes Online Practice Tests
1,001 Practice Questions
Praxis Core dummies
Carla Kirkland
Chan Cleveland
9781119263883
USA $26.99
CAN $31.99
UK £19.99

Available Everywhere Books Are Sold

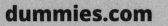

dummies.com

dummies
A Wiley Brand

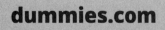
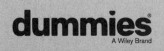